CHOICE READINGS FOR PUBLIC AND PRIVATE ENTERTAINMENTS AND FOR THE USE OF SCHOOLS COLLEGES AND PUBLIC READERS WITH ELOCUTIONARY ADVICE

EDITED BY

ROBERT McLEAN CUMNOCK, A. M.

PROFESSOR OF RHETORIC AND
ELOCUTION, AND DIRECTOR
OF THE SCHOOL OF ORATORY
NORTHWESTERN UNIVERSITY
EVANSTON, ILLINOIS, U. S. A

REVISED AND ENLARGED EDITION

FORTIETH THOUSAND

CHICAGO: A. C. McCLURG
AND CO. . . . . MDCD

PREFACE.

The great wrong practiced upon our youth is that they are led to imitate an interpretation given to them by some person whom they admire, rather than to ascertain and apply the principles which govern the vocal expression of all sentiments and emotions that are conveyed by words.

The evil results of such a course of training might be averted, in a measure, if every teacher of Reading were an artist; but, unfortunately, few have the time or aptitude for such high attainments. The only safe course is to ascertain the principles of vocal expression by careful observation of nature in its best moods and manifestations, and to apply the rules thus obtained to such portions of our Literature as may be easily classified with reference to the sentiment or passion they chiefly express.

In this book are contained selections from a very wide range of English authorship, such as are thought to be the best suited to the purposes of elocutionary training, and public reading and declamation.

An endeavor has also been made to give such specific directions as will aid the intelligent student to acquire a just conception of their sentiment.

The variety of the selections, added to the fact that each has been chosen with reference to its effectiveness and availability, will furnish material for every possible exercise in the ordinary requirements of school life, as well as in the more formal exercise of Public Reading and Declamation.

The elocutionary suggestions will appear as introductions to the various classes of selections in their respective orders:

First.— Pathos.
Second.— Solemnity.
Third.— Serenity, Beauty, Love.
Fourth.— Narrative, Descriptive and Didactic Styles.
Fifth.— Gayety.
Sixth.— Humor.
*Seventh.—*Grand, Sublime and Reverential Styles.
Eighth.— Oratorical Styles.
Ninth.— Abrupt and Startling Styles.
Tenth.— Miscellaneous Selections.

In each class of selections an endeavor has been made to secure just as pleasing and effective pieces as though the choice were unrestricted, and, at the same time, to choose pieces that would serve as types of the sentiment or passion they are intended to illustrate.

If, in some cases, selections do not sustain, from beginning to end, the sentiment that they are intended to illustrate, they are placed where the leading or most characteristic sentiment of the piece would require; and it is thought that, in most cases, the selections are nearly perfect specimens of the several classes in which they are placed.

The compiler acknowledges, with thanks, the kind permission of Messrs. J. R. Osgood & Co., Hurd & Houghton, and D. Appleton & Co., to use the poems of Longfellow, Whittier, Holmes, Cary, Bryant, and others, that are in this volume, and of which they hold the copyright.

R. McL. C.

Evanston, Ill., January, 1878.

PREFACE TO THE REVISED EDITION.

The greatest change in this edition of "Choice Readings" is the introduction of the editor's discussions of the most important topics in Elocution. With this addition the volume can be used as a manual for instruction, as well as a book of selections. The chief difficulties that perplex the student of elocution are treated in language as simple as the technical nature of the subject permits. The main object in the introduction of this new material has been to furnish the student with practical working systems leading up to the certain acquisition of the fundamental excellences of good reading and good speaking. The original order of the chapters is slightly changed; the introductory remarks to each chapter are retained with unimportant modifications.

About one-half of the old selections have been supplanted by new ones which, it is hoped, will prove as stimulating and attractive as their predecessors. The exceptionally strong selections still hold their places in the volume. In the work of preparing this edition the editor received from his associates in the school of oratory valuable assistance, which he here gratefully acknowledges. This revised edition is sent forth with the confident belief that it is a better and more serviceable book than the old one; and it is hoped that, by making the path to success in public speaking more clear and straight, it will meet with public favor and approval.

The editor is greatly indebted to the following publishers for permission to use the selections from works of which they hold the copyright, viz: Harper and Brothers, "The Boy Orator of Zepata City," from *The Exiles*, and "Her First Appearance," from *Van Bibber and Others;* American Publishers' Corporation, "An Invalid in Lodgings," from *A Tillyloss Scandal*, and "Scene from 'The Little Minister'"; The Century Company, "The Two Runaways" and "The Trial of Ben Thomas," from *Two Runaways and Other Stories;* The Bowen-Merrill Company, "The South Wind and the Sun," and "Knee-Deep in June," from *Afterwhiles*, and H. S. Edwards' "Mammy's Li'l' Boy."

R. McL. C.

Evanston, Ill., June, 1898.

CONTENTS.

CONTENTS.

CONTENTS.

CHOICE READINGS.

ENGLISH PRONUNCIATION.

A correct and refined pronunciation of words is one of the foundation stones upon which all elocutionary excellence must be built. However much we may deride the mechanics of speech, we shall be brought, as we grow older and wiser, to acknowledge their great importance. All speaking, however melodious or expressive, that is marred by a careless or provincial pronunciation, must lose a large share of its effectiveness by offending an educated and refined taste. Nothing is truer than the following statement of Alfred Ayres:

"The manner in which one speaks his mother-tongue is looked upon as showing more clearly than any other one thing what his culture is, and what his associations have been."

Perhaps on no subject in the whole range of educational work is there so much variance and uncertainty as on the subject of English vowel sounds. This fault is not to be laid at the door of the student altogether, but rather should be charged up to the halting and conflicting opinions of the dictionaries. A large share of the mischief has arisen from the use of the word *obscure*. This word, as used by orthoëpists, is an extremely unfortunate one, because it destroys all standards of ascertainable truth in pronunciation. What is obscure to one may not be so obscure to another; and hence all standards which should define the sound to be given to the vowel, are completely broken down. We see no higher motive in the use of the word obscure than an easy and comfortable way to get rid of difficulties.

In the presentation of the subject of English phonation,

15

two things are important. First: Simplicity and clearness of statement. Second: A keen and discriminating appreciation of sound. The following table is, in our opinion, the simplest form in which the vowel sounds of the English language can be presented.

TABLE OF VOWEL SOUNDS.

SIMPLE.		DIPHTHONGAL.

1　ạ as in all　　7　ẽ as in term　　13　ā as in ale $=$ ā $+$ ē

2 { ä as in arm　8　ĭ as in pin　　14　ī as in ice $=$ ä $+$ ē
　{ à as in ask　9 { ōō as in ooze　15　ō as in old $=$ ō $+$ ōō

3　ă as in at　　　 { ŏŏ as in look　16　oi as in oil $=$ ạ $+$ ē

4　â as in care　10　ŏ as in ox　　17　ou as in our $=$ ä $+$ ōō

5　ē as in eve　11　ŭ as in up　　18　ū as in use $=$ ĭ $+$ ōō

6　ĕ as in met　12　û as in urge　　　or y $+$ oo

The student will see, by the table, that there are but twelve simple vowel sounds in the language, and six diphthongal sounds—the diphthongs being made by uniting two of the simple sounds. Long ā, however, number thirteen in the table, and long ō, are made by uniting the *name sound* of the letter with one of the simple sounds; thus long ā $=$ ā (the name sound) plus long ē; also long ō $=$ ō (the name sound) plus ōō. In our dictionaries and School Readers the vowel sounds are taught as they appear to the *eye*, and not as they come to the *ear*; thus the u in bury is not a u sound, but a short ĕ as in bĕrrÿ; also the e in pretty is not an e sound, but a short ĭ as prĭttÿ. Hence duplicate sounds enlarge the dictionary list of the vowels. The number of vowel sounds enumerated in dictionaries and School Readers varies from twenty to thirty-three.

By reducing the number of vowels to twelve, we simplify the task of the pupil. It is a much easier matter to get acquainted with twelve sounds than with thirty-three. The following lists of *equivalents* will show, to some extent, the double and triple use of the simple vowel sounds, and will account for the long list of vowel sounds found in our dictionaries.

Equivalents whose pronunciation is indicated without respelling:

　ạ as in ạll is the same sound as ô in ôr and the ô in côugh.

　â as in câre is the same sound as ê in thêre.

ē as in ēve is the same sound as ï in pïque and ee in eel.
ē̃ as in fē̃rn is the same sound as ī in sīr and ȳ in mȳrrh.
ĭ as in ĭll is the same sound as y̆ in hy̆mn.
o͞o as in fo͞od is the same sound as ǫ in dǫ and ṷ in trṷe.
o͝o as in fo͝ot is the same sound as ǫ in wǫlf and ṷ in pṷll.
ŏ as in ŏdd is the same sound as ạ in whạt.
ŭ as in ŭp is the same sound as ȯ in sȯn.
ā as in āle is the same sound as ẹ in ẹight.
ī as in īce is the same sound as ȳ in flȳ.

Words whose vowel sounds cannot be indicated without respelling:

any pronounced ĕny̆.
beau pronounced bō.
boy pronounced boi.
breeches pronounced brĭtchĕz.
bury pronounced bĕrry̆.
busy pronounced bĭzy̆.
says pronounced sĕz.
dew pronounced dū.
hautboy pronounced hō'boi.
pretty pronounced prĭtty̆.
quay pronounced kē.
saith pronounced sĕth.
owl pronounced oul.
sewing pronounced sō'–ĭng.
sergeant pronounced sär'–gĕnt.
word pronounced wûrd.
cough pronounced kạf.

In recent discussions of this subject, the larger share of attention has been directed to the *quantity* of vowels, and the *correct accentuation* of words, rather than to the subtle distinctions of vowel sound which form the basis of refined and elegant speech. The chief reason for this is the ease with which quantity and accentuation may be determined; while on the other hand the difficulty of making sensible and just discriminations, in the finer shades of vowel sound, has kept people from venturing an opinion in that direction.

We will now, as briefly as possible, discuss the vowel sounds, giving special consideration to those that are most frequently mispronounced. In class work, place on the blackboard twenty-five words to illustrate each of the vowel sounds in the table, and practice the pronunciation of

these words in concert until the true sound of each vowel
is fully appreciated. The first vowel is called broad a̤;
marked in the dictionaries with two dots below the letter,
thus, a̤ as in a̤ll. We have little difficulty with this sound.
Avoid, however, making broad a̤ like short ŏ. Do not say
wŏter for wa̤ter, dŏtter for da̤ughter.

LIST OF WORDS FOR PRACTICE.

a̤ll	ba̤ld	fôught	ba̤lsam	la̤wyer	fa̤lconer
appa̤ll	ba̤lk	fôrm	da̤ughter	a̤wful	a̤lbeit
a̤lmost	broa̤d	ôrb	fa̤lchion	qua̤rter	la̤udable
a̤we	bra̤wl	tôrpid	ga̤udy	wa̤ter	la̤udanum
a̤wl	da̤wn	va̤ult	wha̤rf	wa̤rrior	la̤ureate

The second vowel in the table requires special attention. It is called the long Italian ä, and is marked with
two dots above, thus, ä as in ärm. This sound is correctly given when followed by r (as in fär, chärm); but
there are forty or more words in our language in which
the broad sound of a̤ as in a̤ll, or the short sound of
ă as in hăt, is frequently substituted for the sound of
the long Italian ä. Do not say läugh or la̤ugh for
läugh. Let the ear be trained to catch the correct
vowel sound, as heard in ärm, and then secure the
same sound in the list of words given below. The only
way to secure accuracy in the pronunciation of these
doubtful words is *frequent repetition*, until it becomes a
habit to speak them correctly at all times.

LIST OF WORDS FOR PRACTICE.

älms	fläunt	läunch	älmond	däunt	Neväda
äunt	gäpe	läva	läughter	psälm	Alabäma
cälf	gäunt	sälve	läundry	hälf	cantäta
cälm	täunt	suäve	säunter	pälm	promenäde

The next vowel sound that suffers at the hands, or
rather the tongues, of most people, even of those liberally
educated, is the short Italian ȧ. This vowel is the same
sound in *quality* as the long Italian ä, but less in *quantity*,
i.e., the vowel in ȧsk is sounded the same as the vowel in
ärm; the only difference is that the former is shorter than
the latter.

To acquire the correct vowel quality in the pronunciation of these words, a sustained sound of long Italian ä should be made, until the ear catches the precise shade of sound, then a much shorter sound of the same quality should be made, and used in the pronunciation of the words. Strict attention to the quality of vowel sound used, and frequent comparisons with the long-drawn Italian ä sound, and frequent repetition of the list of words given below are all the directions and cautions needed, to enable any one to pronounce these frequently used words correctly.

Do not say ăsk or äsk for ȧsk. The short Italian ȧ is found, chiefly, in monosyllabic words ending in ff, ss, sk, sp, st, ft, nce, nt.

LIST OF WORDS FOR PRACTICE.

ȧsk	fȧst	ȧsp	ȧfter	bȧsket	advȧntage
stȧff	glȧnce	grȧnt	commȧnd	cȧsket	advȧncing
cȧst	hȧsp	grȧss	demȧnd	enhȧnce	commȧnder
clȧss	quȧff	pȧnt	mȧster	mȧsking	pȧssable
shȧft	chȧnt	drȧught	slȧnting	pȧstor	tȧskmȧster

The third vowel in the table is short ă as in căt, băd. We occasionally hear this sound pronounced like short ĕ, thus, cĕt for căt. When short ă is followed by *rr* (as in arrow) or by r and a vowel (as in chărity), it is often incorrectly sounded like â, as in câre.

LIST OF WORDS FOR PRACTICE.

băt	Hărry	păssion	jăsper	căricature
păd	mărry	romănce	păramount	aquătic
găs	lărynx	vălentine	căravan	barbăric
cănt	gămut	cărriage	căssimere	cărrion
thănk	ărid	căssock	clăssify	păssenger
săp	bărrel	dăstard	compărison	pălmistry
dăzzle	bărrow	hărass	chăracter	Măssachusetts

The fourth vowel in the table is frequently mispronounced, and requires special attention. This vowel is marked with a caret over the letter, and is called by some orthöepists the caret â, by others the circumflex â, and by still others the medial â. In some of the northern sections of our country we hear the vowel pronounced like long ā, while the colored population of the South, with rare exceptions, give it the sound of Italian ä. Observe that it is neither pārent nor pärent, but pârent; neither hāre nor här, but hâir.

LIST OF WORDS FOR PRACTICE.

fâir	châir	teâr	scârce	fâre	âir
snâre	bâre	thêre	spâre	scâre	râre
stâre	fâiry	lâir	weâr	beâr	sweâr
shâre	pârent	hâir	squâre	dâre	mâre
pâir	gârish	declâre	prepâre	ensnâre	pârentage

We seldom hear any error in the enunciation of the fifth vowel in the table, long ē as in ēve. When followed by r (as in ēar, fēar) some careless speakers give the vowel a sound that verges toward short ĭ, while others pronounce the vowel with a sound resembling caret â.

LIST OF WORDS FOR PRACTICE.

ēke	nēar	believe	drēary	appēaring	expērience
fēet	pēer	recēive	antique	lēnient	infērior
fēar	quēer	ravine	caprice	carēering	matērial
glēam	rēar	quēry	machine	pēriod	Presbytērian
hēar	tēar	wēary	marine	retrēating	supērior

The sixth vowel in the table, short ĕ as in mĕt, is occasionally mispronounced like long ā in such words as mĕasure, plĕasure. When short ĕ is followed by r, it is frequently given a sound like caret â. Do not say pâril for pĕril nor mâry for mĕrry.

LIST OF WORDS FOR PRACTICE.

ĕbb	hĕdge	rĕnt	mĕasure	mĕrry	clĕrical
bĕck	kĕn	said	plĕasure	pĕril	celĕrity
dĕll	lĕss	saith	trĕasure	stĕrile	hĕrring
fĕd	mĕt	vĕst	bury	tĕrror	kĕr'osene
gĕm	wĕst	whĕn	ferry	vĕry	sevĕrity

The seventh vowel in the table is called the *tilde* ē and ĩ, or, perhaps a better name, the waved ē and ĩ. It is the most delicate vowel sound in the language, and is frequently mispronounced. The error in the pronunciation of this vowel is in making it like the û in ûrge; thus, we are accustomed to pronounce tērm as though it were spelled tûrm. The not overdone difference between these two sets of words $\frac{\text{ēarn}}{\text{ûrn}}$ $\frac{\text{fĭr}}{\text{fûr}}$ indicates the distinction between the correct and incorrect sound of the element. The ē in tērm is a more delicate and closer sound than the û in ûrge. The soft palate and root of the tongue are brought closer together, and the whole surface of the tongue is lifted nearer the roof of the mouth. Do not pronounce hēr like the first syllable of the word hŭrry, nor the word sĭr like the first syllable of sŭrround.

This vowel is always followed by the consonant r, and is usually found in words where the r is not followed by another r, or where the r is not followed by a vowel. Verbs having this sound almost always retain it when inflected or suffixed, even though the r be doubled, as confēr, confērring. Examples where we have short ĕ and ĭ when the r is followed by another r—fĕrry, Jĕrry, mĕrry, bĕrry, mĭrror. Examples where we have short ĕ and ĭ when the r is followed by a vowel—pĕril, spĭrit, mĕrit, vĕry, vĭrulent.

LIST OF WORDS FOR PRACTICE.

ēarn	hēard	nērve	sĭr	thĭrteen	altēr'nately
bĭrd	jērk	pēarl	vērge	cĭrcle	confērring
dĭrge	mĭrth	quĭrk	dĭrt	cērtain	detērring
gērm	lēarn	sērge	bĭrch	ērmine	ēarnestness
fērn	mȳrrh	tērm	pērch	sĭrloin	vērsatile
bĭrth	vērse	gĭrd	fĭrst	kērnel	vĭrtuous

The eighth vowel in the table, short ĭ as in pĭn, is usually pronounced correctly. It is sometimes, however, carelessly pronounced like long ē when followed by the sound of *sh*, as in dish, fish, wish.

LIST OF WORDS FOR PRACTICE.

bĭb	jĭg	schĭsm	dĭvan	condĭtion	ĭrrĭtable
dĭd	kĭck	rhȳthm	mĭrror	suffĭcient	gĭbberish
fĭg	lĭve	dĭsh	mĭnute	elȳsium	vĭrulent
gĭll	mĭdge	fĭsh	ĭsthmus	dĭploma	lȳrical
hĭm	nĭche	wĭsh	spĭrit	dĭdactic	penĭnsula

The ninth vowel in the table is a source of trouble to most people. I find that many speakers are at fault in pronouncing a few words that take the long o͞o as their vowel; for example, bo͞ot, ro͞ot, ho͞of. As a rule, we are apt to shorten the quantity of the long o͞o; and as a corrective the following words ought to be pronounced frequently.

LIST OF WORDS FOR PRACTICE.

ho͞of	ro͞ot	ro͞of	fo͞od	ro͝od	so͞on
rumor	rue	gruel	truce	croup	wo͞of
ruin	routine	true	bo͞ot	mo͞on	fo͞ol
rural	cruel	prune	brute	wo͞o	smo͞oth
ruthless	ro͞om	o͞oze	rule	bo͞om	sho͞ot

What we have said about the long o͞o may be repeated with much more emphasis in the consideration of the short o͝o. In the case of the long o͞o there is a tendency in a few words, like ho͞of and ro͞of, to give the vowel the sound of short ŭ; but in words in which short o͝o is the vowel we more frequently hear the words pronounced with the sound of short ŭ than the proper vowel sound, thus, bŭk for bo͝ok, cŭk for co͝ok. Pronounce frequently the following words, and give to the vowels the shortened form of o͞o in fo͞od.

LIST OF WORDS FOR PRACTICE.

bo͝ok	wolf	bro͝ok	pull	ho͝od	bullion
lo͝ok	sho͝ok	could	put	go͝od	bulwark
ho͝ok	to͝ok	would	full	sto͝od	butcher
co͝ok	wo͝ol	should	push	ro͝ok	forso͝ok
no͝ok	wo͝od	cro͝ok	bush	fo͝ot	willful

The tenth vowel in the table, short ŏ as in ox, is pronounced by careless speakers like short ŭ in such words as frŏm, ŏf, wạs. When short ŏ is followed by rr, or by r and a vowel, there is a tendency to make it like the broad ạ. Avoid saying maurrow for mŏrrow, aurigin for ŏrigin.

LIST OF WORDS FOR PRACTICE.

ŏdd	frŏm	wash	clŏset	fŏrest	cŏrrect
ŏf	dŏll	prŏduct	tŏrrid	fŏreign	ŏrator
ŏff	gŏne	pŏssess	bŏrrow	mŏrals	ŏrigin
clŏth	was	ŏffice	mŏrrow	cŏlumn	cŏronet

The eleventh vowel in the table, short ŭ as in ŭp, is usually pronounced correctly.

LIST OF WORDS FOR PRACTICE.

bŭd	hŭt	wont	onion	hŭrry	cŭrrent
hŭb	jŭg	ŭnder	sŭrrey	scŭrry	bŭrrow
fŭn	mŭff	noŭrish	cŭrry	worry	fŭrrow
gŭn	nŭmb	floŭrish	flŭrry	coŭrage	tŭrret

The twelfth vowel in the table, caret û as in ûrge, is always followed by the consonant r. This sound gives us very little trouble. Occasionally we hear students straining for an over-nice pronunciation of this vowel, endeavoring to give it the sound of waved ē, thus, ērge for ûrge.

LIST OF WORDS FOR PRACTICE.

bûrr	ûrge	lûrch	word	bûrlesque	attorney
cûr	bûrn	sûrge	work	joûrnal	bifûrcate
fûr	cûrd	tûrn	worm	pûrpose	colonel
pûrr	fûrl	dûrst	worst	pûrling	objûrgatory
ûrn	hûrt	cûrst	pûrse	tûrmoil	pûrsuivant

DIPHTHONGS.

The long ā, No. 13 in the table, is made by uniting the original element, or name sound of the letter, with long ē, thus a=a+ē.

LIST OF WORDS FOR PRACTICE.

bābe	breāk	quāke	dāiry	fācial	ā'eronaut
cāpe	lāde	rāge	Māry	pāthos	barbā'rian
dāte	māin	sāfe	prāirie	heinous	canā'ry
fāme	nāve	bāss	vāry	Sārah	vagā'ries
eight	plāgue	grimāce	wāry	wāylāy	pĕrorā'tion

The long ī, No. 14 in the table, is made by uniting Italian ä with long ē, thus ī=ä+ē.

LIST OF WORDS FOR PRACTICE.

bīde	kīne	rhȳme	bīas	bī'cȳcle	declīnable
dȳke	līfe	scȳthe	fīnite	derīsive	deifȳ
fīfe	mīre	gȳves	sē'-nīle	dȳnamite	dīadem
quīte	nīce	thrīve	sȳren	inquīry	eȳing
heīght	pīpe	wīle	cȳcle	īcicle	guīde

The long ō, No. 15 in the table, is made by uniting the name sound of the letter with ŏŏ, thus ō=ō+ŏŏ. The vanish into ŏŏ is slight.

LIST OF WORDS FOR PRACTICE.

bōde	lōbe	bōard	lōre	bōvine	anchō'vy
cōke	nōte	cōurt	rōar	brōoch	histō'rian
dōle	trōw	dōor	shōre	glōry	encō'mium
fōam	wōn't	fōur	swōrd	Dōra	oppō'nent
hōse	yōre	hōard	tōward	Nōrah	zōölogy

The diphthong oi is made by uniting broad a̤ with ē, thus oi=a̤+ē.

LIST OF WORDS FOR PRACTICE.

boy	join	buoyant	cloister	avoirdupois
buoy	Lloyd	alloy	poison	hoidenish
choice	moist	ointment	noisome	clairvoyance
foil	poise	poignant	oyster	loyalty
hoist	void	royal	loiter	reconnoiter

The diphthong ou is made by uniting Italian ä and o͞o, thus ou=ä+o͞o.

LIST OF WORDS FOR PRACTICE.

bough	mount	tower	drowsy	counter	countersign
cowl	now	vouch	fountain	foundling	counselor
doubt	pout	hound	vowel	gouty	cowardice
fowl	rouse	blouse	rowdy	houseless	dowager
house	sour	drought	resound	mouthing	lowering

The diphthong long ū has always been a stumbling block to the most of our public speakers. According to the best orthoëpists, it is equivalent to the sound of the consonant y and oo; thus ū=y+oo. The only way to prove this is to make the sound of y and oo in rapid succession and blend them; or we may say that in pronunciation ū=you. Here the y forms the initial part of the diphthong and ou the oo part. When the long ū stands as a syllable by itself, we experience no difficulty in hearing the diphthongal sound; thus, ed-yoo-cate, yoo-nite, etc. In such cases we never think of dropping the y part of the diphthong, and saying ed-oo-cate; also when long ū does not form a syllable by itself, but is found in combination with certain consonants, we always hear the initial y and the sound of oo; thus, mūte—we never hear the y suppressed and the word pronounced moot; we never hear

beauty pronounced booty, cūte pronounced coot, or pūre
pronounced poor. The trouble in pronouncing this diphthong occurs when any of the following consonants, d, t,
l, n, s, or th happens to come before a long ū; thus, we
are apt to pronounce dūty as though it were spelled dooty
—i. e. we make the long ū in such cases equal to oo; but
it is equal, as we have shown, to y+oo. The question
then to be answered is this, Why do we suppress the y
part of the diphthong whenever d, t, l, n, s, or th happens
to come before a long ū? Simply because d, t, l, n, s, and
th are made in the fore part of the mouth by the tip of
the tongue and teeth, and the y part of the diphthong is
made by the palate. We see plainly that to pass from the
front part of the mouth to the palate is the greatest possible distance in the articulative machinery, hence it is
easier to pass from d, t, l, n, s, and th to the oo sound
than to take up the intermediate y. The rule then in all
cases where d, t, l, n, s, and th precedes the long ū is
this: always introduce the sound of y as the initial part of
the diphthong, with this added caution that it be given
with as slight a sound as possible, to avoid affectation.

LIST OF WORDS FOR PRACTICE.

dūke	thews	dūty	dūet	dūbious	indūbitable
tūne	dew	tūmult	tūtor	tūberose	matūrity
lūte	tūbe	Lūcy	Tūesday	lubricate	illūminate
nūde	Lūke	neūter	nūisance	numerous	innūmerable
sūit	new	Sūsan	Matthew	studious	enthūsiasm
dūe	dūde	tūlip	sūpine	institūte	sūperiority

The pupil must be impressed from the foregoing discussion that the vowels whose pronunciation requires the
most careful attention are the long Italian ä and short
Italian å No. 2, the caret â No. 4, the waved ē and ī No.
7, the long ōō and short ŏŏ No. 9, and the diphthongal
long ū No. 18. In order that the life-long habits of mispronunciation may be amended, continuous daily practice
of the lists of words, with special attention to the five difficult vowel sounds mentioned, is recommended as absolutely necessary. A knowledge of what is right does not
always insure the practice of what is right.

Unless this rigid and continuous practice be kept up
for a long time, the student will find himself unconsciously

slipping back to the old and incorrect pronunciation. The main thing is to keep the subject constantly before the student. This can be done in a very simple and practical way. Let each student procure a piece of cardboard 30x15 inches, and arrange the words for practice in vertical columns. It is not necessary to include all the lists of words in this *chart*, but simply those that illustrate the five vowel sounds that are the most difficult. The chart should be hung on the wall of the study room, and the words printed or written large enough to be seen at a considerable distance. The words should be repeated several times a day until ease and accuracy in their pronunciation is attained. It will require patience and industry to break up long established habits of mispronunciation, but the plan suggested is the simplest and surest method to accomplish the task.

Outline of Chart for the Vowel Sounds.—Practice vowel sounds to secure accuracy in pronunciation.

TABLE OF VOWEL SOUNDS.

SIMPLE.			DIPHTHONGAL.	
1	ạ as in all.	7	ē as in term.	13 ā as in ale$=$ä$+$ē.
2 {	ä as in arm.	8	ĭ as in pin.	14 ī as in ice$=$ä$+$ē.
{	à as in ask.	9	&c.	15 &c. $=$
3	&c.	10		16 $=$
4		11		17 $=$
5		12		18 $=$
6				

Vowel sounds that give us the most trouble in pronunciation:

Long Italian ä.	Short Italian à.	Caret â.	Waved ē and ī.	Long ōō.	Short ŏŏ.	Long ū.
älms	àsk	fâir	ēarn	hōōf	bŏŏk	dūke
äunt	stàff	snâre	bĭrd	rōōm	lŏŏk	tūne
cälf	càst	stâre	dĭrge	ōōze	hŏŏk	lūte
cälm	clàss	shâre	gērm	rumor	cŏŏk	nūde
etc	etc	etc	etc	etc	etc	etc

The full table of vowel sounds should appear on the completed chart, and the vertical columns of words for practice should be filled out.

Constant use of the table of vowel sounds is necessary in order that pupils may be trained to detect vowel sound as rapidly as they read words.

EXAMPLES FOR ILLUSTRATION.

4   8   15   7   18   8   17   2   3 3   6 8 8   18   8   9

There is no virtue without a characteristic beauty to

13   8   2   8 18 11   8   11   10   11   9   3   9   13   11

make it particularly loved of the good, and to make the

3   2   13   10   4   6   6   10   8

bad ashamed of their neglect of it.

The diacritical marks may be used in this exercise, although I prefer the numerals for two reasons. First: It is not necessary, in using the numerals, to respell words like bury, any, etc. Second: Students, who are not sure of their knowledge of vowel sound, can make diacritical marks so ingeniously that no teacher can tell what they mean.

EXAMPLES FOR PRACTICE.

Mark the vowels in the following sentences:
  The mourners went home in the morning.
  Honesty is the best policy.
  Blood, says the pride of life, is more honorable
    than money.

In some of the recently published dictionaries, there is a strong tendency in the direction of current pronunciation. This is to be commended, provided the movement does not become so radical as to interfere seriously with the standards of good taste in pronunciation. We are yielding, I fear, too much to the *easy way* of pronouncing words, and allowing ourselves to hold in light esteem some of the delicate distinctions in vowel sound that have given to cultivated speech its distinctive charm. The duty of the conscientious student of elocution is to conserve all that adds to the grace and finish of human speech, and, at the same time, to avoid the weakness of over-nicety and oddness. We have endeavored in this discussion to present a *positive* and *working* system of English phonation. We have given to each vowel sound a definite existence, and have contended for a phonation clearly outlined and fixed in its quality and quantity.

We have not driven the short Italian ă into obscurity, nor have we seen our way clear to merge the pleasing sound of waved ē and ī into the sound of caret û. We are content to allow the long ū and short ŏ a continuance of their honorable existence, and, though strenuous for the nicest distinctions in phonation, we have not thought it wise to disturb the relationship of the long and the short oo. Although aware that the positions taken are in agreement with the majority of the ablest authorities, yet we are on the anxious seat of improvement, and will welcome any innovation that promises reform, or any change that will insure progress.

It may be of service, in this connection, to offer a few words of advice in the management of Pronunciation Matches. A large proportion of the words that we have seen submitted for tests in pronunciation, have been those seldom or never used. The exercise, to be of the highest educational value, should include only words in current use. We must seek to lift pronunciation from the low level of the puzzle to the higher ground of useful knowledge. It is worse than a waste of time to ask any one to learn the pronunciation of words he never uses himself, and never saw before they were presented for pronunciation. Again, great care should be taken not to condemn a pronunciation because it is not the pronunciation in your dictionary. Perhaps on investigation you will find just as weighty authority approving it as you found condemning it. The only safe and useful thing that can be done in this matter is to prepare a list of common words usually mispronounced, and in the correct pronunciation of which the *authorities are substantially agreed.*

LIST OF WORDS FOR PRONUNCIATION MATCHES.

accent	ăk′-sĕnt (noun)
accent	ăk-sĕn′t (verb)
address	ăd-drĕs′ (both noun and verb)
aforesaid	à-fōr′-sĕd
alias	ā′-lĭ-ăs
allege	ăl-lĕj′
amenable	à-mē′-na-bl
apparatus	ăp-pa-rā′-tŭs

ay or aye	ā (meaning always)
ay or aye	ī (meaning yes)
betrothal	be-trŏth′-al (th asp)
blatant	blā′-tant
breeches	brĭtch′ĕz
brigand	brĭg′-and
chasten	chā′-s′n
chastisement	chăs′-tĭz-mĕnt
cleanly	clēn′-lĭ (adverb)
cleanly	clĕn′-lĭ (adj.)
clique	clēk
condolence	cŏn-dō′-lĕns
demise	dē-mīz′
designate	dĕs′-ĭg-nāt (hissing s)
discourse	dĭs-kōrs′ (noun and verb)
falcon	fạk′n
flaccid	flăk′-sĭd
forensic	fō-rĕn′-sĭk (hissing s)
hypocrisy	hĭ-pŏk′-rĭ-sĭ
idea	ī-dē′-ȧ
impious	ĭm′-pĭ-ŭs
integral	ĭn′-tē-gral
intrinsic	ĭn-trĭn′sĭk (hissing s)
inventory	ĭn′-vĕn-tō-rĭ
javelin	jăv′-lĭn
legislature	lej′-ĭs-lā-tūre
magazine	măg-a-zēn′
patriotism	pā′-trĭ-ot-ism
preface	prĕf′-ās (noun and verb)
presentiment	prē-sĕnt′-ĭ-mĕnt (hissing s)
primary	prī′-ma-rĭ
program	prō′-grăm
prosaic	prō-zā′-ĭk
protestation	prŏt-ĕs-tā′-shŭn
quickening	kwĭk′-nĭng
recess	rē-cĕs′
resource	rē-sōrs′
sedative	sĕd′-a-tĭv
sieve	sĭv
sinecure	sī′-nē-kūr
spectator	spĕk-tā′-tor
swarthy	swarth′-ĭ (th asp)
thither	thĭth′-er (both subvocal th)

truths	truths (th asp)
unfrequented	ŭn-frē-kwĕnt′-ĕd
version	vẽr′-shŭn
yours	ūrz
youths	ūths (th asp)

HOW CAN I BECOME A DISTINCT SPEAKER?

A satisfactory answer to this question must be of great practical value to every lover of good reading and good speaking.

As indistinctness is the prominent fault of public address, so the discovery of a remedy for indistinctness must be to the majority of speakers the most desirable and most useful knowledge. It is a very general belief that indistinctness is a personal disability which can be only partially removed, and that it will ever continue as a hindrance to the public success of the unfortunate individual. The truth is, however, that any person of even feeble and imperfect articulation may become a distinct speaker. A notable case came under my observation and care a few years since. A minister who had been relieved from work because of indistinctness, applied to me for instruction. I found that he had been tormented by his brethren with some such general advice as this: "Speak distinctly." "Do not run your words together," etc. The poor man was not able to profit by such indefinite criticism. He had never been trained to use his articulative organs, and, as is sometimes the case, had become more indistinct in his enunciation during the four years of his ministry. He was helpless, discouraged, brokenhearted; but at the end of two months' practice in the correct and vigorous use of his tongue, teeth, and lips, he went back to work a moderately distinct speaker. He continued to improve, and is now one of the most distinct speakers and one of the most successful ministers in his denomination. I cite this case for the encouragement of all who may be similarly afflicted, and to add emphasis to what follows.

It is not personal endowment that enables one man to speak more distinctly than another, but simply industry.

Genius plays a very small part in the acquisition of a distinct utterance. It is work, intelligently directed and persistently pursued, that masters the difficulties and secures the desired results.

The distinct pronunciation of words depends entirely on a nimble use of the tongue, teeth, lips, and palate. Sound is made in the glottis, and when it reaches the mouth, the tongue, teeth, and lips form it into syllables and words. Now, any exercise which will give the pupil an energetic and rapid use of these organs of articulation will certainly insure distinctness.

Great care, time, and expense are lavished on the rudimentary training of the tyro in piano playing. Weeks, months, and years are given up to exercises to develop strength and dexterity in the use of the fingers, hands, and wrists of the young performer; and yet in ordinary articulation we use our tongue, teeth, and lips as rapidly as the pianist uses his fingers, and expect distinctness in speaking without any preliminary practice. Careful and continued practice in articulation by all public speakers is as necessary as the constant and laborious practice of the piano player to secure perfect technique in playing.

No one knows so well as the painstaking public speaker the truth of the above statement. The fear of indistinctness haunts him in every public effort, and keeps him keyed up to the most exacting demands of his audience. Since indistinctness may be overcome by industry, he can never forgive himself if he falls a victim to his own easy indifference. And it is well that this burden should be laid on all public speakers, for surely nothing is more irritating to an audience than a slipshod, mumbling utterance. Not only is the time of the hearers wasted while listening to such a speaker, but they are, through sympathy for the unfortunate man, subjected to a gratuitous persecution.

I wish to indicate a system of practice which, if diligently pursued, will give the pupil such strength and dexterity in the use of the articulative organs that indistinctness will be impossible.

TABLE OF CONSONANT SOUNDS,

Arranged with reference to the organs by which they are formed.

Lips.	*Lips and Teeth.*	*Teeth and Tongue.*	*Tongue and Palate.*	*Teeth, Tongue and Palate.*
b as in babe m " " maim p " " pipe w " " woe wh " " when	f as in fife v " " valve	th as in thin th " " thine	ch as in church d " " did g " " gag j " " judge k " " cake l " " lull n " " nun ng " " song t " " tent	r as in rap r " " war s " " cease sh " " push y " " yet z " " zone zh " " azure

M, n, and ng are sometimes called nasal consonants.

The First Step in the practice is the mastery of the consonantal elements. The correct pronunciation of the vowel sounds secures elegance and refinement in speech, but distinctness in utterance depends entirely upon the rapid and energetic articulation of the consonants.

A definite knowledge of the position of the tongue teeth and lips, is essential to the accurate production of these consonantal sounds.

The subtonic *b* is made by a firm compression of the lips. The vocal resonance, which is heard in the interior of the head and mouth, reaches a maximum when the lips are suddenly opened. Pronounce the word *babe* and prolong the final *b* until the sound of the consonant is distinctly apprehended.

The subtonic *m* is made by a gentle compression of the lips which forces the vocal resonance through the nostrils. Prolong the final consonant in the word *maim*.

The atonic *p* is formed with the organs in the same position as in making *b*. The lips are intensely compressed, and the maximum of pressure is followed by an aspirated explosion. Pronounce the word *pipe* and execute with special force the final consonant.

The subtonic *w* is the sound of *oo*, with a slight breathing before the vowel. Let the lips be rounded as in pronouncing *oo*, and then draw the lips closer to the teeth, and contract the labial aperture as in whistling. The word *woe* is suggested for practice, *woe=w+o*. Make the sound of *w*, then of *o*, and then blend them.

The diagraph *wh* is regarded by Bell as a whispered form of *w*. In forming it, the lips are closely approximated, and then rapidly separated. Pronounce the word *when*, and endeavor to get the initial sound.

The subtonic *v* is made by placing the ridge of the under lip against the edges of the upper teeth, and forcing the vocalized breath between the teeth. Care should be taken to raise the upper lip in order to prevent its interfering with the upper front teeth. The world *valve* is suggested for practice.

The aspirate *f* is the cognate of *v*, and is made in the same manner, with this difference only, that the lip and teeth are more closely compressed and the unvocalized breath is more forcibly expelled. Pronounce the word *fife* with special force on the final *f*.

The subtonic *th*, which is the occasion of so much trouble to foreigners learning our language, is in reality one of the easiest consonants to produce. The tip of the tongue is pressed forcibly under and against the upper front teeth, the lips are slightly parted, and the vocalized breath is expelled between the teeth. The word *thine* is suggested for practice. The atonic *th* is a forcible aspiration executed with the organs in a similar position, the only difference being the absence of vocality. Practice the word *thin* with special reference to the initial sound.

The atonic *ch* has generally been considered as a compound of *t* and *sh*. This analysis is questioned. The sound is made by placing the tip of the tongue with energy against the interior ridge of upper gum, with the teeth shut. The sudden break of this contact of the organs permits the breath to escape in the sound of the explosive *ch*. Prolong the final *ch* in the word *church*.

The subtonic *d* is made by placing the tip of the tongue with great energy against the interior ridge of gum over the upper front teeth. The soft palate is raised to prevent the passage of air through the nose. The vocal resonance is by these acts of closure arrested until the maximum of pressure results in the explosive *d*. Pronounce *did* until the sound of the final *d* is fully appreciated.

The subtonic *g* is produced by carrying the tongue back in a curved position against the palate, thereby compressing the vocalized breath, which issues in the explosive *g* when the organs relax. Prolong for practice the final *g* in the word *gag*.

The subtonic *j* has generally been regarded as a compound of *d* and *zh*. There is some doubt as to the accuracy of this analysis. The sound is made by arching the fore part of the tongue against the roof of the mouth, forming a temporary contact, which is suddenly broken, allowing the sound to escape with a forcible expulsion. Practice the word *judge* with special reference to the initial sound.

The atonic *k* is made by a movement and position of the tongue and palate similar to that used in producing the subtonic *g*. The compression of breath, however, is much greater, and the consequent explosion more abrupt and forcible. Pronounce the word *cake*, dwelling with special force upon the final consonant.

The subtonic *l* is made by raising the tongue toward the roof of the mouth with the tip against the interior ridge of gum over the front teeth, allowing the vocalized breath to escape over the sides of the tongue. Prolong the final consonant in the word *lull*.

The subtonic *n* is produced by placing the tip of the tongue against the interior ridge of gum immediately above the upper front teeth, thereby obstructing the oral passage, and forcing the vocalized sound through the nose. Prolong the final *n* in the word *nun*.

The subtonic *ng* is made by bringing the root of the tongue into contact with the soft palate, compelling the sound to escape through the nose. The nostrils are partially closed, so that a marked resonance is produced in the nasal cavities. Prolong the *ng* in *song*.

The atonic *t* is made in the same way as the letter *d*, with this difference; in the case of the *t* there is an absence of vocality, and the explosive *t* is heard when the forcible contact of the tip of the tongue with the interior ridge of upper gum is suddenly broken. Pronounce the word *tent* with special reference to the final consonant.

The vibrant *r* is made by placing the tongue with the slightest pressure against the interior ridge of gum over the front teeth, and allowing the vocalized sound to pass over the extreme tip, thereby causing it to vibrate. The trill should never be prolonged. The word *rap* is suggested for practice.

The smooth *r* is made by a gentle vibration of the entire tongue, which is slightly drawn back and lifted near the roof of the mouth. Prolong the final consonant in the word *war*.

The atonic *s* is made by rounding up the tip of the tongue against the interior gum immediately over the front teeth, forming a small aperture for the escape of the breath. The forcible aspiration produced by this partial closure resembles the sound of water under pressure as it escapes from the nozzle of a pipe. Prolong the final consonant in the word *cease* until the true sound of *s* is appreciated.

The atonic *sh* is formed in a manner similar to the subtonic *zh*, the blade of the tongue being well rounded toward the roof of the mouth, and the breath expelled with great force, giving a highly aspirated sound. Prolong the final *sh* in the word *push*.

The consonant *y*, like the *w*, is a vowel with a breathing. The organs are placed in very much the same position in making the *y* as in making long *e*. The palate and the root of the tongue, however, are brought more closely together, so that the initial sound is a mere buzz or breathing. The pressure of the tongue against the teeth is also much greater than in the production of the vowel. Let special attention be paid to the initial sound of the word *yes*.

The subtonic *z* is made with the organs in the same general position as in making the atonic *s*. The pressure, however, is very much less, and the breath is vocalized, not aspirated, sound. Prolong the initial consonant sound in the word *zone*.

The subtonic *zh* is produced by raising the whole fore part of the tongue close to the roof of the mouth, with the teeth nearly shut, and allowing a partially vocal sound to escape between the tongue and the teeth. Prolong the final sound in the first syllable of the word *azure*.

To some the foregoing analysis may seem unnecessarily minute, but exactness in articulation cannot be secured without the closest attention to details in the formation and execution of these consonantal elements. Practice these sounds until they can be made with *precision, rapidity*, and *energy*.

The Second Step is the mastery of final combinations. This is the most important step in the practice, for it is the final consonants that we fail to articulate. The method of practice is as follows: take for example the final combination *ld*.

(1) Articulate the *l*, then the *d*.

(2) Articulate the combination *ld*.

(3) Pronounce the word *bold*.

The order of practice suggested above should be strictly pursued, in order that accuracy may be secured, not only in the articulation of each element, but also in the blending of two or more consonants. The pronunciation of the word is also important in practice, as it constantly calls attention to the measure of energy needed in uttering distinctly the closing sounds of words. Practice the final combinations below in the manner indicated above.

ld—bold, hailed, tolled.

lf—elf, wolf, gulf, sylph.

lk—milk, silk, bulk, hulk.

lm—elm, helm, whelm, film.

lp—help, gulp, alp, scalp.

ls—falls, tells, toils, halls.

lt—fault, melt, bolt, hilt.

lve—elve, delve, revolve.

md—maim'd, claim'd, gloom'd.

ms—streams, gleams, climes.

nd—land, band, and, hand.

ns—dens, runs, gains, gleans.

nk—bank, dank, sank, link.

nce—dance, glance, hence.

nt—ant, want, gaunt, point.

sm—chasm, schism, prism.

sp—asp, clasp, grasp.

st—vast, mast, lest.

ct—act, fact, reject.

pn—op'n, rip'n, weap'n.

kn—tak'n, wak'n, tok'n.

tn—bright'n, tight'n, whit'n.

ble—able, Bible, double.

ple—ample, triple, topple.

bl'd—troubl'd, bubbl'd, doubl'd.

dl'd—cradl'd, saddl'd, idl'd.

mst—arm'st, charm'st.

lst—call'st, heal'st, till'st.
nst—canst, runn'st, gain'st.
dst—midst, call'dst, roll'dst.
rdst—heard'st, guard'st, reward'st.
ngdst—wrong'dst, throng'dst.
rmdst—arm'dst, form'dst.
rndst—learn'dst, scorn'dst.

The Third Step is the pronunciation of words of many syllables. The object of this step is to distribute the articulative energy so that all the syllables of a long word shall be brought out evenly. Frequently we apply so much force to the accented syllable that the syllables immediately preceding and following are imperfectly enunciated. The final syllables also frequently suffer.

Method of practice: pronounce each of the following words five times in rapid succession and with vigorous force. It may be necessary to begin the pronunciation at a slow rate of utterance, and to increase the rate as the pupil gains in articulative energy.

absolutely	antipathy	constitution	multiplication
accessory	apocrypha	lucubration	articulately
accurately	affability	colloquially	disinterestedly
agitated	chronological	indissolubly	congratulatory
adequately	annihilate	temporarily	circumlocution
angularly	apostatize	mythological	disingenuousness
antepenult	innumerable	appropriate	ecclesiastically
revolution	intolerable	assimilate	authoritatively
institution	dishonorable	acquiescence	superiority
deglutition	collaterally	momentarily	incalculable
lugubrious	apologetic	ambiguously	indisputable
necessarily	dietetically	atmospherical	immediately
generally	apocalyptic	allegorical	justificatory
abominably	coagulation	inexplicable	

The Fourth Step is the mastery of difficult combinations in sentences. Rigid personal criticism is necessary at each step. Difficult words and combinations of words should not be passed over or avoided because of inability to master them. It is much better to slacken the speed of utterance and gradually acquire the power of conquering the difficulties. Pronounce the following sentences, increasing the rate of utterance as strength and facility in articulation are acquired.

Amos Ames, the amiable aëronaut, aided in an aërial enterprise at the age of eighty-eight.

Some shun sunshine. Do you shun sunshine?

Fine white wine vinegar with veal.

Bring a bit of buttered brown bran bread.

Geese cackle, cattle low, crows caw, cocks crow.

Eight gray geese in a green field grazing.

Six thick thistle sticks.

Lucy likes light literature.

A big black bug bit a big black bear.

Peter Prangle, the prickly prangly pear picker picked three pecks of prickly prangly pears from the prickly prangly pear trees on the pleasant prairies.

Theophilus Thistle, the successful thistle sifter, in sifting a sieve full of unsifted thistles, thrust three thousand thistles through the thick of his thumb; now if Theophilus Thistle, the successful thistle sifter, in sifting a sieve full of unsifted thistles, thrust three thousand thistles through the thick of his thumb, see that thou, in sifting a sieve full of unsifted thistles, thrust not three thousand thistles through the thick of thy thumb. Success to the successful thistle sifter!

She sells sea-shells. Shall Susan sell sea-shells.

What whim led White Whitney to whittle, whistle, whisper, and whimper, near the wharf where a floundering whale might wheel and whirl?

He sawed six, long, slim, sleek, slender saplings.

Swan swam over the sea. Swan swam back again. Well swam, swan.

Amidst the mists and coldest frosts,
With stoutest wrists and loudest boasts,
He thrusts his fists against the posts
And still insists he sees the ghosts.

The Fifth Step is reading.

Narrative, descriptive, and didactic styles are recommended for practice at first. Newspaper articles, essays, conversations, and biographical sketches should be frequently read aloud, and at sight.

Pursue these directions with patience and diligence, and without a question of doubt your articulation will be improved, and will finally become as distinct and perfect as public speaking and reading demand.

A chart may be made for the consonants similar in size to the one suggested on page 26 for the vowels. It should be hung on the wall of the study-room, and the various exercises in articulation should be practiced *frequently and persistently.*

OUTLINE OF CHART FOR THE CONSONANTAL SOUNDS.

FIRST STEP.—Master consonantal elements.

TABLE OF CONSONANTAL SOUNDS.

Lips.	Lips and Teeth.	Teeth and Tongue.	Tongue and Palate.	Teeth, Tongue, and Palate.
b as in babe m " " maim p " " pipe w " " woe wh " " when	f as in fife v " " valve	th as in thin th " " thine	ch as in church d " " did g " " gag j " " judge k " " cake l " " lull n " " nun ng " " song t " " tent	r as in rap r " " war s " " cease sh " " push y " " yet z " " zone zh " " azure

SECOND STEP.—Master final combinations of consonants.
> ld—bold, fold; lk—milk, silk; lp—help, gulp; nd—land, band.
> lf—elf, wolf; lm—elm, helm; ls—falls, tells; nk—bank, dank, etc.

THIRD STEP.—Master the pronunciation of words of many syllables:
> Absolutely, accessory, accurately, agitated, etc.

FOURTH STEP.—Master difficult combinations in sentences.
> Some shun sunshine, etc.

FIFTH STEP.—Common reading.

Students in making this chart will fill in all vacant spaces under the several *steps* with material for practice.

HOW CAN I BECOME A NATURAL SPEAKER?

Before we attempt to answer this question it would not be irrelevant to investigate certain charges of eccentric and unnatural speaking brought against the ministerial profession, and to enter a protest against the unwise and ferocious methods of criticism prevalent in our day.

There always has been a certain piquant pleasure in criticising the clergy. No opportunity has been allowed to pass unimproved, and advice has been offered *ad nauseam*. If this advice, in all cases, had been discriminating and just, good results might have followed; but alas! the criticism of the elocution of the pulpit has so frequently taken the form of ridicule or indiscriminate condemnation, that nothing has come of it save a prejudiced notion in the public mind that ministers, as a class, are the poorest speakers we have. However general this belief may be, it is very certain that many of our best speakers are in the ranks of the ministry, and must, of necessity, be there as long as the present order of things continues. The minister has altogether the best field for the cultivation of elegant and effective public address; the orderly audience, the church constructed with special reference to speaking, the wide range of topics to be discussed, the important interests involved in the discussion, furnish conditions that no other profession can offer. So far then from believing ministers to be the poorest speakers, we are inclined to believe that they are the best.

Whatever opinion may be entertained with reference to this matter, it is very evident that a fierce and dangerous spirit of fault-finding is prevalent and popular in our day. We live in an age of such large freedom that nobody hesitates to criticise or rather to find fault, forgetting that the rarest and highest ability is required for useful and safe criticism. The true province of the critic is to construct and build up, not to destroy and pull down. However beneficent and helpful constructive criticism might be to society, it is nevertheless true that modern criticism has become essentially destructive. It is popular, in our day, to use the knife, to cut deep, to parade the weakness of public men rather than to construct better men out of what we have. And, although ministers are the targets at which the public especially delight to aim their shafts, it must be confessed that the clergy themselves are often as fierce and heartless in their criticism of one another as are the outsiders. It is not our purpose to stand sponsor for any of the eccentricities or improprieties of pulpit address, nor do we think it wise to allow an indifferent standard of excellence to be set up and go unchallenged; we simply wish to condemn, as dangerous and wicked, the careless, jocose, and irresponsible style of criticism that prevails.

This habit of fault-finding has grown to such an extent that ministers expect it, and indeed frequently invite it, and often act as though they were disappointed if they do not get more than they deserve.

How often do we hear ministers using these inviting words—"Now do not spare me"—"Cut me to pieces"— not knowing that this is the worst kind of criticism. Is it ever helpful to beat a man to pieces, and leave him in weakness to struggle back to his former health and strength? Is it ever cheering or strengthening to tell a man that he is greatly at fault in his reading and speaking, and that he ought to desist from public work until he can acquire a better form, and then to leave him in his discouragement to improve under the gracious and good advice he has received?

To all such reformers we have but one word: never criticise any man's reading or speaking unless you can suggest a better method, and can outline a course of training that will lead to that end. Keeping this principle in view, we will endeavor to discuss our theme: "How can I become a natural speaker?"

An unpleasant melody or intonation of voice has given rise to the phrase—the "ministerial tone." So very few speakers use a melody entirely free from unpleasant tones, that it would be just as proper to speak of the actor's tone, or the lawyer's tone, as to speak of the ministerial tone.

It must be remembered that a sentence may be written out in musical form as well as a song or any other musical composition, the chief difference being this: in the melody of song everything is arbitrary; in the melody of speech everything is voluntary. In other words, when you sing a song you must sing the notes as they are written on the musical staff; in reading an essay you make your own music.

Now it must be very evident that those people who are unable to sing, because of their lack of appreciation of musical sound, must be under great disadvantage in making good music when they speak. It is not necessary, however, that a person should be a good musician or singer in order to be a good speaker. It is only necessary that the speaker should have such an appreciation of musical sound that the variety of intonation employed may be pleasing to the ear. Let it not be imagined, however, that an agreeable melody can be acquired by a few weeks' practice. It may take months and years, and never be thoroughly mastered; but any improvement in this direction is a substantial gain.

The attainment of a pleasing variety of intonation secures two things that are essential to the successful public speaker: first, a well modulated voice, which renders all speech agreeable; second, inflection, which renders all speech effective and intelligent. A careful and continuous study and practice of the following suggestions is recommended for the improvement of the melody of the voice.

The First Step: *Practice Colloquial Reading.*—A number of colloquial selections should be secured. The following are admirable specimens of colloquial style:

A SIMILAR CASE.

Jack, I hear you 've gone and done it,—
 Yes, I know; most fellows will;
Went and tried it once myself, sir,
 Though you see I 'm single still.
And you met her—did you tell me—
 Down at Newport, last July,
And resolved to ask the question
 At a soirée ? So did I.

I suppose you left the ball-room,
　　With its music and its light;
For they say love's flame is brightest
　　In the darkness of the night.
Well, you walked along together,
　　Overhead the starlit sky;
And I'll bet—old man, confess it—
　　You were frightened. So was I.

So you strolled along the terrace,
　　Saw the summer moonlight pour
All its radiance on the waters,
　　As they rippled on the shore,
Till at length you gathered courage,
　　When you saw that none was nigh—
Did you draw her close and tell her
　　That you loved her? So did I.

Well, I need n't ask you further,
　　And I'm sure I wish you joy.
Think I'll wander down and see you
　　When you 're married—eh, my boy?
When the honeymoon is over
　　And you 're settled down, we'll try—
What? the deuce you say! Rejected—
　　You rejected? So was I.

Anonymous.

This selection and the following one should be read
and re-read until the intonations seem as natural as
though you were engaged in a conversation with an old
friend.

OLD CHUMS.

Is it you, Jack? Old boy, is it really you?
　　I should n't have known you but that I was told
You might be expected;—pray, how do you do?
　　But what, under heavens, has made you so old?

Your hair! why, you 've only a little gray fuzz!
　　And your beard 's white! but that can be beautifully
　　　　dyed;
And your legs are n't but just half as long as they was;
　　And then—stars and garters! your vest is so wide.

Is this your hand? Lord, how I envied you that
　In the time of our courting,—so soft, and so small,
And now it is callous inside, and so fat,—
　Well, you beat the very old deuce, that is all.

Turn round! let me look at you! is n't it odd
　How strange in a few years a fellow's chum grows!
Your eye is shrunk up like a bean in a pod,
　And what are these lines branching out from your nose?

Your back has gone up and your shoulders gone down,
　And all the old roses are under the plough;
Why, Jack, if we 'd happened to meet about town,
　I would n't have known you from Adam, I vow!

You 've had trouble, have you? I 'm sorry; but, John,
　All trouble sits lightly at your time of life.
How 's Billy, my namesake? You do n't say he 's gone
　To the war, John, and that you have buried your wife?

Poor Katherine! so she has left you—ah me!
　I thought she would live to be fifty, or more.
What is it you tell me? She *was* fifty-three!
　O no, Jack! she was n't so much by a score.

Well, there 's little Katy,—was that her name, John?
　She 'll rule your house one of these days like a queen.
That baby! good lord! is she married and gone?
　With a Jack ten years old! and a Katy fourteen!

Then I give it up! Why, you 're younger than I
　By ten or twelve years, and to think you 've come back
A sober old greybeard, just ready to die!
　I do n't understand how it is,—do you, Jack?

I 've got all my faculties yet, sound and bright;
　Slight failure my eyes are beginning to hint;
But still, with my spectacles on, and a light
　'Twixt them and the page, I can read any print.

My hearing *is* dull, and my leg is more spare,
　Perhaps, than it was when I beat you at ball;
My breath gives out, too, if I go up a stair,—
　But nothing worth mentioning, nothing at all!

My hair is just turning a little you see,
  And lately I 've put on a broader-brimmed hat
Than I were at your wedding, but you will agree,
  Old fellow, I look all the better for that.

I'm sometimes a little rheumatic 'tis true,
  And my nose is n't quite on a straight line, they say;
For all that, I don't think I've changed much, do you?
  And I don't feel a day older, Jack—not a day.

Alice Cary.

THE BRAKEMAN AT CHURCH.

On the road once more, with Lebanon fading away in the distance, the fat passenger drumming idly on the window-pane, the cross passenger sound asleep, and the tall, thin passenger reading "General Grant's Tour Around the World," and wondering why "Green's August Flower" should be printed above the doors of "A Buddhist Temple at Benares." To me comes the brakeman, and seating himself on the arm of the seat, says, "I went to church yesterday."

"Yes?" I said, with that interested inflection that asks for more. "And what church did you attend?"

"Which do you guess?" he asked.

"Some union mission church," I hazarded.

"No," said he; "I don't like to run on these branch roads very much. I don't often go to church, and when I do, I want to run on the main line, where your run is regular, and you go on schedule time and don't have to wait on connections. I don't like to run on a branch. Good enough, but I don't like it."

"Episcopal?" I guessed.

"Limited express," he said; "all palace cars and two dollars extra for seat, fast time, and only stop at big stations. Nice line, but too exhaustive for a brakeman. All train-men in uniform, conductor's punch and lantern silver-plated, and no train-boys allowed. Then the passengers are allowed to talk back at the conductor, and it makes them too free and easy. No, I could n't stand the palace cars. Rich road, though. Don't often hear of a receiver being appointed for that line. Some mighty nice people travel on it, too."

"Universalist ?" I suggested.

"Broad gauge," said the brakeman; "does too much complimentary business. Everybody travels on a pass. Conductor does n't get a fare once in fifty miles. Stops at flag-stations, and won't run into anything but a union depot. No smoking car on the train. Train orders are rather vague, though, and the train-men don't get along well with the passengers. No, I do n't go to the Universalist, but I know some good men who run on that road."

"Presbyterian ?" I asked.

"Narrow gauge, eh ?" said the brakeman; "pretty track, straight as a rule; tunnel right through a mountain rather than go around it; spirit-level grade; passengers have to show their tickets before they get on the train. Mighty strict road, but the cars are a little narrow; have to sit one in a seat, and no room in the aisle to dance. Then there is no stop-over tickets allowed; got to go straight through to the station you 're ticketed for, or you can't get on at all. When the car is full, no extra coaches; cars built at the shop to hold just so many, and nobody else allowed on. But you don't often hear of an accident on that road. It 's run right up to the rules."

"Maybe you joined the Free Thinkers ?" said I.

"Scrub road," said the brakeman; "dirt road-bed and no ballast; no time-card and no train dispatcher. All trains run wild, and every engineer makes his own time, just as he pleases. Smoke if you want to; kind of go-as-you-please road. Too many side-tracks, and every switch wide open all the time, with the switchman sound asleep and the target lamp dead out. Get on as you please and get off when you want to. Don't have to show your tickets, and the conductor is n't expected to do anything but amuse the passengers. No, sir. I was offered a pass, but I do n't like the line. I do n't like to travel on a road that has no terminus. Do you know, sir, I asked a division superintendent where that road run to, and he said he hoped to die if he knew. I asked him if the general superintendent could tell me, and he said he did n't believe they had a general superintendent, and if they had he did n't know anything more about the road than the passengers. I asked him who he reported to, and he said 'nobody.' I asked a conductor who he got his orders from, and he said he did n't take orders from any living man or dead ghost. And when I asked the engineer who he got his orders from, he said he 'd like to see anybody give him orders; he 'd run the train to suit himself, or he 'd run it into the ditch. Now you see, sir, I'm a railroad man, and I do n't care to run on a road that has no time, makes no connections, runs nowhere, and has no superintendent. It may be all right, but I 've railroaded too long to understand it.''

"Maybe you went to the Congregational church?"

"Popular road,'' said the brakeman; "an old road, too —one of the very oldest in the country. Good road-bed and comfortable cars. Well-managed road, too; directors don't interfere with division superintendents and train orders. Road 's mighty popular, but it 's pretty independent, too. Yes, did n't one of the division superintendents down east discontinue one of the oldest stations on this line two or three years ago? But it 's a mighty pleasant road to travel on—always has such a pleasant class of passengers.''

"Did you try the Methodist?" I said.

"Now you 're shouting!" he said with some enthusiasm. "Nice road, eh? Fast time and plenty of passengers. Engines carry a power of steam, and don't you forget it; steam-gauge shows a hundred and enough all the time. Lively road; when the conductor shouts 'all aboard,' you can hear him at the next station. Every train-light shines like a head-light. Stop-over checks are given on all through tickets; passenger can drop off the train as often as he likes, do the station two or three days, and hop on the next revival train that comes thundering along. Good, whole-souled, companionable conductors; ain't a road in the country where the passengers feel more at home. No passes; every passenger pays full traffic rates for his ticket. Wesleyanhouse air-brakes on all trains, too; pretty safe road, but I did n't ride over it yesterday.''

"Perhaps you tried the Baptist?" I guessed once more.

"Ah, ha!" said the brakeman; "she's a daisy; is n't she? River-road; beautiful curves, sweep around anything to keep close to the river; but it 's all steel rail and rock ballast; single track all the way; and not a sidetrack from the round-house to the terminus. Takes a heap of water to run it, though; double tanks at every station, and there is n't an engine in the shops that can

pull a pound or run a mile with less than two gauges.
But it runs through a lovely country; those river-roads
always do; river on one side and hills on the other, and
it's a steady climb up the grade all the way till the run
ends where the fountain-head of the river begins. Yes,
sir; I'll take the river-road every time for a lovely trip;
sure connections and a good time, and no prairie dust
blowing in at the windows. And yesterday, when the
conductor came around for the tickets with a little basket-
punch, I didn't ask him to pass me, but I paid my fare
like a little man—twenty-five cents for an hour's run
and a little concert by the passengers thrown in. I tell
you, pilgrim, you take the river-road when you want—"

But just here the long whistle from the engine
announced a station, and the brakeman hurried to the
door, shouting:

"Zionsville! the train makes no stops between here
and Indianapolis!"—*Robert J. Burdette.*

Additional selections for practice: "The One Horse
Shay," Oliver Wendell Holmes; "Her Letter," Bret
Harte.

The conversational character of these selections will
assist the reader to a natural and melodious use of the
voice. They will induce him to read as he talks, and will
help him to acquire a variety that is free from false and
affected intonations.

No instruction or advice is valuable just at this point,
save that which inspires patient endeavor, constantly
directs the attention of the pupil to the melody of simple
conversation, and stimulates a desire for perfect freedom
from all that is artificial. After a fair degree of success is
attained in reading these selections, a more difficult list of
pieces should be tried—those involving sentimental and
colloquial qualities.

The Second Step: *Colloquial Selections Involving Sentiment.*

IN AN ATELIER.

I pray you, do not turn your head; and let your hands lie
    folded—so.
It was a dress like this, blood-red, that Dante liked so,
    long ago.
You don't know Dante? Never mind. He loved a lady
    wondrous fair—
His model? Something of the kind. I wonder if she had
    your hair!

I wonder if she looked so meek, and was not meek at all,
    —my dear
I want that side-light on your cheek. He loved her, it is
    very clear,
And painted her, as I paint you; but rather better on the
    whole.
Depress your chin, yes, that will do: he was a painter of
    the soul!

And painted portraits, too, I think, in the Inferno—rather
    good!
I'd make some certain critics blink if I'd his method and
    his mood.
Her name was—Jennie, let your glance rest there by that
    Majolica tray—
Was Beatrice; they met by chance—they met by chance,
    the usual way.

As you and I met, months ago, do you remember? How
    your feet
Went crinkle-crinkle on the snow adown the long gas-
    lighted street!
An instant in the drug store's glare you stood as in a
    golden frame!
And then I swore it—then and there—to hand your sweet-
    ness down to fame.

They met, and loved, and never wed—all this was long
    before our time;
And though they died, they are not dead—such endless
    youth gives 'mortal rhyme!
Still walks the earth, with haughty mien, great Dante, in
    his soul's distress;
And still the lovely Florentine goes lovely in her blood-
    red dress.

You do not understand at all? He was a poet; on his page
He drew her; and though kingdoms fall, this lady lives
    from age to age:
A poet—that means painter too, for words are colors,
    rightly laid;
And they outlast our brightest hue, for ochers crack and
    crimsons fade.

The poets—they are lucky ones! when we are thrust upon
    the shelves,
Our works turn into skeletons almost as quickly as our-
    selves;
For our poor canvas peels at length, at length is prized
    when all is bare:
"What grace!" the critics cry, "what strength!" when
    neither strength nor grace is there.

Ah, Jennie, I am sick at heart, it is so little one can do,
We talk our jargon—live for art! I 'd much prefer to live
    for you.
How dull and lifeless colors are: you smile, and all my
    picture lies:
I wish that I could crush a star to make a pigment for
    your eyes.

Yes, child, I know I 'm out of tune; the light is bad; the
    sky is gray:
I 'll work no more this afternoon, so lay your royal robes
    away.
Besides, you 're dreamy—hand on chin—I know not what
    —not in the vein:
While I would paint Anne Boleyn, you sit there looking
    like Elaine.

Not like the youthful, radiant Queen, unconscious of the
    coming woe,
But rather as she might have been, preparing for the
    headsman's blow.
I see! I 've put you in a miff—sitting bolt upright, wrist on
    wrist.
How should you look? Why, dear as if—somehow—as if
    you 'd just been kissed.

T. B. Aldrich.

AN ORDER FOR A PICTURE.

O good painter, tell me true,
    Has your hand the cunning to draw
    Shapes of things you never saw?
Ay? Well, here is an order for you.

Woods and cornfields a little brown,—
    The picture must not be over-bright,
    Yet all in the golden and gracious light
Of a cloud, when the summer sun is down.
    Alway and alway, night and morn,
    Woods upon woods, with fields of corn
        Lying between them, not quite sere,
And not in the full, thick, leafy bloom,
When the wind can hardly find breathing-room
        Under their tassels,—cattle near,
Biting shorter the short green grass,
And a hedge of sumach and sassafras,
With bluebirds twittering all around—
(Ah, good painter, you can't paint sound!)
    These, and the house where I was born,
Low and little, and black and old,
With children, many as it can hold,
All at the windows open wide,
Heads and shoulders clear outside,
And fair young faces all ablush:
    Perhaps you may have seen, some day,
    Roses crowding the self-same way,
Out of a wilding, wayside bush.

Listen closer. When you have done
    With woods and cornfields and grazing herds,
A lady, the loveliest ever the sun
Looked down upon, you must paint for me;
O, if I only could make you see
    The clear blue eyes, the tender smile,
The sovereign sweetness, the gentle grace,
The woman's soul, and the angel's face
    That are beaming on me all the while!—
    I need not speak these foolish words;
    Yet one word tells you all I would say,—
She is my mother: you will agree
    That all the rest may be thrown away.

Two little urchins at her knee
You must paint, sir: one like me,—
    The other with a clearer brow,
  And the light of his adventurous eyes
  Flashing with boldest enterprise:
At ten years old he went to sea,—
    God knoweth if he be living now,—
  He sailed in the good ship Commodore,—
Nobody ever crossed her track
To bring us news, and she never came back.
  Ah, 'tis twenty long years and more
Since that old ship went out of the bay
  With my great-hearted brother on her deck;
  I watched him till he shrank to a speck,
And his face was toward me all the way.
Bright his hair was, a golden brown,
  The time we stood at our mother's knee:
That beauteous head, if it did go down,
  Carried sunshine into the sea!

Out in the fields one summer night
  We were together, half afraid
Of the corn-leaves' rustling, and of the shade
    Of the high hills, stretching so still and far,—
Loitering till after the low little light
  Of the candle shone through the open door,
And over the haystack's pointed top,
All of a tremble, and ready to drop,
    The first half-hour, the great yellow star
  That we with staring, ignorant eyes,
Had often and often watched to see
  Propped and held in its place in the skies
By the fork of a tall, red mulberry-tree,
  Which close in the edge of our flax-field grew,—
Dead at the top,—just one branch full
Of leaves, notched round, and lined with wool,
  From which it tenderly shook the dew
Over our heads, when we came to play
In its handbreadth of shadow, day after day:—
  Afraid to go home, sir; for one of us bore
A nest full of speckled and thin-shelled eggs,—
The other, a bird, held fast by the legs,
Not so big as a straw of wheat:
The berries we gave her she would n't eat,

But cried and cried, till we held her bill,
So slim and shining, to keep her still.

At last we stood at our mother's knee.
   Do you think, sir, if you try,
    You can paint the look of a lie?
   If you can, pray have the grace
   To put it solely in the face
Of the urchin that is likest me:
    I think 'twas solely mine, indeed:
   But that's no matter,—paint it so;
   The eyes of our mother—(take good heed)—
Looking not on the nestful of eggs,
Nor the fluttering bird, held so fast by the legs,
But straight through our faces down to our lies,
And O, with such injured, reproachful surprise!
   I felt my heart bleed where that glance went, as though
   A sharp blade struck through it.
                    You, sir, know,
   That you on the canvas are to repeat
Things that are fairest, things most sweet,—
Woods and cornfields and mulberry tree,—
The mother,—the lads, with their bird, at her knee:
   But, O, that look of reproachful woe!
High as the heavens your name I'll shout,
   If you paint me the picture, and leave that out.
                      Alice Cary.

JOHN BURNS OF GETTYSBURG.

Have you heard the story the gossips tell
Of Burns of Gettysburg?—No? Ah, well
Brief is the glory that hero earns,
Briefer the story of poor John Burns;
He was the fellow who won renown—
The only man who didn't back down
When the rebels rode through his native town;
But held his own in the fight next day,
When all his townsfolk ran away.
That was in July, sixty-three,—
The very day that General Lee,
The flower of Southern chivalry,
Baffled and beaten, backward reeled
From a stubborn Meade and a barren field.

I might tell how, but the day before,
John Burns stood at his cottage-door,
Looking down the village street,
    Where, in the shade of his peaceful vine,
    He heard the low of his gathered kine,
And felt their breath with incense sweet;
Or, I might say, when the sunset burned
The old farm gable, he thought it turned
The milk that fell in a babbling flood
Into the milk-pail, red as blood;
Or, how he fancied the hum of bees
Were bullets buzzing among the trees.
But all such fanciful thoughts as these
Were strange to a practical man like Burns,
Who minded only his own concerns,
Troubled no more by fancies fine
Than one of his calm-eyed, long-tailed kine—
Quite old-fashioned, and matter-of-fact,
Slow to argue, but quick to act.
That was the reason, as some folks say,
He fought so well on that terrible day.

And it was terrible.   On the right
Raged for hours the heavy fight,
Thundered the battery's double bass—
Difficult music for men to face;
While on the left—where now the graves
Undulate like the living waves
That all the day unceasing swept
Up to the pits the rebels kept—
Round shot plowed the upland glades,
Sown with bullets, reaped with blades;
Shattered fences here and there
Tossed their splinters in the air;
The very trees were stripped and bare;
The barns that once held yellow grain
Were heaped with harvests of the slain;
The cattle bellowed on the plain,
The turkeys screamed with might and main,
And brooding barn-fowl left their rest
With strange shells bursting in each nest.

Just where the tide of battle turns,
Erect and lonely, stood old John Burns.

How do you think the man was dressed?
He wore an ancient, long buff vest,
Yellow as saffron—but his best;
And, buttoned over his manly breast
Was a bright blue coat with a rolling collar,
And large gilt buttons—size of a dollar—
With tails that country-folk called "swaller."
He wore a broad-brimmed, bell-crowned hat,
White as the locks on which it sat.
Never had such a sight been seen
For forty years on the village-green,
Since old John Burns was a country beau,
And went to the "quilting" long ago.

Close at his elbows, all that day
Veterans of the Peninsula,
Sunburnt and bearded, charged away,
And striplings, downy of lip and chin,—
Clerks that the Home Guard mustered in—
Glanced as they passed at the hat he wore,
Then at the rifle his right hand bore,
And hailed him from out their youthful lore,
With scraps of a slangy *répertoire :*
"How are you, White Hat?" "Put her through!"
"Your head's level!" and, "Bully for you!"
Called him "Daddy"—and begged he 'd disclose
The name of the tailor who made his clothes,
And what was the value he set on those;
While Burns, unmindful of jeers and scoff,
Stood there picking the rebels off—
With his long, brown rifle and bell-crown hat,
And the swallow-tails they were laughing at.

'Twas but a moment, for that respect
Which clothes all courage their voices checked;
And something the wildest could understand
Spake in the old man's strong right hand,
And his corded throat, and the lurking frown
Of his eyebrows under his old bell-crown;
Until, as they gazed, there crept an awe
Through the ranks in whispers, and some men saw,
In the antique vestments and long white hair
The Past of the Nation in battle there.
And some of the soldiers since declare

That the gleam of his old white hat afar,
Like the crested plume of the brave Navarre,
That day was their oriflamme of war.
Thus raged the battle. You know the rest:
How the rebels beaten, and backward pressed,
Broke at the final charge and ran.
At which John Burns—a practical man
Shouldered his rifle, unbent his brows,
And then went back to his bees and cows.

That is the story of old John Burns;
This is the moral the reader learns:
In fighting the battle, the question's whether
You 'll show a hat that's white, or a feather.

Bret Harte.

HANNAH JANE.

She is n't half so handsome as when twenty years agone,
At her old home in Piketon, Parson Avery made us one:
The great house crowded full of guests of every degree,
The girls all envying Hannah Jane, the boys all envying
me.

Her fingers then were taper, and her skin as white as milk,
Her brown hair—what a mess it was! and soft and fine as
silk;
No wind-moved willow by a brook had ever such a grace,
The form of Aphrodite, with a pure Madonna face.

She had but meager schooling: her little notes to me,
Were full of crooked pothooks, and the worst orthography:
Her "dear" she spelled with double *e* and "kiss" with but
one *s:*
But when one 's crazed with passion, what 's a letter more
or less?

She blundered in her writing, and she blundered when
she spoke,
And every rule of syntax that old Murray made, she
broke;
But she was beautiful and fresh, and I—well, I was young;
Her form and face o'erbalanced all the blunders of her
tongue.

I was but little better. True, I 'd longer been at school;
My tongue and pen were run, perhaps, a little more by rule;
But that was all. The neighbors round, who both of us
    well knew,
Said—which I believed—she was the better of the two.

All 's changed; the light of seventeen 's no longer in her
    eyes;
Her wavy hair is gone—that loss the coiffeur's art supplies;
Her form is thin and angular; she slightly forward bends;
Her fingers once so shapely, now are stumpy at the ends.

She knows but very little, and in little are we one;
The beauty rare, that more than hid that great defect, is
    gone.
My parvenu relations now deride my homely wife,
And pity me that I am tied to such a clod for life.

I know there is a difference; at reception and levee,
The brightest, wittiest, and most famed of women smile
    on me;
And everywhere I hold my place among the greatest men;
And sometimes sigh, with Whittier's judge, "Alas! it
    might have been."

When they all crowd around me, stately dames and bril-
    liant belles,
And yield to me the homage that all great success com-
    pels,
Discussing art and statecraft, and literature as well,
From Homer down to Thackeray, and Swedenborg on
    "Hell."

I can't forget that from these streams my wife has never
    quaffed,
Has never with Ophelia wept, nor with Jack Falstaff
    laughed;
Of authors, actors, artists—why, she hardly knows the
    names;
She slept while I was speaking on the Alabama claims.

I can't forget—just at this point another form appears—
The wife I wedded as she was before my prosperous years;
I travel o'er the dreary road we traveled side by side,
And wonder what my share would be, if Justice should
    decide.

She had four hundred dollars left her from the old estate;
On that we married, and, thus poorly armored, faced our
  fate.
I wrestled with my books; her task was harder far than
  mine—
'Twas how to make two hundred dollars do the work of
  nine.

At last I was admitted; then I had my legal lore,
An office with a stove and desk, of books perhaps a score;
She had her beauty and her youth, and some housewifely
  skill,
And love for me, and faith in me, and back of that a *will*.

Ah! how she cried for joy when my first legal fight was won,
When our eclipse passed partly by, and we stood in the sun!
The fee was fifty dollars—'twas the work of half a year—
First captive, lean and scraggy, of my legal bow and
  spear.

I well remember when my coat (the only one I had)
Was seedy grown and threadbare, and, in fact, most
  "shocking bad."
The tailor's stern remark when I a modest order made:
"Cash is the basis, sir, on which we tailors do our trade."

Her winter cloak was in his shop by noon that very day;
She wrought on hickory shirts at night that tailor's skill
  to pay;
I got a coat and wore it; but, alas, poor Hannah Jane
Ne'er went to church or lecture, till warm weather came
  again.

Our second season she refused a cloak of any sort,
That I might have a decent suit in which t' appear in
  court;
She made her last year's bonnet do, that I might have a
  hat;—
Talk of the old-time flame-enveloped martyrs after that!

No negro ever worked so hard; a servant's pay to save,
She made herself most willingly a household drudge and
  slave.
What wonder that she never read a magazine or book,
Combining as she did in one, nurse, housemaid, seam-
  stress, cook!

What wonder that the beauty fled that I once so adored!
Her beautiful complexion my fierce kitchen fire devoured;
Her plump, soft, rounded arm, was once too fair to be
    concealed;
Hard work for me that softness into sinewy strength con-
    gealed.

I was her altar, and her love the sacrificial flame;
Ah! with what pure devotion she to that altar came,
And, tearful, flung thereon—alas! I did not know it then—
All that she was, and, more than that, all that she might
    have been!

At last I won success. Ah! then our lives were wider
    parted;
I was far up the rising road; she, poor girl, where we
    started.
I had tried my speed and mettle, and gained strength in
    every race;
I was far up the heights of life—she drudging at the base.

She made me take each fall the stump; she said 't was my
    career,
The wild applause of list'ning crowds was music to my
    ear.
What stimulus had she to cheer her dreary solitude?
For me she lived on gladly, in unnatural widowhood.

She couldn't read my speech; but when the papers all
    agreed
'Twas the best one of the session, those comments she
    could read;
And with a gush of pride thereat, which I had never felt,
She sent them to me in a note with half the words mis-
    spelt.

At twenty-eight the State-house; on the Bench at thirty-
    three;
At forty every gate in life was opened wide to me.
I nursed my powers and grew, and made my point in life;
    but she—
Bearing such pack-horse weary loads, what could a woman
    be?

What could she be! Oh, shame! I blush to think what she
    has been—
The most unselfish of all wives to the selfishest of men.
Yes, plain and homely now she is; she's ignorant, 'tis
    true;
For me she rubbed herself quite out—I represent the two.

Well, I suppose that I might do as other men have done—
First break her heart with cold neglect, then shove her
    out alone.
The world would say 'twas well, and more, would give
    great praise to me,
For having borne with "such a wife" so uncomplainingly.

And shall I? No! The contract 'twixt Hannah, God, and
    me,
Was not for one or twenty years, but for eternity.
No matter what the world may think; I know, down in my
    heart,
That, if either, I'm delinquent; she has bravely done her
    part.

There's another world beyond this; and, on the final day,
Will intellect and learning 'gainst such devotion weigh?
When the great one, made of us two, is torn apart again,
I'll yield the palm, for God is just, and He knows Hannah
    Jane.   *D. R. Locke.*

In these selections an occasional passage of sentiment
occurs that requires a change from a conversational or
staccato to an effusive or flowing form of utterance. To
preserve this smooth utterance and, at the same time,
secure perfect naturalness in the intonations of the voice,
demands a greater degree of skill than the reading of
the purely colloquial styles. The proximity of the colloquial passage to the sentimental will serve as a guide and
help to a natural melody.

The Third Step: *Common Reading.*—We are now prepared to enter upon the practice of narrative, descriptive,
and didactic styles, or what is generally called common
reading. Here the difficulties in securing pleasing variety
are greatly increased. The dignified diction and elaborate
structure of the sentence furnish opportunities for the

display of great taste and skill in the melodious management of the voice. Nothing is more to be prized as an
achievement in elocutionary work than a skillful and
melodious reading of a piece of common English. Such
an acquirement so thoroughly commends itself, because of
its usefulness, that many people wonder why we do not
hear more of it. But like all other good and desirable
things it is not easily secured. It requires patient and
laborious practice to acquire perfect melody in the reading of an essay or a newspaper article.

So difficult is it, that all this preliminary practice of colloquial selections is needful as a preparatory training. I
cannot suggest a better text-book for common reading
than the New Testament.

A few chapters are suggested for practice. The Ser-
mon on the Mount, Matt. v, vi, vii; The Parable of the
Pharisee and the Publican, Luke xviii:9; The Parable of the
Prodigal Son, Luke xv:11; Regeneration, John iii; The
Blind Man Restored to Sight, John ix; Duties Enjoined,
Rom. xii; Charity, 1st Cor. xiii; The Resurrection, 1st
Cor. xv; Faith, Heb. xi; Love, 1st John iv.

Some teachers (whose judgment I greatly respect)
insist that an elaborate system of rules for inflection and
emphasis is the surest way to lead to a natural and pleasing variety of intonation. I admit that success has been
secured by this system of training, but I seriously question the propriety of beginning with rules before the pupil
has been trained to a certain appreciation of musical
variety. The teacher may find an occasional pupil who
will yield to no other treatment than the application of
fixed rules; but such are very rare exceptions. As a
matter of fact, the current melody of a sentence should
not be subjected to rules; for, if it were, you would absolutely fix the intonations of every person, and thereby
destroy all individuality.

I much prefer that the pupil at first should secure a
natural use of his voice, without thought of rules. After
the ear has been trained to a just appreciation of musical
intonations, it will then be time to assist and strengthen
the reader by fixed rules for inflection, cadence, and
emphasis. You will by this method avoid a peculiar mechanical stiffness, that frequently appears in those who
train themselves by rules without any previously acquired

power to execute what the rule requires. Bear in mind constantly this general direction—*read the above chapters as though you were talking in the most direct way to your hearers, and endeavor to impress the truth in as earnest and natural tones as you would use in uttering the same precepts to your personal friends.*

The Fourth Step: *Oratorical Expression.*—Oratory is simply elevated talk, and the same intonations that are used in common reading or conversation should be carried into this style of address. The increase of force, or volume of voice, greatly adds to the difficulty of securing a pleasing variety. It is in this style of composition that speakers are chiefly found guilty of using "tones" or "false notes" or more properly, bad melody. The safest and best advice we can offer to all those who have acquired unfortunate habits of intonation in their public address is this—pursue the system of practice outlined in this discussion until an appreciation of natural melody such as is heard in the ordinary conversation of good speakers is established in your public speaking. A study and practice of the simple and direct form of address found in the orations of Wendell Phillips is recommended; then the more ornate and elaborate styles of Burke and Webster may be attempted.

The Fifth Step: *Grand, Sublime, and Reverential Readings.* — These are probably the most difficult styles in which to secure good melody. In none of the foregoing selections have we used, to any great extent, an effusive utterance; but here it is essential to the expression of the sentiment. The deep orotund voice, rendered with a flowing utterance, offers such opportunities for unpleasant intonations, that very few attain a perfectly musical modulation. An easy way out of the difficulty would be to drop the effusion; but if we do this we sacrifice the sentiment which is the very life of the thought. The only way is to be patient and thorough in the preliminary practice, and to rely upon the cultivated sense of musical sounds thus acquired. To be sure, a less varied melody is required in these styles, but the need of suitable variety is just as imperative here as elsewhere. Because this style of reading is sometimes called monotone, do not conclude that the reader should be monotonous. The reading is made melodious and pleasing by a skillful use of the vanish of the tones in the form of waves. The reading of a large portion of the Old Testament, of the Revelation in the New Testament, the reading of most hymns and of the Liturgy falls under this division.

I have often thought that many of the bad tones used by ministers in the delivery of their sermons could be traced to the frequent use of the reverential style. The remedy for all this is to begin with the simplest forms of reading and lead up to the most difficult; not to reverse the order.

EXERCISES FOR THE DEVELOPMENT OF VOCAL PURITY.

As the body is the instrument used for the production of sound, it is necessary that those parts or muscles of the body which are employed for that purpose should be carefully strengthened and developed, and made subject to the constant control of the will. A physical basis must be laid, before the pupil can acquire a voice suitable for public speaking; and therefore the mastery of exercises in physical culture is an absolute prerequisite to the attainment of a good voice. It is not our purpose to discuss scientifically the laws of sound, or the anatomy of the organs of speech, but to suggest a few practical exercises for students who wish to secure a free and full use of their vocal powers.

One of the first and most imperative demands made upon the public speaker is that his *voice shall be pleasing*. This involves the acquirement of the purest musical quality of tone united with perfect freedom from apparent effort in vocalization. The first step in securing pure tone is to *gain control of the breath*, so that it may flow from the mouth in a perfectly equable stream. This control must be certain and free, and the whole breathing apparatus must be brought, by physical training, under such perfect obedience to the will of the speaker that its action will eventually become largely automatic.

The First Step: Exercises in Physical Culture and Breathing.

Poise.—The head and shoulders should be in such relation to poise that ear, shoulder, hip, and instep shall fall in the same line. An easily balanced position of the parts of the body is essential to free chest expansion and the correct and forcible use of throat and abdominal muscles.

RELAXATION FOR ELASTICITY.

Jaw.—Relax the muscles of the face, beginning with eyelids and eyebrows. Let go all tension until the expression is that of a sleeper, with jaws relaxed and mouth falling open. Move the jaw with the fingers in all directions until it is flexible in joint. Shake relaxed jaws by movement of head sideways and up and down.

Throat.—With the jaw relaxed, open the throat and breathe through it as in snoring. Let head drop forward, throat and neck muscles relaxed. Practice the preceding, letting head fall backward, to right, left, and in oblique directions, until its full weight can be felt.

Tongue.—Let the tongue lie flat in bottom of mouth, tip lightly touching lower teeth; from that position, without arching it, thrust it straight forward and draw it back as far as possible several times. Open the mouth wide, and move the tongue in circular direction, following outline of lips and stretching the muscles at the base of the tongue.

Breathing.—Inhale normal breath slowly, using abdominal, dorsal, and chest muscles in filling the lungs from the lower part to top. Exhale slowly in reverse order. Increase the length of inspirations and expirations, until twenty-five or thirty seconds for each may be easily reached. Inhale slowly through the nostrils for ten, twenty, or thirty seconds. Exhale for the same length of time, using the syllable *hah*, which may be uttered with a gentle aspiration. Repeat this exercise several times, and notice particularly that the stream of air escaping from the mouth is delivered with a *smooth and even flow.*

The Second Step is to vocalize this stream or column of air. The steady management of the air column producing perfect musical vibrations, determines largely the beauty and vocal purity of the tone. It follows then that a regulated emission of the breath becomes an important factor in the production of pure tone. *Sound the tonics ā, ē, ī, ō, ū, ōō, ä.* Inhale freely, and prolong each one of these vowel sounds for ten or twenty seconds. This exercise should be repeated frequently, for it constitutes the beginning and end of training for vocal purity.

All other exercises are, at best, but slight variations of

the above. Bear in mind that it is not multiplicity of exercises that is desirable, but a few well-chosen ones in which the principles of correct vocalization are applied. The ability to sound the tonic $\bar{a}$ for ten or twenty seconds, and from the initiation of the tone to its close to produce perfect musical vibrations, is the surest sign that the pupil is pursuing the most rational and direct course to secure vocal purity. The skillful teacher may assist in relaxing the muscles of the throat, and in placing the tongue and mouth in their proper positions to secure pure tone; but after all is said and done, the instructor cannot, by any physical adjustment of the organs, do more than assist the student in his efforts in vocalization. The mechanism of the human voice is so delicate, and its adjustments are so varied and difficult, that any clumsy attempt to regulate it, as one would tune a piano or a harp, will utterly fail. It will require months and years of practice before the speaker gains free and absolute control of the delicate machinery. Nothing less than untiring patience and industry, united with skillful and careful advice, can master the difficulties. In beginning this exercise, all that the student is required to know is the difference between a harsh and unpleasant sound and a comparatively pure and musical tone. His musical sense, however deficient, can surely detect such a difference.

The Third Step is a slight variation of the preceding exercise, for the purpose of bringing the sound column to the *front part of the mouth.* If the column of sound is directed against the soft palate and the soft walls of the air-chambers above the larynx, a dull, hollow quality of tone will be produced. This is due to the character of the resonating surface against which the column is directed. For clearness, brilliancy, and purity of tone the column should be directed against the hard palate, or sounding-board, in the roof of the mouth. Select a list of words whose initial consonants are made by the lips and teeth. The consonantal combination will aid in bringing the voice forward, and in locating the resonance in its proper place. Pronounce the following words, prolonging the tonic element four or five seconds, constantly endeavoring in your efforts to get the tone more pure and to locate the resonance in the front oral cavity.

māin,	tāme,	fāme,	pāin—pāy,	bāy,	mȧy,	dȧy.
pēel,	mēal,	fēel,	dēal—pīle,	mīle,	fīle,	tīle.
pä,	fä,	mä,	dä —pŏŏh,	bo͞o,	mo͞o,	dō.

The Fourth Step is Reading. Selections involving the sentiments of serenity, beauty, and love, are best suited for exercises in vocal purity. The effusive form of utterance, and the long vowel quantities required for the proper expression of these sentiments, will enable the student to detect harshness or impurity in the tones of his voice.

Singing or chanting exercises may be introduced here, but it is better to use only a few exercises, inasmuch as the same vocal principle enunciated in the *second step* will be repeated with slight variations in all these exercises. As soon as the pupil is aware of the impurity of the tones he is using, and has a clear notion of how to improve the quality of his voice in the use of a few well-chosen exercises, he should be put to the reading of selections. The stimulus of thought and sentiment, and the awakened powers of appreciation, will encourage him in his work, and at the same time furnish as good opportunities for vocal practice as the abstract exercises.

EXAMPLES FOR PRACTICE.

SONG.

When stars are in the quiet skies,
  Then most I pine for thee;
Bend on me then, thy tender eyes,
  As stars look on the sea.
For thoughts, like waves that glide by night,
  Are stillest when they shine;
Mine earthly love lies hushed in light
  Beneath the heaven of thine.

There is an hour when angels keep
  Familiar watch o'er men,
When coarser souls are wrapt in sleep—
  Sweet spirit, meet me then.
There is an hour when holy dreams
  Through slumber fairest glide,
And in that mystic hour it seems
  Thou shouldst be by my side.

The thoughts of thee too sacred are
   For daylight's common beam;
I can but know thee as my star,
   My angel, and my dream!
When stars are in the silent skies,
   Then most I pine for thee;
Bend on me, then, thy tender eyes,
   As stars look on the sea.

                    Sir Edward Lytton.

Frequently test the purity of the tone you are using by prolonging the vowel quantity in certain words, and then use the same pure quality in shortened form for reading—thus, in the first line of the song the words *stars* and *skies* whose vowels are long, may be so used; also in the second line the words *pine* and *thee*, etc.

DRIFTING.

    My soul to-day
    Is far away,
Sailing the Vesuvian Bay;
    My winged boat,
    A bird afloat,
Swims round the purple peaks remote:—

    Round purple peaks
    It sails and seeks
Blue inlets, and their crystal creeks,
    Where high rocks throw,
    Through deeps below,
A duplicated golden glow.

    Far, vague and dim,
    The mountains swim:
While on Vesuvius' misty brim,
    With outstretched hands,
    The gray smoke stands,
O'erlooking the volcanic lands.

    Here Ischia smiles
    O'er liquid miles;
And yonder, bluest of the isles,
    Calm Capri waits,
    Her sapphire gates
Beguiling to her bright estates.

I heed not if
My rippling skiff
Float swift or slow from cliff to cliff;—
With dreamful eyes
My spirit lies
Under the walls of Paradise.

Under the walls
Where swells and falls
The Bay's deep breast at intervals,
At peace I lie,
Blown softly by,
A cloud upon this liquid sky.

The day, so mild,
Is Heaven's own child,
With Earth and Ocean reconciled;—
The airs I feel
Around me steal
Are murmuring to the murmuring keel.

Over the rail
My hand I trail
Within the shadow of the sail,
A joy intense,
The cooling sense,
Glides down my drowsy indolence.

With dreamful eyes
My spirit lies
Where Summer sings and never dies,—
O'erveiled with vines,
She glows and shines
Among her future oil and wines.

Her children hid
The cliffs amid,
Are gamboling with the gamboling kid;
Or down the walls,
With tipsy calls,.
Laugh on the rocks like waterfalls.

The fisher's child,
With tresses wild,
Unto the smooth, bright sand beguiled,

With glowing lips
Sings as she skips,
Or gazes at the far-off ships.

Yon deep bark goes
Where traffic blows,
From lands of sun to lands of snows;—
This happier one,
Its course is run
From lands of snow to lands of sun.

Oh, happy ship,
To rise and dip,
With the blue crystal at your lip!
Oh, happy crew,
My heart with you
Sails, and sails, and sings anew!

No more, no more
The worldly shore
Upbraids me with its loud uproar!
With dreamful eyes
My spirit lies
Under the walls of Paradise.

Thomas Buchanan Read.

PASSING AWAY.

Was it the chime of a tiny bell
    That came so sweet to my dreaming ear,
Like the silvery tones of a fairy's shell,
    That he winds on the beach so mellow and clear,
When the winds and the waves lie together asleep,
And the moon and the fairy are watching the deep,
        She dispensing her silvery light,
        And he his notes as silvery quite,
While the boatman listens and ships his oar,
To catch the music that comes from the shore?—
        Hark! the notes on my ear that play,
        Are set to words: as they float, they say,
            "Passing away! passing away!"

But, no; it was not a fairy's shell,
  Blown on the beach, so mellow and clear:
Nor was it the tongue of a silver bell
  Striking the hours that fell on my ear,
As I lay in my dream: yet was it a chime
That told of the flow of the stream of Time;
For a beautiful clock from the ceiling hung,
And a plump little girl for a pendulum, swung;
    (As you 've sometimes seen, in a little ring
    That hangs in his cage, a canary bird swing;)
    And she held to her bosom a budding bouquet,
    And as she enjoyed it, she seemed to say,
      "Passing away! passing away!"

Oh, how bright were the wheels, that told
  Of the lapse of time as they moved round slow!
And the hands, as they swept o'er the dial of gold,
  Seemed to point to the girl below.
And lo! she had changed;—in a few short hours,
Her bouquet had become a garland of flowers,
That she held in her outstretched hands, and flung
This way and that, as she, dancing, swung
In the fullness of grace and womanly pride,
That told me she soon was to be a bride;
    Yet then, when expecting her happiest day,
    In the same sweet voice I heard her say,
      "Passing away! passing away!"

While I gazed on that fair one's cheek, a shade
  Of thought, or care, stole softly over,
Like that by a cloud in a summer's day made,
  Looking down on a field of blossoming clover.
The rose yet lay on her cheek, but its flush
Had something lost of its brilliant blush;
  And the light in her eye, and the light on the wheels,
That marched so calmly round above her,
  Was a little dimmed—as when evening steals
Upon noon's hot face:—yet one could n't but love her;
    For she looked like a mother whose first babe lay
    Rocked on her breast, as she swung all day;
    And she seemed in the same silver tone to say,
      "Passing away! passing away!"

While yet I looked, what a change there came!
  Her eye was quenched and her cheek was wan;
Stooping and staffed was her withered frame,
  Yet just as busily swung she on:
The garland beneath her had fallen to dust;
The wheels above her were eaten with rust;
The hands, that over the dial swept,
Grew crook'd and tarnished, but on they kept;
And still there came that silver tone
From the shriveled lips of the toothless crone,
    (Let me never forget, to my dying day,
    The tone or the burden of that lay)—
      "PASSING AWAY! PASSING AWAY!"
                                    John Pierpont.

FROM THE LOTOS-EATERS.

How sweet it were, hearing the downward stream
With half-shut eyes ever to seem
Falling asleep in a half-dream!
  To dream and dream, like yonder amber light,
  Which will not leave the myrrh-bush on the height;
To hear each other's whispered speech;
  Eating the Lotos day by day,
To watch the crisping ripples on the beach,
  And tender curving lines of creamy spray;
To lend our hearts and spirits wholly
To the influence of mild-minded melancholy;
To muse and brood and live again in memory,
With those old faces of our infancy
Heaped over with a mound of grass,
Two handfuls of white dust, shut in an urn of brass!
                                    Lord Tennyson.

FROM ROMEO AND JULIET.

Rom. It is my lady; O, it is my love!
      O, that she knew she were!—
      She speaks, yet she says nothing; what of that?
      Her eye discourses, I will answer it.
      I am too bold, 'tis not to me she speaks:
      Two of the fairest stars in all the heaven,

Having some business, do entreat her eyes
To twinkle in their spheres till they return.
What if her eyes were there, they in her head?
The brightness of her cheek would shame those
    stars,
As daylight doth a lamp; her eyes in heaven
Would through the airy region stream so bright,
That birds would sing, and think it were not
    night.

Jul. Wilt thou be gone? it is not yet near day:
It was the nightingale, and not the lark,
That pierced the fearful hollow of thine ear;
Nightly she sings on yon pomegranate-tree:
Believe me, love, it was the nightingale.

Rom. It was the lark, the herald of the morn,
No nightingale: look, love, what envious streaks
Do lace the severing clouds in yonder east;
Night's candles are burnt out, and jocund day
Stands tiptoe on the misty mountain-tops.
I must be gone and live, or stay and die.

                              William Shakespeare.

THE BROOKSIDE.

I wandered by the brookside,
    I wandered by the mill;
I could not hear the brook flow,—
    The noisy wheel was still;
There was no burr of grasshopper,
    No chirp of any bird,
But the beating of my own heart
    Was all the sound I heard.

I sat beneath the elm tree;
    I watched the long, long shade,
And, as it grew still longer,
    I did not feel afraid;
For I listened for a footfall,
    I listened for a word,—
But the beating of my own heart
    Was all the sound I heard.

He came not,—no, he came not,—
  The night came on alone,—
The little stars sat one by one,
  Each on his golden throne;
The evening wind passed by my cheek,
  The leaves above were stirred,
But the beating of my own heart
  Was all the sound I heard.

Fast, silent tears were flowing,
  When something stood behind;
A hand was on my shoulder,—
  I knew its touch was kind;
It drew me nearer,—nearer,—
  We did not speak one word,
For the beating of our own hearts
  Was all the sound we heard.
                              Lord Houghton.

EXERCISES FOR THE DEVELOPMENT OF VOCAL ENERGY.

In the discussion of purity of tone, we confined ourselves to selections that required subdued or moderate volumes of voice, for two reasons: first, because we seldom use, in the ordinary affairs of life, anything more than moderate force; second, because it is easier to secure purity of tone with the moderate forces of voice than with the louder or more impassioned. Nevertheless, it is necessary to cultivate the louder forces of voice, and though the much greater portion of our literature is rendered with moderate volumes, yet the louder forces are needed for public address and for the expression of the more elevated forms of thought.

The First Step in securing vocal energy is the mastery of those physical exercises that relate to the development of strength in the action of the diaphragm and the muscular walls of the abdomen; the development of the muscles of the chest, and the expansion of the lungs; the development of elasticity in the muscles of the trunk, and flexibility in the muscles of the thorax and the throat.

PHYSICAL EXERCISES.

To develop upper chest muscles.—Raise arms sideways, shoulders high, elbows straight, hands clenched, knuckles toward floor. Make as many small circles with arms from shoulder as possible, while inhaling one full deep breath slowly.

Inhale full deep breath while raising arms slowly sideways to meet overhead. Keep hips back, head up, weight forward, and elbows perfectly straight. Exhale while arms come down slowly to position. This exercise fills the lungs completely, and gives the greatest strength and freedom to the respiratory muscles. Repeat the same lying with the back flat on the floor.

Abdominal muscles.—Inhale and hold breath while bending at the waist line, first to the right, then to the left. Repeat, bending to the front and back at the waist. Lying flat on the back, keep the heels together on the floor, fold arms across chest, and rise to sitting position.

Use the abdominal muscles in the exercise of panting like a dog, closing the exercise by one quick expulsion of the remaining breath. Let the throat muscles be free. Whisper the following commands with free, open position of throat, and strong, quick action of abdominal muscles:

Forward, the Light Brigade!
Charge for the guns!

"My bannerman, advance!
I see," he cried, "their column shake;
Now, gallants! for your ladies' sake,
Upon them with the lance!"

Not a minute more to wait!
Let the captains all and each
Shove ashore, then blow up, burn the vessels on the
 beach!

In the exercises for purity of tone, the resonance was confined to the cavities of the mouth, nose, and pharynx, and hence it is called *head tone.* In the following exercises, the resonance will be felt in all the air-chambers of the body, especially in the large cavity of the chest, and this is known by the term *chest tone.*

The Second Step is to vocalize the vowels or numerals expulsively and explosively. An expulsive sound is a short shout, having a very appreciable vanish; an explosive sound is a pistol-like report, having little appreciable vanish.

EXERCISES FOR PRACTICE.

1. Repeat the word *ŭp* five times expulsively.
2. Repeat the word *ŭp* five times explosively.
3. Repeat each one of the vowels ā, ē, ī, ō, ū, and the

numerals up to ten, five times expulsively, and then as often explosively.

4. Repeat the *vowels* and *numerals* and the word *ŭp* expulsively and explosively as many times as you can with one breath. Avoid all severe strain upon the muscles or lungs in continuing the repetitions.

5. Join the word *ŭp* with the combinations pā, fā, mā, dā, bā, thus: ŭp-pā, ŭp-pē, ŭp-pī, ŭp-pō, ŭp-pū—ŭp-fā, ŭp-fē, ŭp-fī, ŭp-fō, ŭp-fū, etc. Repeat these combinations expulsively and explosively.

6. Join the word *ŭp* with the first ten numerals, thus: ŭp-one, ŭp-two, ŭp-three, etc. Repeat expulsively and explosively.

7. Alternate this exercise, first vowels, then numerals.

8. Shout with sustained force or the calling voice the vowels ā, ē, ī, ō, ū. Prolong each vowel five or ten seconds.

9. Shout with sustained force the numerals up to ten.

10. Read in the calling voice the following sentences:
Ho! Ship ahoy!
Katherine, Queen of England, come into the court!
Awake, arise, or be forever fallen!
Thou, too, sail on, O Ship of State!
Jove with us, Jove with us!
Forward, the Light Brigade!
Blow on! This is the land of liberty!
Olea! for Castile!
Charge, Chester, charge! On, Stanley, on!

The Third Step is to secure variety in force. Next to indistinctness, which must be acknowledged the cardinal fault in public speaking, comes *the lack of variety in force*. Most speakers, to put it in the language of the people, have a big voice and a little one. Very few intermediate volumes are cultivated, and the consequence is that the speaking is all of the same strength and thickness—like a rope. As well expect an orchestra to render a great musical composition without reading between the lines and observing the moderate, forte, and fortissimo directions, as to expect a great masterpiece of oratory to be successfully delivered without regard to the lights and shades of varying force. Variety in the speaking voice is secured: first, by melodious intonations, or using different notes on the musical scale in uttering the various words of a sentence; second, by increasing or decreasing the volume of voice, as the impassioned or the didactic portions of the selection demand. The latter form of variety is the one most sadly neglected, and for the cultivation of which we offer a few simple and practical suggestions. The following diagram will give the pupil some idea of the wide range of force that should be cultivated.

(· · · · · · ·)(· · · · · · · ·)(• • • • • •)(● • • • • ●)(●● ●●)

Very soft.   Soft.   Moderate.   Loud.   Very loud.

It is quite possible, by beginning with the group of moderate forces and increasing the volume until you reach the loudest, to produce thirty different degrees, which can be clearly appreciated by the ear.

EXERCISES FOR PRACTICE.

Sound the vowels, numerals, or single words, beginning with the moderate volumes, and increasing in force until you reach the maximum of your power. Thus:

1. Sound the vowel *ā* or the numeral *one*, or the word *louder*, as many times as you can, increasing in power with each successive effort.

2. Pronounce the following sentences or phrases in the same way. Begin with moderate force, and increase in volume of voice as you proceed:

EXAMPLES.

I impeach him!

The war must go on.

The love of liberty.

The living love of liberty.

Independence now, and Independence forever.

Our native land.

Our home, and native land.

The student should be careful not to be over-ambitious in the use of this exercise. It is best to begin with five repetitions of each phrase or sentence, and to increase the number of repetitions as he acquires power of voice. Never continue the exercise for more than two minutes at any one time. Practice frequently, but for short periods. This caution is necessary, that the student may avoid straining the vocal organs or the lungs.

3. Having mastered the previous exercises, the student is now prepared to render the climactic paragraph.

EXAMPLES FOR PRACTICE.

FROM ORATION ON THE IMPEACHMENT OF WARREN HASTINGS.

Therefore, it is with confidence that, ordered by the Commons of Great Britain, I impeach Warren Hastings of high crimes and misdemeanors.

I impeach him in the name of the Commons of Great Britain in Parliament assembled, whose parliamentary trust he has abused.

I impeach him in the name of the Commons of Great Britain, whose national character he has dishonored.

I impeach him in the name of the people of India, whose laws, rights, and liberties he has subverted.

I impeach him in the name of the people of India, whose property he has destroyed, whose country he has laid waste and desolate.

I impeach him in the name of human nature itself, which he has cruelly outraged, injured, and oppressed, in both sexes. And I impeach him in the name and by the virtue of those eternal laws of justice, which ought equally to pervade every age, condition, rank, and situation in the world.—*Edmund Burke.*

FROM ORATION ON WASHINGTON.

But the same impartial history will record more than one ineffaceable stain upon his character, and never, to the end of time, never on the page of historian, poet, or philosopher; never till a taste for true moral greatness is eaten out of the hearts of men by a mean admiration of success and power; never in the exhortations of the prudent magistrate counseling his fellow-citizens for their good; never in the dark ages of national fortune, when anxious patriots explore the annals of the past for examples of public virtue; never in the admonition of the parent forming the minds of his children by lessons of fireside wisdom; never, O never, will the name of Napoleon, nor of any of the other of the famous conquerors of ancient and modern days, be placed upon a level with Washington's.—*Edward Everett.*

FROM ORATION ON IDOLS.

Nothing of this now; nothing but incessant eulogy. But not a word of one effort to lift the yoke of cruel or unequal legislation from the neck of its victim; not one attempt to make the code of his country wiser, purer, better; not one effort to bless his times or breathe a higher moral purpose into the community. Not one blow struck for right or for liberty, while the battle of the giants was going on about him; not one patriotic act to stir the hearts of his idolaters; not one public act of any kind whatever about whose merit friend or foe could even quarrel, unless when he scouted our great charter as a glittering generality, or jeered at the philanthropy which tried to practice the sermon on the mount.—*Wendell Phillips.*

FROM ORATION ON LAFAYETTE.

And what was it, fellow-citizens, which gave to our Lafayette his spotless fame? The love of liberty. What has consecrated his memory in the hearts of good men? The love of liberty. What nerved his youthful arm with strength, and inspired him, in the morning of his days, with sagacity and counsel? The living love of liberty. To what did he sacrifice power, and rank, and country, and freedom itself? To the horror of licentiousness,—to the sanctity of plighted faith,—to the love of liberty protected by law. Thus the great principle of your Revolutionary fathers, and of your Pilgrim sires, was the rule of his life—*the love of liberty protected by law.*—*Edward Everett.*

THE CURSE OF MARINO FALIERO.

Ye elements! in which to be resolved
I hasten, let my voice be as a spirit
Upon you!—Ye blue waves! which bore my banner,
Ye winds! which fluttered o'er as if ye loved it,
And filled my swelling sails, as they were wafted
To many a triumph! Thou, my native earth,
Which I have bled for! and thou foreign earth,
Which drank this willing blood from many a wound!
Ye stones, in which my gore will not sink, but
Reek up to heaven! Ye skies, which will receive it!
Thou sun! which shinest on these things, and Thou!
Who kindlest and who quenchest suns!—attest!
I am not innocent, but are these guiltless?
I perish, but not unavenged; far ages
Float up from the abyss of time to be,
And show these eyes, before they close, the doom
Of this proud city; and I leave my curse
On her and hers forever.

Lord Byron.

Be careful to economize the voice so as to reserve sufficient force for the closing sentence of the period. Gradually increase the volume as the thought and language become more intense and fervid.

SHORT DAILY DRILL TO SECURE VOCAL ENERGY.

First step—two minutes in deep breathing.
Second step—two minutes in deep reading.
Third step—two minutes in shouting.
Fourth step—four minutes in oratorical speaking.

This drill requires but ten minutes of time, and should be repeated three times a day by those who desire to cultivate a voice for public speaking. The time given, or which should be given, by every student to physical exercise exceeds the time required for this drill, and as speaking is one of the very best kinds of bodily exercise, this drill may be made to serve as a physical, as well as a vocal exercise.

The First Step is two minutes in deep breathing. The object is to get into the *habit* of filling all the cells of the lungs with air. People, as a rule, breathe superficially, using the air-cells in the upper part of the lungs, and seldom making use of the cells in the lower part. Exercises in deep breathing, covering a considerable period of time, so accustom the lungs to full inspiration, that they in time adapt themselves to the new condition of things, and become practically automatic in their action. This result is of great practical value to the speaker, as it insures a sufficient supply of breath for all the requirements of long clauses and sentences, without taxing the mind in the operation. In short, it becomes a fixed habit of the lungs to keep themselves well filled.

BREATHING EXERCISE.

Inhale slowly for ten, twenty, or thirty seconds; exhale for the same length of time. If thirty seconds of time are used for inhalation, it will be a quite sure test that the lungs are being well filled. An equal amount of time for exhalation will give the student excellent practice in the management of the breath.

The Second Step is two minutes in deep reading. The object of this step is to get easy control of the lower notes of the scale, and thereby secure body or fullness of voice by amplitude of resonance in the large cavity of the chest.

EXAMPLES FOR PRACTICE.

FROM CHILDE HAROLD.

Roll on, thou deep and dark blue Ocean—roll!
   Ten thousand fleets sweep over thee in vain,
Man marks the earth with ruin—his control
   Stops with the shore;—upon the watery plain
   The wrecks are all thy deed, nor doth remain
A shadow of man's ravage, save his own,
   When for a moment, like a drop of rain,
He sinks into thy depths with bubbling groan,
Without a grave, unknelled, uncoffined, and unknown.

Thou glorious mirror, where the Almighty's form
    Glasses itself in tempests; in all time,
Calm or convulsed—in breeze or gale or storm,
    Icing the pole, or in the torrid clime
    Dark heaving;—boundless, endless, and sublime—
The image of Eternity—the throne
    Of the Invisible; even from out thy slime
The monsters of the deep are made; each zone
Obeys thee: thou goest forth, dread, fathomless, alone.
Lord Byron.

FROM THE BURIAL OF MOSES.

O, lonely tomb in Moab's land,
    O, dark Beth-peor's hill,
Speak to these curious hearts of ours,
    And teach them to be still.
God hath His mysteries of Grace—
    Ways that we cannot tell;
He hides them deep, like the secret sleep
    Of him He loved so well.
Mrs. Cecil Francis Alexander.

FROM HYMN TO MONT BLANC.

Thou, too, hoar Mount! with thy sky-pointing peaks,
Oft from whose feet the avalanche, unheard,
Shoots downward, glittering through the pure serene,
Into the depth of clouds that veil thy breast—
Thou, too, again, stupendous Mountain! thou
That as I raise my head, awhile bowed low
In adoration, upward from thy base
Slow traveling with dim eyes suffused with tears,
Solemnly seemest, like a vapory cloud,
To rise before me—Rise, O ever rise!
Rise like a cloud of incense, from the earth!
Thou kingly Spirit throned among the hills,
Thou dread ambassador from earth to heaven,
Great Hierarch! tell thou the silent sky,
And tell the stars, and tell yon rising sun,
Earth, with her thousand voices, praises God.
Samuel Taylor Coleridge.

FROM ADDRESS TO THE SUN.

O thou that rollest above, round as the shield of my
  fathers!
Whence are thy beams, O Sun! thy everlasting light!

Ossian.

FROM HYMN TO THE NIGHT.

Peace! Peace! Orestes-like I breathe this prayer!
  Descend with broad-winged flight,
The welcome, the thrice-prayed for, the most fair,
  The best-beloved Night!

Henry Wadsworth Longfellow.

FROM THE BUILDING OF THE SHIP.

  The ocean old,
  Centuries old,
  Strong as youth, and as uncontrolled,
  Paces restless to and fro,
  Up and down the sands of gold.
His beating heart is not at rest;
  And far and wide,
  With ceaseless flow,
  His beard of snow
Heaves with the heaving of his breast.

Henry Wadsworth Longfellow.

The Third Step is two minutes in shouting. The
object of this step is to secure the maximum of power in
vibration and resonance.

EXAMPLE FOR PRACTICE.

FROM THE BUILDING OF THE SHIP.

Thou, too, sail on, O Ship of State!
Sail on, O Union, strong and great!
Humanity, with all its fears,
With all the hopes of future years,
Is hanging breathless on thy fate!

We know what Master laid thy keel,
What workmen wrought thy ribs of steel,
Who made each mast, and sail, and rope,
What anvils rang, what hammers beat,
In what a forge, and what a heat,
Were shaped the anchors of thy hope!

Fear not each sudden sound and shock;
'Tis of the wave, and not the rock;
'Tis but the flapping of the sail,
And not a rent made by the gale!
In spite of rock and tempest's roar,
In spite of false lights on the shore,
Sail on, nor fear to breast the sea!
Our hearts, our hopes, are all with thee:
Our hearts, our hopes, our prayers, our tears,
Our faith triumphant o'er our fears,
Are all with thee,—are all with thee!
　　　　　　　—Henry Wadsworth Longfellow.

The Fourth Step is four minutes in oratorical speaking. As the chief aim in all this training for vocal energy has been to prepare students for the exacting demands of public speaking, we select, as our last exercise in this drill, the oration. (See introductory remarks to the chapter "Oratorical Styles," page 309).

EXAMPLES FOR PRACTICE.

FROM THE ORATION INCENTIVES TO DUTY.

Go forth into the many mansions of the house of life: scholars! store them with learning; jurists! build them with justice; artists! adorn them with beauty; philanthropists! let them resound with love. Be servants of truth, each in his vocation; doers of the word and not hearers only. Be sincere, pure in heart, earnest, enthusiastic. A virtuous enthusiasm is always self-forgetful and noble. It is the only inspiration now vouchsafed to man. Like Pickering, blend humanity with learning. Like Story, ascend above the Present, in place and time. Like Allston, regard fame only as the eternal shadow of excellence. Like Channing, bend in adoration before the right. Cultivate alike the wisdom of experience and the wisdom of hope. Mindful of the Future, do not neglect the Past: awed by the majesty of Antiquity, turn not with indifference from the Future. True wisdom looks to the ages before us, as well as behind us. Like the Janus of the Capitol, one front thoughtfully regards the Past, rich with experience, with memories, with the priceless traditions of virtue; the other is earnestly directed to the All Hail Hereafter, richer still with its transcendent hopes and unfulfilled prophecies.

. We stand on the threshold of a new age, which is preparing to recognize new influences. The ancient divinities of Violence and Wrong are retreating to their kindred darkness.

> There's a fount about to stream,
> There's a light about to beam,
> There's a warmth about to glow,
> There's a flower about to blow;
> There's a midnight blackness changing
>   Into gray;
> Men of thought, and men of action,
>   *Clear the way.*
>
> Aid the dawning, tongue and pen;
> Aid it, hopes of honest men;
> Aid it, paper; aid it, type;
> Aid it, for the hour is ripe,
> And our earnest must not slacken,
>   Into play;
> Men of thought, and men of action,
>   *Clear the way.*

The age of Chivalry has gone. An age of Humanity has come. The Horse, whose importance, more than human, gave the name to that early period of gallantry and war, now yields his foremost place to Man. In serving him, in promoting his elevation, in contributing to his welfare, in doing him good, there are fields of bloodless triumph, nobler far than any in which the bravest knight ever conquered. Here are spaces of labor, wide as the world, lofty as heaven. Let me say, then, in the benison once bestowed upon the youthful knight,—Scholars! jurists! artists! philanthropists! heroes of a Christian age, companions of a celestial knighthood, "Go forth, be brave, loyal, and successful!"

And may it be our office to-day to light a fresh beacon-fire on the venerable walls of Harvard, sacred to Truth, to Christ, and the Church,—to Truth Immortal, to Christ the Comforter, to the Holy Church Universal. Let the flame spread from steeple to steeple, from hill to hill, from island to island, from continent to continent, till the long lineage of fires shall illumine all the nations of the earth; animating them to the holy contests of KNOWLEDGE, JUSTICE, BEAUTY, LOVE.—*Charles Sumner.*

ADDRESS AT THE DEDICATION OF GETTYS-BURG CEMETERY.

Fourscore and seven years ago our fathers brought forth upon this continent a new nation, conceived in liberty, and dedicated to the proposition that all men are created equal. Now we are engaged in a great civil war, testing whether that nation, or any nation, so conceived and so dedicated, can long endure. We are met on a great battlefield of that war. We are met to dedicate a portion of it as the final resting-place of those who here gave their lives that that nation might live.

It is altogether fitting and proper that we should do this. But in a larger sense we cannot dedicate, we cannot consecrate, we cannot hallow this ground. The brave men, living and dead, who struggled here, have consecrated it far above our power to add or detract. The world will little note, nor long remember what we say here, but it can never forget what they did here.

It is for us, the living, rather to be dedicated here to the unfinished work they have thus far so nobly carried on. It is rather for us to be here dedicated to the great task remaining before us, that from these honored dead we take increased devotion to the cause for which they gave the last full measure of devotion; that we here highly resolve that these dead shall not have died in vain, that the nation shall, under God, have a new birth of freedom, and that the government of the people, by the people, and for the people, shall not perish from the earth.—*Abraham Lincoln.*

SOUTH CAROLINA AND MASSACHUSETTS.

[From a speech in defense of the Union and the Constitution, delivered in the Senate of the United States, January 26, 1830.]

The eulogium pronounced by the honorable gentleman on the character of the State of South Carolina, for her Revolutionary and other merits, meets my hearty concurrence. I shall not acknowledge that the honorable member goes before me in regard for whatever of distinguished talent or distinguished character South Carolina has produced. I claim part of the honor; I partake in the pride, of her great names. I claim them for countrymen, one and all,—the Laurenses, the Rutledges, the Pinckneys, the Sumters, the Marions,—Americans all, whose fame is no more to be hemmed in by State lines, than their talents and patriotism were capable of being circumscribed within the same narrow limits.

In their day and generation, they served and honored the country, and the whole country; and their renown is of the treasures of the whole country. Him whose honored name the gentleman himself bears,—does he esteem me less capable of gratitude for his patriotism, or sympathy for his sufferings, than if his eyes had first opened upon the light of Massachusetts, instead of South Carolina? Sir, does he suppose it in his power to exhibit a Carolina name so bright as to produce envy in my bosom? No, sir; increased gratification and delight, rather. I thank God, that, if I am gifted with little of the spirit which is able to raise mortals to the skies, I have yet none, as I trust, of that other spirit which would drag angels down.

When I shall be found, sir, in my place here in the Senate, or elsewhere, to sneer at public merit because it happens to spring up beyond the limits of my own State or neighborhood; when I refuse, for any such cause, or for any cause, the homage due to American talent, to elevated patriotism, to sincere devotion to liberty and the country; or, if I see an uncommon endowment of heaven, —if I see extraordinary capacity and virtue in any son of the South, and if, moved by local prejudice or gangrened by State jealousy, I get up here to abate the tithe of a hair from his just character and just fame,—may my tongue cleave to the roof of my mouth!

Sir, let me recur to pleasing recollections; let me indulge in refreshing remembrances of the past; let me remind you that, in early times, no States cherished greater harmony, both of principle and feeling, than Massachusetts and South Carolina. Would to God that harmony might again return! Shoulder to shoulder they went through the Revolution; hand in hand they stood round the administration of Washington, and felt his own great arm lean on them for support. Unkind feeling, if it exist, alienation and distrust, are the growth, unnatural to such soils, of false principles since sown. They are weeds, the seeds of which that same great arm never scattered.

Mr. President, I shall enter on no encomium upon Massachusetts; she needs none. There she is. Behold her, and judge for yourselves. There is her history; the world knows it by heart. The past, at least, is secure. There is Boston, and Concord, and Lexington, and Bunker Hill; and there they will remain forever. The bones of her sons, fallen in the great struggle for Independence, now lie mingled with the soil of every State, from New England to Georgia; and there they will lie forever.

And, sir, where American Liberty raised its first voice, and where its youth was nurtured and sustained, there it still lives, in the strength of its manhood, and full of its original spirit. If discord and disunion shall wound it; if party strife and blind ambition shall hawk at and tear it; if folly and madness, if uneasiness under salutary and necessary restraint, shall succeed in separating it from that Union by which alone its existence is made sure,—it will stand, in the end, by the side of that cradle in which its infancy was rocked; it will stretch forth its arm, with whatever of vigor it may still retain, over the friends who gather round it, and it will fall at last, if fall it must, amid the proudest monuments of its own glory, and on the very spot of its origin.—*Daniel Webster.*

FROM ORATION ON TOUSSAINT L'OUVERTURE.

If I were to tell you the story of Napoleon, I should take it from the lips of Frenchmen, who find no language rich enough to paint the great captain of the nineteenth century. Were I to tell you the story of Washington, I should take it from your hearts,—you, who think no marble white enough on which to carve the name of the Father of his country. But I am to tell you the story of a negro, Toussaint L'Ouverture, who has left hardly one written line. I am to glean it from the reluctant testimony of his enemies, men who despised him because he was a negro and a slave, hated him because he had beaten them in battle.

Cromwell manufactured his own army. Napoleon, at the age of twenty-seven, was placed at the head of the best troops Europe ever saw. Cromwell never saw an army till he was forty; this man never saw a soldier till he was fifty. Cromwell manufactured his own army—out of what? Englishmen,—the best blood in Europe. Out of the middle class of Englishmen,—the best blood of the island. And with it he conquered what? Englishmen,—their equals. This man manufactured his army out of what? Out of what you call the despicable race of negroes, debased, demoralized by two hundred years of slavery, one hundred thousand of them imported into the island within four years, unable to speak a dialect intelligible even to each other. Yet out of this mixed, and, as you say, despicable mass, he forged a thunderbolt and hurled it at what? At the proudest blood in Europe, the Spaniard, and sent him home conquered; at the most warlike blood in Europe, the French, and put them under his feet; at the pluckiest blood in Europe, the English, and they skulked home to Jamaica. Now, if Cromwell was a general, at least this man was a soldier.—*Wendell Phillips.*

THE ELEVATED CONVERSATIONAL VOICE.

It frequently happens that a speaker is put at a great disadvantage in being compelled to speak in a large auditorium on a purely didactic subject. The nature of the theme requires that the speaker should talk. In fact, the great majority of addresses, sermons, arguments, etc., in their inception, and well on to the first third of their contents, are largely didactic, and must be delivered with a conversational voice, or at least with conversational intonations and inflections. If an attempt be made to employ an impassioned utterance, suitable to the expression of the loftiest patriotism, for the conveyance of purely mechanical or scientific information, it will prove such a ridiculous misfit that its repetition will be improbable. If your theme is unemotional, you must be content to use the conversational voice, even if the people in the back seats are unable to hear your words. If, then, a large share of public speaking is upon subjects that appeal to the understanding, and not to the emotions, and in consequence must be delivered in the conversational voice, it follows that any system of practice that will strengthen or increase the body of this voice, so that the speaker can be easily heard in large audience rooms, must be of vital importance. The result desired is not a distinct quality of voice like the conversational or the orotund, but rather a blend of these two qualities, like the blending of the flute and the reed tones of an orchestra or organ. The elevated conversational voice, then, is a blending of the head and chest resonance. That this can be done, and still preserve the essential characteristics of the conversational quality is true, because the conversational quality predominates in the blend, while the orotund quality is simply used to give greater fullness and body to the predominant quality.

SUGGESTIONS FOR THE ACQUIREMENT OF THE ELEVATED CONVERSATIONAL VOICE.

A full and free use of orotund quality should be acquired so that the student can produce the resonant chest tones as easily as the lighter head tones. Then, selecting those passages in addresses or orations that are conversational or didactic, he should aim to deliver them as if he were conversing with a large audience, rather than with a few friends. The effort to make his voice carry to the distant portions of the auditorium will call into use occasionally the orotund quality to give fullness and carrying power to the voice, while the character of the thought he is expressing will keep him steadily in a conversational relation to his audience.

EXAMPLES FOR PRACTICE.

CRIME ITS OWN DETECTER.

Against the prisoner at the bar, as an individual, I cannot have the slightest prejudice; I would not do him the smallest injury or injustice. But I do not affect to be indifferent to the discovery and the punishment of this deep guilt. I cheerfully share in the opprobrium, how much soever it may be, which is cast on those who feel and manifest an anxious concern, that all who had a part in planning, or a hand in executing, this deed of midnight assassination, may be brought to answer for their enormous crime at the bar of public justice.

Gentlemen, this is a most extraordinary case. In some respects it has hardly a precedent anywhere—certainly none in our New England history. This bloody drama exhibited no suddenly excited, ungovernable rage. The actors in it were not surprised by any lion-like temptation springing upon their virtue, and overcoming it before resistance could begin. Nor did they do the deed to glut savage vengeance, or satiate long-settled and deadly hate. It was a cool, calculating, money-making murder. It was all "hire and salary, not revenge." It was the weighing of money against life; the counting out of so many pieces of silver against so many ounces of blood.—*Daniel Webster.*

FROM ORATION ON THE CENTENNIAL OF THE BIRTH OF O'CONNELL.

I think I do not exaggerate when I say that never since God made Demosthenes has He made a man better fitted for a great work than O'Connell.

You may say that I am partial to my hero; but John Randolph of Roanoke, who hated an Irishman almost as much as he did a Yankee, when he got to London and heard O'Connell, the old slaveholder threw up his hands and exclaimed, "This is the man, those are the lips, the most eloquent that speak English in my day!" and I think he was right.

Webster could address a bench of judges; Everett could charm a college; Choate could delude a jury; Clay could magnetize a senate, and Tom Corwin could hold the mob in his right hand; but no one of these men could do more than this one thing. The wonder about O'Connell was that he could out-talk Corwin, he could charm a college better than Everett, and leave Henry Clay himself far behind in magnetizing a senate.

It has been my privilege to hear all the great orators of America who have become singularly famed about the world's circumference. I know what was the majesty of Webster; I know what it was to melt under the magnetism of Henry Clay; I have seen eloquence in the iron logic of Calhoun; but all three of these men never surpassed and no one of them ever equaled the great Irishman. I have hitherto been speaking of his ability and success, I will now consider his character.

To show you that he never took a leaf from our American gospel of compromise, that he never filed his tongue to silence on one truth fancying so to help another, let me compare him to Kossuth, whose only merits were his eloquence and his patriotism. When Kossuth was in Faneuil Hall, he exclaimed, "Here is a flag without a stain, a nation without a crime!" We abolitionists appealed to him, "O, eloquent son of the Magyar, come to break chains, have you no word, no pulse-beat for four millions of negroes bending under a yoke ten times heavier than that of Hungary?" He exclaimed, "I would forget anybody, I would praise anything, to help Hungary!'' O'Connell never said anything like that.

When I was in Naples I asked Sir Thomas Fowell Buxton, ''Is Daniel O'Connell an honest man?'' ''As honest a man as ever breathed,'' said he, and then he told me the following story: ''When, in 1830, O'Connell first entered Parliament, the anti-slavery cause was so weak that it had only Lushington and myself to speak for it, and we agreed that when he spoke I should cheer him up, and when I spoke he should cheer me, and these were the only cheers we ever got. O'Connell came with one Irish member to support him. A large party of members (I think Buxton said twenty-seven) whom we called the West India interest, the Bristol party, the slave party, went to him, saying, 'O'Connell, at last you are in the House with one helper—if you will never go down to Freemason's Hall with Buxton and Brougham, here are twenty-seven votes for you on every Irish question. If you work with those abolitionists, count us always against you.'

'' It was a terrible temptation. How many a so-called statesman would have yielded! O'Connell said, 'Gentlemen, God knows I speak for the saddest people the sun sees; but may my right hand forget its cunning and my tongue cleave to the roof of my mouth, if to help Ireland —even Ireland—I forget the negro one single hour.'

''From that day,'' said Buxton, '' Lushington and I never went into the lobby that O'Connell did not follow us.''

And then besides his irreproachable character, he had what is half the power of a popular orator, he had a majestic presence. In youth he had the brow of a Jupiter, and the stature of Apollo. A little O'Connell would have been no O'Connell at all. Sydney Smith says of Lord John Russell's five feet, when he went down to Yorkshire after the Reform Bill had passed, the stalwart hunters of Yorkshire exclaimed, ''What, that little shrimp, *he* carry the Reform Bill!'' ''No, no,'' said Smith, ''he *was* a large man, but the labors of the bill shrunk him.'' You remember the story that Russell Lowell tells of Webster when we in Massachusetts were about to break up the Whig party. Webster came home to Faneuil Hall to protest, and four thousand Whigs came out to meet him. He lifted up his majestic presence before that sea of human faces, his brow charged with thunder, and said, ''Gentle-

men, I am a Whig; a Massachusetts Whig; a Revolutionary Whig; a Constitutional Whig; a Faneuil Hall Whig;
and if you break up the Whig party, where am *I* to go?''
"And," says Lowell, "we all held our breath, thinking
where he *could* go." "But," says Lowell, "if he had been
five feet three, we should have said, confound you, who do
you suppose cares where you go?" Well, O'Connell had
all that, and then he had what Webster never had, and
what Clay had, the magnetism and grace that melt a
million souls into his.

When I saw him he was sixty-five, lithe as a boy. His
every attitude was beauty, his every gesture grace. Why,
Macready or Booth never equaled him.

It would have been a pleasure even to look at him if he
had not spoken at all, and all you thought of was a grey-
hound. And then he had, what so few American speakers
have, a voice that sounded the gamut. I heard him once
in Exeter Hall say, "Americans, I send my voice career-
ing like the thunderstorm across the Atlantic, to tell
South Carolina that God's thunderbolts are hot, and to
remind the negro that the dawn of his redemption is drawing near;" and I seemed to hear his voice reverberating
and re-echoing back to London from the Rocky Mountains.

And then, with the slightest possible flavor of an Irish
brogue, he would tell a story that would make all Exeter
Hall laugh, and the next moment there were tears in his
voice, like an old song, and five thousand men would be
in tears. And all the while no effort—he seemed only
breathing.

> " As effortless as woodland nooks
> Send violets up and paint them blue."
>
> *Wendell Phillips.*

DESCRIPTION OF WEBSTER'S SPEECH IN REPLY TO HAYNE.

It was Tuesday, January the 26th, 1830,— a day to be
hereafter forever memorable in Senatorial annals, that the
Senate resumed the consideration of Foote's resolution.

There never was before, in the city, an occasion of so
much excitement. Multitudes of strangers had for two
or three days previous been rushing into the city, and the

hotels overflowed. As early as nine o'clock of this morning, crowds poured into the Capitol in hot haste; at twelve o'clock, the hour of meeting, the Senate chamber—its galleries, floor, and even lobbies—was filled to its utmost capacity. The very stairways were dark with men, who clung to one another like bees in a swarm. The House of Representatives was early deserted, an adjournment could hardly have made it emptier.

Seldom, if ever, has speaker in this or any other country had more powerful incentives to exertion. A subject, the determination of which involved the most important interests; even the duration of the Republic. Competitors unequaled in reputation, ability, or position; a name to make still more glorious or lose forever; and an audience comprising not only persons of this country, most eminent in intellectual greatness, but representatives of other nations where the art of eloquence had flourished for ages. *All* the soldier seeks in opportunity was here.

Mr. Webster perceived and felt equal to the destinies of the moment. The very greatness of the hazard exhilarated him. His spirits rose with the occasion. He awaited the time of onset with a stern, impatient joy. A confidence in his own resources springing from no vain estimate of his power, but the legitimate offspring of previous severe mental discipline, sustained and excited him. He had gauged his opponent, his subject, and himself. He never rose on an ordinary occasion to address an ordinary audience more self-possessed. There was no tremulousness in his voice nor manner; nothing hurried, nothing simulated. The calmness of superior strength was visible everywhere; in countenance, voice, and bearing.

Mr. Webster rose and addressed the Senate. His exordium is known by heart everywhere: "Mr. President, when the mariner has been tossed, for many days in thick weather and on an unknown sea, he naturally avails himself of the first pause in the storm, the earliest glance of the sun, to take his latitude and ascertain how far the elements have driven him from his true course. Let us imitate this prudence, and, before we float farther on the waves of this debate, refer to the point from which we departed, that we may, at least, be able to conjecture where we now *are*. I ask for the reading of the resolution before the Senate."

There wanted no more to enchain the attention. There was a spontaneous, though silent, expression of eager approbation, as the orator concluded these opening remarks, and while the clerk read the resolution many attempted the impossibility of getting nearer the speaker. Every head was inclined toward him, every ear turned in the direction of his voice, and that deep, sudden, mysterious silence followed, which always attends fullness of emotion. From the sea of upturned faces before him, the orator beheld his thoughts reflected as from a mirror. The varying countenance, the suffused eye, the earnest smile, the ever attentive look, assured him of his audience's entire sympathy. If among his hearers there were those who affected at first an indifference to his glowing thoughts and fervent words, the difficult mask was soon laid aside, and profound, undisguised, devoted attention followed. Those who had doubted Mr. Webster's ability to cope with and overcome his opponents were fully satisfied of their error before he had proceeded far in his speech. Their fears soon took another direction. When they heard his sentences of powerful thought, towering in accumulative grandeur, one above the other, as if the orator strove, Titan-like, to reach the very Heavens themselves; they were giddy with an apprehension that he would break down in his flight; they dared not believe that genius, learning, and intellectual endowment, however uncommon that was simply mortal, could sustain itself long in a career seemingly so perilous; they feared an Icarian fall. What New England heart was there but throbbed with vehement, tumultuous, irrepressible emotions as he dwelt upon New England struggles and New England triumphs during the war of the Revolution?

There was scarcely a dry eye in the Senate; all hearts were overcome; grave judges and men grown old in dignified life turned aside their heads to conceal the evidences of their emotion. In one corner of the gallery was clustered a group of Massachusetts men; they had hung from the first moment upon the words of the speaker, with feelings variously but always warmly excited, deepening in intensity as he proceeded. At first, while the orator was going through his exordium, they held their breath and hid their faces, mindful of the savage attack upon him and New England, and the fearful

odds against him, her champion:—as he went deeper into
his speech they felt easier; when he turned Hayne's flank
on Banquo's ghost they breathed freer and deeper. But
now as he alluded to Massachusetts, their feelings were
strained to their highest tension, and when the orator,
concluding this encomium òf the land of his birth, turned,
unintentionally, or otherwise, his burning eye full upon
them, they shed tears like girls. The exulting rush of
feeling with which he went through the peroration threw
a glow over his countenance, like inspiration—eye, brow,
each feature, every line of his face seemed touched as
with a celestial fire. The swell and roll of his voice
struck upon the ears of the spell-bound audience, in deep
and melodious cadence, as waves upon the shore of the
far-resounding sea. The Miltonic grandeur of his words
was the fit expression of his thought, and raised his hearers up to his theme. His voice, exerted to its utmost
power, penetrated every recess and corner of the Senate—
penetrated even the ante-rooms and stairways, as he
pronounced in the deepest tones of pathos these words of
solemn significance:

"When my eyes turn to behold for the last time the
sun in heaven, may they not see him shining on the broken and.dishonored fragments of a once glorious Union;
on States dissevered, discordant, belligerent; on a land
rent with civil feuds, or drenched, it may be, in fraternal
blood. Let their last feeble and lingering glance rather
behold the gorgeous ensign of the Republic, now known
and honored throughout the earth, still full. hjgh advanced; its arms and trophies streaming in all their
original luster; not a stripe erased or polluted; not a
single star obscured; bearing for its motto no such miserable interrogatory as "What is all this worth?" nor
those other words of delusion and folly, of Liberty first,
and Union afterwards, but everywhere, spread all over in
characters of living light, and blazing on all its ample
folds, as they float over the sea and over the land, and in
every wind under the whole heavens, that other sentiment dear to every American heart,—Liberty AND Union,
—now and forever,—one and inseparable."

The speech was over, but the tones of the orator still
lingered upon the ear, and the audience, unconscious of
the close, remained in their positions. The agitated coun-

tenance, the heaving breast, the suffused eye, attested the continued influence of the spell upon them. Hands that in the excitement of the moment had sought each other still remained closed in an unconscious grasp. Eye still turned to eye, to receive and repay mutual sympathy, and everywhere around seemed forgetfulness of all but the orator's presence and words.—*Charles W. March.*

The last two selections, in the main, are good illustrations of elevated conversational address. A few passages requiring the fullest orotund quality are retained to preserve the symmetry and completeness of the selections.

PRACTICAL SUGGESTIONS ON EMPHASIS, INFLECTION AND CADENCE.

General treatises and lectures on elocution are of no great value to anybody. They may entertain popular audiences, and excite interest in good reading and speaking; but they do not, as a rule, touch upon the difficulties that perplex public speakers, nor do they offer specific directions for the attainment of desirable results. On the other hand, there is danger in following implicitly a highly-elaborated system. The enthusiastic student of elocutionary science may so expand his theories as clearly to invade the domain of individual taste, where no *ipse dixit* should be tolerated. Knowledge with discretion is needed that the pretension of ignorance and the folly of empiricism may be avoided. These cautions are called forth by the difficulties that surround the subject under discussion. It is one that requires all the knowledge and skill of the experienced teacher, who appreciates the limitations of elocutionary science.

It is not our purpose to discuss, at great length, the topics of emphasis, inflection, and cadence, but simply to make a few practical suggestions, as we have previously intimated.

EMPHASIS.

Correct emphasis in reading and speaking cannot be too highly commended. It demonstrates, at once, the intelligence of the speaker, and gives certainty of meaning to the thought expressed. It would be a questionable use of time to endeavor, by any set of rules, to indicate to students the emphatic words of a sentence. In every sentence there are one or more words upon which the meaning of the sentence turns. If the student has not sufficient intelligence to discover these words, it is very evident that he should continue his preparatory education. But when the meaning of the author is clearly apprehended, and the important words are made to stand out by the application of emphasis, then the significance of this agent of expression is seen and felt. It frequently happens that two speakers of equal intelligence and skill will emphasize a sentence or a verse from the Bible differently. This is not to be discouraged. It is rather to be encouraged, for truth is many-sided, and in this way we may see it from different intellectual standpoints. The main thing for the student, however, is to get a clear idea of the meaning of the text, and then to emphasize those words that will set forth with certainty the thought he wishes to express. Important as is the suggestion in the last sentence, it is nevertheless true that there is more practical difficulty in getting students to apply emphasis correctly, than in getting them to think the sentence clearly. This is due, in large measure, to two causes: first, lack of knowledge; second, complicated elocutionary requirements. How, then, is the application of emphasis retarded by lack of knowledge? In that students are ignorant of the vocal instrumentalities by which words are emphasized. The vocal agencies used for emphasis are: first, slide; second, pause; third, pitch; fourth, force; fifth, time; sixth, quality.

FIRST.—The emphasis of the *slide* is a downward or an upward stroke of the voice, passing through the interval of a third, fifth, or octave on the musical scale, the length of the slide being determined by the intensity of the thought or emotion.

SECOND.—The emphasis of *pause* is a sudden stop in speech, thereby exciting attention and giving weight or emphasis to the word momentarily withheld.

THIRD.—The emphasis of *pitch* is a sudden change from the general pitch to a much higher or lower pitch, thereby arresting the attention, and giving significance to the words thus uttered.

FOURTH.—The emphasis of *force* is the utterance of certain words with greater loudness, thereby calling attention to their importance.

FIFTH.—The emphasis of *time* is the retardation of the general rate of utterance, thereby calling attention to the words drawn out or retarded.

SIXTH.—The emphasis of *quality* is the change from a comparatively smooth and pleasant quality of voice to a harsh or aspirated quality. The abrupt change makes the word thus roughened or aspirated distinctively emphatic.

These are the chief instrumentalities used to give significance to the utterance of words, and the effective use of them should be more frequently taught and illustrated.

The second cause interfering with the application of emphasis, is complicated elocutionary requirements. It has always been a source of regret that certain writers on elocution have insisted that several vocal elements must enter into every effort in emphasis. To require a student to combine three or four of the different kinds of emphasis previously enumerated in every attempt to designate an important word, is as unnecessary as it is unwarranted, and must result either in making the student tired, or in producing a combination or blend of vocal elements that nobody wants to hear. It is not denied that several of these forms of emphasis frequently combine to produce an emphatic result; but one of the forms so predominates in the vocal effect, that the others require no very serious consideration. If we give attention to the leading form we employ, and make that the chief vocal agent of emphasis, we greatly simplify the requirements, and release the student from a system too elaborate for practical use. It is not improbable that this combination plan of emphasis has so weakened our interest in the study of any one kind, that we have become ignorant of the powers that lie hidden in the emphasis of the slide and the pause.

INFLECTION, OR THE EMPHASIS OF THE SLIDE.

Inflection, or slide, is an uninterrupted upward or downward stroke of the voice on the musical scale. The emphasis of the slide is the most important form because it is the most frequently used. In all oral communications in the everyday affairs of life, as well as in all common reading, this is the form of emphasis used to designate the words that give definiteness and certainty to our thought. In unimpassioned speech, or in common reading, the slide is three notes in length, and is called the slide of the *third*. In elevated or impassioned styles, the length of the slide is five or eight notes, called respectively the slide of the *fifth* and the *octave*. Any word receiving this stroke or slide of the voice is so distinguished or made prominent by the vocal effect, that we call it an emphatic word. When we speak of sending a word home, the sending power is the emphatic stroke or slide.

ILLUSTRATIVE EXAMPLES.

But _some_ man will say, _How_ are the dead raised up,

and with what _body_ do they come?

But if our gospel be _hid,_ it is _hid_ to them who are _lost._

For as many as are _led_ by the Spirit of God, they are

the _sons_ of God.

O death, _where_ is. thy sting? O grave, where is _thy_

victory?

It is important to note that the slide begins above the level of the ordinary pitch and extends to an equal distance below it. This is necessary that the slide may be made to harmonize with the current melody. If the slide should be made so that the vocal stroke is entirely below the level of the ordinary pitch, thus, $- - - \backslash - - \backslash - -$ $- \backslash$, the reading would become heavy and plunging. If, on the other hand, the slide is made above the line, thus, $- \backslash - - - \backslash - - \backslash$, the reading would become light and unimpressive.

ILLUSTRATIVE EXAMPLES OF THE FIFTH AND OCTAVE.

FROM THE BURIAL MARCH OF DUNDEE.

" Soldiers! I have sworn a vow.

Ere the evening star shall glisten

On Schiehallion's lofty brow,

Either we shall rest in triumph,

Or another of the Græmes

Shall have died in battle-harness

For his Country and King James!

Think upon the Royal Martyr,—

Think of what his race endure,—

Think of him whom butchers murdered

On the field of Magus Muir:—

By his sacred blood I charge ye,

By the ruined hearth and shrine,—

By the blighted hopes of Scotland,

By your injuries and mine,—

Strike this day as if the anvil

Lay beneath your blows the while,

Be they covenanting traitors,

Or the brood of false Argyle!

Strike! and drive the trembling rebels

Backwards o'er the stormy Forth;

Let them tell their pale Convention

How they fared within the North.

Let them tell that Highland honor

Is not to be bought nor sold,

That we *scorn* their Prince's anger

As we *loathe* his foreign gold.

Strike! and when the fight is over,

If ye look in vain for me,
Where the dead are lying thickest,
Search for him that was Dundee!"

William E. Aytoun.

FROM CORIOLANUS.

Aufidius. "Name not the god,
Thou boy of tears.

Coriolanus. *Measureless liar!* thou hast made my heart

Too great for what *contains it.*

Boy! Cut me to *pieces,* Volscians: men and *lads,*

Stain *all* your edges on me. *Boy!*

If you have writ your annals true, 't is there

That, like an eagle in a dovecot, I

Fluttered   your Volscians in   Corioli:

Alone   I did it.—   Boy!"

William Shakespeare.

CADENCE.

Cadence is the name given to the closing melody of sentences. There are two kinds of cadence—partial and complete. Complete cadence is used at periods where the whole thought has been expressed. Partial cadence is used at semicolons and colons, where complete thought has been expressed, but not the whole thought of the paragraph.

It may be well to inquire why we use a falling inflection or complete cadence at a period. Usually at a period complete thought has been expressed, and the utmost closing musical effect is required to indicate that completion. If then, at a period, the falling inflection is required because complete thought has been expressed, we might expect that, at a comma, which indicates simply a grammatical division, the opposite or rising reflection would be required; which is really the case. The rise, however, is so slight that it may be indicated by a horizontal line, thus ——; signifying that the voice is suspended. If then a suspension of voice is used at a comma, and a full cadence at a period, what form of closing melody should be used at semicolons and colons? The answer is a Partial Cadence. It must be distinctly understood that we make use of the punctuation marks here simply to make the discussion more definite. If a comma were used to indicate a grammatical division simply, and a semicolon or a colon to indicate complete thought and yet not the whole thought, and a period to indicate fully completed thought, we should get on with the marks without trouble; but the laws for punctuation, unfortunately, are not yet fixed, or universally observed, and hence the only safe guide in reading is to follow the sense. The partial cadence is used so frequently in paragraphic writing, that it would be well briefly to investigate the structure of the paragraphic sentence. It is a series of simple sentences, each making complete sense in itself, bound together for the cumulative effect of the whole series.

EXAMPLE.

"Doing well is the cause of a just sense of elevation of character; it clears and strengthens the spirits; it gives higher reaches of thought; it widens our benevolence; and makes the current of our peculiar affections swift and deep."

Take the first sentence in the paragraph "Doing well is the cause of a just sense of elevation of character." Here is a complete thought which might be severed from its connections, and made to terminate with a full cadence; yet it is not the whole thought contained in the paragraph. The elocutionary requirements, then, are that a closing vocal effect must be employed here to indicate completed thought, and a rising effect to anticipate the sentences that are to follow. The partial cadence, then, is a closing and a rising vocal effect combined—a melody that closes up what has been said, and suspends the mind in anticipation of what is to follow. The form of musical notation indicating the partial cadence may be usually written

thus, Sometimes we hear a melody that may

be written thus, or thus, It is

well, however, to leave the whole matter of melody, as well as the number of words or syllables required for its execution, to the individual taste of the speaker. The thing of importance is the general principle, which is clear, viz., that a closing and a suspensive inflection must be secured. By turning the concrete or stem of the last note down, we secure a closing effect or falling inflection; and by placing the radical or bulb of the last note higher on the musical scale than the previous note, we secure a suspensive inflection.

ILLUSTRATIVE EXAMPLES.

Doing well is the cause of a just sense of elevation of *character;* it clears and strengthens the *spirits;* it
gives higher reaches of *thought;* it widens our *benevolence;*
and makes the current of our peculiar affections
swift and deep.

I have roamed through the world to find hearts nowhere warmer than *hers;* soldiers nowhere *braver;*
patriots nowhere *purer;* wives and
mothers nowhere *truer;* maidens nowhere *lovelier;*
green valleys and bright rivers nowhere greener or
brighter.

It is important to note that, as the thought and language become more intense and fervid, there is a change
or variety in the melody of the cadence. In the natural
rise of climactic intensity, as in the last illustrative example, the Partial Cadence might be written in musical
form, thus, maidens nowhere *lovelier.*

The same principle evidently obtains, but, in its application, the musical form is changed. This is an important fact, and relieves the ear from the constant recurrence of the same musical effect, which is extremely annoying to people of cultivated taste.

It now remains for us to discuss the *complete cadence.* This occurs at the close of sentences and paragraphs, and is preceded by the penultimate slide. The penultimate slide is an upward movement of the voice, and occurs generally on the last word or words of the penultimate clause. The special function of the penultimate slide is to lift the voice up on the musical scale so that the descent on the last clause may be more impressive and perceptible to the ear. If, in the delivery of a climactic paragraph, the voice be allowed to move on to the end without any special rise, and the closing cadence be immediately applied, the suddenness and abruptness of the descent will fail to produce the pleasing impression of repose and completion. In order to secure the most satisfactory results, the voice must reach the line of full repose by successive descents at the longest possible intervals. The penultimate slide has been aptly called "the flourish of the period."

ILLUSTRATIVE EXAMPLE.

But the same impartial history will record more than

one ineffaceable stain upon his *character;* and *never* to

the end of *time;* *never* on the page of historian,

poet or *philosopher;* *never* till a taste for true moral great-

ness is eaten out of the hearts of men by a mean admiration of success and power; never in the exhortations of

the prudent magistrate counseling his fellow-citizens

for their good; never in the dark ages of national fortune,

when anxious patriots explore the annals of the past for

examples of public virtue; never in the admonition of

the parent forming the minds of his children by lessons

of fireside wisdom; never, O never, will the name of

Napoleon, nor of any of the other of the famous conquer-

ors of ancient and modern days be placed upon a

level

with

Washington's.

The recurring word *never* receives the emphatic slide of the fifth, increasing to the octave on the last repetition of *never;* the words *Napoleon* and *other* receive the stroke of the fifth, while the sentences of the paragraph are closed with partial cadences; and the penultimate slide, preparatory to the complete cadence, occurs on the words *modern days.*

The penultimate slide is not confined to oratorical selections, but occurs in all common reading, though applied in a more subdued form and with a shortened upward stroke. In grand, sublime and reverential styles, its use is indispensable.

The fullest cadential melody is the "Triad of the Cadence," or three successive downward steps on the musical scale, thus: "Doing well makes the current of our

peculiar *affections* ♪ swift

♪ and

♪ deep."

In the best manuals of elocution may be found a full discussion of the various forms of complete cadence: the Monad, Duad, Triad, Tetrad and Pentad forms. However, the triad form is recommended for general use as the most pleasing and satisfactory, even if we are obliged to use words instead of syllables in executing the successive downward steps, and sometimes are obliged to sacrifice a trifle in strength for the sake of melodious closing effects. If the question is asked, Would you ever use a monad or duad form of cadence? I should answer, Yes; but for general practical use the triad is preferred for reasons stated. This, like all other ideas in this discussion, is offered as a suggestion rather than as a general law, and for the following reason: in all matters of melody, whether current or closing, the student must be allowed the largest possible liberty consistent with a cultivated musical taste.

EXPRESSION.

By Expression we mean the utterance of words with their accompanying emotions. We do not develop the full thought of an emotional selection by the mere repetition of the words. If we did, the tenderest pathos and the sublimest passion would alike sink to the level of the most common talk. The temper or emotion which is the life of the thought, and which seeks conveyance in the words, must be expressed before the meaning of the author can be made known.

A knowledge, then, of the laws of Expression is necessary to the proper interpretation of thought. The method proposed in this book for the attainment of such knowledge has taken shape in my daily experience as a teacher, and has no greater merit than its practicability. No merely arbitrary rules are of value here. Nature must ever be the great teacher, and he who observes most clearly her best manifestations must be, of necessity, the best fitted to deduce the laws that underlie and control those manifestations.

It is, however, of great importance to the student of Elocution to remember that there is a certain best way to render every emotion, and having mastered one selection of a great class, the power has been acquired to render all selections of that type. By pursuing such a method, the reader will be lifted from the contemplation of a single piece to the class of which it is a specimen, and eventually to a classified knowledge of the laws that develop every sentiment and passion of the human soul.

NARRATIVE, DESCRIPTIVE, AND DIDACTIC STYLES.

This class of selections includes all that is generally designated as *common reading*, viz. : conversations, essays, newspaper composition, or any selection which is intended simply to convey information to the mind. So frequent is the use of this style of address that more than two-thirds of everything the professional man has to utter falls under this head, and in non-professional life nearly every thing that is spoken. The excellences of common reading may be compassed by observing the following suggestions:

FIRST—Purity of tone.

SECOND—Variety of tone.

THIRD—Distinctness of enunciation.

Purity of tone is of as much importance in common reading as in the rendering of sentiment. Every tone should fall from the lips like the tinkle of a coin upon the table. A clear, musical and crystalline articulation is the highest charm of common reading.

Variety of tone is an element not to be overlooked. An essay can be written out in musical forms as well as an oratorio, and he who makes the best music is, other things being equal, the best reader. A well-modulated voice traversing the musical scale with happy intonations renders common reading not only interesting, but highly artistic and charming. The only caution necessary is that over-much variety may render the reading fantastic and flippant.

Distinctness of enunciation must always be strictly demanded. As a rule, we enunciate the first parts of our words distinctly, but the last parts are frequently blurred, or left untouched. The only relief in such cases is a thorough drill in the consonantal elements, until firmness, accuracy and force are developed in enunciation. The last syllable in a word should be brought out as distinctly as the first, and the middle syllables as distinctly as the last.

The question may be raised, are Narrative, Descriptive and Didactic styles all read in the same manner? Narrative and Descriptive Readings, appealing in many instances to feeling and imagination for their chief effects, abound in vivid and varied tones associated with the different moods of sympathy and emotion; while Didactic subjects, being usually directed to the reason and judgment through the understanding, hold a more steady, uniform and regulated course of utterance, adapted to a clear, distinct and pointed conveyance of thought to the intellect.

NARRATIVE, DESCRIPTIVE AND DIDACTIC SELECTIONS.

HAMLET'S INSTRUCTIONS TO THE PLAYERS.

Speak the speech I pray you, as I pronounced it to you, —trippingly on the tongue; but if you mouth it, as many of our players do, I had as lief the town-crier spake my lines. Nor do not saw the air too much with your hand thus, but use all gently; for in the very torrent, tempest, and, as I may say, whirlwind of your passion, you must acquire and beget a temperance, that may give it smoothness. Oh! it offends me to the soul to hear a robustious periwig-pated fellow tear a passion to tatters,—to very rags,—to split the ears of the groundlings; who, for the most part, are capable of nothing but inexplicable dumb show and noise. I would have such a fellow whipped for o'erdoing Termagant: it out-herods Herod. Pray you, avoid it.

Be not too tame, neither, but let your own discretion be your tutor. Suit the action to the word; the word to the action; with this special observance — that you o'erstep not the modesty of nature: for anything so overdone is from the purpose of playing; whose end, both at the first and now, was, and is, to hold, as 'twere, the mirror up to nature;—to show virtue her own feature; scorn her own image; and the very age and body of the time, his form and pressure. Now this, overdone or come tardy off, though it make the unskillful laugh, can not but make the judicious grieve; the censure of which one, must, in your allowance, o'erweigh a whole theater of others. Oh! there be players, that I have seen play, and heard others praise, and that highly, not to speak it profanely, that, neither having the accent of Christians, nor the gait of Christian, pagan, or man, have so strutted and bellowed, that I have thought some of nature's journeymen had made men, and not made them well,—they imitated humanity so abominably!

William Shakespeare.

BOOKS.

Studies serve for delight, for ornament, and for ability. Their chief use for delight is in privateness, and retiring; for ornament, is in discourse; and for ability, is in the judgment and disposition of business; for expert men can execute, and perhaps judge of particulars, one by one; but the general counsels, and the plots and marshalling of affairs, come best from those that are learned.

To spend too much time in studies, is sloth; to use them too much for ornament, is affectation; to make judgment wholly by their rules, is the humor of a scholar; they perfect nature, and are perfected by experience—for natural abilities are like natural plants, that need pruning by study; and studies themselves do give forth directions too much at large, except they be bounded in by experience. Crafty men contemn studies, simple men admire them, and wise men use them, for they teach not their own use; but that is a wisdom without them, and above them, won by observation. Read not to contradict and confute, nor to believe and take for granted, nor to find talk and discourse, but to weigh and consider. Some books are to be tasted, others to be swallowed, and some few to be chewed and digested: that is, some books are to be read only in parts; others to be read, but not curiously; and some few to be read wholly, and with diligence and attention. Some books also may be read by deputy and extracts made of them by others; but that would be only in the less important arguments, and the meaner sort of books; else distilled books are, like common distilled waters, flashy things.   Reading maketh a full man, conference a ready man, and writing an exact man; and, therefore, if a man write little, he had need have a great memory; if he confer little, he had need have a present wit; and if he read little, he had need have much cunning, to seem to know that he doth not.   Histories make men wise; poets witty; the mathematics subtle; natural philosophy deep; moral grave; logic and rhetoric, able to contend.

Francis Bacon.

THE CHILD-WIFE.

All this time I had gone on loving Dora harder than ever.   If I may so express it, I was steeped in Dora. I was not merely over head and ears in love with her, I was saturated through and through.   I took night walks to Norwood where she lived, and perambulated round and round the house and garden for hours together, looking through crevices in the palings, using violent exertions to get my chin above the rusty nails on the top, blowing kisses at the lights in the windows, and romantically calling on the night to shield my Dora,—I don't exactly know from what,—I suppose from fire, perhaps from mice, to which she had a great objection.

Dora had a discreet friend, comparatively stricken in years, almost of the ripe age of twenty, I should say, whose name was Miss Mills.   Dora called her Julia.   She was the bosom friend of Dora.   Happy Miss Mills!

One day Miss Mills said: "Dora is coming to stay with me.   She is coming the day after to-morrow.   If you would like to call, I am sure papa would be happy to see you."

I passed three days in a luxury of wretchedness.   At last, arrayed for the purpose, at a vast expense, I went to Miss Mills's, fraught with a declaration.   Mr. Mills was not at home.   I didn't expect he would be.   Nobody wanted *him*.   Miss Mills was at home.   Miss Mills would do.

I was shown into a room upstairs, where Miss Mills and Dora were.   Dora's little dog Jip was there.   Miss Mills was copying music, and Dora was painting flowers.   What were my feelings when I recognized flowers I had given her!

Miss Mills was very glad to see me, and very sorry her

papa was not at home, though I thought we all bore that with fortitude. Miss Mills was conversational for a few minutes, and then laying down her pen, got up and left the room.

I began to think I would put it off till to-morrow.

"I hope your poor horse was not tired when he got home at night from that picnic," said Dora, lifting up her beautiful eyes. "It was a long way for him."

I began to think I would do it to-day.

"It was a long way for *him*, for *he* had nothing to uphold him on his journey."

"Was n't he fed, poor thing?" asked Dora.

I began to think I would put it off till to-morrow.

"Ye—yes, he was well taken care of. I mean he had not the unutterable happiness that I had in being so near to you."

I saw now that I was in for it, and it must be done on the spot.

"I do n't know why you should care for being near me," said Dora, "or why you should call it a happiness. But, of course, you do n't mean what you say. Jip, you naughty boy, come here!"

I do n't know how I did it, but I did it in a moment.

I intercepted Jip. I had Dora in my arms. I was full of eloquence. I never stopped for a word. I told her how I loved her. I told her I should die without her. I told her that I idolized and worshiped her. Jip barked madly all the time. My eloquence increased, and I said, if she would like me to die for her, she had but to say the word, and I was ready. I had loved her to distraction every minute, day and night, since I first set eyes upon her. I loved her at that moment to distraction. I should always love her, every minute, to distraction. Lovers had loved before, and lovers would love again; but no lover had ever loved, might, could, would, or should ever love, as I loved Dora. The more I raved, the more Jip barked. Each of us in his own way got more mad every moment.

Well, well: Dora and I were sitting on the sofa, by and by, quiet enough, and Jip was lying in her lap winking peacefully at me. It was off my mind. I was in a state of perfect rapture. Dora and I were engaged.

Charles Dickens.

GEORGE THE THIRD.

We have to glance over sixty years in as many minutes. To read the mere catalogue of characters who figured during that long period, would occupy our allotted time, and we should have all text and no sermon. England has to undergo the revolt of the American colonies; to submit to defeat and separation; to shake under the volcano of the French Revolution; to grapple and fight for the life with her gigantic enemy Napoleon; to gasp and rally after that tremendous struggle. The old society, with its courtly splendors, has to pass away; generations of statesmen to rise and disappear; Pitt to follow Chatham to the tomb; the memory of Rodney and Wolfe to be superseded by Nelson's and Wellington's glory; the old poets who unite us to Queen Anne's time to sink into their graves; Johnson to die, and Scott and Byron to arise, Garrick to delight the world with his dazzling dramatic genius, and Kean to leap on the stage and take possession of the astonished theater. Steam has to be invented; kings to be beheaded, banished, deposed, restored; Napoleon to be but an episode, and George III. is to be alive through all these varied changes, to accompany his people through all these revolutions of thought, government, society,— to survive out of the old world into ours.

His mother's bigotry and hatred George inherited with the courageous obstinacy of his own race; but he was a firm believer where his fathers had been free-thinkers, and a true and fond supporter of the Church, of which he was the titular defender. Like other dull men, the king was all his life suspicious of superior people. He did not like Fox; he did not like Reynolds; he did not like Nelson, Chatham, Burke: he was testy at the idea of all innovations, and suspicious of all innovators. He loved mediocrities; Benjamin West was his favorite painter; Beattie was his poet. The king lamented, not without pathos, in his after life, that his education had been neglected. He was a dull lad, brought up by narrow-minded people. The cleverest tutors in the world could have done little probably to expand that small intellect, though they might have improved his tastes and taught his perceptions some generosity.

George married the Princess Charlotte of Mecklenburg-Strelitz, and for years they led the happiest, simplest lives, sure, ever led by married couple. It is said the king winced when he first saw his homely little bride; but, however that may be, he was a true and faithful husband to her, as she was a faithful and loving wife. They had the simplest pleasures,—the very mildest and simplest,—little country dances, to which a dozen couple were invited, and where the honest king would stand up and dance for three hours at a time to one tune; after which delicious excitement they would go to bed without any supper (the Court people grumbling sadly at that absence of supper), and get up quite early the next morning, and perhaps the next night have another dance; or the queen would play on the spinnet,—she played pretty well, Haydn said; or the king would read to her a paper out of the *Spectator*, or perhaps one of Ogden's sermons. O Arcadia! what a life it must have been!

The theater was always his delight. His bishops and clergy used to attend it, thinking it no shame to appear where that good man was seen. He is said not to have cared for Shakespeare or tragedy much; farces and pantomimes were his joy; and especially when clown swallowed a carrot or a string of sausages, he would laugh so outrageously that the lovely princess by his side would have to say, "My gracious monarch, do compose yourself." But he continued to laugh, and at the very smallest farces, as long as his poor wits were left him.

"George, be a king!" were the words which his mother was forever croaking in the ears of her son; and a king the simple, stubborn, affectionate, bigoted man tried to be.

He did his best,—he worked according to his lights: what virtue he knew, he tried to practice; what knowledge he could master, he strove to acquire. But, as one thinks of an office almost divine, performed by any mortal man, — of any single being pretending to control the thoughts, to direct the faith, to order implicit obedience of brother millions; to compel them into war at his offense or quarrel; to command, "In this way you shall trade, in this way you shall think; these neighbors shall be your allies, whom you shall help,—these others your enemies, whom you shall slay at my orders; in this way you shall worship God;"—who can wonder that, when such a man as George took such an office on himself, punishment and humiliation should fall upon people and chief?

Yet there is something grand about his courage. The battle of the king with his aristocracy remains yet to be told by the historian who shall view the reign of George more justly than the trumpery panegyrists who wrote immediately after his decease. It was he, with the people to back him, that made the war with America; it was he and the people who refused justice to the Roman Catholics; and on both questions he beat the patricians. He bribed, he bullied, he darkly dissembled on occasion; he exercised a slippery perseverance, and a vindictive resolution, which one almost admires as one thinks his character over. His courage was never to be beat. It trampled North underfoot; it bent the stiff neck of the younger Pitt; even his illness never conquered that indomitable spirit. As soon as his brain was clear, it resumed the scheme, only laid aside when his reason left him: as soon as his hands were out of the strait-waistcoat, they took up the pen and the plan which had engaged him up to the moment of his malady. I believe, it is by persons believing themselves in the right, that nine-tenths of the tyranny of this world has been perpetrated. Arguing on that convenient premise, the Dey of Algiers would cut off twenty heads of a morning; Father Dominic would burn a score of Jews in the presence of the Most Catholic King, and the Archbishops of Toledo and Salamanca sing Amen. Protestants were roasted, Jesuits hung and quartered at Smithfield, and witches burned at Salem; and all by worthy people, who believed they had the best authority for their actions. And so with respect to old George, even Americans whom he hated and who conquered him, may give him credit for having quite honest reasons for oppressing them.

Of little comfort were the king's sons to the king. But the pretty Amelia was his darling; and the little maiden, prattling and smiling in the fond arms of that old father, is a sweet image to look on.

From November, 1810, George III. ceased to reign. All the world knows the story of his malady; all history presents no sadder figure than that of the old man, blind and deprived of reason, wandering through the rooms of his palace, addressing imaginary parliaments, reviewing fancied troops, holding ghostly courts. I have seen his picture as it was taken at this time, hanging in the apartment of his daughter, the Landgravine of Hesse Homburg, —amidst books and Windsor furniture, and a hundred fond reminiscences of her English home. The poor old father is represented in a purple gown, his snowy beard falling over his breast,—the star of his famous Order still idly shining on it. He was not only sightless,—he became utterly deaf. All light, all reason, all sound of human voices, all the pleasures of this world of God, were taken from him. Some slight lucid moments he had; in one of which, the queen, desiring to see him, entered the room, and found him singing a hymn, and accompanying himself at the harpsichord. When he had finished, he knelt down and prayed aloud for her, and then for his family, and then for the nation, concluding with a prayer for himself, that it might please God to avert His heavy calamity from him, but if not, to give him resignation to submit. He then burst into tears, and his reason again fled.

What preacher need moralize on this story; what words save the simplest are requisite to tell it? It is too terrible for tears. The thought of such a misery smites me down in submission before the Ruler of kings and men, the Monarch Supreme over empires and republics, the inscrutable Dispenser of life, death, happiness, victory. "O brothers," I said to those who heard me first in America,—"O brothers! speaking the same dear mother tongue, —O comrades! enemies no more, let us take a mournful hand together as we stand by this royal corpse, and call a truce to battle! Low he lies to whom the proudest used to kneel once, and who was cast lower than the poorest; dead, whom millions prayed for in vain. Driven off his throne, buffeted by rude hands; with his children in revolt; the darling of his old age killed before him untimely; our Lear hangs over her breathless lips and cries, 'Cordelia, Cordelia, stay a little!'

> 'Vex not his ghost—oh! let him pass—he hates him
> That would upon the rack of this tough world
> Stretch him out longer!'

Hush! Strife and Quarrel, over the solemn grave! Sound, Trumpets, a mournful march. Fall, Dark Curtain, upon his pageant, his pride, his grief, his awful tragedy!"

William Makepeace Thackeray.

THE BIRTH OF DOMBEY.

Rich Mr. Dombey sat in the corner of his wife's darkened bedchamber in the great arm-chair by the bedside, and rich Mr. Dombey's Son lay tucked up warm in a little basket, carefully placed on a low settee in front of the fire and close to it, as if his constitution were analogous to that of a muffin, and it was essential to toast him brown while he was very new.

Rich Mr. Dombey was about eight-and-forty years of age. Rich Mr. Dombey's Son, about eight-and-forty minutes.

Mr. Dombey, exulting in the long-looked-for event,— the birth of a son —jingled his heavy gold watch-chain as he sat in his blue coat and bright buttons by the side of the bed, and said:—

"Our house of business will once again be not only in name but in fact Dombey and Son; Dombey and Son! He will be christened Paul, of course. His father's name, Mrs. Dombey, and his grandfather's! I wish his grandfather were alive this day!" And again he said, "Dombey and Son."

Those three words conveyed the one idea of Mr. Dombey's life. The earth was made for Dombey and Son to trade in, and the sun and moon were made to give them light. Common abbreviations took new meanings in his eyes, and had sole reference to them. A. D. had no concern with anno Domini, but stood for anno Dombei—and Son.

He had been married ten years, and, until this present day on which he sat jingling his gold watch-chain in the great arm-chair by the side of the bed, had had no issue.

—To speak of. There had been a girl some six years before, and she, who had stolen into the chamber unobserved, was now crouching in a corner whence she could see her mother's face. But what was a girl to Dombey and Son!

Mr. Dombey's cup of satisfaction was so full, however, that he said: "Florence, you may go and look at your pretty brother, if you like. Do n't touch him!"

Next moment the sick lady had opened her eyes and seen the little girl; and the little girl had run towards her; and, standing on tiptoe, to hide her face in her embrace, had clung about her with a desperate affection very much at variance with her years. The lady herself seemed to faint.

"O Lord bless me!" said Mr. Dombey, "I do n't like the look of this. A very ill-advised and feverish proceeding having this child here. I had better ask Doctor if he 'll have the goodness to step up stairs again; " which he did, returning with the Doctor himself, and closely followed by his sister, Mrs. Chick, a lady rather past the middle age than otherwise, but dressed in a very juvenile manner, who flung her arms around his neck, and said:—

"My dear Paul! This last child is quite a Dombey! He 's such a perfect Dombey!"

"Well, well! I think he *is* like the family. But what is this they have told me, since the child was born, about Fanny herself. How is Fanny?"

"My dear Paul, there 's nothing whatever wrong with Fanny. Take my word, nothing whatever. An effort is necessary. That 's all. Ah! if dear Fanny were a Dombey! But I dare say, although she is not a born Dombey herself, she 'll make an effort; I have no doubt she 'll make an effort. Knowing it to be required of her, as a duty, of course she 'll make an effort. And that effort she must be encouraged, and really, if necessary, urged to make. Now, my dear Paul, come close to her with me."

The lady lay immovable upon her bed, clasping her little daughter to her breast. The girl clung close about her, with the same intensity as before, and never raised her head, or moved her soft cheek from her mother's face, or looked on those who stood around, or spoke, or moved, or shed a tear.

There was such a solemn stillness round the bed, and the Doctor seemed to look on the impassive form with so much compassion and so little hope, that Mrs. Chick was for a moment diverted from her purpose. But presently summoning courage, and what she called presence of mind, she sat down by the bedside, and said, in the tone of one who endeavors to awaken a sleeper,—

"Fanny! Fanny!"

There was no sound in answer but the loud ticking of Mr. Dombey's watch and the Doctor's watch, which seemed in the silence to be running a race.

"Fanny, my dear, here's Mr. Dombey come to see you. Won't you speak to him? They want to lay your little boy in bed,—the baby, Fanny, you know; you have hardly seen him yet, I think,—but they can't till you rouse yourself a little. Don't you think it's time you roused yourself a little? Eh?"

No word or sound in answer. Mr. Dombey's watch and the Doctor's watch seemed to be racing faster.

"Now really, Fanny my dear, I shall have to be quite cross with you if you don't rouse yourself. It's necessary for you to make an effort, and perhaps a very great and painful effort, which you are not disposed to make; but this is a world of effort, you know, Fanny, and we must never yield when so much depends upon us. Come! Try! I must really scold you if you don't. Fanny! Only look at me; only open your eyes to show me that you hear and understand me; will you? Good Heaven, gentlemen, what is to be done?"

The physician, stooping down, whispered in the little girl's ear. Not having understood the purport of his whisper, the little creature turned her deep, dark eyes towards him.

The whisper was repeated.

"Mamma!"

The little voice, familiar and dearly loved, awakened some show of consciousness, even at that ebb. For a moment, the closed eyelids trembled, and the nostril quivered, and the faintest shadow of a smile was seen.

"Mamma! O dear mamma! O dear mamma!"

The Doctor gently brushed the scattered ringlets of the child aside from the face and mouth of the mother. And thus, clinging fast to that frail spar within her arms, the mother drifted out upon the dark and unknown sea that rolls round all the world.

Charles Dickens.

SCENE AT DOCTOR BLIMBER'S.

At length Mr. Dombey, one Saturday, when he came down to Brighton to see Paul, who was then six years old, resolved to make a change, and enroll him as a small student under Doctor Blimber.

Whenever a young man was taken in hand by Doctor Blimber, he might consider himself sure of a pretty tight squeeze. The Doctor only undertook the charge of ten young gentlemen, but he had always ready a supply of learning for a hundred, and it was at once the business and delight of his life to gorge the unhappy ten with it.

In fact Doctor Blimber's establishment was a great hot-house, in which there was a forcing apparatus incessantly at work. All the boys blew before their time. Mental green peas were produced at Christmas, and intellectual asparagus all the year round. No matter what a young gentleman was intended to bear, Doctor Blimber made him bear to pattern, somehow or other.

This was all very pleasant and ingenious, but the system of forcing was attended with its usual disadvantages. There was not the right taste about the premature productions; and they did n't keep well. Moreover, one young gentleman, with a swollen nose and an excessively large head (the oldest of the ten who had "gone through" everything), suddenly left off blowing one day, and remained in the establishment a mere stalk. And people did say that the Doctor had rather overdone it with young Toots, and that when he began to have whiskers he left off having brains.

The Doctor was a portly gentleman in a suit of black, with strings at his knees, and stockings below them. He had a bald head, highly polished; a deep voice; and a chin so very double, that it was a wonder how he ever managed to shave into the creases.

His daughter, Miss Blimber, although a slim and grace-ful maid, did no soft violence to the gravity of the Doctor's house. There was no light nonsense about Miss Blimber. She kept her hair short and crisp, and wore spectacles, and she was dry and sandy with working in the graves of deceased languages. None of your live languages for Miss Blimber. They must be dead,—stone dead,

—and then Miss Blimber dug them up like a Ghoul. Mrs. Blimber, her mamma, was not learned herself, but she pretended to be, and that answered just as well. She said at evening parties, that, if she could have known Cicero, she thought she could have died contented.

As to Mr. Feeder, B.A., Doctor Blimber's assistant, he was a kind of human hand-organ, with a little list of tunes at which he was continually working, over and over again, without any variation.

To Doctor Blimber's Paul was taken by his father, on an appointed day. The Doctor was sitting in his portentous study, with a globe at each knee, books all around him; Homer over the door and Minerva on the mantel-shelf. "And how do you do, sir?" he said to Mr. Dombey, "and how is my little friend?" When the Doctor left off, the great clock in the hall seemed (to Paul, at least) to take him up, and to go on saying, over and over again, "How, is, my, lit,tle, friend; how, is, my, lit,tle, friend?"

"Mr. Dombey," said Dr. Blimber, "you would wish my little friend to acquire—"

"Everything, if you please, Doctor."

"Yes," said the Doctor, who, with his half-shut eyes, seemed to survey Paul with a sort of interest that he might attach to some choice little animal he was going to stuff,—"yes, exactly. Ha! We shall impart a great variety of information to our little friend, and bring him quickly forward, I dare say. Permit me. Allow me to present Mrs. Blimber and my daughter Cornelia, who will be associated with the domestic life of our young Pilgrim to Parnassus."

"Now, Dombey," said Miss Blimber, "I'm going out for a constitutional."

Paul wondered what that was, and why she did n't send the footman out to get it in such unfavorable weather. But he made no observation on the subject, his attention being devoted to a little pile of new books, on which Miss Blimber appeared to have been recently engaged.

"These are yours, Dombey. I am going out for a constitutional; and while I am gone, that is to say in the interval between this and breakfast, Dombey, I wish you to read over what I have marked in these books, and to tell me if you quite understand what you have got to learn."

They comprised a little English, and a deal of Latin,—names of things, declensions of articles and substantives, exercises thereon, and rules,—a trifle of orthography, a glance at ancient history, a wink or two at modern ditto, a few fables, two or three weights and measures, and a little general information. When poor little Dombey had spelt out number two, he found he had no idea of number one; fragments of which afterwards obtruded themselves into number three, which slided into number four, which grafted itself on to number two. So that it was an open question with him whether twenty Romuluses made a Remus, or hic hæc hoc was troy weight, or a verb always agreed with an ancient Briton, or three times four was Taurus, a bull.

Such spirits as little Dombey had he soon lost, of course. But he retained all that was strange and old and thoughtful in his character; and even became more strange and old and thoughtful. He loved to be alone, and liked nothing so well as wandering about the house by himself, or sitting on the stairs listening to the great clock in the hall. He was intimate with all the paper-hangings in the house; he saw things that no one else saw in the patterns; and found out miniature tigers and lions running up the bedroom walls.

And so the solitary child lived on and on, surrounded by the arabesque work of his musing fancy, and still no one understood him. He grew fond, now, of a large engraving that hung upon the staircase, where, in the center of the group, one figure that he knew—a figure with a light about its head, benignant, mild, merciful—stood pointing upward. He watched the waves and clouds at twilight with his earnest eyes, and breasted the window of his solitary room when birds flew by, as if he would have emulated them and soared away.

Charles Dickens.

DEATH OF PAUL DOMBEY.

Little Dombey had never risen from his little bed. He lay there, listening to the noises in the street, quite tranquilly; not caring much how the time went, but watching it and watching everything.

When the sunbeams struck into his room through the rustling blinds, and quivered on the opposite wall, like golden water, he knew that evening was coming on, and that the sky was red and beautiful. As the reflection died away, and a gloom went creeping up the wall, he watched it deepen, deepen, deepen into night. Then he thought how the long unseen streets were dotted with lamps, and how the peaceful stars were shining overhead. His fancy had a strange tendency to wander to the river, which he knew was flowing through the great city; and now he thought how black it was, and how deep it would look reflecting the hosts of stars; and, more than all, how steadily it rolled away to meet the sea.

"Floy! What *is* that?"

"Where, dearest?"

"There! at the bottom of the bed."

"There's nothing there, except papa!"

The figure lifted up its head and rose, and, coming to the bedside, said:

"My own boy! Do n't you know me?"

Paul looked it in the face. Before he could reach out both his hands to take it between them and draw it towards him, the figure turned away quickly from the little bed, and went out at the door.

The next time he observed the figure sitting at the bottom of the bed, he called to it.

"Do n't be so sorry for me, dear papa. Indeed, I am quite happy!"

His father coming and bending down to him, he held him round the neck, and repeated these words to him several times, and very earnestly; and he never saw his father in his room again at any time, whether it were day or night, but he called out, "Do n't be so sorry for me! Indeed, I am quite happy!"

How many times the golden water danced upon the

wall, how many nights the dark river rolled towards the sea in spite of him, Paul never sought to know.

One night he had been thinking of his mother and her picture in the drawing-room downstairs. The train of thought suggested to him to inquire if he had ever seen his mother. For he could not remember whether they had told him, yes or no; the river running very fast, and confusing his mind.

"Floy, did I ever see mamma?"

"No, darling; why?"

"Did I never see any kind face, like a mamma's, looking at me when I was a baby, Floy?"

"O yes, dear!"

"Whose, Floy?"

"Your old nurse's. Often."

"And where is my old nurse? Show me that old nurse, Floy, if you please!"

"She is not here, darling. She shall come to-morrow."

"Thank you, Floy!"

Little Dombey closed his eyes with these words, and fell asleep. When he awoke, the sun was high, and the broad day was clear and warm. Then he awoke,— woke mind and body,—and sat upright in his bed. He saw them now about him. There was no great mist before them, as there had been sometimes in the night. He knew them every one, and called them by their names.

"And who is this? Is this my old nurse?" asked the child, regarding, with a radiant smile, a figure coming in.

Yes, yes. No other stranger would have shed those tears at sight of him, and called him her dear boy, her pretty boy, her own poor blighted child. No other woman would have stooped down by his bed, and taken up his wasted hand, and put it to her lips and breast, as one who had some right to fondle it. No other woman would have so forgotten everybody there but him and Floy, and been so full of tenderness and pity.

"Floy! this is a kind, good face! I am glad to see it again. Do n't go away, old nurse. Stay here! Good by!"

"Good by, my child?" cried Mrs. Pipchin, hurrying to his bed's head. "Not good by?"

"Ah, yes! Good by!—Where is papa?"

His father's breath was on his cheek before the words

had parted from his lips.   The feeble hand waved in the
air, as if it cried, "Good by!" again.

"Now lay me down; and, Floy, come close to me, and
let me see you."

Sister and brother wound their arms around each other,
and the golden light came streaming in, and fell upon
them, locked together."

"How fast the river runs, between its green banks and
the rushes, Floy! But, it 's very near the sea now.   I
hear the waves! They always said so!"

Presently he told her that the motion of the boat upon
stream was lulling him to rest.   Now the boat was out at
sea.   And now there was a shore before him.   Who stood
on the bank!—

"Mamma is like you, Floy.   I know her by the face!"

The golden ripple on the wall came back again, and
nothing else stirred in the room.   The old, old fashion!
The fashion that came in with our first garments, and will
last unchanged until our race has run its course, and the
wide firmament is rolled up like a scroll.   The old, old
fashion,—Death!

O, thank God, all who see it, for that older fashion yet,
of immortality! And look upon us, Angels of young
children, with regards not quite estranged, when the
swift river bears us to the ocean!

Charles Dickens.

THE CHARCOAL MAN.

Though rudely blows the wintry blast,
And sifting snows fall white and fast,
Mark Haley drives along the street,
Perched high upon his wagon seat;
His somber face the storm defies,
And thus from morn till eve he cries,—
    "Charco'! charco'!"
While echo faint and far replies,—
    "Hark, O! hark, O!"
"Charco'!"—"Hark, O!"—Such cheery sounds
Attend him on his daily rounds.

The dust begrimes his ancient hat;
His coat is darker far than that;
'Tis odd to see his sooty form
All speckled with the feathery storm;
Yet in his honest bosom lies
Nor spot nor speck,—though still he cries,—
"Charco'! charco'!"
And many a roguish lad replies,—
   "Ark, ho! ark, ho!"
"Charco'!"—"Ark, ho!"—Such various sounds
Announce Mark Haley's morning rounds.

Thus all the cold and wintry day
He labors much for little pay;
Yet feels no less of happiness
Than many a richer man, I guess,
When through the shades of eve he spies
The light of his own home, and cries,—
   "Charco'! charco'!"
And Martha from the door replies,—
   "Mark, ho! Mark, ho!"
"Charco'!"—"Mark, ho!"—Such joy abounds
When he has closed his daily rounds.

The hearth is warm, the fire is bright
And while his hand, washed clean and white,
Holds Martha's tender hand once more,
His glowing face bends fondly o'er
The crib wherein his darling lies,
And in a coaxing tone he cries,
"Charco'! charco'!"
And baby with a laugh replies,—
   "Ah, go! ah, go!"
"Charco'!"—"Ah, go!"—while at the sounds
The mother's heart with gladness bounds.

Then honored be the charcoal man!
Though dusty as an African,
'Tis not for you, that chance to be
A little better clad than he,
His honest manhood to despise,

Although from morn till eve he cries,—
　"Charco'! charco'!"
While mocking echo still replies,—
　"Hark, O! hark, O!"
"Charco'!"—"Hark, O!"—Long may the sounds
Proclaim Mark Haley's daily rounds!

J. T. Trowbridge.

SCENE AT THE NATURAL BRIDGE.

The scene opens with a view of the great Natural Bridge in Virginia. There are three or four lads standing in the channel below looking up with awe to that vast arch of unhewn rocks, which the Almighty bridged over those everlasting butments, "when the morning stars sung together."

It is almost five hundred feet from where they stand, up those perpendicular bulwarks of limestone, to the key-rock of that vast arch, which appears to them only the size of a man's hand. The silence of death is rendered more impressive by the little stream that falls from rock to rock down the channel. The sun is darkened, and the boys have unconsciously uncovered their heads, as if standing in the presence-chamber of the majesty of the whole earth.

At last this feeling begins to wear away; they begin to look around them; they find that others have been there before them. They see the names of hundreds cut in the limestone butments. A new feeling comes over their young hearts, and their knives are in their hands in an instant. "What man has done, man can do," is their watchword, while they draw themselves up, and carve their names a foot above those of a hundred full-grown men who have been there before them.

They are all satisfied with this feat of physical exertion, except one.

He grasped his knife with a firmer hand, and clinging to a little jutting crag, he cuts a gain into the limestone, about a foot above where he stands; he then reaches up and cuts another for his hands.

'Tis a dangerous adventure; but as he puts his feet and hands into those gains, and draws himself up carefully to his full length, he finds himself a foot above every name chronicled in that mighty wall. While his companions are regarding him with concern and admiration, he cuts his name in rude capitals, large and deep into that flinty album.

His knife is still in his hand, and strength in his sinews, and a new created aspiration in his heart. Again he cuts another niche, and again he carves his name in larger capitals. This is not enough. Heedless of the entreaties of his companions, he cuts and climbs again. The gradations of his ascending scale grow wider apart. He measures his length at every gain he cuts. The voices of his friends wax weaker and weaker, till their words are finally lost on his ear.

He now, for the first time, cast a look beneath him. Had that glance lasted a moment, that moment would have been his last. He clings with a convulsive shudder to his little niche in the rock. An awful abyss awaits his almost certain fall. He is faint with severe exertion, and trembling from the sudden view of the dreadful destruction to which he is exposed. His knife is worn half way to the haft. He can hear the voices, but not the words, of his terror-stricken companions below! What a moment! There is no retracing his steps. It is impossible to put his hand into the same niche with his feet, and retain his slender hold a moment.

His companions instantly perceive this new and fearful dilemma, and await his fall with emotions that "freeze their young blood." He is too high, too faint, to ask for his father and mother. But one of his companions anticipates his desire. Swift as the wind, he bounds down the channel, and the situation of the ill-fated boy is told upon his father's hearthstone.

Minutes of almost eternal length roll on, and there are hundreds standing in that rocky channel, and hundreds on the bridge above, all holding their breath, and awaiting the fearful catastrophe. The poor boy hears the hum of new and numerous voices both above and below. He can distinguish the tones of his father, who is shouting, with all the energy of despair," William! William! don't look down! We are all here praying for you! Don't look down! Keep your eye towards the top!"

The boy did n't look down. His eye is fixed like a flint towards heaven, and his young heart on Him who reigns there. He grasps again his knife. He cuts another niche, and another foot is added to the hundreds that remove him from the reach of human help from below. How carefully he uses his wasting blade! How anxiously he selects the softest places in that vast pier! How he avoids every flinty grain! How he economizes his physical powers, resting a moment at each gain he cuts! How every motion is watched from below! There stand his father, mother, brother, and sister, on the very spot, where, if he falls, he will not fall alone.

Fifty more gains must be cut before the longest rope can reach him. His wasting blade strikes again into the limestone. Spliced ropes are ready in the hands of those who are leaning over the outer edge of the bridge. Two minutes more and all must be over. The blade is worn to the last half inch. The boy's head reels; his eyes are starting from their sockets. His last hope is dying in his heart; his life must hang on the next gain he cuts. That niche is the last.

At the last faint gash he makes, his knife—his faithful knife—falls from his little nerveless hand, and ringing along the precipice, falls at his mother's feet. An involuntary groan of despair runs like a death-knell through the channel below, and all is still as the grave. At the height of nearly three hundred feet, the devoted boy lifts his hopeless heart, and closes his eyes to commend his soul to God.

'Tis but a moment—there! one foot swings off—he is reeling—trembling—toppling over into eternity! Hark! a shout falls on his ear from above. The man who is lying with half his length over the bridge, has caught a glimpse of the boy's head and shoulders. Quick as thought the noosed rope is within reach of the sinking youth. With a faint convulsive effort, the swooning boy drops his arms into the noose. Darkness comes over him, and with the words God—Mother—the tightening rope lifts him out of his last shallow niche. Not a lip moves while he is dangling over that fearful abyss; but when a sturdy Virginian reaches down and draws up the lad, and holds him up in his arms before the tearful, breathless multitude, such shouting—such leaping and weeping for joy—never greeted the ear of a human being so recovered from the yawning gulf of eternity.

Elihu Burritt.

DICK SWIVELLER AND THE MARCHIONESS.

One circumstance troubled Mr. Swiveller's mind very much, and that was that the small servant always remained somewhere in the bowels of the earth, and never came to the surface unless the single gentleman rang his bell, when she would answer it and immediately disappear again. She never went out, or came into the office, or had a clean face, or took off the coarse apron, or looked out of any one of the windows, or stood at the street door for a breath of air, or had any rest or enjoyment whatever. Nobody ever came to see her, nobody spoke of her, nobody cared about her.

"Now," said Dick, walking up and down with his hands in his pockets, "I'd give something—if I had it—to know how they use that child, and where they keep her. My mother must have been a very inquisitive woman; I have no doubt I'm marked with a note of interrogation somewhere—upon my word, I should like to know how they use her!"

After running on, in this way, for some time, Mr. Swiveller softly opened the office door, with the intention of darting across the street for a glass of the mild porter. At that moment he caught a parting glimpse of the brown head-dress of Miss Brass flitting down the kitchen stairs. "And by Jove!" thought Dick, "she's going to feed the small servant. Now or never!"

First peeping over the hand-rail and allowing the head-dress to disappear in the darkness below, he groped his way down, and arrived at the door of a back kitchen immediately after Miss Brass had entered the same, bearing in her hand a cold leg of mutton. It was a very dark, miserable place, very low and very damp: the walls disfigured by a thousand rents and blotches. The water was trickling out of a leaky butt, and a most wretched cat was lapping up the drops with the sickly eagerness of starvation. Everything was locked up; the coal-cellar, the candle-box, the salt-box, the meat-safe, were all padlocked. There was nothing that a beetle could have lunched upon. The pinched and meager aspect of the place would have killed a chameleon: he would have known, at the first mouthful, that the air was not eatable, and must have given up the ghost in despair.

While these acts and deeds were in progress in and out of the office of Sampson Brass, Richard Swiveller, being often left alone therein, began to find the time hang heavy on his hands. For the better preservation of his cheerfulness, therefore, and to prevent his faculties from rusting, he provided himself with a cribbage-board and pack of cards, and accustomed himself to play at cribbage with a dummy, for twenty, thirty, or sometimes even fifty thousand pounds a side, besides many hazardous bets to a considerable amount.

As these games were very silently conducted, notwithstanding the magnitude of the interest involved, Mr. Swiveller began to think that on those evenings when Mr. and Miss Brass were out (and they often went out now) he heard a kind of snorting or hard-breathing sound in the direction of the door, which, it occurred to him, after some reflection, must proceed from the small servant, who always had a cold from damp living. Looking intently that way one night, he plainly distinguished an eye gleaming and glistening at the keyhole; and having now no doubt that his suspicions were correct, he stole softly to the door, and pounced upon her before she was aware of his approach.

"Oh! I did n't mean any harm indeed, upon my word I did n't, it 's so very dull downstairs. Please do n't tell upon me, please do n't."

"Tell upon you!" said Dick. "Do you mean to say you are looking through the keyhole for company?"

"Yes, upon my word I was."

"How long have you been cooling your eye there?"

"Oh, ever since you first began to play them cards, and long before."

"Well,—come in. Here, sit down, and I 'll teach you how to play."

"Oh! I durst n't do it. Miss Sally 'ud kill me, if she know'd I come up here."

"Have you got a fire downstairs?"

"A very little one."

"Miss Sally could n't kill me if she know'd I went down there, so I 'll come," said Richard, putting the cards in his pocket. "Why, how thin you are! What do you mean by it?"

"It ain't my fault."

"Could you eat any bread and meat?" said Dick, taking down his hat. "Yes? Ah! I thought so. Did you ever taste beer?"

"I had a sip of it once."

"Here's a state of things!" cried Mr. Swiveller, raising his eyes to the ceiling. "She *never* tasted it—it can't be tasted in a sip! Why, how old are you?"

"I don't know."

Mr. Swiveller opened his eyes very wide, and appeared thoughtful for a moment; then, bidding the child mind the door until he came back, vanished straightway.

Presently he returned, followed by the boy from the public-house, who bore in one hand a plate of bread and beef, and in the other a great pot, filled with some very fragrant compound, which sent forth a grateful steam, and was indeed choice purl, made after a particular recipe which Mr. Swiveller had imparted to the landlord, at a period when he was deep in his books and desirous to conciliate his friendship. Relieving the boy of his burden at the door, and charging his little companion to fasten it to prevent surprise, Mr. Swiveller followed her into the kitchen.

"There!" said Richard, putting the plate before her. "First of all clear that off, and then you'll see what's next."

The small servant needed no second bidding, and the plate was soon empty.

"Next," said Dick, handing the purl, "take a pull at that; but moderate your transports, you know, for you're not used to it. Well, is it good?"

"Oh! isn't it?" said the small servant.

Mr. Swiveller appeared gratified beyond all expression by this reply, and took a long draught himself. These preliminaries disposed of, he applied himself to teaching her the game, which she soon learnt tolerably well, being both sharp-witted and cunning.

Mr. Swiveller and his partner played several rubbers with varying success, until the loss of three sixpences, the gradual sinking of the purl, and the striking of ten o'clock, combined to render that gentleman mindful of the flight of time, and the expediency of withdrawing before Mr. Sampson and Miss Sally Brass returned.

"With which object in view, Marchioness," said Mr. Swiveller gravely, "I shall ask your ladyship's permission to put the board in my pocket, and to retire from the presence when I have finished this tankard; merely observing, Marchioness, that since life, like a river, is flowing, I care not how fast it rolls on, ma'am, on, while such purl on the bank still is growing, and such eyes light the waves as they run. Marchioness, your health. You will excuse my wearing my hat, for the palace is damp, and the marble floor is—if I may be allowed the expression—sloppy."

He gave utterance to these apologetic observations, and slowly sipped the last choice drops of nectar.

"The Baron Sampsono Brasso and his fair sister are (you tell me) at the Play?" said Mr. Swiveller, leaning his left arm heavily upon the table, and raising his voice and his right leg after the manner of a theatrical bandit.

The Marchioness nodded.

"Ha!" said Mr. Swiveller, with a portentous frown. "'Tis well, Marchioness!—but no matter. Some wine there. Ho!" He illustrated these melodramatic morsels, by handing the tankard to himself with great humility, receiving it haughtily, drinking from it thirstily, and smacking his lips fiercely.

The small servant, who was not so well acquainted with theatrical conventionalities as Mr. Swiveller (having indeed never seen a play, or heard one spoken of, except by chance through chinks of doors and in other forbidden places), was rather alarmed by demonstrations so novel in their nature, and showed her concern so plainly in her looks, that Mr. Swiveller felt it necessary to discharge his brigand manner, for one more suitable to private life, as he asked, "Do they often go where glory waits 'em, and leave you here?"

"Oh, yes; I believe you they do. Miss Sally's such a one-er for that, she is."

"Such a what?" said Dick.

"Such a one-er," returned the Marchioness.

"Is Mr. Brass a wunner?"

"Not half what Miss Sally is, he isn't. Bless you, he'd never do anything without her."

"Oh! He would n't, would n't he?"

"Miss Sally keeps him in such order. He always asks her advice, he does; and he catches it sometimes. Bless you, you would n't believe how much he catches it."

"I suppose," said Dick, "that they consult together, a good deal, and talk about a great many people—about me, for instance, sometimes, eh, Marchioness?"

The Marchioness nodded amazingly.

"Complimentary?" said Mr. Swiveller.

The Marchioness changed the motion of her head, which had not yet left off nodding, and suddenly began to shake it from side to side, with a vehemence which threatened to dislocate her neck.

"Humph;" Dick muttered. "Would it be any breach of confidence, Marchioness, to relate what they say of the humble individual who has now the honor to—?"

"Miss Sally says you 're a funny chap," replied his friend.

"Well, Marchioness," said Mr. Swiveller, "that 's not uncomplimentary. Merriment, Marchioness, is not a bad or degrading quality. Old King Cole was himself a merry old soul, if we may put any faith in the pages of history."

"But she says that you an't to be trusted."

"Why, really, Marchioness," said Mr. Swiveller, thoughtfully; "several ladies and gentlemen—not exactly professional persons, but tradespeople, ma'am, trades-people — have made the same remark. The obscure citizen who keeps the hotel over the way, inclined strongly to that opinion to-night when I ordered him to prepare the banquet. It 's a popular prejudice, Mar-chioness; and yet I am sure I do n't know why, for I have been trusted in my time to a considerable amount, and I can safely say that I never forsook my trust until it deserted me—never. Mr. Brass is of the same opinion, I suppose?"

His friend nodded again, with a cunning look which seemed to hint that Mr. Brass held stronger opinions on the subject than his sister; and seeming to recollect herself, added imploringly, "But do n't you ever tell upon me, or I shall be beat to death."

"Marchioness," said Mr. Swiveller, rising, "the word of a gentleman is as good as his bond—sometimes better, as in the present case, where his bond might prove a doubtful sort of security. I am your friend, and I hope we shall play many more rubbers together in this same saloon. But, Marchioness,'' added Richard, stopping in his way to the door, and wheeling slowly round upon the small servant, who was following with the candle; "it occurs to me that you must be in the constant habit of airing your eye at keyholes, to know all this.''

"I only wanted,'' replied the trembling Marchioness, "to know where the key of the safe was hid; that was all; and I would n't have taken much, if I had found it— only enough to squench my hunger.''

"You did n't find it then?'' said Dick. "But of course you did n't, or you'd be plumper. Good night, Marchioness. Fare thee well—and if for ever, then for ever, fare thee well.''

Charles Dickens.

TULKINGHORN, THE LAWYER, AND MADE- MOISELLE HORTENSE.

Mr. Tulkinghorn, the Lawyer, smoke-dried and faded, dwelling among mankind, but not consorting with them, aged without experience of genial youth, and so long used to make his cramped nest in holes and corners of human nature that he had forgotten its broader and better range, comes sauntering home.

The lamplighter is skipping up and down his ladder on Mr. Tulkinghorn's side of the fields, when that high priest of noble mysteries arrives at his own dull court-yard. He ascends the door-steps, unlocks his door, gropes his way into his murky rooms, lights his candles, and looks about him. He then takes a small key from his pocket, unlocks a drawer in which there is another key, which unlocks a chest in which there is another, and so comes to the cellar key, with which he prepares to descend to the regions of old wine. He is going toward the door with a candle in his hand, when a knock comes.

"Who 's this?—Ay, ay, Mistress, it 's you, is it? You appear at a good time. I have just been hearing of you. Now! What do you want?''

He stands the candle on the chimney-piece, in the

clerk's hall, and taps his dry cheek with the key, as he addresses these words of welcome to Mademoiselle Hortense. That feline personage, with her lips tightly shut, and her eyes looking out at him sideways, softly closes the door before replying.

"I have had a great deal of trouble to find you, sir."

"*Have* you?"

"I have been here very often, sir. It has always been said to me, he is not at home, he is engage, he is this, he is that, he is not for you."

"Quite right, and quite true."

"Not true. Lies!"

"Now, Mistress," says the lawyer, tapping the key hastily upon the chimney-piece, "if you have anything to say, say it, say it."

"Sir, you have not use me well. You have been mean and shabby."

"Mean and shabby, eh?" returns the lawyer, rubbing his nose with the key.

"Yes. What is it that I tell you? You know you have. You have attraped me—catched me—to give you information; you have asked me to show you the dress of mine my lady must have worn that night; you have prayed me to come in it here to meet that boy—Say! Is it not?"

"You are a vixen, a vixen!—Well wench, well. I paid you."

"You paid me! Two sovereign! I have not change them, I re-fuse them, I de-spise them, I throw them from me! Now! You have paid me? Eh, my God, O yes!"

Mr. Tulkinghorn rubs his head with the key, while she entertains herself with a sarcastic laugh.

"You must be rich, my fair friend, to throw money about in that way!"

"I *am* rich; I am very rich in hate. I hate my lady, of all my heart. You know that."

"Know it? How should I know it?"

"Because you have known it perfectly, before you prayed me to give you that information. Because you have known perfectly that I was en-r-r-r-raged!"

"Oh! I knew that, did I?"

"Yes, without doubt. I am not blind. You have made sure of me because you knew that. You had reason! I det-est her."

"Having said this, have you anything else to say, Mademoiselle?"

"I am not yet placed. Place me well. Find me a good condition! If you cannot, or do not choose to do that, employ me to pursue her, to chase her, to disgrace and to dishonor her. I will help you well, and with a good will. It is what *you* do. Do I not know that?"

"You appear to know a good deal."

"Do I not? Is it that I am so weak as to believe, like a child, that I come here in that dress to receive that boy, only to decide a little bet, a wager? Eh, my God, O yes!"

"Now, let us see how this matter stands."

"Ah! Let us see."

"You come here to make a remarkably modest demand, which you have just stated, and it not being conceded, you will come again."

"And again, and yet again. And yet again. And many times again. In effect, forever!"

"And not only here, but you will go to Mr. Snagsby's, too, perhaps? That visit not succeeding either, you will go again, perhaps?"

"And again. And yet again. And yet again. And many times again. In effect, forever."

"Very well. Now, Mademoiselle Hortense, let me recommend you to take the candle and pick up that money of yours. I think you will find it behind the clerk's partition in the corner yonder."

She merely throws a laugh over her shoulder and stands her ground with folded arms.

"You will not, eh!"

"No, I will not!"

"So much the poorer you; so much the richer I! Look, Mistress, this is the key of my wine cellar. It is a large key, but the keys of prisons are larger. In this city there are houses of correction (where the treadmills are for women), the gates of which are very strong and heavy, and no doubt the keys, too. I am afraid a lady of your spirit and activity would find it an inconvenience to have one of those keys turned upon her for any length of time. What do you think?"

"I think that you are a miserable wretch."

"Probably, but I do n't ask what you think of myself; I ask what you think of the prison."

"Nothing. What does it matter to me?"

"Why, it matters this much, Mistress, the law is so despotic here, that it interferes to prevent any of our good English citizens from being troubled, even by a lady's visits, against his desire. And, on his complaining that he is so troubled, it takes hold of the troublesome lady, and shuts her up in prison under hard discipline. Turns the key upon her, Mistress." Illustrating with the cellar key.

"Truly! that is droll! But—my faith!—still what does it matter to me?"

"My fair friend, make another visit here, or at Mr. Snagsby's, and you shall learn."

"In that case you will send me to the prison, perhaps?"

"Perhaps.—In a word, Mistress, I am sorry to be impolite, but if you ever present yourself uninvited here —or there—again, I will give you over to the police. Their gallantry is great, but they carry troublesome people through the streets in an ignominious manner; strapped down on a board, my good wench."

"I will prove you, I will try if you dare to do it!"

"And if," pursues the lawyer, without minding her, "I place you in that good condition of being locked up in jail, it will be some time before you find yourself at liberty again."

"I will prove you."

"And now," proceeds the lawyer, still without minding her, "you had better go. Think twice before you come here again."

"Think you twice two hundred times!"

"You were dismissed by your lady, you know," Mr. Tulkinghorn observes, following her out upon the staircase, "as the most implacable and unmanageable of women. Now turn over a new leaf, and take warning by what I say to you. For what I say I mean; and what I threaten, I will do, Mistress."

"Oh! I will prove you—you miserable wretch—I will prove you."

When she is gone, he goes down to the cellar, and returning with his cobweb-covered bottle, devotes himself to a leisurely enjoyment of its contents.

Charles Dickens.

PASSAGE OF THE REFORM BILL.

Such a scene as the division of last Tuesday I never saw, and never expect to see again. If I should live fifty years, the impression of it will be as fresh and sharp in my mind as if it had just taken place. It was like seeing Cæsar stabbed in the Senate-house, or seeing Oliver taking the mace from the table; a sight to be seen only once, and never to be forgotten.

The crowd overflowed the House in every part. When the strangers were cleared out and the doors locked, we had six hundred and eighty members present—more by fifty-five than ever were in a division before.

The ayes and noes were like two volleys of cannon from opposite sides of a field of battle.

When the opposition went out into the lobby, an operation which took up twenty minutes or more, we spread ourselves over the benches on both sides of the House; for there were many of us who had not been able to find a seat during the evening. When the doors were shut we began to speculate on our numbers. Everybody was desponding. "We have lost it. We are only two hundred and eighty at most. I do not think we are two hundred and fifty. They are three hundred. Alderman Thompson has counted them. He says they are two hundred and ninety-nine." This was the talk on our benches. I wonder that men who have been long in Parliament do not acquire a better *coup d'œil* for numbers. The House, when only the ayes were in it, looked to me a very fair House, much fuller than it generally is even on debates of considerable interest.

I had no hope, however, of three hundred. As the tellers passed along our lowest row on the left-hand side, the interest was insupportable—two hundred and ninety-one—two hundred and ninety-two—we were all standing up and stretching forward, telling with the tellers.

At three hundred there was a short cry of joy—at three hundred and two another—suppressed, however, in a moment; for we did not yet know what the hostile force might be.

We knew, however, that we could not be severely beaten. The doors were thrown open, and in they came.

Each of them, as he entered, brought some different report of their numbers. It must have been impossible, as you may conceive, in the lobby, crowded as they were, to form any exact estimate.

First we heard that they were three hundred and three; then that number rose to three hundred and ten; then went down to three hundred and seven. Alexander Barry told me that he had counted, and that they were three hundred and four. We were all breathless with anxiety, when Charles Wood, who stood near the door, jumped up on a bench and cried out, "They are only three hundred and one." We set up a shout that you might have heard to Charing Cross, waving our hats, stamping against the floor, and clapping our hands. The tellers scarcely got through the crowd; for the House was thronged up to the table, and all the floor was fluctuating with heads like the pit of a theater. But you might have heard a pin drop as Duncannon read the numbers. Then again the shouts broke out, and many of us shed tears. I could scarcely refrain—and the jaw of Peel fell; and the face of Twiss was as the face of a damned soul; and Herries looked like Judas taking his necktie off for the last operation.

We shook hands and clapped each other on the back, and went out laughing, crying, and huzzaing into the lobby. And no sooner were the outer doors opened than another shout answered that within the House. All the passages and the stairs into the waiting-rooms were thronged by people who had waited till four in the morning to know the issue.

We passed through a narrow lane between two thick masses of them; and all the way down they were shouting and waving their hats, till we got into the open air. I called a cabriolet, and the first thing the driver asked was, "Is the bill carried?"

"Yes, by one."

"Thank God for it, sir!"

And away I rode to Gray's Inn—and so ended a scene which will probably never be equaled till the reformed Parliament wants reforming; and that, I hope, will not be till the days of our grandchildren.

Lord Macaulay.

SCENE FROM IVANHOE.

The scene is a turret chamber of Torquilstone castle. The characters are Ivanhoe, who has been so severely wounded that he cannot leave his couch, and the Jewess Rebecca, who is caring for him. Both have been made captive by Front-de-Bœuf, the lord of the castle. The incident is the siege of the stronghold by King Richard in the disguise of the Black Knight. Rebecca stands at a lattice window, protecting herself with an ancient buckler, and reports the progress of the attack to the wounded knight.

"The skirts of the wood seem lined with archers, although only a few are advanced from its dark shadow."

"Under what banner?" asked Ivanhoe.

"Under no ensign of war which I can observe," answered Rebecca.

"A singular novelty," muttered the knight, "to advance to storm such a castle without pennon or banner displayed! Seest thou who they be that act as leaders?"

"A knight, clad in sable armor, is the most conspicuous," said the Jewess; "he alone is armed from head to heel, and seems to assume the direction of all around him."

"What device does he bear on his shield?" replied Ivanhoe.

"Something resembling a bar of iron, and a padlock painted blue on the black shield."

"A fetterlock and shacklebolt azure," said Ivanhoe; "I know not who may bear the device, but well I ween it might now be mine own. Canst thou not see the motto?"

"Scarce the device itself at this distance," replied Rebecca; "but when the sun glances fair upon his shield, it shows as I tell you."

"Seem there no other leaders?" exclaimed the anxious inquirer.

"None of mark and distinction that I can behold from this station," said Rebecca; "but, doubtless, the other side of the castle is also assailed They appear even now to be preparing to advance—God of Zion protect us! What a dreadful sight! Those who advance first bear huge shields and defenses made of plank; the others fol-

low, bending their bows as they come on. They raise
their bows! God of Moses, forgive the creatures thou
hast made!''

"And I must lie here like a bed-ridden monk,''
exclaimed Ivanhoe, "while the game that gives me
freedom or death is played out by the hand of others!
Look from the window once again, kind maiden, but
beware that you are not marked by the archers beneath.
Look out once more and tell me if they yet advance to the
storm.''

"What dost thou see, Rebecca?'' again demanded the
wounded knight.

"Nothing but the cloud of arrows flying so thick as to
dazzle mine eyes, and to hide the bowmen who shoot
them.''

"That cannot endure," said Ivanhoe; "if they press
not right on to carry the castle by pure force of arms, the
archery may avail little against stone walls and bulwarks.
Look for the Knight of the Fetterlock, fair Rebecca,
and see how he bears himself; for as the leader is, so will
his followers be.''

"I see him not," said Rebecca.

"Foul craven!" exclaimed Ivanhoe; "does he blench
from the helm when the wind blows highest?''

"He blenches not! he blenches not!" said Rebecca.
"I see him now; he leads a body of men close under the
outer barrier of the Barbican. They pull down the piles and
palisades; they hew down the barriers with axes. His
high black plume floats abroad over the throng, like a
raven over the field of the slain. They have made a
breach in the barriers—they rush in—they are thrust
back! Front-de-Bœuf heads the defenders; I see his
gigantic form above the press. They throng again to
the breach, and the pass is disputed hand to hand, and
man to man. God of Jacob! it is the meeting of two
fierce tides—the conflict of two oceans moved by adverse
winds!''

She turned her head from the lattice, as if unable
longer to endure a sight so terrible.

"Look forth again, Rebecca," said Ivanhoe, mistak-
ing the cause of her retiring; "the archery must in some
degree have ceased, since they are now fighting hand to
hand. Look again; there is now less danger.''

Rebecca again looked forth, and almost immediately exclaimed, "Holy prophets of the law! Front-de-Bœuf and the Black Knight fight hand to hand on the breach, amid the roar of their followers, who watch the progress of the strife — Heaven strike with the cause of the oppressed and of the captive!" She then uttered a loud shriek, and exclaimed, "He is down!—he is down!"

"Who is down?" cried Ivanhoe; "for our dear Lady's sake, tell me which has fallen!"

"The Black Knight," answered Rebecca, faintly; then instantly again shouted with joyful eagerness—"But no! —but no!—the name of the Lord of Hosts be blessed!— he is on foot again, and fights as if there were twenty men's strength in his single arm. His sword is broken— he snatches an ax from a yeoman—he presses Front-de-Bœuf with blow on blow. The giant stoops and totters like an oak under the steel of the woodman—he falls—he falls."

"Front-de-Bœuf?" exclaimed Ivanhoe.

"Front-de-Bœuf!" answered the Jewess; "his men rush to the rescue, headed by the haughty Templar—their united force compels the champion to pause. They drag Front-de-Bœuf within the walls."

"The assailants have won the barriers, have they not?" said Ivanhoe.

"They have—they have!" exclaimed Rebecca—"and they press the besieged hard upon the outer wall; some plant ladders, some swarm like bees, and endeavor to ascend upon the shoulders of each other—down go stones, beams, and trunks of trees upon their heads, and as fast as they bear the wounded to the rear, fresh men supply their places in the assault—Great God! hast Thou given men Thine own image, that it should be thus cruelly defaced by the hands of their brethren!"

"Think not of that," said Ivanhoe; "this is no time for such thoughts—Who yield?—who push their way?"

"The ladders are thrown down," replied Rebecca, shuddering; "the soldiers lie groveling over them like crushed reptiles—The besieged have the better."

"Saint George strike for us!" exclaimed the knight; "do the false yeomen give way?"

"No!" exclaimed Rebecca, "they bear themselves right yeomanly—the Black Knight approaches the postern with his huge ax—the thundering blows which he deals, you may hear them above all the din and shouts of the battle. Stones and beams are hailed down on the bold champion—he regards them no more than if they were thistle-down or feathers!''

"By Saint John of Acre,''said Ivanhoe, raising himself joyfully on his couch, "methought there was but one man in England that might do such a deed!''

"The postern gate shakes,'' continued Rebecca; "it crashes—it is splintered by his blows—they rush in—the outwork is won—Oh, God!—they hurl the defenders from the battlements—they throw them into the moat—Oh, men, if ye be indeed men, spare them that can resist no longer!''

"The bridge—the bridge which communicates with the castle—have they won the bridge?'' exclaimed Ivanhoe.

"No,'' replied Rebecca, "the Templar has destroyed the plank on which they crossed—few of the defenders escaped with him into the castle—the shrieks and cries which you hear tell the fate of the others—Alas! I see it is still more difficult to look upon victory than upon battle.''

"What do they now, maiden?'' said Ivanhoe; "look forth yet again—this is no time to faint at bloodshed.''

"It is over for the time,'' answered Rebecca; "our friends strengthen themselves within the outwork which they have mastered, and it affords them so good a shelter from the foemen's shot, that the garrison only bestow a few bolts on it from interval to interval, as if rather to disquiet than effectually to injure them.''

"Our friends,'' said Ivanhoe, "will surely not abandon an enterprise so gloriously begun and so happily attained. O no! I will put my faith in the good knight whose ax hath rent heart-of-oak and bars of iron. Singular,'' he again muttered to himself, "if there be two who can do a deed of such *derring-do!** a fetterlock, and a shacklebolt on a field-sable—what may that mean? Seest thou naught else, Rebecca, by which the Black Knight may be distinguished?''

"Nothing,'' said the Jewess; "all about him is black as the wing of the night raven. Nothing can I spy that can mark him further—but having once seen him put forth

*Derring-do—desperate courage.

his strength in battle, methinks I could know him again among a thousand warriors. He rushes to the fray as if he were summoned to a banquet. There is more than mere strength, there seems as if the whole soul and spirit of the champion were given to every blow which he deals upon his enemies. God assoilzie him of the sin of bloodshed! it is fearful, yet magnificent, to behold how the arm and heart of one man can triumph over hundreds."

"Rebecca," said Ivanhoe, "thou hast painted a hero; surely they rest but to refresh their force, or to provide the means of crossing the moat. Under such a leader as thou hast spoken this knight to be, there are no craven fears, no cold-blooded delays, no yielding up a gallant emprize; since the difficulties which render it arduous, render it also glorious. I swear by the honor of my house —I vow by the name of my bright lady-love, I would endure ten years' captivity to fight one day by that good knight's side in such a quarrel as this!"

At this moment the door of the apartment flew open, and the Black Knight rushed in, seized upon Ivanhoe, and bore him off in his arms.

Sir Walter Scott.

INTERVIEW BETWEEN AARON BURR AND MARY SCUDDER.

Mary entered the room where Burr was seated, and wished him good morning, in a serious and placid manner, in which there was not the slightest trace of embarrassment or discomposure.

"Shall I have the pleasure of seeing your fair companion this morning?" said Burr, after some moments of indifferent conversation.

"No, sir; Madame de Frontignac desires me to excuse her to you."

"Is she ill?" said Burr with a look of concern.

"No, Mr. Burr, she prefers not to see you."

Burr gave a start of well-bred surprise, and Mary added,—"Madame de Frontignac has made me familiar with the history of your acquaintance with her, and you will therefore understand what I mean, Mr. Burr, when I say, that, during the time of her stay with us, we should prefer not to receive calls from you."

"Your language, Miss Scudder, has certainly the merit of explicitness."

"I intend it shall have, sir," said Mary tranquilly; "half the misery in the world comes of want of courage to speak and to hear the truth plainly and in a spirit of love."

"I am gratified that you add the last clause, Miss Scudder; I might not otherwise recognize the gentle being whom I have always regarded as the impersonation of all that is softest in woman. I have not the honor of understanding in the least the reason of this apparently capricious sentence, but I bow to it in submission."

"Mr. Burr," said Mary, walking up to him, and looking him full in the eyes, with an energy that for the moment bore down his practiced air of easy superiority, "I wish to speak to you for a moment, as one immortal soul should to another, without any of those false glosses and deceits which men call ceremony and good manners. You have done a very great injury to a lovely lady, whose weakness ought to have been sacred in your eyes. Precisely because you are what you are,—strong, keen, penetrating, and able to control and govern all who come near you,—because you have the power to make yourself agreeable, interesting, fascinating, and to win esteem and love,—just for that reason you ought to hold yourself the guardian of every woman, and treat her as you would wish any man to treat your own daughter. I leave it to your conscience, whether this is the manner in which you have treated Madame de Frontignac."

"Upon my word, Miss Scudder," began Burr, "I cannot imagine what representations our mutual friend may have been making. I assure you our intercourse has been as irreproachable as the most scrupulous could desire."

"Irreproachable!—scrupulous!—Mr. Burr, you know that you have taken the very life out of her. You men can have everything,—ambition, wealth, power; a thousand ways are open to you; women have nothing but their heart; and when that is gone, all is gone. Mr. Burr, you remember the rich man who had flocks and herds, but nothing would do for him but he must have the one little ewe-lamb which was all his poor neighbor had. Thou art the man! You have stolen all the love she had to give,—all that she had to make a happy home; and you can never give her anything in return, without endangering her purity and her soul,—and you knew you could not. I know you men think this is a light matter; but it is death to us. What will this woman's life be? One long struggle to forget; and when you have forgotten her, and are going on gay and happy,—when you have thrown her very name away as a faded flower, she will be praying, hoping, fearing for you; though all men deny you, yet will not she. Yes, Mr. Burr, if ever your popularity and prosperity should leave you, and those who now flatter should despise and curse you, she will always be interceding with her own heart and with God for you, and making a thousand excuses where she cannot deny; and if you die, as I fear you have lived, unreconciled to the God of your fathers, it will be in her heart to offer up her very soul for you, and to pray that God will impute all your sins to her, and give you heaven. Oh, I know this, because I have felt it in my own heart!" and Mary threw herself passionately down into a chair, and broke into an agony of uncontrolled sobbing.

Burr turned away, and stood looking through the window; tears were dropping silently, unchecked by the cold, hard pride which was the evil demon of his life.

In a few moments Mary rose with renewed calmness and dignity, and, approaching him, said,—"Before I wish you good morning, Mr. Burr, I must ask pardon for the liberty I have taken in speaking so very plainly."

"There is no pardon needed, my dear child," said Burr; and turning, he bowed, and was gone.

Harriet Beecher Stowe.

GAYETY.

In this class of selections the same suggestions that were made on the subject of common reading are pertinent and practical. However, greater variety of intonation, a quicker movement, and a higher pitch, are required. Flexibility of voice is indispensable, so that the slides of the fifth and octave may be easily reached, while the voice remains free from strain and harshness.

GAY AND ANIMATED SELECTIONS.

THE DAFFODILS.

I wandered lonely as a cloud
  That floats on high o'er vales and hills,
When all at once I saw a crowd,—
  A host of golden daffodils
Beside the lake, beneath the trees,
Fluttering and dancing in the breeze.

Continuous as the stars that shine
  And twinkle on the Milky Way,
They stretched in never-ending line
  Along the margin of a bay;
Ten thousand saw I, at a glance,
Tossing their heads in sprightly dance.

The waves beside them danced, but they
  Outdid the sparkling waves in glee;
A poet could not but be gay
  In such a jocund company;
I gazed—and gazed—but little thought
What wealth the show to me had brought.

For oft, when on my couch I lie,
  In vacant or in pensive mood,

They flash upon that inward eye
   Which is the bliss of solitude;
And then my heart with pleasure fills,
And dances with the daffodils.
                William Wordsworth.

CUPID SWALLOWED.

T' other day, as I was twining
Roses for a crown to dine in,
What, of all things, midst the heap,
Should I light on, fast asleep,
But the little desperate elf,—
The tiny traitor,—Love himself!
By the wings I pinched him up
Like a bee, and in a cup
Of my wine I plunged and sank him;
And what d' ye think I did?—I drank him!
Faith, I thought him dead. Not he!
There he lives with tenfold glee;
And now this moment, with his wings,
I feel him tickling my heart-strings.
                   Leigh Hunt.

THE SOUTH WIND AND THE SUN.

O the South Wind and the Sun!
How each loved the other one—
   Full of fancy—full of folly—
Full of jollity and fun!
How they romped and ran about,
Like two boys when school is out,
   With glowing face, and lisping lip,
Low laugh, and lifted shout!

And the South Wind—he was dressed
With a ribbon round his breast
   That floated, flopped and fluttered
In a riotous unrest;

And a drapery of mist,
From the shoulder and the wrist
  Flowing backward with the motion
Of the waving hand he kissed.

And the Sun had on a crown
Wrought of gilded thistle-down,
  And a scarf of velvet vapor,
And a raveled-rainbow gown;
And his tinsel-tangled hair,
Tossed and lost upon the air,
  Was glossier and flossier
Than any anywhere.

And the South Wind's eyes were two
Little dancing drops of dew,
  As he puffed his cheeks, and pursed his lips,
And blew, and blew, and blew!
And the Sun's—like diamond-stone,
Brighter yet than ever known,
  As he knit his brows and held his breath,
And shone, and shone, and shone!

And this pair of merry fays
Wandered through the summer days;
  Arm in arm they went together
Over heights of morning haze—
Over slanting slopes of lawn
They went on, and on, and on,
  Where the daisies looked like star-tracks
Trailing up and down the dawn.

And where'er they found the top
Of a wheat-stalk droop and lop,
  They chucked it underneath the chin
And praised the lavish crop,
Till it lifted with the pride
Of the heads it grew beside,
  And then the South Wind and the Sun
Went onward satisfied.

And the humming-bird, that hung
Like a jewel up among
  The tilted honeysuckle-horns,
They mesmerized, and swung
In the palpitating air,
Drowsed with odors strange and rare,
  And, with whispered laughter, slipped away
And left him hanging there.

By the brook with mossy brink,
Where the cattle came to drink,
  They trilled, and piped, and whistled
With the thrush and bobolink,
Till the kine, in listless pause,
Switched their tails in mute applause,
  With lifted head and dreamy eyes,
And bubble-dripping jaws.

And where the melons grew,
Streaked with yellow, green, and blue,
  These jolly sprites went wandering
Through spangled paths of dew.
And the melons, here and there,
They made love to, everywhere,
  Turning their pink souls to crimson
With caresses fond and fair.

Over orchard walls they went,
Where the fruited boughs were bent
  Till they brushed the sward beneath them
Where the shine and shadow blent;
And the great green pear they shook
Till the sallow hue forsook
  Its features, and the gleam of gold
Laughed out in every look.

And they stroked the downy cheek
Of the peach, and smoothed it sleek,
  And flushed it into splendor;
And, with many an elfish freak,

Gave the russet's rust a wipe—
Prankt the rambo with a stripe,
    And the winesap blushed its reddest
As they spanked the pippins ripe.

And the golden-banded bees,
Droning o'er the flowery leas,
    They bridled, reined, and rode away
Across the fragrant breeze,
Till in hollow oak and elm
They had groomed and stabled them
    In waxen stalls that oozed with dews
Of rose and lily stem.

Where the dusty highway leads,
High above the wayside weeds,
    They sowed the air with butterflies
Like blooming flower-seeds,
Till the dull grasshopper sprung
Half a man's height up, and hung
    Tranced in the heat, with whirring wings,
And sung, and sung, and sung!

And they heard the killdee's call,
And afar, the waterfall,
    But the rustle of a falling leaf
They heard above it all;
And the trailing willow crept
Deeper in the tide that swept
    The leafy shallop to the shore,
And wept, and wept, and wept!

And the fairy vessel veered
From its moorings—tacked and steered
    For the center of the current—
Sailed away and disappeared:
And the burthen that it bore
From the long-enchanted shore—
    "Alas! the South Wind and the Sun!"
I murmur evermore.

For the South Wind and the Sun,
Each so loves the other one,
   For all his jolly folly,
And frivolity and fun,
That our love for them they weigh
As their fickle fancies may,
   And when at last we love them most,
They laugh and sail away.

James Whitcomb Riley.

SONG OF THE BROOK.

I come from haunts of coot and hern:
   I make a sudden sally
And sparkle out among the fern,
   To bicker down a valley.

By thirty hills I hurry down,
   Or slip between the ridges,
By twenty thorps, a little town,
   And half a hundred bridges,

Till last by Philip's farm I flow
   To join the brimming river;
For men may come and men may go,
   But I go on forever.

I chatter over stony ways,
   In little sharps and trebles;
I bubble into eddying bays,
   I babble on the pebbles.

With many a curve my banks I fret
   By many a field and fallow,
And many a fairy foreland set
   With willow-weed and mallow.

I chatter, chatter, as I flow
  To join the brimming river;
For men may come and men may go,
  But I go on forever.

I wind about, and in and out,
  With here a blossom sailing,
And here and there a lusty trout,
  And here and there a grayling.

And here and there a foamy flake
  Upon me, as I travel
With many a silvery waterbreak
  Above the golden gravel,

And draw them all along, and flow
  To join the brimming river;
For men may come and men may go,
  But I go on forever.

I steal by lawns and grassy plots;
  I slide by hazel covers;
I move the sweet forget-me-nots
  That grow for happy lovers.

I slip, I slide, I gloom, I glance,
  Among my skimming swallows;
I make the netted sunbeams dance
  Against my sandy shallows.

I murmur under moon and stars
  In brambly wildernesses;
I linger by my shingly bars;
  I loiter round my cresses;

And out again I curve and flow
  To join the brimming river;
For men may come and men may go,
  But I go on forever.

                              Lord Tennyson.

THE BALLAD OF THE BROOK.

Oh, it was a dainty maid that went a-maying in the morn,
  A dainty, dainty maiden of degree;
The ways she took were merry, and the ways she missed
    forlorn,
  And the laughing water tinkled to the sea.

The little leaves above her loved the dainty, dainty maid,
  The little winds they kissed her, every one;
At the nearing of her little feet the flowers were not afraid,
  And the water lay a-wimpling in the sun.

Oh, the dainty, dainty maid to the borders of the brook,
  Lingered down as lightly as the breeze;
And the shy water-spiders quit their scurrying to look,
  And the happy water whispered to the trees.

She was fain to cross the brook, was the dainty, dainty maid,
  But first she lifted up her elfin eyes
To see if there were cavalier or clown anear to aid,
  And the water-bubbles blinked in surprise.

The brook bared its pebbles to persuade her dainty feet,
  But the dainty, dainty maid was not content;
She had spied a simple country lad (for dainty maid unmeet),
  And the shy water twinkled as it went.

As the simple lad drew nigh, then this dainty, dainty maid,
  Oh, maidens, well you know how it was done!
Stood a-gazing at her feet, until he saw she was afraid
  Of the water there a-wimpling in the sun.

Now that simple lad had in him all the making of a man,
  And he stammered, " I had better lift you over."
Said the dainty, dainty maid, " Do you really think you can?"
  And the water hid its laughter in the clover.

So he carried her across, with his honest eyes cast down,
  And his foolish heart a-quaking with delight,

And the maid, she looked him over with her elfin eyes of
    brown,
  And the limpid water giggled at his plight.

He reached the other side; he set down the dainty maid;
  But he trembled so he could n't speak a word;
Then the dainty, dainty maid, "Thank you, sir! Good-day!"
    she said,
  And the water-bubbles chuckled as they heard.

Oh, she tripped away so lightly, a-maying in the morn,
  That dainty, dainty maiden of degree;
But she left the simple country lad a-sighing and forlorn,
  Where the mocking water twinkled to the sea.
                      Charles G. D. Roberts.

TO A SKYLARK.

Hail to thee, blithe Spirit!
  Bird thou never wert,
That from heaven, or near it,
  Pourest thy full heart
In profuse strains of unpremeditated art.

Higher still and higher
  From the earth thou springest,
Like a cloud of fire,
  The blue deep thou wingest,
And singing still dost soar, and soaring ever singest.

In the golden lightning
  Of the setting sun,
O'er which clouds are brightening,
  Thou dost float and run,
Like an embodied joy whose race is just begun.

The pale purple even
  Melts around thy flight;
Like a star of heaven,
  In the broad daylight
Thou art unseen, but yet I hear thy shrill delight.

Keen as are the arrows
Of that silver sphere,
Whose intense lamp narrows
In the white dawn clear,
Until we hardly see, we feel that it is there.

All the earth and air
With thy voice is loud,
As, when night is bare,
From one lonely cloud
The moon rains out her beams, and heaven is overflow'd.

What thou art we know not;
What is most like thee?
From rainbow clouds there flow not
Drops so bright to see
As from thy presence showers a rain of melody.

Teach us, sprite or bird,
What sweet thoughts are thine:
I have never heard
Praise of love or wine
That panted forth a flood of rapture so divine.

Chorus hymeneal,
Or triumphal chant,
Matched with thine, would be all
But an empty vaunt,—
A thing wherein we feel there is some hidden want.

What objects are the fountains
Of thy happy strain?
What fields, or waves, or mountains?
What shapes of sky or plain?
What love of thine own kind? what ignorance of pain?

Teach me half the gladness
That thy brain must know,
Such harmonious madness
From my lips would flow,
The world should listen then, as I am listening now.
Percy Bysshe Shelley.

RIDING DOWN.

Oh, did you see him riding down,
And riding down while all the town
Came out to see, came out to see,
And all the bells rang mad with glee?

Oh, did you hear those bells ring out,
The bells ring out, the people shout?
And did you hear that cheer on cheer
That over all the bells rang clear?

And did you see the waving flags,
The fluttering flags, the tattered flags?
Red, white, and blue, shot through and through,
Baptized with battle's deadly dew.

And did you hear the drums' gay beat,
The drums' gay beat, the bugles sweet,
The cymbals' clash, the cannons' crash
That rent the sky with sound and flash?

And did you see me waiting there,
Just waiting there and watching there?
One little lass amid the mass
That pressed to see the hero pass.

And did you see him smiling down?
And smiling down, as riding down
With slowest pace, with stately grace,
He caught the vision of a face,—

My face uplifted, red and white,—
Turned red and white with sheer delight
To meet the eyes, the smiling eyes,
Outflashing in their swift surprise?

Oh, did you see how swift it came,
How swift it came like sudden flame,—
That smile to me, to only me,
The little lass who blushed to see?

And at the windows all along,
Oh, all along, a lovely throng
Of faces fair beyond compare
Beamed out upon him riding there.

Each face was like a radiant gem,—
A sparkling gem, and yet for them
No swift smile came like sudden flame;
No arrowy glance took certain aim.

He turned away from all their grace,
From all that grace of perfect face;
He turned to me, to only me,—
The little lass who blushed to see.

Nora Perry.

HUMOR.

The upper tones of the voice are peculiarly those of Humor. A sudden flight on the musical scale, from a comparatively low note to a very high one, is usually provocative of mirth.

The greatest possible variety in intonation, united with an airiness of movement and an approach to a laughing utterance, are the principal requirements of Humorous Reading.

HUMOROUS SELECTIONS.

A SENATOR ENTANGLED.

The Countess di Nottinero was not exactly a Recamier, but she was a remarkably brilliant woman, and the acknowledged leader of the liberal part of Florentine society.

The good Senator had never before encountered a thorough woman of the world, and was as ignorant as a child of the innumerable little harmless arts by which the power of such a one is extended and secured. At last the Senator came to this conclusion,—*La Cica* was desperately in love with him.

She appeared to be a widow. At least she had no husband that he had ever seen. Now, if the poor *Cica* was hopelessly in love, it must be stopped at once. But let it be done delicately, not abruptly.

One evening they walked on the balcony of *La Cica's* noble residence. She was sentimental, devoted, charming.

The conversation of a fascinating woman does not sound so well when it is reported as it is when uttered. Her power is in her tone, her glance, her manner. Who can catch the evanescent beauty of her expression or the deep tenderness of her well modulated voice?—who indeed?

"Does ze scene please you, my Senator?"

"Very much indeed."

"Youar countryman haf tol me zey would like to stay here alloway."

"It is a beautiful place."

"Did you aiver see anythin moaire loafely?" And the Countess looked full in his face.

"Never," said the Senator, earnestly. The next instant he blushed. He had been betrayed into a compliment.

The Countess sighed.

"Helas! my Senator, that it is not pairmitted to mortals to sociate as zey would laike."

"'Your Senator,'" thought the gentleman thus addressed; "how fond, how tender,—poor thing! poor thing!"

"I wish that Italy was nearer to the States," said he.

"How I adamair youar style of mind, so different from ze Italiana! You are so strong,—so nobile. Yet would I laike to see moar of ze poetic in you."

"I always loved poetry, marm," said the Senator, desperately.

"Ah—good—nais – eccelente. I am plees at zat," cried the Countess, with much animation. "You would loafe it moar eef you knew Italiano. Your langua ees not sufficient musicale for poatry."

"It is not so soft a language as the *I*talian."

"Ah—no—not so soft. Very well. And what theenka you of ze Italiano?"

"The sweetest language I ever heard in all my born days."

"Ah now—you hev not heard much of ze Italiano, my Senator."

"I have heard you speak often," said the Senator, naïvely.

"Ah, you compliment! I sot you was aboove flattera."

And the Countess playfully tapped his arm with her little fan.

"What Ingelis poet do you loafe best?"

"Poet? English poet?" said the Senator, with some surprise. "O—why, marm, I think Watts is about the best of the lot.

"Watt? Was he a poet? I did not know zat. He who invented ze stim-injaine? And yet if he was a poet, it is naturale zat you loafe him best."

"Steam-engine? O no! This one was a minister."

"A meeneestaire? Ah! an abbc? I know him not. Yet I haf read mos of all youar poets."

"He made up hymns, marm, and psalms,—for instance, 'Watts' Divine Hymns and Spiritual Songs.'"

"Songs? Spirituelle? Ah, I mus at once procuaire ze works of Watt, which was favorit poet of my Senator."

"A lady of such intelligence as you would like the poet Watts," said the Senator, firmly. "He is the best known by far of all our poets."

"What! better zan Shakespeare, Milton, Bairon? You much surprass me."

"Better known and better loved than the whole lot. Why, his poetry is known by heart through all England and America."

"Merciful Heaven! what you tell me! ees eet possible! An yet he is not known here efen by name. It would please me mooch, my Senator, to haire you make one quotatione. Know you Watt? Tell to me some words of his which I may remembaire."

"I have a shocking bad memory."

"Bad memora! O, but you remember somethin, zis mos beautiful charm nait—you haf a nobile soul—you mus be affecta by beauty—by ze ideal. Make for a me one quotatione."

And she rested her little hand on the Senator's arm, and looked up imploringly in his face.

The Senator looked foolish. He felt even more so. Here was a beautiful woman, by act and look showing a tender interest in him. Perplexing,—but very flattering, after all. So he replied,—

"You will not let me refuse you anything."

"Aha! you are vera willin' to refuse. It is difficulty for me to excitaire youar regards. You are fill with the grands ideas. But come,—will you spik for me some from your favorit Watt?"

"Well, if you wish it so much," said the Senator, kindly; and he hesitated.

"Ah,—I do wis it so much!"

"Ehem!"

"Begin," said the Countess. "Behold me. I listen. I hear every sin, and will remembaire it forava."

The only thing that the Senator could think of was a verse which had been running in his head for the last few days, its measured rhythm keeping time with every occupation:—

"'My willing soul would stay—'"

"Stop one moment," said the Countess. "I weesh to learn it from you;" and she looked fondly and tenderly up, but instantly dropped her eyes.

"'Ma willina sol wooda sta—'"

"'In such a frame as this,'" prompted the Senator.

"'Een socha framas zees.' Wait—'Ma willina sol wooda sta in socha framas zees.' Ah, appropriat! but could I hope zat you were true to zose lines, my Senator? Well?"

"'And sit and sing herself away,'" said the Senator, in a faltering voice, and breaking out into a cold perspiration for fear of committing himself by such uncommonly strong language.

"Ansit ansin hassaf awai," repeated the Countess, her face lighting up with a sweetly conscious expression.

The Senator paused.

"Well?"

"I—ehem! I forget."

"Forget? Impossible!"

"I do really."

"Ah now! Forget! I see by youar face—you desave. Say on."

The Countess again gently touched his arm with both of her little hands, and held it as though she would clasp it.

"Have you fear? Ah, cruel!"

The Senator turned pale, but, finding refusal impossible, boldly finished:—

"'To everlasting bliss'—there!"

"'To affarlastin blees thar.' Stop. I repeat it all: 'Ma willina sol wooda sta in socha framas zees, ansit ansin hassaf awai to affarlastin blees thar.' Am I right?"

"Yes," said the Senator, meekly.

"I knew you war a poetic sola," said the Countess, confidingly. "You are honesto—true—you cannot desave. When you spik I can beliv you. Ah, my Senator! an you can spik zis poetry!—at soch a taime! I nefare knew befoare zat you wos so impassione!—an you air so artaful! You breeng ze confersazione to beauty—to poatry—to ze poet Watt—so you may spik verses mos impassione! Ah! what do you mean? Santissima madra! how I wish you spik Italiano."

The Countess drew nearer to him, but her approach only deepened his perplexity.

"How that poor thing does love me!" sighed the Senator.

" Law bless it! she can't help it,—can't help it nohow. She is a goner; and what can I do? I 'll have to leave Florence."

The Countess was standing close beside him in a tender mood waiting for him to break the silence. How could he? He had been uttering words which sounded to her like love; and she—" a widow! a widow! a widow! wretched man that I am!"

There was a pause. The longer it lasted the more awkward the Senator felt. What upon earth was he to do or say? What business had he to go and quote poetry to widows? What an old fool he must be! But the Countess was very far from feeling awkward. Assuming an elegant attitude she looked up, her face expressing the tenderest solicitude.

" What ails my Senator? "

" Why, the fact is, marm—I feel sad—at leaving Florence. I must go shortly. My wife has written summoning me home. The children are down with the measles."

O base fabrication! O false Senator! There was n't a word of truth in that remark. You spoke so because you wished *La Cica* to know that you had a wife and family. Yet it was very badly done.

La Cica changed neither her attitude nor her expression. Evidently the existence of his wife and the melancholy situation of his unfortunate children awakened no sympathy.

" But, my Senator—did you not say you wooda seeng yousellef away to affarlastin blees? "

" O marm, it was a quotation,—only a quotation."

But at this critical juncture the conversation was broken up by the arrival of a number of ladies and gentlemen.

James de Mille.

HENRY V.'S WOOING.

SCENE.—*An Apartment in the French King's Palace.—King Henry, Katherine, and Alice her Gentlewoman.*

King Henry. Fair Katherine, and most fair!
Will you vouchsafe to teach a soldier terms,
Such as will enter a lady's ear,
And plead his love-suit to her gentle heart?

Kath. Your majesty shall mock at me; I cannot speak your England.

K. Hen. O fair Katherine, if you will love me soundly with your French heart, I will be glad to hear you confess it brokenly with your English tongue. Do you like me, Kate?

Kath. Pardonnez moy, I cannot tell vat is—like me.

K. Hen. An angel is like you, Kate; and you are like an angel.

Kath. Que dit-il? que je suis semblable à les anges?

Alice. Ouy, vrayment, sauf vostre Grace, ainsi dit-il.

K. Hen. I said so, dear Katherine, and I must not blush to affirm it.

Kath. O bon Dieu! les langues des hommes sont pleines de tromperies.

K. Hen. What says she, fair one? that the tongues of men are full of deceit?

Alice. Ouy; dat de tongues of de mans is be full of deceits; dat is de Princess.

K. Hen. The Princess is the better Englishwoman. I' faith, Kate, my wooing is fit for thy understanding: I am glad thou canst speak no better English; for if thou couldst, thou wouldst find me such a plain king that thou wouldst think I had sold my farm to buy my crown. I know no ways to mince it in love, but directly to say—I love you: then, if you urge me further than to say—Do you in faith? I wear out my suit. Give me your answer; I' faith, do, and so clap hands and a bargain. How say you, lady?

Kath. Sauf vostre Honneur, me understand well.

K. Hen. Marry, if you would put me to verses, or to dance for your sake, Kate, why you undid me: for the one, I have neither words nor measure; and for the other, I have no strength in measure, yet a reasonable measure in strength. If I could win a lady at leap-frog, or by vaulting into my saddle with my armor on my back, under the correction of bragging be it spoken, I should quickly leap into a wife; or, if I might buffet for my love, or bound my horse for her favors, I could lay on like a butcher, and sit like a jack-an-apes, never off: but, before God, Kate, I cannot look green-ly, nor gasp out my eloquence, nor I have no cunning in protestation; only down-right oaths, which I never use till urged, nor never break for urging. If thou canst love a fel-low of this temper, Kate, whose face is not worth sun-burning, that never looks in his glass for love of anything he sees there, let thine eye be thy cook. I speak to thee plain soldier; if thou canst love me for this, take me; if not, to say to thee that I shall die, is true; but for thy love, by the Lord, no; yet I love thee, too. And, while thou liv'st, dear Kate, take a fellow of plain and uncoined constancy, for he perforce must do thee right, because he hath not the gift to woo in other places; for these fellows of infinite tongue, that can rhyme themselves into ladies' favors, they do always reason themselves out again. What! a speaker is but a prater; a rhyme is but a ballad. A good leg will fall, a straight back will stoop, a black beard will turn white, a curled pate will grow bald, a fair face will wither, a full eye will wax hollow; but a good heart, Kate, is the sun and the moon; or, rather, the sun, and not the moon, for it shines bright, and never changes, but keeps his course truly. If thou would have such a one, take me: and take me, take a soldier; take a soldier, take a king; and what say'st thou then to my love? speak, my fair, and fairly, I pray thee.

Kath. Is it possible dat I should love de enemy of France?

K. Hen. No; it is not possible you should love the enemy of France, Kate; but in loving me, you should love the friend of France, for I love France so well that I will not part with a village of it; I will have it all mine; and, Kate, when France is mine and I am yours, then yours is France and you are mine.

Kath. I cannot tell vat is dat.

K. Hen. No, Kate? I will tell thee in French, which I am sure will hang upon my tongue like a new-married wife about her husband's neck, hardly to be shook off. *Quand j'ay la possession de France, et quand vous avez le possession de moy* (let me see, what then? Saint Denis be my speed!)— *donc vostre est France et vous estes mienne.* It is as easy for me, Kate, to conquer the Kingdom, as to speak so much more French. I shall never move thee in French, unless it be to laugh at me.

Kath. Sauf vostre Honneur, le François que vous parlez est meilleur que l' Anglois lequel je parle.

K. Hen. No, faith, is 't not, Kate; but thy speaking of my tongue, and I thine, most truly falsely, must needs be granted to be much at one. But, Kate, dost thou understand thus much English? Canst thou love me?

Kath. I cannot tell.

K. Hen. Can any of your neighbors tell, Kate? I 'll ask them. Come, I know thou lovest me, and at night, when you come into your closet, you'll question this gentlewoman about me; and I know, Kate, you will to her, dispraise those parts in me that you love with your heart; but, good Kate, mock me mercifully, the rather, gentle Princess, because I love thee cruelly. If ever thou be'st mine, Kate (as I have a saving faith within me tells thou shalt), I get thee with scambling. But what say'st thou, my fair flower-de-luce?

Kath. I do not know dat.

K. Hen. No; 'tis hereafter to know, but now to promise. How answer you, *la plus belle Katherine du monde, mon très chère et divin déese?*

Kath. Your *Majesté* have *fausse* French enough to deceive de most *sage damoiselle* dat is *en France.*

K. Hen. Now, fie upon my false French! By mine honor, in true English, I love thee, Kate: by which honor I dare not swear thou lovest me; yet my blood begins to flatter me thou dost, notwithstanding the poor and untempering effect of my visage. I was created with a stubborn outside, with an aspect of iron, that, when I come to woo ladies, I fright them. But, in faith, Kate, the elder I wax, the better I shall appear: my comfort is, that old age, that ill layer-up of beauty, can do no more spoil upon my face; thou hast me, if thou hast me, at the worst; and thou shalt wear me, if thou wear me, better and better. And therefore tell me, most fair Katherine, will you have me? Put off your maiden blushes; avouch the thoughts of your heart with the looks of an empress; take me by the hand and say—Harry of England, I am thine: which word thou shalt no sooner bless my ear withal, but I will tell thee aloud—England is thine, Ireland is thine, France is thine, and Henry Plantagenet is thine. Who, though I speak it before his face, if he be not fellow with the best King, thou shalt find the best king of good fellows. Come, your answer in broken music, for thy voice is music, and thy English broken; therefore, Queen of all Katherines, break thy mind to me in broken English: wilt thou have me?

Kath. Dat is as it shall please de *Roy mon père.*

K. Hen. Nay it will please him well, Kate: it shall please him, Kate.

Kath. Den it shall also content me.

K. Hen. Upon that I kiss your hand, and I call you— my queen.

William Shakespeare.

WIDOW MALONE.

Did you hear of the Widow Malone,
                    Ohone!
Who lived in the town of Athlone,
                    Alone!
        O, she melted the hearts
        Of the swains in them parts:
So lovely the Widow Malone,
                    Ohone!
So lovely the Widow Malone.

Of lovers she had a full score,
                    Or more,
And fortunes they all had galore,
                    In store;
        From the minister down
        To the clerk of the Crown,
All were courting the Widow Malone,
                    Ohone!
All were courting the Widow Malone.

But so modest was Mistress Malone
                    'T was known!
That no one could see her alone,
                    Ohone!
        Let them ogle and sigh,
        They could ne'er catch her eye,
So bashful the Widow Malone,
                    Ohone!
So bashful the Widow Malone.

Till one Misther O'Brien, from Clare,
                    (How quare!
It 's little for blushing they care
                    Down there.)
        Put his arm round her waist,—
        Gave ten kisses at laste,—
"O," says he, "you 're my Molly Malone,
                    My own!"
"O," says he, "you 're my Molly Malone".

And the widow they all thought so shy,
　　　　My eye!
Ne'er thought of a simper or sigh,—
　　　　For why?
　　But, "Lucius," says she,
　　"Since you 've now made so free,
You may marry your Mary Malone,
　　　　Ohone!
You may marry your Mary Malone."

There 's a moral contained in my song,
　　　　Not wrong;
And one comfort, it 's not very long,
　　　　But strong.
　　If for widows you die,
　　Learn to kiss, not to sigh;
For they 're all like sweet Mistress Malone,
　　　　Ohone!
O they 're all like sweet Mistress Malone.
　　　　　　　　　　Charles Lever.

THE BALLAD OF THE OYSTERMAN.

It was a tall young oysterman lived by the river-side,
His shop was just upon the bank, his boat was on the tide;
The daughter of a fisherman, that was so straight and slim,
Lived over on the other bank, right opposite to him.

It was the pensive oysterman that saw a lovely maid,
Upon a moonlight evening, a-sitting in the shade;
He saw her wave her handkerchief, as much as if to say,
"I 'm wide awake, young oysterman, and all the folks away."

Then up arose the oysterman and to himself said he:
"I guess I 'll leave the skiff at home, for fear that folks
　　should see;
I read it in the story-book, that, for to kiss his dear,
Leander swam the Hellespont,—and I will swim this here."

And he has leaped into the waves, and crossed the shining
  stream,
And he has clambered up the bank, all in the moonlight
  gleam;
O there were kisses sweet as dew, and words as soft as rain,—
But they have heard her father's step, and in he leaps again!

Out spoke the ancient fisherman,—"O what was that, my
  daughter?"
" 'Twas nothing but a pebble, sir, I threw into the water."
"And what is that, pray tell me, love, that paddles off so
  fast?"
"It's nothing but a porpoise, sir, that's been a-swimming
  past."

Out spoke the ancient fisherman,—"Now bring me my har-
  poon!
I'll get into my fishing-boat, and fix the fellow soon."
Down fell that pretty innocent, as falls a snow-white lamb,
Her hair drooped round her pallid cheeks, like sea-weed on
  a clam.

Alas for those two loving ones! she waked not from her
  swound,
And he was taken with the cramp, and in the waves was
  drowned;
But Fate has metamorphosed them, in pity of their woe,
And now they keep an oyster-shop for mermaids down
  below.   *Oliver Wendell Holmes.*

THE LOW-BACKED CAR.

When first I saw sweet Peggy,
  'Twas on a market day:
A low-backed car she drove, and sat
  Upon a truss of hay;
But when that hay was blooming grass,
  And decked with flowers of spring,
No flower was there that could compare
  With the blooming girl I sing.

As she sat in the low-backed car,
The man at the turnpike bar
      Never asked for the toll,
      But just rubbed his owld poll,
And looked after the low-backed car.

In battle's wild commotion,
      The proud and mighty Mars
With hostile scythes demands his tithes
      Of death in warlike cars;
While Peggy, peaceful goddess,
      Has darts in her bright eye,
That knock men down in the market town,
      As right and left they fly;
While she sits in her low-backed car,
Than battle more dangerous far,—
      For the doctor's art
      Cannot cure the heart,
That is hit from that low-backed car.

Sweet Peggy round her car, sir,
      Has strings of ducks and geese,
But the scores of hearts she slaughters
      By far outnumber these;
While she among her poultry sits,
      Just like a turtle-dove,
Well worth the cage, I do engage,
      Of the blooming god of Love!
While she sits in her low-backed car,
The lovers come near and far,
      And envy the chicken
      That Peggy is pickin',
As she sits in her low-backed car.

O, I 'd rather own that car, sir,
      With Peggy by my side,
Than a coach and four, and gold *galore*,
      And a lady for my bride;
For the lady would sit forninst me,
      On a cushion made with taste,
While Peggy would sit beside me,
      With my arm around her waist,

While we drove in the low-backed car,
To be married by Father Mahar;
   O, my heart would beat high
   At her glance and her sigh,—
Though it beat in a low-backed car!
                  Samuel Lover.

THE BIRTH OF SAINT PATRICK.

On the eighth day of March it was, some people say,
Saint Patrick at midnight he first saw the day;
While others declare 'twas the ninth he was born,
And 'twas all a mistake between midnight and morn;
For mistakes will occur in a hurry and shock,
And some blamed the baby—and some blamed the clock—
Till with all their cross-questions sure no one could know
If the child was too fast, or the clock was too slow.

Now the first faction-fight in owld Ireland, they say,
Was all on account of Saint Patrick's birthday.
Some fought for the eighth,—for the ninth more would die,
And who would n't see right, sure they blackened his eye!
At last, both the factions so positive grew,
That each kept a birthday, so Pat then had two,
Till Father Mulcahy, who showed them their sins,
Said, " No one could have two birthdays, but a twins."

Says he, " Boys, do n't be fightin' for eight or for nine,
Do n't be always dividin'—but sometimes combine;
Combine eight with nine, and seventeen is the mark,
So let that be his birthday,"—" Amen," says the clerk.
" If he was n't a twins, sure our history will show
That, at least, he 's worth any two saints that we know!"
Then they all got blind dhrunk.—which complated their bliss,
And we keep up the practice from that day to this.
                  Samuel Lover.

THE COURTIN'.

God makes sech nights, all white an' still
  Fur 'z you can look or listen,
Moonshine an' snow on field an' hill,
  All silence an' all glisten.

Zekle crep' up quite unbeknown
  An' peeked in thru' the winder,
An' there sot Huldy all alone,
  'Ith no one nigh to hender.

A fireplace filled the room's one side
  With half a cord o' wood in—
There warn't no stoves (tell comfort died)
  To bake ye to a puddin'.

The wa'nut logs shot sparkles out
  Towards the pootiest, bless her,
An' leetle flames danced all about
  The chiny on the dresser.

Agin the chimbley crook-necks hung,
  An' in amongst 'em rusted
The ole queen's arm that gran'ther Young
  Fetched back from Concord busted.

The very room, coz she was in,
  Seemed warm from floor to ceilin',
An' she looked full ez rosy agin
  Ez the apples she was peelin'.

'Twas kin' o' kingdom-come to look
  On sech a blesséd creetur,
A dogrose blushin' to a brook
  Ain't modester nor sweeter.

He was six foot o' man, A 1,
  Clean grit an' human natur';
None could n't quicker pitch a ton
  Nor dror a furrer straighter.

He'd sparked it with full twenty gals,
  Had squired 'em, danced 'em, druv 'em,
Fust this one, an' then thet, by spells—
  All is, he could n't love 'em.

But long o' her his veins 'ould run
  All crinkly like curled maple,
The side she breshed felt full o' sun,
  Ez a south slope in Ap'il.

She thought no v'ice hed 'sech a swing
  Ez hisn in the choir;
My! when he made Ole Hundred ring,
  She *knowed* the Lord was nigher.

An she'd blush scarlit, right in prayer,
  When her new meetin'-bunnet
Felt somehow thru' its crown a pair
  O' blue eyes sot upon it.

Thet night, I tell ye, she looked *some!*
  She seemed to 've gut a new soul,
For she felt sartin-sure he'd come,
  Down to her very shoe-sole.

She heered a foot, an' knowed it tu,
  A-raspin' on the scraper,—
All ways to once her feelin's flew
  Like sparks in burnt-up paper.

He kin' o' l'itered on the mat,
  Some doubtfle o' the sekle,
His heart kep' goin' pity-pat,
  But hern went pity Zekle.

An' yit she gin her cheer a jerk
  Ez though she wished him furder,
An' on her apples kep' to work,
  Parin' away like murder.

"You want to see my Pa, I s'pose?"
  "Wal . . . no . . . I come designin'"—
"To see my Ma?   She's sprinklin' clo'es
  Agin to-morrer's i'nin'."

To say why gals acts so or so,
  Or do n't 'ould be presumin';
Mebby to mean *yes* an' say *no*
  Comes nateral to women.

He stood a spell on one foot fust,
  Then stood a spell on t'other,
An' on which one he felt the wust
  He could n't ha' told ye nuther.

Says he, " I 'd better call agin;"
  Says she, " Think likely, Mister;"
Thet last word pricked him like a pin,
  An' . . . Wal, he up an' kist her.

When Ma bimeby upon 'em slips,
  Huldy sot pale ez ashes,
All kin' o' smily 'roun the lips
  An' teary 'roun the lashes.

For she was jes' the quiet kind
  Whose naturs never vary,
Like streams that keep a summer mind
  Snowhid in Jenooary.

The blood clost roun' her heart felt glued
  Too tight for all expressin',
Tell mother see how metters stood,
  An gin 'em both her blessin'.

Then her red come back like the tide
  Down to the Bay o' Fundy,
An' all I know is they was cried
  In meetin' come nex' Sunday.
James Russell Lowell.

KITTY OF COLERAINE.

As beautiful Kitty one morning was tripping
　　With a pitcher of milk, from the fair of Coleraine,
When she saw me she stumbled, the pitcher it tumbled,
　　And all the sweet buttermilk watered the plain.

" O, what shall I do now?—'twas looking at you now!
　　Sure, sure, such a pitcher I 'll ne'er meet again!
'Twas the pride of my dairy: O Barney M'Cleary!
　　You 're sent as a plague to the girls of Coleraine."

I sat down beside her, and gently did chide her,
　　That such a misfortune should give her such pain.
A kiss then I gave her; and ere I did leave her,
　　She vowed for such pleasure she 'd break it again.

'Twas hay-making season—I can't tell the reason—
　　Misfortunes will never come single, 'tis plain;
For very soon after poor Kitty's disaster
　　The devil a pitcher was whole in Coleraine.
　　　　　　　　　　　　　Charles Dawson Shanly.

OUR GUIDE IN GENOA AND ROME.

European guides know about enough English to tangle
everything up so that a man can make neither head nor tail
of it. They know their story by heart,—the history of every
statue, painting, cathedral, or other wonder they show you.
They know it and tell it as a parrot would,—and if you interrupt, and throw them off the track, they have to go back
and begin over again. All their lives long, they are employed
in showing strange things to foreigners and listening to their
bursts of admiration.

It is human nature to take delight in exciting admiration.
It is what prompts children to say "smart" things, and do
absurd ones, and in other ways "show off" when company
is present. It is what makes gossips turn out in rain and
storm to go and be the first to tell a startling bit of news.

Think, then, what a passion it becomes with a guide, whose privilege it is, every day, to show to strangers wonders that throw them into perfect ecstasies of admiration! He gets so that he could not by any possibility live in a soberer atmosphere.

After we discovered this, we *never* went into ecstasies any more,—we never admired anything,—we never showed any but impassible faces and stupid indifference in the presence of the sublimest wonders a guide had to display. We had found their weak point. We have made good use of it ever since. We have made some of these people savage, at times, but we have never lost our serenity.

The doctor asks the questions generally, because he can keep his countenance, and look more like an inspired idiot, and throw more imbecility into the tone of his voice than any man that lives. It comes natural to him.

The guides in Genoa are delighted to secure an American party, because Americans so much wonder, and deal so much in sentiment and emotion before any relic of Columbus. Our guide there fidgeted about as if he had swallowed a spring mattress. He was full of animation,—full of impatience. He said:

"Come wis me, genteelmen!—come! I show you ze letter writing by Christopher Colombo!—write it himself!—write it wis his own hand!—come!"

He took us to the municipal palace. After much impressive fumbling of keys and opening of locks, the stained and aged document was spread before us. The guide's eyes sparkled. He danced about us and tapped the parchment with his finger:—

"What I tell you, genteelmen! Is it not so? See! handwriting Christopher Colombo!—write it himself!"

We looked indifferent,—unconcerned. The doctor examined the document very deliberately, during a painful pause. Then he said, without any show of interest,—

"Ah,—Ferguson,—what—what did you say was the name of the party who wrote this?"

"Christopher Colombo! ze great Christopher Colombo!"

Another deliberate examination.

"Ah,—did he write it himself, or, or—how?"

"He write it himself!—Christopher Colombo! he's own handwriting, write by himself!"

Then the doctor laid the document down and said,—

"Why, I have seen boys in America only fourteen years old that could write better than that."

"But zis is ze great Christo—"

"I do n't care who it is! It's the worst writing I ever saw. Now you must n't think you can impose on us because we are strangers. We are not fools, by a good deal. If you have got any specimens of penmanship of real merit, trot them out!—and if you have n't, drive on!"

We drove on. The guide was considerably shaken up, but he made one more venture. He had something which he thought would overcome us. He said,—

"Ah, genteelmen, you come wis me! I show you beautiful, O, magnificent bust Christopher Colombo!—splendid, grand, magnificent!"

He brought us before the beautiful bust,—for it *was* beautiful,—and sprang back and struck an attitude:—

"Ah, look, genteelmen!—beautiful, grand,—bust Christopher Colombo!—beautiful bust, beautiful pedestal!"

The doctor put up his eye-glass,—procured for such occasions:—

"Ah,—what did you say this gentleman's name was?"

"Christopher Colombo! ze great Christopher Colombo!"

"Christopher Colombo,—the great Christopher Colombo. Well, what did *he* do?"

"Discover America!—discover America, O, ze devil!"

"Discover America. No,—that statement will hardly wash. We are just from America ourselves. We heard nothing about it. Christopher Colombo,—pleasant name,—is—is he dead?"

"O, corpo di Baccho!—three hundred year!"

"What did he die of?"

"I do not know. I cannot tell."

"Small-pox, think?"

"I do not know, genteelmen,—I do not know *what* he die of."

"Measles, likely?"

"Maybe,—maybe. I do *not* know,—I think he die of somethings."

"Parents living?"

"Im-posseeble!"

"Ah,—which is the bust and which is the pedestal?"

"Santa Maria!—*zis* ze bust!—*zis* ze pedestal!"

"Ah, I see, I see—happy combination,—very happy combination indeed. Is—is this the first time this gentleman was ever on a bust?"

That joke was lost on the foreigner,—guides cannot master the subtleties of the American joke.

We have made it interesting for this Roman guide. Yesterday we spent three or four hours in the Vatican again, that wonderful world of curiosities. We came very near expressing interest sometimes, even admiration. It was hard to keep from it. We succeeded, though. Nobody else ever did, in the Vatican museums. The guide was bewildered, nonplussed. He walked his legs off, nearly, hunting up extraordinary things, and exhausted all his ingenuity on us, but it was a failure; we never showed any interest in anything. He had reserved what he considered to be his greatest wonder till the last,—a royal Egyptian mummy, the best preserved in the world, perhaps. He took us there. He felt so sure, this time, that some of his old enthusiasm came back to him:

"See, genteelmen!—Mummy! Mummy!"

The eye-glass came up as calmly, as deliberately as ever.

"Ah,—Ferguson,—what did I understand you to say the gentleman's name was?"

"Name?—he got no name! Mummy!—'Gyptian mummy!"

"Yes, yes. Born here?"

"No. *'Gyptian* mummy."

"Ah, just so. Frenchman, I presume?"

"No!—*not* Frenchman, not Roman!—born in Egypta!"

"Born in Egypta. Never heard of Egypta before. Foreign locality, likely. Mummy,—mummy. How calm he is, how self-possessed! Is—ah!—is he dead?"

"O, *sacre bleu!* been dead three thousan' year!"

The doctor turned on him savagely:—

"Here, now, what do you mean by such conduct as this? Playing us for Chinamen because we are strangers and trying to learn! Trying to impose your vile second-hand carcasses on *us!* Thunder and lightning! I've a notion to—to— If you've got a nice *fresh* corpse, fetch him out!—or, by George, we'll brain you!"

We make it exceedingly interesting for this Frenchman. However, he has paid us back, partly, without knowing it. He came to the hotel this morning to ask if we were up, and he endeavored, as well as he could, to describe us, so that the landlord would know which persons he meant. He finished with the casual remark that we were lunatics. The observation was so innocent and so honest that it amounted to a very good thing for a guide to say.

Our Roman Ferguson is the most patient, unsuspecting, long-suffering subject we have had yet. We shall be sorry to part with him. We have enjoyed his society very much. We trust he has enjoyed ours, but we are harassed with doubts.

Samuel L. Clemens.

THE SUBSCRIPTION LIST.

On the Sunday in question, Father Phil intended delivering an address to his flock from the altar, urging them to the necessity of bestirring themselves in the repairs of the chapel, which was in a very dilapidated condition, and at one end let in the rain through its worn-out thatch. A subscription was necessary: and to raise this among a very impoverished people was no easy matter. The weather happened to be unfavorable, which was most favorable to Father Phil's purpose, for the rain dropped its arguments through the roof upon the kneeling people below, in the most convincing manner; and as they endeavored to get out of the wet, they pressed round the altar as much as they could, for which they were reproved very smartly by his Reverence in the very midst of the mass. These interruptions occurred sometimes in the most serious places, producing a ludicrous effect, of which the worthy Father was quite unconscious, in his great anxiety to make the people repair the chapel.

A big woman was elbowing her way towards the rails of the altar, and Father Phil, casting a sidelong glance at her, sent her to the right-about, while he interrupted his appeal to Heaven to address her thus:—

"*Agnus Dei*— You'd bether jump over the rails of the althar, I think. Go along out o' that; there's plenty o' room in the chapel below there—"

Then he would turn to the altar, and proceed with the service, till, turning again to the congregation, he perceived some fresh offender.

"*Orate fratres!*— Will you mind what I say to you, and

go along out of that, there's room below there. Thrue for you, Mrs. Finn,—it's a shame for him to be thramplin' on you. Go along, Darby Casy, down there, and kneel in the rain,—it's a pity you have n't a decent woman's cloak under you, indeed!—*Orate fratres!*"

Then would the service proceed again, till the shuffling of feet edging out of the rain would disturb him, and, casting a backward glance, he would say,—

"I hear you there,—can't you be quiet, and not be disturbin' my mass, you haythens?"

Again he proceeded, till the crying of a child interrupted him. He looked round quickly—

"You'd betther kill the child, I think, thramplin' on him, Lavery. Go out o' that,—your conduct is scandalous.— *Dominus vobiscum!*"

Again he turned to pray, and after some time he made an interval in the service to address his congregation on the subject of the repairs, and produced a paper containing the names of subscribers to that pious work who had already contributed, by way of example to those who had not.

"Here it is," said Father Phil,—"here it is, and no denying it,—down in black and white; but if they who give are down in black, how much blacker are those who have not given at all! But I hope they will be ashamed of themselves when I howld up those to honor who have contributed to the uphowlding of the house of God. And is n't it ashamed o' yourselves you ought to be, to lave His house in such a condition? and does n't it rain a'most every Sunday, as if He wished to remind you of your duty?—are n't you wet to the skin a'most every Sunday? O, God is good to you! to put you in mind of your duty, giving you such bitther cowlds that you are coughing and sneezin' every Sunday to that degree that you can't hear the blessed mass for a comfort and a benefit to you; and so you'll go on sneezin' until you put a good thatch on the place, and prevent the appearance of the evidence from Heaven against you every Sunday, which is condemning you before your faces, and behind your backs, too; for don't I see this minit a strame o' wather that might turn a mill running down Micky Mackavoy's back, between the collar of his coat and his shirt?"

Here a laugh ensued at the expense of Micky Mackavoy,

who certainly *was* under a very heavy drip from the imperfect roof.

"And is it laughing you are, you haythens?" said Father Phil, reproving the merriment which he himself had purposely created, *that he might reprove it.* "Laughing is it you are, at your backslidings and insensibility to the honor of God, —laughing because when you come here to be saved, you are lost entirely with the wet, and how, I ask you, are my words of comfort to enter your hearts when the rain is pouring down your backs at the same time? Sure I have no chance of turning your hearts while you are under rain that might turn a mill,—but once put a good roof on the house, and I will inundate you with piety! Maybe it's Father Dominick you would like to have coming among you, who would grind your hearts to powdher with his heavy words." (Here a low murmur of dissent ran through the throng.) "Ha! ha! so you would n't like it, I see,—very well, very well,—take care then, for I find you insensible to my moderate reproofs, you hard-hearted haythens, you malefacthors and cruel persecuthors, that won't put your hands in your pockets because your mild and quiet poor fool of a pasthor has no tongue in his head! I say your mild, quiet, poor fool of a pasthor (for I know my own faults partly, God forgive me!) and I can't spake to you as you deserve, you hard-living vagabonds, that are as insensible to your duties as you are to the weather. I wish it was sugar or salt that you are made of, and then the rain might melt you if I could n't; but no, them naked rafthers grins in your face to no purpose,—you chate the house of God,—but take care, maybe you won't chate the Divil so aisy." (Here there was a sensation.) "Ha! ha! that makes you open your ears, does it? More shame for you; you ought to despise that dirty enemy of man, and depend on something better,—but I see I must call you to a sense of your situation with the bottomless pit undher you, and no roof over you. O dear! dear! dear! I'm ashamed of you,—throth, if I had time and sthraw enough, I'd rather thatch the place myself than lose my time talking to you; sure the place is more like a stable than a chapel. O, think of that!—the house of God to be like a stable!—for though our Redeemer was born in a stable, that is no reason why you are to keep His house always like one.

"And now I will read you the list of subscribers, and it

will make you ashamed when you hear the names of several good and worthy Protestants in the parish, and out of it, too, who have given more than the Catholics."

SUBSCRIPTION LIST

For the Repairs and Enlargement of Ballyslough-Gutthery Chapel.

PHILIP BLAKE, P. P.

Micky Hickey, £0 7s. 6d. "He might as well have made it ten shillings; but half a loaf is betther than no bread."

"Plaze your Reverence," says Mick, from the body of the chapel, "sure seven and sixpence is more than half of ten shillings." (A laugh.)

"O, how witty you are! Faith, if you knew your prayers as well as your arithmetic, it would be betther for you, Micky."

Here the Father turned the laugh against Mick.

Billy Riley, £0 3s. 4d. "Of course he means to subscribe again?"

John Dwyer, £0 15s. "That's something like! I'll be bound he's only keeping back the odd five shillings for a brush full o' paint for the althar; it's as black as a crow, instead o' being as a dove."

He then hurried over rapidly some small subscribers as follows:

Peter Hefferman, £0 1s. 8d.

James Murphy, £0 2s. 6d.

Mat Donovan, £0 1s. 3d.

Luke Dannelly, £0 3s. 0d.

Jack Quigly, £0 2s. 1d.

Pat Finnegan, £0 2s. 2d.

EDWARD O'CONNOR, Esq., £2 0s. 0d. "There's for you! Edward O'Connor, Esq.,—*a Protestant in the parish*,—two pounds."

"Long life to him!" cried a voice in the chapel.

"Amen!" said Father Phil; "I'm not ashamed to be clerk to so good a prayer."

Nicholas Fagan, £0 2s. 6d.

Young Nicholas Fagan, £0 5s. 0d. "Young Nick is betther than owld Nick, you see."

Tim Doyle, £0 7s. 4d.

Owny Doyle, £1 0s. 0d. "Well done, Owny na Coppal,—

you deserve to prosper, for you make good use of your thrivings."

Simon Leary, £0 2s. 6d.; Bridget Murphy, £0 10s. 0d. "You ought to be ashamed o' yourself, Simon; a lone widow-woman gives more than you."

Simon answered, "I have a large family, sir, and she has no childhre."

"That's not her fault," said the priest,—"and maybe she'll mend o' that yet." This excited much merriment, for the widow was buxom, and had recently buried an old husband, and, by all accounts, was cocking her cap at a handsome young fellow in the parish.

Judy Moylan, £0 5s. 0d. "Very good, Judy; the women are behaving like gentlemen; they'll have their reward in the next world."

Pat Finnerty, £0 8s. 4d. "I'm not sure if it is 8s. 4d. or 3s. 4d., for the figure is blotted, but I believe it is 8s. 4d."

"It was three and fourpence I gave your Reverence," said Pat, from the crowd.

"Well, Pat, as I said eight and fourpence, you must not let me go back o' my word, so bring me five shillings next week."

"Sure, you wouldn't have me pay for a blot, sir?"

"Yis, I would,—that's the rule of backgammon, you know, Pat. When I hit the mark, you pay for it."

Here his Reverence turned round, as if looking for some one, and called out, "Rafferty! Rafferty! Rafferty! Where are you, Rafferty?"

An old, gray-headed man appeared, bearing a large plate, and Father Phil continued,—

"There, now, be active—I'm sending him among you, good people, and such as cannot give as much as you would like to be read before your neighbors, give what little you can towards the repairs, and I will continue to read out the names by way of encouragement to you, and the next name I see is that of Squire Egan. Long life to him!"

SQUIRE EGAN, £5 0s. 0d. "Squire Egan—five pounds—listen to that—*a Protestant in the Parish!*—five pounds! Faith, the Protestants will make you ashamed of yourselves if you don't take care."

Mrs. Flanagan, £2 0s. 0d. "Not her own parish, either,—a kind lady."

James Milligan, of Roundtown, £1 0s. 0d. "And here I

must remark that the people of Roundtown has not been backward in coming forward on this occasion. I have a long list from Roundtown,— I will read it separate." He then proceeded at a great pace, jumbling the town and the pounds and the people in the most extraordinary manner: "James Milligan, of Roundtown, one pound ; Darby Daly, of Roundtown, one pound ; Sam Finnigan, of Roundtown, one pound ; James Casey, of Roundpound, one town? Kit Dwyer, of Townpound, one round — pound, I mane ; Pat Roundpound — Pounden, I mane — Pat Pounden a pound of Poundtown also — there's an example for you!—

"But what are you about, Rafferty? I do n't like the sound of that plate of yours,— you are not a good gleaner,— go up first into the gallery there, where I see so many good-looking bonnets,— I suppose they will give something to keep their bonnets out of the rain, for the wet will be into the gallery next Sunday if they do n't. I think that is Kitty Crow I see, getting her bit of silver ready ; them ribbons of yours cost a thrifle, Kitty — Well, good Christians, here is more of the subscription for you.

Matthew Lavery, £0 2s. 6d. "*He* does n't belong to Roundtown,— Roundtown will be renowned in the future ages for the support of the church. Mark my words! Roundtown will prosper from this day out,— Roundtown will be a rising place."

Mark Hennessy, £0 2s. 6d.; Luke Clancy, £0 2s. 6d.; John Doolin, £0 2s. 6d. "One would think they all agreed only to give two and sixpence apiece. And they comfortable men, too! And look at their names,— Matthew, Mark, Luke and John,— the names of the blessed Evangelists, and only ten shillings among them! O, they are apostles not worthy the name,— we 'll call them the poor apostles from this out!" (Here a low laugh ran through the chapel.) "Do you hear that, Matthew, Mark, Luke, and John? Faith! I can tell you that name will stick to you." (Here the laugh was louder.)

A voice, when the laugh subsided, exclaimed, "I 'll make it ten shillin's, your Reverence."

"Who 's that?" said Father Phil.

"Hennessy, your Reverence."

"Very well, Mark. I suppose Matthew, Luke, and John will follow your example?"

"We will, your Reverence."

"Ha! I thought you made a mistake; we'll call you now the faithful apostles,—and I think the change in the name is better than seven and sixpence apiece to you.

"I see you in the gallery there, Rafferty. What do you pass that well-dressed woman for? thry back—Ha! see that, she had her money ready if you only asked her for it,—don't go by that other woman there—O ho! So you won't give anything, ma'am? You ought to be ashamed of yourself. There is a woman with an elegant sthraw bonnet, and she won't give a farthing. Well now,—after that remember,—I give it from the althar, that from this day out sthraw bonnets pay fi'penny pieces."

Thomas Durfy, Esq., £1 0s. 0d. "It's not his parish, and he's a brave gentleman."

Miss Fanny Dawson, £1 0s. 0d. "*A Protestant, out of the parish*, and a sweet young lady, God bless her! O faith, the Protestants is shaming you!"

Dennis Fannin, £0 7s. 6d. "Very good indeed, for a working mason."

Jemmy Riley, £0 5s. 0d. "Not bad for a hedge carpenther."

"I gave you ten, plaze your Reverence," shouted Jemmy; "and by the same token, you may remember it was on the Nativity of the blessed Vargin, sir, I gave you the second five shillin's."

"So you did, Jemmy," cried Father Phil, "I put a little cross before it, to remind me of it; but I was in a hurry to make a sick call when you gave it to me, and forgot it afther: and indeed myself doesn't know what I did with that same five shillings."

Here a pallid woman, who was kneeling near the rails of the altar, uttered an impassioned blessing, and exclaimed, "O, that was the very five shillings, I'm sure, you gave to me that very day, to buy some little comforts for my poor husband, who was dying in the fever!" and the poor woman burst into loud sobs as she spoke.

A deep thrill of emotion ran through the flock as this accidental proof of their poor pastor's beneficence burst upon them; and as an affectionate murmur began to arise above the silence which that emotion produced, the burly Father Philip blushed like a girl at this publication of his charity, and even at the foot of that altar where he stood, felt something like shame in being discovered in the commission of that virtue so highly commended by the Providence to whose worship that altar was raised. He uttered a hasty " Whisht, whisht! " and waved with his outstretched hands his flock into silence.

In an instant one of those sudden changes so common to an Irish assembly, and scarcely credible to a stranger, took place. The multitude was hushed, the grotesque of the subscription list had passed away and was forgotten, and that same man and that same multitude stood in altered relations, —*they* were again a reverent flock, and *he* once more a solemn pastor; the natural play of his nation's mirthful sarcasm was absorbed in a moment in the sacredness of his office; and with a solemnity befitting the highest occasion, he placed his hands together before his breast, and, raising his eyes to heaven, he poured forth his sweet voice, with a tone of the deepest devotion, in that reverential call for prayer, " *Orate, fratres!* "

The sound of a multitude gently kneeling down followed, like the soft breaking of a quiet sea on a sandy beach; and when Father Philip turned to the altar to pray, his pent-up feelings found vent in tears, and while he prayed he wept.

I believe such scenes as this are not of unfrequent occurrence in Ireland,—that country so long suffering, so much maligned, and so little understood.

Samuel Lover.

A FRENCHMAN ON MACBETH.

An enthusiastic French student of Shakespeare thus comments on the tragedy of Macbeth:—

" Ah! your Mossieu' Shak-es-pier! He is gr-r-aä-nd — mysterieuse — soo-blime! You 'ave reads ze Macabess? — ze scene of ze Mossieu' Macabess vis ze Vitch — eh? Superb sooblimitée! W'en he say to ze Vitch, ' Ar-r-roynt ze, Vitch! ' she go away: but what she *say* when she go away? She say she will do s'omesing dat aves got no naäme! ' Ah, ha!' she say, ' I go, like ze r-r-aä-t vizout ze tail *but* I'll do! I'll *do!* I'll DO!' *W'at* she do? Ah, ha! — voila le graand mystérieuse Mossieu' Shak-es-pier! She not *say* what she do!"

This *was* "grand," to be sure; but the prowess of Mac-

beth, in his "bout" with Macduff, awakens all the mercurial
Frenchman's martial ardor:—

"Mossieu' Macabess, he see him come, clos' by; he say
(proud *empressement*), 'Come o-o-n, Mossieu' Macduffs, and
d — d be he who first say *Enoffs!*,' Zen zey fi-i-ght — moche.
Ah, ha! — voila! Mossieu' Macabess, vis his br-r-ight
r-r-apier 'pink' him, vat you call, in his body. He 'ave gots
mal d'estomac: he say, vis grand simplicité, '*Enoffs!*' What
for he say ' Enoffs?' 'Cause he *got* enoffs — plaänty; and he
*ex*pire, r-r-ight away, 'mediately, pretty quick! Ah, mes amis,
Mossieu' Shak-es-pier is rising man in La Belle France!"

Anonymous.

THE WHITE SQUALL.

On deck, beneath the awning,
I dozing lay and yawning;
It was the gray of dawning,
   Ere yet the sun arose;
And above the funnel's roaring,
And the fitful wind's deploring,
I heard the cabin snoring
   With universal nose.
I could hear the passengers snorting,—
I envied their disporting,—
Vainly I was courting
   The pleasure of a doze.

So I lay, and wondered why light
Came not, and watched the twilight,
And the glimmer of the skylight
   That shot across the deck;
And the binnacle, pale and steady,
And the dull glimpse of the dead-eye,
And the sparks in fiery eddy
   That whirled from the chimney neck.
In our jovial floating prison
There was sleep from fore to mizzen,
And never a star had risen
   The hazy sky to speck.

Strange company we harbored,
We'd a hundred Jews to larboard,
Unwashed, uncombed, unbarbered,—
　　Jews black and brown and gray.
With terror it would seize ye,
And make your souls uneasy
To see those Rabbis greasy,
　　Who did naught but scratch and pray.
Their dirty children puking,—
Their dirty saucepans cooking,—
Their dirty fingers hooking
　　Their swarming fleas away.

To starboard Turks and Greeks were,—
Whiskered and brown their cheeks were—
Enormous wide their breeks were,—
　　Their pipes did puff away;
Each on his mat allotted
In silence smoked and squatted,
Whilst round their children trotted
　　In pretty, pleasant play.

He can't but smile who traces
The smiles of those brown faces,
And the pretty, prattling graces
　　Of those small heathens gay.

And so the hours kept tolling;
And through the ocean rolling
Went the brave Iberia bowling,
　　Before the break of day,—
When a squall, upon a sudden,
Came o'er the waters scudding;
And the clouds began to gather,
And the sea was lashed to lather,
And the lowering thunder grumbled,
And the lightning jumped and tumbled,
And the ship, and all the ocean,
Woke up in wild commotion.

Then the wind set up a howling,
And the poodle dog a yowling,
And the cocks began a crowing,
And the old cow raised a lowing,

As she heard the tempest blowing;
And fowls and geese did cackle,
And the cordage and the tackle
Began to shriek and crackle;
And the spray dashed o'er the funnels,
And down the deck in runnels;
And the rushing water soaks all,
From the seamen in the fo'ksal
To the stokers, whose black faces
Peer out of their bed-places;
And the captain he was bawling,
And the sailors pulling, hauling,
And the quarter-deck tarpauling
Was shivered in the squalling;
And the passengers awaken,
Most pitifully shaken;
And the steward jumps up, and hastens
For the necessary basins.

Then the Greeks they groaned and quivered,
And they knelt and moaned and shivered,
As the plunging waters met them,
    And splashed and overset them;
And they called in their emergence
Upon countless saints and virgins;
And their marrowbones are bended,
And they think the world is ended.
And the Turkish women for'ard
Were frightened and behorrored;
And, shrieking and bewildering,
The mothers clutched their children;
The men sang " Allah! Illah!
Mashallah Bismillah!"
As the warring waters doused them,
And splashed them and soused them;
And they called upon the Prophet,
Who thought but little of it.

Then all the fleas in Jewry
Jumped up and bit like fury;
And the progeny of Jacob
Did on the main-deck wake up,
(I wot those greasy Rabbins

Would never pay for cabins;)
And each man moaned and jabbered in
His filthy Jewish gabardine,
In woe and lamentation,
And howling consternation.
And the splashing water drenches
Their dirty brats and wenches;
And they crawl from bales and benches,
In a hundred thousand stenches.

This was the white squall famous,
Which latterly o'ercame us,
And which all will well remember,
On the 28th September;
When a Prussian captain of Lancers
(Those tight-laced, whiskered prancers)
Came on the deck astonished,
By that wild squall admonished,

And wondering cried, " Potz tausend,
Wie ist der Stürm jetzt brausend?"
And looked at Captain Lewis,
Who calmly stood and blew his
Cigar in all the bustle,
And scorned the tempest's tussle.
And oft we've thought hereafter
How he beat the storm to laughter;
For well he knew his vessel
With that vain wind could wrestle;
And when a wreck we thought her,
And doomed ourselves to slaughter,
How gayly he fought her,
And through the hubbub brought her,
And as the tempest caught her,
Cried, "George, some brandy and water!"

And when, its force expended,
The harmless storm was ended,
And as the sunrise splendid
    Came blushing o'er the sea,—
I thought, as day was breaking,
My little girls were waking,
And smiling, and making
    A prayer at home for me.

                    William Makepeace Thackeray.

THE RATIONALISTIC CHICKEN.

Most strange!
Most queer—although most excellent a change!
Shades of the prison-house, ye disappear!
My fettered thoughts have won a wider range,
   And, like my legs, are free;
No longer huddled up so pitiably;
Free now to pry and probe, and peep and peer,
   And make these mysteries out.
Shall a free-thinking chicken live in doubt?
For now in doubt undoubtedly I am;
  This problem's very heavy on my mind;
And I'm not one to either shirk or sham;
  I won't be blinded, and I won't be blind!
   Now, let me see:
First, I would know how did I get in there?
   Then, where was I of yore?
Besides, why did n't I get out before?
   Dear me!
Here are three puzzles (out of plenty more),
Enough to give me pip upon the brain!
   But let me think again!
How do I know I ever was inside?
Now I reflect, it is, I do maintain,
Less than my reason, and beneath my pride,
   To think that I could dwell
In such a paltry, miserable cell
   As that old shell.
Of course I could n't! How could I have lain—
Body and beak and feathers, legs and wings,
And my deep heart's sublime imaginings—
   In there?
I meet the notion with profound disdain;
It 's quite incredible; since I declare
(And I 'm a chicken that you can't deceive),
What I can't understand I won't believe!

Where did I come from, then? Ah, where indeed?
This is a riddle monstrous hard to read.
   I have it! Why, of course,
All things are moulded by some plastic force

Out of some atoms somewhere up in space,
Fortuitously concurrent anyhow.
      There now!
That 's plain as is the beak upon my face.
      What's that I hear?
My mother cackling at me—just her way,
So prejudiced and ignorant, I say,
So far behind the wisdom of the day.

      What 's old I can't revere.
Hark at her. " You 're a silly chick, my dear,
      That 's quite as plain, alack!
As is the piece of shell upon your back!"
How bigoted! Upon my back, indeed!
      I do n't believe it 's there;
For I can't see it; and I do declare,
      For all her fond deceivin',
What I can't see I never will believe in!

                    Anonymous.

A CRITICAL SITUATION.

As Harris and I sat, one morning, at one of the small round tables of the great Hote Schweitzerhof in Lucerne, watching the crowd of people, coming, going, or breakfasting, and at the same time endeavoring to guess where such and such a party came from, I said:

"There is an American party."

"Yes—but name the State."

I named one State, he named another. We agreed upon one thing, however—that the young girl with the party was very beautiful and very tastefully dressed. But we disagreed as to her age. I said she was eighteen, Harris said she was twenty. The dispute between us waxed warm, and I finally said, with a pretense of being in earnest—

"Well, there is one way to settle the matter—I will go and ask her."

Harris said, sarcastically, " Certainly, that is the thing to do. All you need to do is to use the common formula over here: go and say, 'I'm an American!' Of course, she will be glad to see you."

Then he hinted that perhaps there was no great danger of my venturing to speak to her.

I said, "I was only talking—I did n't intend to approach her, but I see that you do not know what an intrepid person I am. I am not afraid of any woman that walks. I will go and speak to this young girl."

The thing I had in mind was not difficult. I meant to address her in the most respectful way and ask her to pardon me if her strong resemblance to a former acquaintance of mine was deceiving me; and when she should reply that the name I mentioned was not the name she bore, I meant to beg pardon again, most respectfully, and retire. There would be no harm done. I walked to her table, bowed to the gentleman, then turned to her, and was about to begin my little speech when she exclaimed:

"I knew I was n't mistaken—I told John it was you! John said it probably was n't, but I knew I was right. I said you would recognize me presently and come over; and I'm glad you did, for I should n't have felt much flattered if you had gone out of this room without recognizing me. Sit down, sit down—how odd it is—you are the last person I was ever expecting to see again."

This was a stupefying surprise. It took my wits clear away, for an instant. However, we shook hands cordially all around, and sat down. But truly this was the tightest place I ever was in. I seemed to vaguely remember the girl's face, now, but I had no idea where I had seen it before, or what name belonged with it. I immediately tried to get up a diversion about Swiss scenery, to keep her from launching into topics that might betray that I did not know her; but it was of no use, she went right along upon matters which interested her more:

"O dear! what a night that was, when the sea washed the forward boats away—do you remember it?"

"Oh! do n't I!" said I—but I did n't. I wished the sea had washed the rudder and the smoke-stack and the captain away—then I could have located this questioner.

"And do n't you remember how frightened poor Mary was, and how she cried?"

"Indeed I do!" said I. "Dear me, how it all comes back!"

I fervently wished it would come back—but my memory was a blank. The wise way would have been to frankly own up; but I could not bring myself to do that, after the young girl had praised me so for recognizing her; so I went on, deeper and deeper into the mire, hoping for a chance clue but never getting one. The unrecognizable continued, with vivacity:

"Do you know, George married Mary after all?"

"Why, no! Did he?"

"Indeed he did. He said he did not believe she was half as much to blame as her father was, and I thought he was right. Did n't you?"

"Of course he was. It was a perfectly plain case. I always said so."

"Why, no you did n't—at least that summer."

"Oh! no, not that summer. No, you are perfectly right about that. It was the following winter that I said it."

"Well, as it turned out, Mary was not in the least to blame—it was all her father's fault—at least his and old Darley's."

It was necessary to say something—so I said:

"I always regarded Darley as a troublesome old thing."

"So he was; but then they always had a great affection for him, although he had so many eccentricities. You remember that when the weather was the least cold he would try to come into the house."

I was rather afraid to proceed. Evidently Darley was not a man—he must be some other kind of animal—possibly a dog, maybe an elephant. However, tails are common to all animals, so I ventured to say:

"And what a tail he had!"

"One! He had a thousand!"

This was bewildering. I did not quite know what to say, so I only said:

"Yes, he was pretty well fixed in the matter of tails."

"For a negro, and a crazy one at that, I should say he was," said she.

It was getting pretty sultry for me. I said to myself, "Is it possible she is going to stop there, and wait for me to speak? If she does, the conversation is blocked. A negro with a thousand tails is a topic which a person cannot talk upon fluently and instructively without more or less preparation. As to diving rashly into such a vast subject—"

But here, to my gratitude, she interrupted my thought by saying:

" Yes, when it came to tales of his crazy woes, there was simply no end to them if anybody would listen. His own quarters were comfortable enough, but when the weather was cold, the family was sure to have his company—nothing could keep him out of the house. But they always bore it kindly because he had saved Tom's life, years before. You remember Tom?"

"Oh! perfectly. Fine fellow he was, too."

"Yes, he was. And what a pretty little thing his child was?"

"You may well say that. I never saw a prettier child."

"I used to delight to pet it and dandle it and play with it."

"So did I."

"You named it. What was that name? I can't call it to mind."

It appeared to me that the ice was getting pretty thin here. I would have given something to know what the child's sex was. However, I had the good luck to think of a name that would fit either sex—so I brought it out:

"I named it Frances."

"For a relative, I suppose? But you named the one that died, too—the one that I never saw. What did you call that one?"

I was out of neutral names, but as the child was dead and she had never seen it, I thought I might risk a name for it and trust to luck; therefore I said:

"I called that one Thomas Henry."

She said, musingly:

"That is very singular — very singular."

I sat still and let the cold sweat run down. I was in a good deal of trouble, but I believed I could worry through if she would n't ask me to name any more children. I wondered where the lightning was going to strike next. She was still ruminating over that last child's title, but presently she said:

"I have always been sorry you were away at the time — I would have had you name my child."

"Your child! Are you married?"

"I have been married thirteen years."

"Christened, you mean?"

"No, married. The youth by your side is my son."

"It seems incredible — even impossible. I do not mean

any harm by it, but would you mind telling me if you are any over eighteen?—that is to say, will you tell me how old you are?"

"I was just nineteen the day of the storm we were talking about. That was my birthday."

That did not help matters much, as I did not know the date of the storm. I tried to think of some non-committal thing to say, to keep up my end of the talk and render my poverty in the matter of reminiscences as little noticeable as possible, but I seemed to be about out of non-committal things. I was about to say, "You haven't changed a bit since then"—but that was risky. I thought of saying, "You have improved ever so much since then"—but that would not answer, of course. I was about to try a shy at the weather, for a saving change, when the girl slipped in ahead of me and said:

"How I have enjoyed this talk over those happy old times—haven't you?"

"I never have spent such a half hour in all my life before!" said I, with emotion; and I could have added, with a near approach to truth, "and I would rather be scalped than spend another one like it." I was grateful to be through with the ordeal, and was about to make my good-byes and get out, when the girl said:

"But there is one thing that is ever so puzzling to me."

"Why, what is that?"

"That dead child's name. What did you say it was?"

Here was another balmy place to be in; I had forgotten the child's name; I hadn't imagined it would be needed again. However, I had to pretend to know, anyway, so I said:

"Joseph William."

The youth at my side corrected me and said:

"No—Thomas Henry."

I thanked him—in words—and said, with trepidation:

"Oh! yes—I was thinking of another child that I named —I have named a great many, and I got them confused— this one was named Henry Thompson—"

"Thomas Henry," calmly interposed the boy.

I thanked him again—strictly in words—and stammered out:

"Thomas Henry—yes, Thomas Henry was the poor child's name. I named him for Thomas—er—Thomas Carlyle, the great author, you know—and Henry–er–er–Henry the Eighth. The parents were very grateful to have a child named Thomas Henry."

"That makes it more singular than ever," murmured my beautiful friend.

"Does it? Why?"

"Because when the parents speak of that child now, they always call it Susan Amelia."

That spiked my gun. I could not say anything. I was entirely out of verbal obliquities; to go further would be to lie, and that I would not do; so I simply sat still and suffered—sat mutely and resignedly there, and sizzled—for I was being slowly fried to death in my own blushes. Presently the enemy laughed a happy laugh and said:

"I have enjoyed this talk over old times, but you have not. I saw very soon that you were only pretending to know me, and so as I had wasted a compliment on you in the beginning, I made up my mind to punish you. And I have succeeded pretty well. I was glad to see that you knew George and Tom and Darley, for I had never heard of them before, and therefore could not be sure that you had; and I was glad to learn the names of those imaginary children, too. One can get quite a fund of information out of you if one goes at it cleverly. Mary and the storm, and the sweeping away of the forward boats, were facts—all the rest was fiction. Mary was my sister; her full name was Mary ——. Now do you remember me?"

"Yes," I said, "I do remember you now; and you are as hard-hearted as you were thirteen years ago in that ship, else you would n't have punished me so. You have n't changed your nature nor your person, in any way at all; you look just as young as you did then, you are just as beautiful as you were then, and you have transmitted a deal of your comeliness to this fine boy. There—if that speech moves you any, let 's fly the flag of truce, with the understanding that I am conquered and confess it."

All of which was agreed to and accomplished on the spot.

Samuel L. Clemens.

"IMPH-M."

When I was a laddie lang syne at the schule,
The maister aye ca'd me a dunce an' a fule;
For somehoo his words I could ne'er un'erstan',
Unless when he bawled, "Jamie, haud oot yer han'!"
      Then I gloom'd, and said, " Imph-m,"
      I glunch'd, and said, "Imph-m "—
I wasna owre proud, but owre dour to say—A-y-e!

Ae day a queer word, as lang-nebbits' himsel',
He vow'd he would thrash me if I wadna spell,
Quo I, " Maister Quill," wi' a kin' o' a swither,
" I 'll spell ye the word if ye 'll spell me anither:
      Let's hear ye spell ' Imph-m,'
      That common word ' Imph-m,'
That auld Scotch word ' Imph-m,' ye ken it means A-y-e!"

Had ye seen hoo he glour'd, hoo he scratched his big pate,
An' shouted, " Ye villain, get oot o' my gate!
Get aff to your seat! yer the plague o' the schule!
The de'il o' me kens if yer maist rogue or fule!"
      But I only said, " Imph-m,"
      That pawkie word "Imph-m,"
He couldna spell "Imph-m," that stands for an A-y-e!

An' when a brïsk wooer, I courted my Jean—
O'Avon's braw lasses the pride an' the queen—
When neath my gray plaidie, wi' heart beatin' fain,
I speired in a whisper if she'd be my ain,
      She blushed, an' said, " Imph-m,"
      That charming word "Imph-m,"
A thousan' times better an' sweeter than A-y-e!

Just ae thing I wanted my bliss to complete—
Ae kiss frae her rosy mou', couthie an' sweet—
But a shake o' her head was her only reply—
Of course, that said No, but I kent she meant A-y-e,
      For her twa een said " Imph-m,"
      Her red lips said, " Imph-m,"
Her hale face said "Imph-m," an " Imph-m " means A-y-e!
                     Anonymous.

THE ONE-HOSS SHAY; OR, THE DEACON'S MASTERPIECE.

A LOGICAL STORY.

Have you heard of the wonderful one-hoss shay,
That was built in such a logical way,
It ran a hundred years to a day,
And then of a sudden, it—ah, but stay,
I 'll tell you what happened without delay,
Scaring the parson into fits,
Frightening people out of their wits,—
Have you ever heard of that I say?

Seventeen hundred and fifty-five,
Georgius Secundus was then alive,—
Snuffy old drone from the German hive.
That was the year when Lisbon-town
Saw the earth open and gulp her down,
And Braddock's army was done so brown,
Left without a scalp to its crown.
It was on the terrible earthquake day
That the Deacon finished the one-hoss shay.

Now, in building of chaises, I tell you what,
There is always *somewhere* a weakest spot,—
In hub, tire, felloe, in spring or thill,
In panel, or crossbar, or floor, or sill,
In screw, bolt, thorough-brace,—lurking still,
Find it somewhere you must and will,—
Above or below, or within or without,—
And that 's the reason, beyond a doubt,
A chaise *breaks down* but does n't *wear out.*

But the Deacon swore (as Deacons do,
With an "I dew vum," or an "I tell *yeou*,")
He would build one shay to beat the taown
'N' the keounty 'n' all the kentry raoun';
It should be so built that it *could n'* break daown;
—"Fur," said the Deacon, "'t 's mighty plain
That the weakes' place mus' stan' the strain;
'N' the way t' fix it, uz I maintain,
                    Is only jest
T' make that place uz strong uz the rest."

So the Deacon inquired of the village folk
Where he could find the strongest oak,
That could n't be split nor bent nor broke,—
That was for spokes and floor and sills;
He sent for lancewood to make the thills;
The crossbars were ash from the straightest trees;
The panels of whitewood, that cuts like cheese,
But lasts like iron for things like these;
The hubs of logs from the "Settler's ellum,"—
Last of its timber,—they could n't sell 'em,
Never an axe had seen their chips,
And the wedges flew from between their lips,
Their blunt ends frizzled like celery-tips;
Step and prop-iron, bolt and screw,
Spring, tire, axle, and linchpin, too,
Steel of the finest, bright and blue;
Thorough-brace bison-skin, thick and wide;
Boot, top, dasher, from tough old hide
Found in the pit when the tanner died.
That was the way he "put her through."—
'There!" said the Deacon, "naow she 'll dew!"

Do! I tell you, I rather guess
She was a wonder, and nothing less!
Colts grew horses, beards turned gray,
Deacon and deaconess dropped away,
Children and grandchildren,—where were they?
But there stood the stout old one-hoss shay
As fresh as on Lisbon-earthquake day!

EIGHTEEN HUNDRED;—it came and found
The Deacon's masterpiece strong and sound.
Eighteen hundred increased by ten;—
" Hahnsum kerridge " they called it then.
Eighteen hundred and twenty came;—
Running as usual; much the same.
Thirty and forty at last arrive,
And then come fifty, and FIFTY-FIVE.

Little of all we value here
Wakes on the morn of its hundredth year
Without both feeling and looking queer.

In fact, there's nothing that keeps its youth,
So far as I know, but a tree and truth.
(This is a moral that runs at large;
Take it.—You're welcome.—No extra charge.)

FIRST OF NOVEMBER,—the Earthquake day,—
There are traces of age in the one-hoss shay,
A general flavor of mild decay,
But nothing local as one may say.
There could n't be,—for the Deacon's art
Had made it so like in every part
That there was n't a chance for one to start.
For the wheels were just as strong as the thills,
And the floor was just as strong as the sills,
And the panels just as strong as the floor,
And the whippletree neither less nor more,
And the back crossbar as strong as the fore,
And spring and axle and hub *encore*.
And yet, *as a whole*, it is past a doubt
In another hour it will be *worn out!*

First of November, 'Fifty-five!
This morning the parson takes a drive.
Now, small boys, get out of the way!
Here comes the wonderful one-hoss shay,
Drawn by a rat-tailed, ewe-necked bay.
"Huddup!" said the parson.—Off went they.
The parson was working his Sunday's text,—
Had got to fifthly, and stopped perplexed
At what the—Moses was coming next.
All at once the horse stood still,
Close by the meetin'-house on the hill.
—First a shiver, and then a thrill,
Then something decidedly like a spill,—
And the parson was sitting upon a rock,
At half-past nine by the meetin'-house clock,—
Just the hour of the Earthquake shock!
—What do you think the parson found,
When he got up and stared around?
The poor old chaise in a heap or mound,
As if it had been to the mill and ground!
You see, of course, if you're not a dunce,

How it went to pieces all at once,—
All at once, and nothing first,—
Just as bubbles do when they burst.

End of the wonderful one-hoss shay.
Logic is logic. That's all I say.
Oliver Wendell Holmes.

LADY TEAZLE AND SIR PETER.

(*Scenes from "School for Scandal."*)

ACT II. SCENE I.

Sir P. Lady Teazle, Lady Teazle, I'll not bear it!

Lady T. Sir Peter, Sir Peter, you may bear it or not, as you please; but I ought to have my own way in everything; and, what's more, I will, too. What though I was educated in the country, I know very well that women of fashion in London are accountable to nobody after they are married.

Sir P. Very well, ma'am, very well; so a husband is to have no influence, no authority?

Lady T. Authority! No, to be sure; if you wanted authority over me, you should have adopted me, and not married me; I am sure you were old enough.

Sir P. Old enough! ay, there it is! Well, well, Lady Teazle, though my life may be made unhappy by your temper, I'll not be ruined by your extravagance.

Lady T. My extravagance! I'm sure I'm not more extravagant than a woman ought to be.

Sir P. No, no, madam, you shall throw away no more sums on such unmeaning luxury. 'Slife! to spend as much to furnish your dressing-room with flowers in winter as would suffice to turn the Pantheon into a greenhouse, and give a fête champêtre at Christmas!

Lady T. Sir Peter, am I to blame because flowers are dear in cold weather? You should find fault with the climate, and not with me. For my part, I'm sure, I wish it was spring all the year round, and that roses grew under our feet!

Sir P. Zounds, madam! if you had been born to this, I

should n't wonder at your talking thus ; but you forget what your situation was when I married you.

Lady T. No, no, I do n't; 'twas a very disagreeable one, or I should never have married you.

Sir P. Yes, yes, madam, you were then in somewhat a humbler style,— the daughter of a plain country Squire. Recollect, Lady Teazle, when I first saw you sitting at your tambour, in a pretty, figured linen gown, with a bunch of keys at your side ; your hair combed smooth over a roll, and your apartment hung round with fruits in worsted, of your own working.

Lady T. O, yes! I remember it very well, and a curious life I led. My daily occupation to inspect the dairy, superintend the poultry, make extracts from the family receipt-book,— and comb my Aunt Deborah's lap-dog.

Sir P. Yes, yes, ma'am, 'twas so, indeed!

Lady T. And then, you know, my evening amusements : To draw patterns for ruffles, which I had not materials to make up ; to play Pope Joan with the curate ; to read a sermon to my aunt ; or to be stuck down to an old spinet to strum my father to sleep after a fox-chase.

Sir P. I am glad you have so good a memory. Yes, madam, these were the recreations I took you from ; but now you must have your coach — *vis-à-vis* — and three powdered footmen before your chair ; and, in the summer, a pair of white cats to draw you to Kensington Gardens. No recollection, I suppose, when you were content to ride double, behind the butler, on a docked coach-horse.

Lady T. No, I swear I never did that! I deny the butler and the coach-horse.

Sir P. This, madam, was your situation ; and what have I done for you? I have made you a woman of fashion, of fortune, of rank; in short, I have made you my wife.

Lady T. Well then, and there is but one thing more you can make me, and add to the obligation, and that is —

Sir P. My widow, I suppose?

Lady T. Hem! hem!

Sir P. I thank you, madam, but do n't flatter yourself ; for, though your ill conduct may disturb my peace of mind, it shall never break my heart, I promise you ; however, I am equally obliged to you for the hint.

Lady T. Then why will you endeavor to make yourself

so disagreeable to me, and thwart me in every little elegant expense?

Sir P. 'Slife, madam! I say, had you any of these little elegant expenses when you married me?

Lady T. Lud, Sir Peter! would you have me be out of the fashion?

Sir P. The fashion, indeed! What had you to do with the fashion before you married me?

Lady T. For my part, I should think you would like to have your wife thought a woman of taste.

Sir P. Ay, there again! taste! Zounds, madam! you had no taste when you married me.

Lady T. That's very true, indeed, Sir Peter; and, after having married you, I should never pretend to taste again, I allow. But now, Sir Peter, since we have finished our daily jangle, I presume I may go to my engagement at Lady Sneerwell's?

Sir P. Ay, there's another precious circumstance,— a charming set of acquaintances you have made there!

Lady T. Nay, Sir Peter, they are all people of rank and fortune, and remarkably tenacious of reputation.

Sir P. Yes, egad, they are tenacious of reputation with a vengeance; for they don't choose anybody should have a character but themselves. Such a crew! Ah! many a wretch has rid on a hurdle who has done less mischief than these utterers of forged tales, coiners of scandal, and clippers of reputation.

Lady T. What! would you restrain the freedom of speech?

Sir P. Ah! they have made you just as bad as any one of the society.

Lady T. Why, I believe I do bear a part with a tolerable grace.

Sir P. Grace, indeed!

Lady T. But I vow I bear no malice against the people I abuse. When I say an ill-natured thing, 'tis out of pure good-humor; and I take it for granted, they deal exactly in the same manner with me. But, Sir Peter, you know you promised to come to Lady Sneerwell's, too.

Sir P. Well, well; I'll call in just to look after my own character.

Lady T. Then indeed you must make haste after me, or you'll be too late. So, good-bye to ye! [*Exit Lady* TEAZLE.

Sir P. So! I have gained much by my intended expostulation; yet with what a charming air she contradicts every thing I say, and how pleasingly she shows her contempt for my authority! Well, though I can't make her love me, there is great satisfaction in quarrelling with her; and I think she never appears to such advantage as when she is doing every thing in her power to plague me. [*Exit.*]

Act III. Scene i.

Sir P. Was ever man so crossed as I am? Every thing conspiring to fret me! I had not been involved in matrimony a fortnight, before her father, a hale and hearty man, died, on purpose, I believe, for the pleasure of plaguing me with the care of his daughter. [*Lady* Teazle *sings without.*] But here comes my helpmate! She appears in great good-humor. How happy I should be if I could tease her into loving me, though but little!

Enter Lady Teazle.

Lady T. Lud! Sir Peter, I hope you have n't been quarrelling with Maria? It is not using me well to be ill-humored when I am not by.

Sir P. Ah! Lady Teazle, you might have the power to make me good-humored at all times.

Lady T. I am sure I wish I had; for I want you to be in a charming sweet temper at this moment. Do be good-humored now, and let me have two hundred pounds, will you?

Sir P. Two hundred pounds! What, ain't I to be in a good-humor without paying for it? But speak to me thus, and i' faith there 's nothing I could refuse you. You shall have it; [*Gives her notes.*] but seal me a bond of repayment.

Lady T. O no! there, my note of hand will do as well. [*Offering her hand.*]

Sir P. And you shall no longer reproach me with not giving you an independent settlement. I mean shortly to surprise you: but shall we always live thus, hey?

Lady T. If you please. I 'm sure I do n't care how soon we leave off quarrelling, provided you 'll own you were tired first.

Sir P. Well, then let our future contest be, who shall be most obliging.

Lady T. I assure you, Sir Peter, good-nature becomes you. You look now as you did before we were married, when you used to walk with me under the elms, and tell me stories of what a gallant you were in your youth; and chuck me under the chin, you would; and ask me if I thought I could love an old fellow, who would deny me nothing; did n't you?

Sir P. Yes, yes; and you were as kind and attentive—

Lady T. Ay, so I was, and would always take your part, when my acquaintance used to abuse you, and turn you into ridicule.

Sir P. Indeed!

Lady T. Ay, and when my cousin Sophy has called you a stiff, peevish old bachelor, and laughed at me for thinking of marrying one who might be my father, I have always defended you, and said I did n't think you so ugly by any means.

Sir P. Thank you.

Lady T. And I dared say you 'd make a very good sort of a husband.

Sir P. And you prophesied right; and we shall now be the happiest couple—

Lady T. And never differ again. [*Both sit.*]

Sir P. No, never!—though at the same time, indeed, my dear Lady Teazle, you must watch your temper very seriously; for in all our little quarrels, my dear, if you recollect, my love, you always begin.

Lady T. I beg your pardon, my dear Sir Peter; indeed, you always gave the provocation.

Sir P. Now see, my angel! take care,—contradicting is n't the way to keep friends.

Lady T. Then do n't you begin it, my love!

Sir P. There, now! you—you are going on. You do n't perceive, my life, that you are just doing the very thing which you know always makes me angry.

Lady T. Nay, you know if you will be angry without any reason, my dear—

Sir P. There! now you want to quarrel again.

Lady T. No, I am sure I do n't; but if you will be so peevish—

Sir P. There now! who begins first?

Lady T. Why, you, to be sure. [*Both start up.*] I said nothing; but there 's no bearing your temper.

Sir P. No, no, madam; the fault's in your own temper.

Lady T. Ay, you are just what my cousin Sophy said you would be.

Sir P. Your cousin Sophy is a forward, impertinent gypsy.

Lady T. You are a great bear, I'm sure, to abuse my relations.

Sir P. Now, may all the plagues of marriage be doubled on me, if ever I try to be friends with you any more.

Lady T. So much the better.

Sir P. No, no, madam; 'tis evident you never cared a pin for me, and I was a madman to marry you,—a pert, rural coquette, that had refused half the honest squires in the neighborhood.

Lady T. And I am sure I was a fool to marry you,—an old dangling bachelor, who was single at fifty, only because he never could meet with any one who would have him.

Sir P. Ay, ay, madam; but you were pleased enough to listen to me; you never had such an offer before.

Lady T. No? did n't I refuse Sir Tivy Terrier, who everybody said would have been a better match? for his estate is just as good as yours, and he has broke his neck since we have been married.

Sir P. I have done with you, madam! You are an unfeeling, ungrateful—but there's an end of everything. I believe you capable of everything that is bad. Yes, madam, I now believe the reports relative to you and Charles, madam. Yes, madam, *you* and Charles are—not without grounds—

Lady T. Take care, Sir Peter! you had better not insinuate any such thing! I'll not be suspected without cause, I promise you.

Sir P. Very well, madam! very well! A separate maintenance as soon as you please! Yes, madam, or a divorce! I'll make an example of myself for the benefit of all old bachelors. Let us separate, madam.

Lady T. Agreed, agreed! And, now, my dear Sir Peter, we are of a mind once more, we may be the happiest couple, and never differ again, you know,—ha! ha! ha! Well, you are going to be in a passion, I see, and I shall only interrupt you; so, bye, bye. [*Exit.*

Sir P. Plagues and tortures! Can't I make her angry, either? O, I am the most miserable fellow! but I'll not bear her presuming to keep her temper. [*Exit.*

Richard Brinsley Sheridan.

THE BOOK CANVASSER.

He came into my office with a portfolio under his arm. Placing it upon the table, removing a ruined hat, and wiping his nose upon a ragged handkerchief that had been so long out of the wash that it was positively gloomy, he said: " Mr. ——, I'm canvassing for the National Portrait Gallery; splendid work; comes in numbers, fifty cents apiece; contains pictures of all the great American heroes, from the earliest times down to the present day. Everybody subscribing for it, and I want to see if I can't take your name.

"Now, just cast your eyes over that," he said, opening his book and pointing to an engraving. " That's—lemme see—yes, that's Columbus; perhaps you've heard sumfin' about him? The publisher was telling me to-day before I started out that he discovered— No; was it Columbus that dis— Oh! yes. Columbus, he discovered America—was the first man here. He came over in a ship, the publisher said, and it took fire, and he stayed on deck because his father told him to, if I remember right, and when the old thing busted to pieces he was killed. Handsome picture, ain't it? Taken from a photograph, all of 'em are; done especially for this work. His clothes are kinder odd, but they say that's the way they dressed in them days. Look at this one. Now is n't that splendid? William Penn, one of the early settlers. I was reading t' other day about him. When he first arrived he got a lot of Indians up a tree, and when they shook some apples down, he set one on top of his son's head, and shot an arrow plump through it and never fazed him. They say it struck them Indians cold; he was such a terrific shooter. Fine countenance, has n't he? Face shaved clean; he did n't wear a moustache, I believe, but he seems to have let himself out on hair. Now, my view is, that every man ought to have a picture of that Patriarch so's to see how the fust settlers looked and what kind of weskets they yoused to wear. See his legs, too! Trousers a little short, maybe, as if he was going to wade in a creek; but he's all there. Got some kind of a paper in his hand, I see. Subscription list, I reckon. Now, how does that strike you? There's something nice. That I think, is—is—that a—a— yes, to be sure, Washington—you recollect him, of course? Some people call him Father of his Country, George—Washington. Had no middle name, I believe. He lived about two hundred years ago and he was a fighter. I heard the publisher telling a man about him crossing the Delaware River up yer at Trenton, and seems to me, if I recollect right, I've read about it myself. He was courting some girl on the Jersey side, and he used to swim over at nights to see her when the old man was asleep. The girl's family were down on him, I reckon. He looks like a man to do that, do n't he? He's got it in his eye. If it'd been me I'd gone over on a bridge, but he probably wanted to show off afore her; some men are so reckless, you know. Now, if you'll conclude to take this, I'll get the publisher to write out some more stories about him, and bring 'em round to you, so's you can study up on him. I know he did ever so many other things, but I've forgot 'em; my memory's so awful poor.

"Less see! Who have we next? Ah, Franklin! Benjamin Franklin! He was one of the old original pioneers, I think. I disremember exactly what he is celebrated for, but I think it was a flying a—oh! yes, flying a kite, that's it. The publisher mentioned it. He was out one day flying a kite, you know, like boys do nowadays, and while she was a flickering up in the sky, and he was giving her more string, an apple fell off a tree, and hit him on the head;—then he discovered the attraction of gravitation, I think they call it. Smart, was n't it? Now, if you or me'd a been hit, it'd just a made us mad like as not and set us a ravin'. But men are so different. One man's meat's another man's pison. See what a double chin he's got. No beard on him, either, though a goatee would have been becoming to such a round face. He has n't got on a sword, and I reckon he was no soldier;—fit some when he was a boy, maybe, or went out with the home-guard, but not a regular warrior. I ain't one, myself, and I think all the better of him for it. Ah, here we are! Look at that! Smith and Pocahontas! John Smith! Is n't that gorgeous? See how she kneels over him, and sticks out her hands while he lays on the ground, and that big fellow with a club tries to hammer him up. Talk about woman's love! There it is for you. Modocs, I believe. Anyway, some Indians out West there, somewheres; and the publisher tells me that Captain Shackanasty, or whatever his name is there, was going to bang old Smith over the head with a log of wood, and this here girl she was sweet on Smith, it appears, and she broke loose, and jumped forward and says to the man with the stick, 'Why do n't you let John alone? Me and him are going to marry, and if you kill him, I 'll never speak to you as long as I live,' or words like them, and so the man he give it up, and both of them hunted up a preacher and were married and lived happy ever afterward. Beautiful story, is n't it? A good wife she made him, too, I' ll bet, if she was a little copper-colored. And do n't she look just lovely in that picture? But Smith appears kinder sick, evidently thinks his goose is cooked, and I do n't wonder, with that Modoc swooping down on him with such a discouraging club. And now we come to—to ah—to—Putnam —General Putnam:--he fought in the war, too; and one day a lot of 'em caught him when he was off his guard, and they tied him flat on his back on a horse and then licked the horse like the very mischief. And what does that horse do but go pitching down about four hundred stone steps in front of the house, with General Putnam lying there nearly skeered to death. Leastways the publisher said somehow that way, and I oncet read about it myself. But he came out safe, and I reckon sold the horse and made a pretty good thing of it. What surprises me is he did n't break his neck, but maybe it was a mule, for they 're pretty sure footed, you know. Surprising what some of these men have gone through, ain't it? Turn over a couple of leaves. That 's General Jackson. My father shook hands with him once. He was a fighter, I know. He fit down in New Orleans. Broke up the rebel Legislature, and then when the Ku Kluxes got after him he fought 'em behind cotton breastworks and licked 'em 'til they could n't stand. They say he was terrific when he got real mad. Hit straight from the shoulder and fetched his man every time. Andrew, his fust name was; and look how his hair stands up. And then, here 's John Adams and Daniel Boone and two or three pirates, and a whole lot more pictures, so you see it's cheap as dirt. Lemme have your name, won't you?"   *Max Adeler.*

BY TELEPHONE.

When the young ladies who were spending the summer at the Seaside Hotel, at Sandy Beach, resolved to get up a fair, they had no heartier helper than Mr. Samuel Brassy, a young gentleman recently graduated from Columbia College. He was alert, energetic, ingenious, and untiring; and when at last the fair was opened, the young ladies declared that they did not know what they should have done without him.

Mr. Samuel Brassy was on friendly, if not familiar, terms with Mrs. Martin, her charges, the three Miss Pettitoes, and her niece, Miss Bessie Martin. Toward the three Miss Pettitoes he was kind, but to Miss Bessie Martin he was devoted. He hovered about her as though he had words of deepest import trembling on his tongue; but when he sat beside her on the piazza, or danced with her in the Virginia Reel of a Saturday night, or walked to church with her of a Sunday morning, he found that he had nothing to say for himself.

Miss Martin treated him as she treated other young men. She allowed him to assist her in the organization of a post-office department in the fair, of which she was to be post-mistress. At Sam Brassy's suggestion the post-office had been arranged as the public pay-station for the Seaside Hotel Telephone Co. He had set up a toy telephone in the post-office with a line extending to a summer-house, about two hundred feet from the hotel. Any person paying twenty-five cents at the post-office was entitled to go to the summer-house and hold a conversation by wire. The questions which a casual converser might choose to put were answered promptly and pointedly, for Bessie Martin was a quick-witted and keen-sighted girl.

So it happened that the telephone was a captivating novelty, and Miss Bessie's conversation charmed many a quarter into the box.

Sam himself was constant in his attendance at the post-office. He did not seem altogether pleased at the continual use of the telephone. As the evening wore on, a shadow of resolution deepened on his face. About ten o'clock the ball-room began to empty, as the crowd gathered in the dining-room, where the drawing of the grand prize was to take place. A subscription had been opened for a pair of handsome vases which Mr. Martin had presented, and every subscriber had been given a numbered ticket; and now, on the last evening of the fair, there was to be a "casting of lots" to discover to whom the vases might belong. The interest in the result was so intense that most of the ladies who had stalls abandoned them for a while and deserted to the dining-room. Then Mr. Samuel Brassy stepped up to the window of the post-office.

"Are you going to see the drawing of the prize, Miss Bessie?"

"No; I shall stick to my post."

"That's all right, then here's my quarter."

So saying he placed the coin before her, and then he hurried away. Miss Bessie Martin was left alone in the corner of the ball-room. She was counting up her gains, when the telephone bell rang sharply. Before she could put the money down and go to the instrument, there came a second impatient ting-a-ling.

"Somebody seems to be in a hurry," she said, as she took her station before the box and held the receiver to her ear.

"Hello! hello! Oh, it's you, is it, Mr. Brassy?"

* * * * * * * *

"Yes; I wondered why you ran off so suddenly."

* * * * * * * *

"You have paid your quarter and you can talk just two minutes."

* * * * * * *

"Of course, I did not mean that. You ought to know me better."

* * * * *

"What did you say?"

* * * * * * *

"Not lately."

* * * * *

"Yes, she had on a blue dress, and I thought she looked like a fright; didn't you?"

* * * *

"Who were you looking at, then?"

* * * * *

"Oh, Mr. Brassy!"

* * * *

"No, they are not here now."

* * * * * * *

"There's nobody here at all."

* * * * * *

"Yes, I'm *all* alone.   There is n't a creature in sight."

* * * * * *

"I love secrets!   Tell me."

* * * * * *

"Tell me now."

* * * * *

"Why can't you tell me now?   I'm just dying to know."

* * * * *

"No, there is n't anybody here at all—nobody—nobody."

* * * * * * * *

"How poetic you are to-night."

* * * * * * *

"I just dote on poetry."

* * * * * * * *

"Oh, Mr. Brassy!"

* * * * * * *

"You take me by surprise."

* * * * *

"I never thought of such a thing."

* * * * *

"You do!"

* * * *

"With your whole heart?"

* * * *

"I do n't know what to say."

* * * * * * *

"But I can't say 'yes' all at once."

* * * * * * *

"Well, I won't say 'no.'"

* * * * *

"But I really must have time to think."

* * * *

"No, no, no!   I can't give you an answer right away."

* * * * * *

"Well, if you must—you can ask Auntie—"

* * * * * * *

"Yes, yes, I 'm all alone still."

* * * * *

"Good-bye, Sam!"

* * * * * * * *

Miss Bessie Martin turned away from the instrument with

a flush on her cheek and a light in her eye. Just then Mr. Samuel Brassy rushed in through the open door, flew across the ball-room, and disappeared within the post-office. A minute later a throng of people began to pour back from the dining-room, and there were frequent calls for " Sam " and " Mr. Brassy."

With heightened color and ill-concealed excitement, Mr. Samuel Brassy came out of the post-office. He found himself face to face with Mr. Martin, who held out his hand and cried, "I congratulate you, Sam." "How—how did you know anything about it?" Before Mr. Martin could reply, Mr. Harry Brackett and the three Miss Pettitoes came forward. Mr. Brackett bore in his arms the pair of vases.

Then Mr. Brassy knew why Mr. Martin had congratulated him. "You have won the prize," cried Harry Brackett. "I have for a fact," Sam Brassy answered, looking at Miss Bessie Martin.

Anonymous.

BOUNDING THE UNITED STATES.

Among the legends of our late Civil War, there is a story of a dinner-party, given by the Americans residing in Paris, at which were propounded sundry toasts, concerning not so much the past and present as the expected glories of the great American nation. In the general character of these toasts, geographical considerations were very prominent, and the principal fact which seemed to occupy the minds of the speakers was the unprecedented *bigness* of our country.

" Here's to the United States!" said the first speaker,— "bounded on the north by British America, on the south by the Gulf of Mexico, on the east by the Atlantic, and on the west by the Pacific Ocean!" " But," said the second speaker, "this is far too limited a view of the subject, and, in assigning our boundaries, we must look to the great and glorious future, which is prescribed for us by the manifest destiny of the Anglo-Saxon race. Here's to the United States!— bounded on the north by the North Pole, on the south by the South Pole, on the east by the rising, and on the west by the setting, sun!"

Emphatic applause greeted the aspiring prophecy. But

here arose the third speaker, a very serious gentleman, from the far West. " If we are going," said this truly patriotic American, " to lessen the historic past and present, and take our manifest destiny into account, why restrict ourselves within the narrow limits assigned by our fellow-countryman, who has just sat down? I give you the United States! — bounded on the north by the Aurora Borealis, on the south by the precession of the equinoxes, on the east by the primeval chaos, and on the west by the Day of Judgment!"

John Fiske.

AN INVALID IN LODGINGS.

Until my system collapsed, my landlady only spoke of me as her parlor. At intervals I had communicated with her through the medium of Sarah Ann, the servant, and, as her rent was due on Wednesday, could I pay my bill now? Except for these monetary transactions, my landlady and I were total strangers, and, though I sometimes fell over her children in the lobby, that led to no intimacy. Even Sarah Ann never opened her mouth to me. She brought in my tea, and left me to discover that it was there. My first day in lodgings I said " Good-morning " to Sarah Ann, and she replied, " Eh? " " Good-morning," I repeated, to which she answered contemptuously, " Oh, ay." For six months I was simply the parlor, but then I fell ill, and at once became an interesting person.

Sarah Ann found me shivering on the sofa one hot day a week or more ago, beneath my rug, two coats, and some other articles. My landlady sent up some beef-tea, in which she has a faith that is pathetic, and then, to complete the cure, she appeared in person. She has proved a nice, motherly old lady, but not cheerful company.

" Where do you feel it worst, sir? " she asked.

I said it was bad all over, but worst in my head.

" On your brow? "

" No, on the back of my head."

" It feels like a lump of lead? "

" No, like a furnace."

" That 's just what I feared," she said. " It began so with him."

"With whom?"

"My husband. He came in one day, five years ago, complaining of his head, and in three days he was a corpse."

"What?"

"Don't be afraid, sir. Maybe it isn't the same thing."

"Of course it isn't. Your husband, according to the story you told me when I took these rooms, died of fever."

"Yes, but the fever began just in this way. It carried him off in no time. You had better see a doctor, sir. Doctor was no use in my husband's case, but it is a satisfaction to have him."

Here Sarah Ann, who had been listening with mouth and eyes wide open, suddenly burst into tears, and was led out of the room, exclaiming, "Him such a quiet gentleman, and he never flung nothing at me."

Though I knew that I had only caught a nasty cold, a conviction in which the doctor confirmed me, my landlady stood out for its being just such another case as her husband's, and regaled me for hours with reminiscences of his rapid decline. If I was a little better one day, alas! he had been a little better the day before he died; and if I answered her peevishly, she told Sarah Ann that my voice was going. She brought the beef-tea up with her own hand, her countenance saying that I might as well have it, though it could not save me. Sometimes I pushed it away untasted (how I loathe beef-tea now!) when she whispered something to Sarah Ann that sent that tender-hearted maid howling once more from the room.

"He's supped it all," Sarah Ann said, one day, brightening.

"That's a worse sign," said her mistress, "than if he hadn't took none."

I lay on a sofa, pulled close to the fire, and when the doctor came my landlady was always at his heels, Sarah Ann's dismal face showing at the door. The doctor is a personal friend of my own, and each day he said I was improving a little.

"Ah, doctor!" my landlady said, reprovingly.

"He does it for the best," she exclaimed to me, "but I don't hold with doctors as deceive their patients. Why don't he speak out the truth like a man? My husband were told the worst, and so he had time to reconcile himself."

On one of these occasions I summoned up sufficient

energy to send her out of the room; but that only made matters worse.

"Poor gentleman!" I heard her say to Sarah Ann; "he is very violent to-day. I saw he were worse the moment I clapped eyes on him. Sarah Ann, I should n't wonder though we had to hold him down yet."

About an hour afterwards she came in to ask me if I "had come more round to myself," and when I merely turned round on the sofa for reply, she said, in a loud whisper, to Sarah Ann, that I "were as quiet as a lamb now." Then she stroked me and went away.

So attentive was my landlady that she was a ministering angel. Yet I lay on that sofa plotting how to get her out of the room. The plan that seemed the simplest was to pretend sleep, but it was not easily carried out. Not getting any answer from me, she would approach on tiptoe and lean over the sofa, listening to hear me breathe. Convinced that I was still living, she and Sarah Ann began a conversation in whispers, of which I or the deceased husband was the subject. The husband had slept a good deal, too, and it was n't a healthy sign.

"It is n't a good sign," whispered my landlady, "though them as know no better might think it is. It shows he 's getting weaker. When they takes to sleeping in the daytime, it 's only because they do n't have the strength to keep awake."

"Oh, missus!" Sarah Ann would say.

"Better face facts, Sarah Ann," replies my landlady.

In the end I had generally to sit up and confess that I heard what they were saying. My landlady evidently thought this another bad sign.

I discovered that my landlady held receptions in another room, where visitors came who referred to me as her "trial." When she thought me distinctly worse, she put on her bonnet and went out to disseminate the sad news. It was on one of these occasions that Sarah Ann, who had been left in charge of the children, came to me with a serious request.

"Them children," she said, "want awful to see you, and I sort of promised to bring 'em in, if so you did n't mind."

"But, Sarah Ann, they have seen me often, and, though I 'm a good deal better, I do n't feel equal to speaking to them."

Sarah Ann smiled pityingly when I said I felt better, but

she assured me the children only wanted to look at me. I refused her petition, but, on my ultimatum being announced to them, they set up such a roar that, to quiet them, I called them in.

They came one at a time. Sophia, the eldest, came first. She looked at me very solemnly, and then said bravely that if I liked she would kiss me. As she had a piece of flannel tied round her face, and was swollen in the left cheek, I declined this honor, and she went off much relieved. Next came Tommy, who sent up a shriek as his eyes fell on me, and had to be carried off by Sarah Ann. Johnny was bolder and franker, but addressed all his remarks to Sarah Ann. First, he wanted to know if he could touch me, and, being told he could, he felt my face all over. Then, he wanted to see the "spouter." The "spouter" was a spray through which Sarah Ann blew coolness on my head, and Johnny had heard of it with interest. He refused to leave the room until he had been permitted to saturate me and my cushion.

I am so much better now that even my landlady knows I am not dying. I suppose she is glad that it is so, but at the same time she resents it. There is an impression in the house that I am a fraud. They call me by my name as yet, but soon again I shall be the parlor.

J. M. Barrie.

SAUNDERS McGLASHAN'S COURTSHIP.

Saunders McGlashan was a hand-loom weaver in a rural part of Scotland. In his early youth his father died and left him with the care of his mother and the younger children. He was a gray-haired man now. The bairns were married and awa'. His old mother, on whom he had lavished the most tender care, was lying beside his father in the kirkyard. He returned to the house alone. He sat down in his father's chair, crowned with a priceless crown of deserved blessing, but there was no voice to welcome him.

"What 'll I dae?" he said. "I think I 'll just keep the hoose mysel'."

But when winter set in, his trials began. One dark morning he awoke and said: "What needs I lie gautin' here? I 'll rise and get a licht." So he got his flint and steel and tinder box, and set to work. The sparks from the flint and steel would not ignite the tinder. He struck vehemently, missed the flint, and drove the steel deep into his knuckles. " I said in my haste this mornin' that I wud hae a wife, and noo I say in my solemn leisure, this very day I shall have a wife."

Instinct told him that when he went a-wooing his best dress should go on; and looking in the glass he said: " I canna gang to see the lassies wi' a beard like that." The shaving done, he rubbed his chin, saying with great simplicity, " I think that should dae for the lassies noo." Then he turned and admired himself in the glass, for vanity is the last thing that dies in a man.

" Ye 're no a very ill-looking man after a' Saunders; but it 's a' very weel bein' guid lookin' and well-drest, but what woman am I gaun to seek for my wife? "

He got at length a paper and pencil and wrote down with great deliberation six female names in large half-text, carefully dotting all the " i's " and stroking all the " t's " and surveyed the list as follows:

" That's a' the women I mind about. There's no great choice among them; let me see," putting on his spectacles, "it's no wise-like gaun courtin' when a body needs to wear specs. Several o' them I've never spoken till, but I suppose that's of no consequence in this case. There's Mary Young; she's not very young at ony rate. Elspeth McFarlane; but she's blind o' the recht e'e, and it's not necessary that Saunders McGlashan should marry an imperfect woman. Kirsty Forsyth; she 's been married twice already, an' surely twa men 's enough for ony woman. Mary Morrison, a bonnie woman; but she 's gotten a confounded lang tongue, an' they say the hair upon her heid's no her ain hair. I 'm certain it's her ain tongue at ony rate! Jeannie Millar, wi' plenty o' siller—not to be despised. Janet Henderson, wi' plenty o' love. I ken that she has a gude heart, for she was kind to her mither lang bedfast. Noo which o' thae six will I go to first? I think the first four can bide a wee, but the last twa— siller and love! love and siller! Eh, wadna it be grand if a person could get them baith! but that's no allowed in the Christian dispensation. The patriarchs had mair liberty. Abraham wud just hae ta 'en them baith, but I 'm no Abraham. If I bring Janet Henderson to my fireside and she sits at that side darnin' stockin' and I sit at this side readin' after my day's wark, an' I lauch ower to her an' she lauchs ower tae me, isna that heaven upon earth? A body can get on in this warld withoot siller, but they canno get on in the warld withoot love. I'll gie Janet Henderson the first offer."

He put on his best Sabbath-day hat and issued forth into the street. Instantly at all the windows commanding a view of the street there were female noses flattened against the panes. Voices might be heard crying, "Mither! mither! mither! Come here! come here! Look! look! look! There's Saunders McGlashan wi' his beard aff, and his Sabbath-day claes on in the middle of the week! He's lookin' awfu' melancholy. I wonder wha's dead."

Quite unconscious of the sensation he was creating, he walked gravely on toward the house of Janet Henderson.

"Lord preserve me, Saunders, is that you? A sicht o' you's guid for sair een! Come awa into the fire. What's up wi' ye the day, Saunders? Ye're awfu' weel lickit up, ye are. I never saw you lookin' sae handsome. What is't ye're after?"

"I'm gaun aboot seeking a wife."

"Eh, Saunders, if that's what ye want, ye needna want that very lang, I'm thinkin'."

"But ye dinna seem to understand me; it's you I want for my wife."

"Saunders McGlashan! think shame o' yoursel', makin' a fool o' a young person in that manner."

"I'm makin' nae fool o' ye, Janet. This very day I'm determined to hae a wife. You are the first that I have spoken till. I houp there's nae offense, Janet. I meant nae offense. Eh! oh! very well; if that's the way o't, it canna be helped;" and, slowly unfolding the paper which he had taken from his waistcoat pocket, "I have several other women's names markit down here tae ca' upon."

She saw the man meant business, stopped her spinning, looked down, was long lost in thought, raised her head, and broke the silence as follows:

"Saunders (ahem!) McGlashan (ahem!), I've given your serious offer great reflection. I've spoken to my heart, and the answer's come back to my tongue. I'm sorry tae hurt your feelin's, Saunders, but what the heart speaketh the tongue repeateth. A body maun act in thae matters according to their conscience, for they maun gie an account at the last. So I think, Saunders,—I think I'll just—I'll just—" covering her face with her apron—"I'll just tak' ye. Eh! Saunders, gae 'wa' wi' ye! gae 'wa'!"

But the maiden did not require to resist, for he made no attack, but solemnly sat in his seat and solemnly said: "I'm rale muckle obleeged to ye, Janet. It'll no be necessary to ca' on ony o' thae ither lassies noo!"

He rose, thinking it was all over, and turned toward the door; but the maiden was there first, with her back at the door, and said: "Lord preserve me! what have I done? If my neebors come tae ken that I've ta'en you at the very first offer, they'll point the finger of scorn at me and say, ahint my back, as lang as I live, 'that woman was deein' for a man;' so ye maun come every day for the next month, and come in daylicht, so they'll a' see ye comin' an' gaun, and they'll say, 'that woman's no easy courtit, I can tell ye. The puir man's wearin' his shoon aff his feet!' For, Saunders, though I'll be your wife, Saunders, I'm determined to hae my dues o' courtship a' the same."

She lit the lamp of love in his heart at last. For the first time in his long life he felt the unmistakable, holy, heavenly glow; his heart broke into a full storm of love, and, stooping down, he took her yielding hand in his, and said: "Yes, I wull; yes, I wull! I'll come twice every day, my Jo! my Jo—Jaanet!"

Before the unhappy man knew where he was, he had kissed the maiden, who was long expecting it. But the man blushed crimson, feeling guilty of a crime which he thought no woman could forgive, for it was the first kiss he had gotten or given in fifty long years, while the woman stood with a look of supreme satisfaction, and said to him:

"Eh! Saunders McGlashan, isna that rale refreshin'?"

Anonymous.

A GOWK'S ERRANT.

In the village of S——, Perthshire, lived Willie Waddel, wright-joiner, coffin-maker, etc. An honest, hardworking chiel' was Willie. A neebor o' his had occasion to be owre ae mornin' at Dauvid Grant's, and fan him in a sair state about the loss o' a coo that had choked hersel' wi' a turnip thro' the nicht.

Dauvid had two or three acres o' lan' about twa miles frae S——, and was thocht tae ha'e some bawbees i' the bank, and tho' he had only himsel' and Janet, his wife, tae keep, yet the loss o' a coo was a gey serious maiter.

After he had heard o' Dauvid's lamentations, and had set aff on the road hame, he thocht tae himsel' he micht mak' a guid lauch ower puir Dauvid's misfortin'. It was the first o' April; and if he could manage to send Willie Waddel ower tae Dauvid Grant's wi' the strauchtin'-board on a gowk's errant, garran him believe Janet was deid instead o' the coo, it would be a gran' joke. It was nae sunner thocht upon than it was wrocht upon. As soon as he got to S—— he gaes awa' up tae a wee widden erection Willie had dignified wi' the name o' the warkshop.

"Weel, Willie, what are ye busy wi' the day?" quo' he, as he entered.

"No muckle,"· says Willie; "jist makin' a wee chair for Sandy MacGregor's youngest ane."

"Ye'll hae tae let that stan' the noo then, I doot, an' tak' in han' wi' a job that's in a greater hurry, but ane ye'll no like sae weel, I'm thinkin'."

"Od, it'll be a queer job I'll no like the noo, and wark sae slack. Let's hear what it is, man."

"Weel, ye'll tak' yer strauchtin'-boord and gae a wa' ower tae Dauvid Grant's. He's fau' in wi a sair loss, puir man, och, hon', death's aye busy."

"What!" cries Willie, "is Janet dead? What was the maiter? What did she dee of?"

"She choked herself."

"Losh, that's extraordinar'! Dauvid will miss her sair; she was a clever-handed woman was Janet. I'll awa ower this meenit," and, throwing down his hammer, he hurried tae the hoose, and bade his mither mak' his parritch and get oot his Sunday claes as soon as possible, as he was wanted in a hurry at Dauvid Grant's. Away he gaes, wi' his boord ower his shouther, and wi' nae mair idea he was gaun a gouk's errant than the man i' the mune. When he got tae the hoose he set the boord doon at the door, and steppin' in got Dauvid takin' a reek o' the pipe.

"Who's a wi' ye the day?" quo' Willie.

"Jist middlin; but tak' a sate an' rest ye."

"I'm real vexed tae hear o' yer loss. Ye'll miss her sair, I hae nae doot."

"It's a bit hard job for me, but I maun try an' bear it. Ye ken we're tell't tae bear oor trials wi' patience."

"I'm vera glad ye tak' that view o't, for I was feart ye micht brak doon a'thegither."

"Hoot, Willie, there's nae fear o' that. I maun look about an' see an' get anither, for I canna well want ane."

"'Deed, that's true enough, but ye'll no' be in a hurry for awhile."

"Od, I dinna ken; the sunner the better, I think. I dinna see ony use o' puttin' aff time; in fact, I hae my e'en on ane already, but I am feared she's a wee ower auld."

"I would na thocht they were sae easy gotten," says Willie.

"Man, when ye hae twa or three bawbees i' yer pouch, ye can get pick an' waie o' them. Sae, I'll tak' time an' see I get a guid ane when I'm at it."

"Weel, Dauvid, I think ye micht let the ane ye hae decently awa' afore ye think o' fillin' her place."

"I dinna see hoo that wad mak' muckle difference; hoo-ever, I was jist intendin' tae howk a hole in the yaird this afternin, an' pit her in 't. Ye see I canna sell her noo, folks are sae strict."

"Dauvid Grant! dae ye no' think burnin' shame o' yerself tae speak tae me in that manner, and ye an elder o' the kirk? But I'll no' let the maiter rest like that; I'll awa' tae the minister an' gie him an account o' yer conduct, ye auld shameless heathen." And wi' that he oot at the door. The minister saw him comin', and said:

"Well, William, what's the matter?"

"There is something wrang. I wish ye wid come awa' over tae Dauvid Grant's, for I think he's gaen oot o' his judgment."

"What is wrong with David?"

"Weel, ye see, his wife, Janet, is deid; she choked hersel' thro' the nicht, an' I was sent for tae gae ower wi' the strauchtin'-boord. Well, when I gaed in, judge o' my surprise when he began tellin' me he had the thochts o' gettin' anither wife as soon as possible—in fact, he has his e'en on ane a'ready; and when I telt him he micht aye get the ane he had awa' first, od, if the man didna tell me he would pit her in a hole in the yaird if he couldna sell her. But he's demented; his grief has turned his brain, I think."

"David's wife dead! I'm surprised that I had not heard of it. I'll get my hat and go along with you," said the minister. When they got back they found Dauvid steppin' thro' the floor, perplexed at Willie's proceedings.

"I'm grieved to hear of your sad affliction," the minister began; "and I am surprised you did not send for me."

"I canna understandin' what ye're makin' sic a work aboot. It's me that'll hae tae bear the loss, an' I was na thinkin' o' havin' ony bother aboot it," said Dauvid.

"After what has fallen from your own lips, I see there is no use trying to reason with you. I am sorry to think such a man as you are—a member of my church—I will call a meeting and have you expelled," said the minister.

"Ye can ca' a meetin' o' the Presbytery gin ye like, for onything I care."

"I shall stay here no longer to be insulted!" cried the minister, when he was stopped by Willie.

"Od, sir, ye canna richty leave the hoose until we come tae some kind o' an understandin'. Ye see, I has broucht ower my strauchtin'-boord, an' I'll awa' an' get some o' the neebors, an' get her laid oot in a respectable an' Christian-like manner."

"Strauchtin'-boord for a coo! Lay her oot in a Christian-like manner! What on earth does the man mean!" said Dauvid.

"What dae I mean! Yer wife lyin' deid here, an' you hae the impudence tae speer what I mean!" said Willie.

"My wife dead! Hae ye ta'en leave o' yer senses, man?"

"I'm afraid there's some mistake here. Is your wife dead, David?" said the minister.

"Gouid be thankit, no, sir; at least she wasna twa hours syne."

"And where is she?"

"Oh! she gaed awa' ower tae her brother's. Ye see, Nellie's lady's deid and left her sax hunner pounds, so Janet gaed awa' ower tae hear o' the news. But wha' sent ye here wi' the boord?" quo' Dauvid.

"Od, Peter Low cam' up tae the shop this mornin', an' telt me tae come awa' wi' the boord, as ye had met wi' a sair loss."

"Did he say Janet was deid?"

"Noo, he didna' jist say that when I mind, but of course I thoucht it could be nae ither body."

"I see it a' noo!" cried Dauvid, fa'in into a chair roarin' an' lauchin'. "Low was ower here this mornin', an' I was tellin' him aboot the death o' a coo, an' the rogue has gaen and made a gowk o' puir Willie ower the head o' it. Did it never strike ye, Willie, that this was the first o' April?"

"Never until this minute!" exclaimed Willie. "Weel, that cow's the gowan. Od, he has sent me a gowk's errant, an' nae mistak'."

"Good-bye, good-bye," cries the minister, rinnin' oo' at the door, and they heard him lauchin' a' the way tae the manse.

"Weel, Willie," observed Dauvid, "ye hae done me mar guid than onything I hae got this while. But dinna look so sheepish, man ; there's nae harm done. I'm thinkin' o' gaun ower tae Janet's brither's, an' ye'll come awa' ower wi' me, and see Nellie."

After some coaxin' Willie consented tae gae wi' him, for he had a soft side tae Nellie, and was na' ill tae persuade.

On the road Dauvid wid stop every wee bit and ejaculate, "Strauchtin'-boord for a coo! Dacency and Christianity!" and syne roar as if he was gaun intae a fit. At last Willie told him, unless he'd compose himsel' an' not say a word aboot it when they gaed tae the house, he wadna gae anither fit. At last Dauvid promised to say nothing about it. When they got there Willie was puzzled what tae dae wi' the boord, for he had brought it wi' him as it was a bit on the road hame. However, he got it smuggled in ahint the door, an' in they went. Willie got a hearty welcome frae the old folks, and a kind glance from Nellie.

After they had got their dinner, an' Nellie an' Willie close thegither in the corner, wi' his han' in hers, the servant lassie cam' in runnin' an' cryin':

"O mistress, wha's deid? wha's deid? because I was ahint the door for the besom, and there's a strauchtin'-boord there."

Dauvid, wha was twistin' in his chair wi' a face like a nar'wast win', burst out wi' a roar o' lauchin', an' screeched an' yelled an' cried, "O Willie! hae mercy, an' let me tell them, or I'll burst."

"Tell them, an' be hanged tae ye," says Willie, i' the pet. "As well tell them noo, for they'll soon hear on't at any rate."

After Dauvid had telt them the story ye could hae tied them a' wi' a strae, an' Willie caught the infection an' lauched as loud as any o' them. Willie left for hame, wi' mony kind invitations no tae be a stranger among them, which he took advantage of, an' at last got Nellie for a wife.

He's noo in Dundee, in a big way o' daein', an' tae a' accounts Nellie's six hunner pounds hae doubled itself. His customers are sometimes surprised when he gaes for the strauchtin'-boord to see Willie turn red i' the fac' and Nellie fa' intae the lauchin ; but they dinna a' ken what you an' me kens.

Anonymous.

THE TWO RUNAWAYS.

Years ago there dwelt in Middle Georgia a wealthy but eccentric bachelor planter, known by the name of Major Crawford Worthington. He was the owner of a number of slaves, to whom, on the whole, he was very kind. One of them, named Isam, had been with him from childhood; in fact, they had sort of grown up together. Isam had an annual runaway freak, which usually lasted about a fortnight. The strangeness of this action on the part of his slave troubled the Major more than a little, not that he cared an iota for his loss of time, nor for his bad example, but it galled him to think that there was anything in connection with a negro which he could not fathom. At last the Major struck upon a plan whereby he should solve the mystery, and he accordingly threatened Isam with dire punishment if he should go off another time without letting him know. The threat had the desired effect; the Major was duly informed; whereupon, to the astonishment of the negro, the master signified his intention to accompany him on his expedition, and accordingly the two runaways started. For nearly two weeks they remained in the woods, only a few miles distant from their home, where they lived in a semi-civilized state, hunting, fishing, and foraging; both, indeed, enjoying themselves hugely. A day or two prior to their return, they had been out foraging for dinner, and were on their way to camp, heavily laden with their spoils. The two had just reached the edge of the canebrake, beyond which lay the camp, and were entering the narrow path, when a magnificent buck came sweeping through, and collided with Isam with such force and suddenness as to crush and spatter his watermelons into a pitiful ruin, and throw the negro violently to the ground. Instantly the frightened man seized the threatening antlers and held on, yelling lustily for help. The deer made several ineffectual efforts to free himself, during which he dragged the negro right and left without difficulty, but, finding escape impossible, turned fiercely upon his unwilling captor, and tried to drive the terrible horns through his writhing body.

"O Lord! O Lord!" screamed Isam; "O Lord! Mass' Craffud, cum holp me tu'n dis buck loos'."

The laugh died away from Major Worthington's lips. None knew better than he the danger into which Isam had plunged. Not a stick, brush, stone, or weapon of any description was at hand, except his small pocketknife. Hastily opening that, he rushed upon the deer. Isam's eyes were bursting from their sockets, and appealed piteously for the help his stentorian voice was frantically imploring, until the woods rang with his agony. Major Worthington caught the nearest antler with his left hand, and made a fierce lunge at the animal's throat. But the point of the knife was missing, and only a trifling wound was inflicted. The next instant, the deer met the new attack with a rush that carried Isam with it, and thrust the Major to the ground, the knife falling out of reach. Seeing this, the negro let go his hold, rolled out of the way, and with a mighty effort literally ran upon the top of a branching haw-bush, where he lay spread out like a bat, and moaning piteously.

"Stick ter 'im, Mass' Craffud, stick ter 'im! Wo' deer! wo' deer! Stick ter 'im, Mass' Craffud."

And the Major stuck. Retaining his presence of mind, he threw his left arm over the deer's neck, and, still holding with his right the antler, looked about for Isam, who had so mysteriously disappeared.

"Stick ter 'im, Mass' Craffud, stick ter 'im. Hit's better fur one ter die den bofe! Hole 'im, Mass' Craffud, hole 'im! Wo' deer! wo' deer! Stick ter 'im, Mass' Craffud, steddy! Look out fur es ho'n! Wo' deer! Steddy, Mass' Craffud!"

By this time the struggles of the beast had again ceased, and, wearied from his double encounter, he stood with his head pulled down to the ground half astride the desperate man, who was holding on for life. Whether Major Worthington was frightened or not it is hard to say; probably he was; but there was no doubt about his being angry when he saw Isam spread out in the haw-bush, and heard his address. As soon as he caught his breath, he burst forth with:

"You black rascal! why do n't you come—down out of that—bush and help—me?" Isam's face was pitiful in its expression. His teeth chattered, and he fairly shook the bush with his trembling.

"Don', Mass' Craffud, don'; you ain' got no time ter cuss now. Lif' up yo' voice en' pray! Ef ev'r er man had er call ter pray, you dun got it now."

"If ever—I get loose from this—brute—you scoundrel— I'll not leave a—whole bone in your body!"

"Don' say dat, Mass' Craffud, don'! you must n't let de sun go down on yo' wraf! O Lord! don' you mine nuth'n he es er sayin' now, cos he ain' 'spons'b'l'. Ef de bes' aingil you got wuz down dere in his fix, dey ain' no tell'n' w'at ud happ'n, er w'at sorter langwidge he'd let loos'. Wo' deer! wo' deer! Stick ter 'im, Mass' Craffud, stick ter 'im. Steddy, deer! steddy, Mass' Craffud!"

Again the deer commenced to struggle, and by this time the Major's breath was almost gone, and his anger had given way to unmistakable apprehension. He realized that he was in a most desperate plight, and that the only hope of rescue lay in the frightened negro up in the haw-bush. He changed his tactics when the deer rested again.

"Isam," he said, gently.

"Yes, honey."

"Isam, come and help me, old fellow."

"Mass' Craffud, dere ain' nuthin' I woodn' do fur you, but hit's better fur one ter die'n two. Hit's a long sight better."

"But there is no danger, Isam ; none whatever. Just you come down and with your knife hamstring the brute. I'll hold him."

"No, sah! no, sah! no, sah!" said Isam, loudly, and with growing earnestness. "No, sah! it won' wuk! no, sah! You er in fur hit now, Mass' Craffud, en' et can't be holped. Dere ain' nuthin' kin save yer but de good Lord, en' He ain' go'n'ter, less'n you ax 'im 'umble like, en' er b'liev'n 'en es mussy. I prayed w'en I wuz down dere, Mass' Craffud, dat I did, en' look w'at happ'n. Didn' He sen' you like er aingil, en' didn' He git me up hyah safe en' wholesum? Dat He did, en' He nev'r spec' dis nigg'r war go'n'ter fling esse'f und'r dat deer arter He trubbl' Hisse'f to show 'im up hyah. Stick ter 'im, Mass' Craffud, stick ter 'im. Wo' deer! wo' deer! Look ou' fur es ho'n! Stick ter 'im, Mass' Craffud. Dere, now—t'ank de Lord!"

Again the Major got a breathing-spell. The deer, in his struggles, had gotten under the haw-bush, and the Major renewed his earnest negotiations.

"Isam, if you will get down—and cut this brute's legs— I will give you your freedom."

Isam answered with a groan.

"And fifty acres—of land." Again that pitiful moan.

"And—a mule and a—year's rations." The Major paused from force of circumstances. After awhile the answer came:

"Mass' Craffud?"

"Well?"

"You know dis nigg'r b'en hard-work'n en' hones' en' look atter you en' yo'n all es life."

"Yes, Isam," said the Major, "you have been—a faithful, honest—nigger." There was another pause. Perhaps this was too much for Isam. But he continued after a little while:

"Well, lemme tell you, honey, dere ain' nuthin' you got er kin git w'at'll tem' dis nigg'r ter git down dere. W'y," and his voice assumed a most earnest and argumentative tone, "deed 'n hit ud be 'sultin' de Lord. Ain' He dun got me up hyar out'n de way, en' don' He 'spec' me fur ter stay? You reck'n He got nuth'n 'tall ter do but keep puttin' Isam back up er tree? No, sah! He dun 'ten ter me, en' ef you got enny dif'culty, you en' de deer kin fight it out. Hit's my bizness jes ter keep er prayin'. Wo' deer! wo' deer! Steddy, Mass' Craffud. Dere now—tank de Lord!"

Again the Major defeated the beast's struggles, and there came a truce. But the man was well-nigh exhausted, and saw that unless something was done in his behalf he must soon yield up the fight. So he decided to touch the negro's superstitious side:

"Isam," he said, slowly and impressively. But Isam was praying. The Major could hardly trust his ears when he heard the words:

"But, Lord, don' let 'm 'peer'sh fo' yo' eyes. He's b'en er bad man. He cuss 'n' sware, 'n' play keerds, 'n' bet on horse-race, 'n' drink whisky——"

"Isam——"

"En' he steal—goodness, he tek ter steal'n' like er duck ter water. Roast'n yers, watermilluns, chick'n—nuthin' too bad fur 'im——"

"Isam——"

The word came upward in tones of thunder. Even Isam was obliged to regard it.

"Yes, sah?"

"Isam, I am going to die."

Isam gave a yell that ought to have been heard a mile away.

"Oh! do n't let 'im die! Skeer 'im, skeer 'im, Lord; but don' let 'im die!"

"Yes," continued the Major, "I am going to die; but let me tell you something, Isam. I have been looking into this beast's eyes until I recognize him." A sound came from the haw-bush like the hiss of a snake, as the negro with ashen face and beaded brow gasped out an unintelligible word. The right chord had been touched at last. "You remember Dr. Sam, who died last year?" Isam's only reply was a moan that betrayed an agony too deep for expression. "Well, this is Dr. Sam; he got loose the other day when the plug fell out of the tree, and he and I will never give you another hour of peace as long as you live."

The sentence was never finished. With a shriek that was blood-curdling in its intensity of fear and horror, the negro came crashing down through the bush with his hands full of leaves, straight upon the deer.

This was the crisis.

The frightened animal made one desperate plunge, taking the startled Major by surprise, and the next instant found himself free. He did not remain upon the scene, or he would have beheld the terrified negro get upon his feet, run round in a frenzy of terror, and close his last circle at the foot of the bush, up which he scurried again like a squirrel, old as he was. The Major lay flat upon his back, after trying in vain to rise. Then the reaction came. He fixed his eye upon the negro above, and laughed until the tears washed the dirt from his face; and Isam, holding his head up so that his vision could encompass the narrow horizon, said slowly and impressively:

"Mass' Craffud, ef de Lord had n't 'sist'd on Isam cum'n down ter run dat deer off, 'spec' by dis time you'd been er flopp'n yo' wings up yander, er else sput'n on er gridi'on down yander." And from his elevated perch Isam indicated the two extremes of eternity with an eloquent sweep of his hand.

But the Major had small time for laughter or recrimination. In the distance there rang out faintly the full-mouthed cry of a hound. Isam heard it. For him it was at once a welcome and a stimulating sound. Gliding to the ground, he helped the wearied Major to his feet, and started on a run for the boat, crying:

"Run, Mass' Craffud! wors'n er deer 's cummin'. Hit 's dem folks w'at know about dat corn 'en watermilluns ye tuke from dere patch, 'en yer can't 'splain nuthin' ter er houn' dog."

Broken down as he was, the Major realized that there was wisdom in the negro's words, and followed as best he could. The camp traps were thrown into the boat, and the little bark was launched. A minute later the form of a great, thirsty-looking hound appeared on the scene. But the hunters who came after found naught beyond the signs of a camp.

How Isam ever settled his difficulty needs no explanation. But it may interest the reader to know that one day he bore a message and a check that settled the corn and melon debt; and they tell it in Middle Georgia that every year thereafter, until the war-cloud broke over the land, whenever the catalpa worm crept upon the leaf, two runaways fled from Wood-haven and dwelt in the swamps, "loos' en free."

H. S. Edwards.

A STUDY IN NERVES.

A small door at the right of the pulpit opened, and he walked to his place before the altar. It had already been indicated by an inconspicuous chalk mark on the floor. His best man followed a little behind him at an interval which had required frequent rehearsing the evening before. He did not catch his chalk mark for an instant, and overstepped it, but he retreated cautiously, still facing the enemy, and carefully covered it with his foot.

People had been pouring into the church for the last half hour. At last all those who had been invited had been given the front seats. There was a slight flutter in the audience when the bride's mother and her two married sisters were escorted to their seats on the opposite side of the aisle from that set apart for the bridegroom's family, in the suggestively antagonistic manner which is customary when two houses are about to be united.

From his chalk mark by the altar he gazed rather unin-
telligently at the blur of faces turned towards him. Why
should they all be staring at him? Was his cravat slipping
up over his collar? Only a hoarse but reassuring "You're
all right, old man!" brought his wandering hand back to
his side again. But why did n't the music begin?

The vast aggregated stare of the throng in front of him
gradually resolved itself into its elements. It struck him
that every one seemed remarkably solemn, as if it were an
occasion for sadness rather than for smiles. Why could n't
they look pleasant about it? Then it occurred to him that
he felt solemn himself, and the cheerful and sympathetic
grin on the face of one of his still-bachelor classmates, whom
he had suddenly discovered, seemed decidedly out of place
and frivolous.

But none the less, something seemed required of him.
Should he grin back, or should he merely wink in acknowl-
edgment? The rehearsal had not prepared him for this
emergency. He shirked the responsibility of deciding, and
looked away.

Why did n't the music begin? Why did n't they open those
doors? Had anything gone wrong? Had any one arrived
at the last moment to announce some good cause why they
two should not be joined together in holy wedlock? No,
thank heaven, he could face the world on that score. None
the less, he felt that it must be fearfully late. Yet he had
been told that everything was all ready, and that it was time
for him to take his place on his chalk mark. What were
they waiting for? Had he not waited long enough already?

Why did n't the music begin? If he could only look at
his watch and see what time it really was, it would relieve his
mind. He remembered that he had never seen it done, and
kept his hands fast at the seams of his trousers, out of temptation.

Suddenly the doors were pushed back and the bridal
party appeared in the opening. Behind the double file of
somber-hued ushers his eye caught a bit of color from the
dress of one of the bridesmaids, and then rested for a moment upon a little cloud of pure swanlike white. Thank
heaven, there she was. And as she was there, why did n't the
music begin? The tallest usher changed his position, and
the little white cloud disappeared behind his broad black
shoulder. Confound him, why could n't he stand still, when

that was the first glimpse he had had of her for goodness
only knew how long!

There they all stood in the doorway, his seven best friends
and the girl's usher. He supposed there was no reason now,
from his point of view, why that unfortunate should not be
one of his friends, too. He felt that he had never appreciated the fellow's good qualities so strongly as at that moment. He remembered that when she had at first spoken to
him of her usher he had suggested to her the inadvisability
of inviting a man to be present at his own funeral, and how
she had insisted that her usher she would have. There he
was, so why did n't the music begin?

He saw the black back of the organist suddenly fill out as
with the responsibility of his exalted position, and the next
instant the familiar "tum-tum-ti-tum" pealed through the
church. He felt that his troubles were over, for anything
was better than that silent staring.

For a moment he could not make out what had all at
once changed the appearance of things so much. Then he
discovered that the sea of faces had turned into an equally
bewildering exhibition of back hair. What was the matter
with his mind, anyway? Why could n't he stop thinking?

"Tum-tum-ti-tum." The music not only had begun, but
it seemed to him as if it had always been playing. Why did
they not start? What was the use of all that rehearsing if
they did n't know what to do when the time came? "Tum-
tum-ti-tum," played the organist.

It seemed an easy matter for eight grown men to walk up
a broad aisle together, two by two, a certain distance apart.
They had done it half a dozen times the night before. It
was perfectly simple. They were to be two pews apart. Or
was it three pews? "Ti-tum-tum-ti-tum."

He did n't know which it was, but it was no affair of his,
anyway. All he had to do was to stay on his chalk mark
until it was time for him to go to that other chalk mark over
there to receive her. There it was, a little rubbed out, to be
sure, but seeming to him like the guiding star to the path
of matrimony, and to it he had hitched his wagon. A
scarcely breathed "They 're off !" at his elbow, brought him
back to earth again. They were coming through the door.
It was two pews apart after all. He knew he had been right.
He noticed that the girl's usher seemed as cheerful as could
be expected of him. He wondered how he would feel if he

had to change places with him. How had it happened that their places were not changed? He knew that he was a better fellow than the girl's usher, of course, but how had he managed to make her believe it? He knew better men than he who had been girls' ushers in their time.

"Tum-tum-ti-tum."

The two ushers in the lead were within twenty feet of him. Why did n't they move faster? It made him nervous to see them advancing upon him like that. It was like the car of Juggernaut or the inexorable march of time. They were bringing him the happiness of his whole life. Why did n't they bring it to him faster? There they were, coming at him in the same relentless way. All of them were the pendulum, swinging nearer and nearer, to push him into the pit.

"Tum-tum-ti-tum-tum."

The two ushers in the lead were so near him that he could see the pearls on the pins he had given them. There she was, Heaven bless her! What was the sense of all this bother? Why could n't he rush down the aisle and get her, all by himself? His eye fell upon the relentless chalk mark before him, and he shifted his weight uneasily from one foot to the other.

The two files of ushers had begun to deploy on either side of him, each man trying to keep one eye on his alignment, and with the other to steer for the haven of his own particular chalk mark. As the last one disappeared from view behind him, he felt that he never wanted to see one of them again after the way they had just treated him. The next moment the bridesmaids were tripping by him, guided to their positions by that unerring instinct in regard to all that pertains to weddings, which is every woman's birthright.

Then the final "tum-tum-ti-tum" rang out triumphantly into every corner of the church. He rushed to the now benignly-inviting chalk mark, and in an instant her hand was in his own.

Anonymous.

PICKWICK IN THE WRONG BEDROOM.

Having carefully drawn the curtains of his bed on the outside, Mr. Pickwick sat down on the rush-bottomed chair, and leisurely divested himself of his shoes and gaiters. He then took off and folded up his coat, waistcoat, and neck-cloth, and slowly drawing on his tasseled nightcap, secured it firmly on his head by tying beneath his chin the strings which he always had attached to that article of dress. It was at this moment that the absurdity of his recent bewilderment struck upon his mind. Throwing himself back in the rush-bottomed chair, Mr. Pickwick laughed to himself so heartily that it would have been quite delightful to any man of well-constituted mind to have watched the smiles that expanded his amiable features as they shone forth from beneath the nightcap.

"It is the best idea," said Mr. Pickwick to himself, smil-ing till he almost cracked the nightcap strings, "it is the best idea, my losing myself in this place, and wandering about those staircases, that I ever heard of. Droll, droll, very droll." Here Mr. Pickwick smiled again, a broader smile than before, and was about to continue the process of undressing, in the best possible humor, when he was sud-denly stopped by a most unexpected interruption, to-wit, the entrance into the room of some person with a candle, who, after locking the door, advanced to the dressing-table and set down the light upon it.

The smile that played on Mr. Pickwick's features was instantaneously lost in a look of the most unbounded and wonder-stricken surprise. The person, whoever it was, had come in so suddenly and with so little noise, that Mr. Pick-wick had had no time to call out, or oppose their entrance. Who could it be? A robber? Some evil-minded person who had seen him come upstairs with a handsome watch in his hand, perhaps. What was he to do?

The only way in which Mr. Pickwick could catch a glimpse of his mysterious visitor with the least danger of being seen himself, was by creeping on to the bed, and peeping out from between the curtains on the opposite side. To this manœuvre he accordingly resorted. Keeping the curtains carefully closed with his hand, so that nothing more of him could be seen than his face and nightcap, and putting on his spectacles, he mustered up courage and looked out.

Mr. Pickwick almost fainted with horror and dismay. Standing before the dressing glass was a middle-aged lady, in yellow curl-papers, busily engaged in brushing what ladies call their "back hair." However the unconscious middle-aged lady came into that room, it was quite clear that she contemplated remaining there for the night; for she had brought a rush-light and shade with her, which, with praiseworthy precaution against fire, she had stationed in a basin on the floor, where it was glimmering away like a gigantic lighthouse in a particularly small piece of water.

"Bless my soul," thought Mr. Pickwick, "what a dreadful thing!"

"Hem!" said the lady; and in went Mr. Pickwick's head, with automaton-like rapidity.

"I never met with anything so awful as this," thought poor Mr. Pickwick, the cold perspiration starting in drops upon his nightcap. "Never. This is fearful."

It was quite impossible to resist the urgent desire to see what was going forward. So out went Mr. Pickwick's head again. The prospect was worse than before. The middle-aged lady had finished arranging her hair; had carefully enveloped it in a muslin nightcap with a small plaited border, and was gazing pensively on the fire.

"This matter is growing alarming," reasoned Mr. Pickwick with himself. "I can't allow things to go on in this way. By the self-possession of that lady, it is clear to me that I must have come into the wrong room. If I call out she'll alarm the house; but if I remain here, the consequences will be still more frightful."

Mr. Pickwick, it is quite unnecessary to say, was one of the most modest and delicate-minded of mortals. The very idea of exhibiting his nightcap to a lady overpowered him, but he had tied those confounded strings in a knot, and do what he would, he couldn't get it off. The disclosure must be made. There was only one other way of doing it. He shrunk behind the curtains, and called out very loudly:

"Ha—hum!"

That the lady started at this unexpected sound was evident, by her falling up against the rushlight shade; that she persuaded herself it must have been the effect of imagination was equally clear, for when Mr. Pickwick, under the impression that she had fainted away stone-dead from fright, ventured to peep out again, she was gazing pensively on the fire as before.

"Most extraordinary female this," thought Mr. Pickwick, popping in again. "Ha—hum!"

These last sounds, so like those in which, as legends inform us, the ferocious giant Blunderbore was in the habit of expressing his opinion that it was time to lay the cloth, were too distinctly audible to be again mistaken for the workings of fancy.

"Gracious Heaven!" said the middle-aged lady. "What is that?"

"It's—it's—only a gentleman, ma'am," said Mr. Pickwick from behind the curtains.

"A gentleman!" said the lady, with a terrific scream.

"It's all over!" thought Mr. Pickwick.

"A strange man!" shrieked the lady. Another instant and the house would be alarmed. Her garments rustled as she rushed toward the door.

"Ma'am," said Mr. Pickwick, thrusting out his head in the extremity of his desperation, "Ma'am!"

Now, although Mr. Pickwick was not actuated by any definite object in putting out his head, it was instantaneously productive of a good effect. The lady, as we have already stated, was near the door. She must pass it, to reach the staircase, and she would most undoubtedly have done so by this time, had not the sudden apparition of Mr. Pickwick's nightcap driven her back into the remotest corner of the apartment, where she stood, staring wildly at Mr. Pickwick, while Mr. Pickwick in his turn stared wildly at her.

"Wretch," said the lady, covering her eyes with her hands, "what do you want here?"

"Nothing, ma'am; nothing whatever, ma'am," said Mr. Pickwick earnestly.

"Nothing!" said the lady, looking up.

"Nothing, ma'am, upon my honor," said Mr. Pickwick, nodding his head so energetically that the tassel of his nightcap danced again. "I am almost ready to sink, ma'am, beneath the confusion of addressing a lady in my nightcap (here the lady hastily snatched off hers), but I can't get it off, ma'am (here Mr. Pickwick gave it a tremendous tug, in proof of the statement). It is evident to me, ma'am, now, that I have mistaken this bedroom for my own. I had not been here five minutes, ma'am, when you suddenly entered it."

"If this improbable story be really true, sir," said the lady, sobbing violently, "you will leave it instantly."

"I will, ma'am, with the greatest pleasure," replied Mr. Pickwick.

"Instantly, sir," said the lady.

"Certainly, ma'am," interposed Mr. Pickwick very quickly. "Certainly, ma'am. I—I—am very sorry, ma'am," said Mr. Pickwick, making his appearance at the bottom of the bed, "to have been the innocent occasion of this alarm and emotion; deeply sorry, ma'am."

The lady pointed to the door. One excellent quality of Mr. Pickwick's character was beautifully displayed at this moment, under the most trying circumstances. Although he had hastily put on his hat over his nightcap, after the manner of the old patrol; although he carried his shoes and gaiters in his hand, and his coat and waistcoat over his arm, nothing could subdue his native politeness.

"I am exceedingly sorry, ma'am," said Mr. Pickwick, bowing very low.

"If you are, sir, you will at once leave the room," said the lady.

"Immediately, ma'am; this instant, ma'am," said Mr. Pickwick, opening the door and dropping both his shoes with a crash in so doing.

"I trust, ma'am," resumed Mr. Pickwick, gathering up his shoes, and turning round to bow again: "I trust, ma'am, that my unblemished character, and the devoted respect I entertain for your sex, will plead as some slight excuse for this—" But before Mr. Pickwick could conclude the sentence the lady had thrust him into the passage, and locked and bolted the door behind him.

*   *   *   *   *   *

"Sam," said Mr. Pickwick, suddenly appearing before him, "where's my bedroom?"

Mr. Weller stared at his master with the most emphatic surprise; and it was not until the question had been repeated three several times, that he turned round and led the way to the long-sought apartment.

"Sam," said Mr. Pickwick as he got into bed, "I have

made one of the most extraordinary mistakes to-night, that ever were heard of."

"Wery likely, sir," replied Mr. Weller, drily.

"But of this I am determined, Sam," said Mr. Pickwick; "that if I were to stop in this house for six months, I would never trust myself about it, alone, again."

"That's the wery prudentest resolution as you could come to, sir," replied Mr. Weller. "You rayther want somebody to look arter you, sir, wen your judgment goes out a wisitin'."

"What do you mean by that, Sam?" said Mr. Pickwick. He raised himself in bed and extended his hand, as if he were about to say something more; but suddenly checking himself, turned round, and bade his valet "Good-night."

"Good-night, sir," replied Mr. Weller. He paused when he got outside the door—shook his head—walked on—stopped—snuffed the candle—shook his head again—and finally proceeded slowly to his chamber, apparently buried in the profoundest meditation.

Charles Dickens.

PATHOS.

The proper rendition of all pieces of *pure pathos* demands chiefly three conditions:

First, Natural voice.

Second, Effusive utterance.

Third, Slide of semitone.

First.—By natural voice we mean the conversational voice, or the voice we all have by nature. Great care should be taken to secure the purest tone, free from all nasal, guttural and pectoral qualities of voice. A clear, pleasant and musical tone is indispensable in securing the best effects.

Second.—The utterance must be effusive, *i. e.*, flowing from the mouth in a continuous stream of sound. If a staccato or commonplace style of utterance is indulged in, the reading will necessarily degenerate into mere talk, and crush out all sympathetic feeling.

Third.—In ordinary, unimpassioned speech, the voice passes through the interval of *one tone* on the musical scale, in the utterance of each word, thus:

"That quarter   most the   skilful Greeks   an - noy,

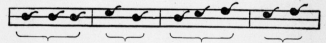

Monotone. Falling Ditone. Rising Tritone. Rising Ditone.

Where   yon wild   fig trees join the   walls   of Troy."

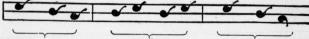

Falling Tritone.   Alternation.   Triad of the Cadence.

The radical pitch is represented by the heads of the notes, and the concrete pitch by the short stems of the notes, which, on observation, will be seen to pass to the note above or below the radical. In short, it is impossible for us to utter a word in unimpassioned speech, from its initiation to its close, without passing up or down the musical scale *one tone*. However, in all plaintive and deeply pathetic moods of mind, we find, on investigation, that the slides of the voice are one-half as long as they are in ordinary discourse. This unconscious slide of the voice on the *minor chord*, as exhibited in the plaintive cry of the child, or the weeping utterance of the bereaved mother, is the chief characteristic of voice necessary to the expression of all pathetic selections.*

The student should now select one of the pieces given under this head, and endeavor to secure the effects which must follow from a careful application of the foregoing suggestions.

It will be found of great service in the acquirement of the semitonic slide, to practice the musical scale, and oftentimes the sympathetic study of a piece, thoroughly saturated with pathetic emotion, is the best aid in the acquisition of the characteristics of voice necessary to the effective rendition of this important class of selections.†

SELECTION FROM ENOCH ARDEN.

He called aloud for Miriam Lane, and said,
" Woman, I have a secret—only swear,
Before I tell you—swear upon the book,
Not to reveal it till you see me dead."
" Dead," clamor'd the good woman; " hear him talk!
I warrant, man, that we shall bring you round."
" Swear," added Enoch, sternly, " on the book."
And on the book, half-frighted, Miriam swore.
Then Enoch, rolling his gray eyes upon her,
" Did you know Enoch Arden, of this town? "
" Know him?" she said; " I knew him far away.

---

* It may be well to note that this pathetic slide is not measured by a half tone in all cases, but follows the voice in all its movements up and down the scale on the third, fifth and octave, always vanishing, however, on a minor chord.

† Exercises on the vowels should constantly be used, or the vowel sounds in the selections you are rendering. Prolong each vowel with as pure and even a tone as possible, in order that the vocal organs may be trained to the manufacture of the clearest musical sounds, thereby ridding the voice of all harsh and unpleasant qualities. Evenness and steadiness of tone can only be secured by perfect control in the management of the breath.

Ay, ay, I mind him coming down the street;
Held his head high, and cared for no man, he."
Slowly and sadly Enoch answer'd her:
" His head is low, and no man cares for him.
I think I have not three days more to live;
I am the man." At which the woman gave
A half incredulous, half hysterical cry.
"You Arden, you! nay,—sure he was a foot
Higher than you be." Enoch said again,
"My God has bow'd me down to what I am;
My grief and solitude have broken me;
Nevertheless, know you that I am he
Who married—but that name has twice been changed—
I married her who married Philip Ray.
Sit, listen!" Then he told her of his voyage,
His wreck, his lonely life, his coming back,
His gazing in on Annie, his resolve,
And how he kept it. As the woman heard,
Fast flow'd the current of her easy tears,
While in her heart she yearn'd incessantly
To rush abroad, all round the little haven,
Proclaiming Enoch Arden and his woes.
But, awed and promise-bounden, she forbore,
Saying only, " See your bairns before you go!
Eh, let me fetch 'em, Arden," and arose,
Eager to bring them down, for Enoch hung
A moment on her words, but then replied:
"Woman, disturb me not now at the last,
But let me hold my purpose till I die.
Sit down again; mark me and understand,
While I have power to speak. I charge you now,
When you shall see her, tell her that I died
Blessing her, praying for her, loving her;
Save for the bar between us, loving her
As when she laid her head beside my own.
And tell my daughter, Annie, whom I saw
So like her mother, that my latest breath
Was spent in blessing her and praying for her.
And tell my son that I died blessing him.
And say to Philip that I blessed him, too;
He never meant us anything but good.
But if my children care to see me dead,
Who hardly knew me living, let them come,

I am their father ; but she must not come,
For my dead face would vex her after-life.
And now there is but one of all my blood
Who will embrace me in the world-to-be:
This hair is his; she cut it off and gave it,
And I have borne it with me all these years,
A'nd thought to bear it with me to my grave ;
But now my mind is changed, for I shall see him,
My babe in bliss: wherefore, when I am gone,
Take, give her this, for it may comfort her;
It will, moreover, be a token to her
That I am he."

    He ceased; and Miriam Lane
Made such a voluble answer, promising all,
That once again he roll'd his eyes upon her,
Repeating all he wish'd, and once again
She promised.

    Then; the third night after this,
While Enoch slumber'd, motionless and pale,
And Miriam watched and dozed at intervals,
There came so loud a calling of the sea
That all the houses in the haven rang.
He woke, he rose, he spread his arms abroad,
Crying, with a loud voice, "A sail! a sail!
I am saved!" And so fell back and spoke no more.

So passed the strong, heroic soul away.
       Lord Tennyson.

LONGING FOR HOME.

A song of a boat:—
 There was once a boat on a billow:
Lightly she rocked to her port remote,
And the foam was white in her wake like snow,
And her frail mast bowed when the breeze would blow,
 And bent like a wand of willow.

I shaded mine eyes one day when a boat
    Went curtseying over the billow;
I marked her course 'til a dancing mote
She faded out on the moonlit foam,
And I stayed behind in the dear loved home;
    And my thoughts all day were about the boat,
        And my dreams upon the pillow.

I pray you hear my song of a boat,
    For it is but short:—
My boat, you shall find none fairer afloat,
    In river or port.
Long I looked out for the lad she bore,
    On the open desolate sea,
And I think he sailed to the heavenly shore,
    For he came not back to me—
                    Ah me!

A song of a nest:
    There was once a nest in a hollow;
    Down in the mosses and knot-grass pressed,
Soft and warm, and full to the brim.
Vetches leaned over it purple and dim,
    With buttercup buds to follow.

I pray you, hear my song of a nest,
    For it is not long:—
You shall never light, in a summer quest,
    The bushes among—
Shall never light on a prouder sitter,
    A fairer nestful, nor ever know
A softer sound than their tender twitter,
    That wind-like did come and go.

I had a nestful once of my own,
    Ah happy, happy I!
Right dearly I loved them; but when they were grown,
    They spread out their wings to fly.
O, one after one they flew away
    Far up to the heavenly blue,
To the better country, the upper day,
    And—I wish I was going, too.

I pray you, what is the nest to me,
   My empty nest?
And what is the shore where I stood to see
   My boat sail down to the west?
Can I call that home where I anchor yet,
   Though my good man has sailed?
Can I call that home where my nest was set,
   Now all its hope hath failed?

Nay, but the port where my sailor went,
   And the land where my nestlings be;
There is the home where my thoughts are sent,
   The only home for me—
               Ah me.
                    Jean Ingelow.

CONNOR.

"To the memory of Patrick Connor; this simple stone **was** erected by his fellow-workmen."

Those words you may read any day upon a white slab in a cemetery not many miles from New York; but you might read them an hundred times without guessing at the little tragedy they indicate, without knowing the humble romance which ended with the placing of that stone above the dust of one poor humble man.

In his shabby frieze jacket and mud-laden brogans, he was scarcely an attractive object as he walked into Mr. Bawne's great tin and hardware shop one day, and presented himself at the counter with an

"I 've been tould ye advertized for hands, yer honor."

"Fully supplied, my man," said Mr. Bawne, not lifting his head from his account book.

"I 'd work faithfully, sir, and take low wages, till I could do better, and I 'd learn—I would that."

It was an Irish brogue, and Mr. Bawne always declared that he never would employ an incompetent hand.

Yet the tone attracted him. He turned briskly, and with his pen behind his ear, addressed the man, who was only one of fifty who had answered his advertisement for four workmen that morning—

"What makes you expect to learn faster than other folks —are you any smarter?"

"I 'll not say that," said the man; "but I 'd be wishing to, and that would make it aisier."

"Are you used to the work?"

"I 've done a bit of it."

"Much?"

"No, yer honor, I 'll tell no lie, Tim O'Toole had n't the like of this place; but I know a bit about tins."

"You are too old for an apprentice, and you 'd be in the way, I calculate," said Mr. Bawne, looking at the brawny arms and bright eyes that promised strength and intelligence. "Besides, I know your countrymen—lazy, good-for-nothing fellows, who never do their best. No, I 've been taken in by Irish hands before, and I won't have another."

"The Virgin will have to be after bringing them over to me in her two arms, thin," said the man, despairingly; "for I 've tramped all the day for the last fortnight, and niver a job can I get, and that 's the last penny I have, yer honor, and it 's but a half one."

As he spoke he spread his palm open, with an English half-penny in it.

"Bring whom over?" asked Mr. Bawne, arrested by the odd speech, as he turned upon his heel and turned back again.

"Jist Nora and Jamesy."

"Who are they?"

"The wan 's me wife, the other me child," said the man. "O masther, just thry me. How 'll I bring 'em over to me, if no one will give me a job? I want to be airning, and the whole big city seems against it, and me with arms like them."

He bared his arms to the shoulder as he spoke, and Mr. Bawne looked at them, and then at his face.

"I 'll hire you for a week," he said; "and now, as it 's noon, go down to the kitchen and tell the girl to get you some dinner—a hungry man can't work."

With an Irish blessing, the new hand obeyed, while Mr. Bawne, untying his apron, went upstairs to his own meal. Suspicious as he was of the new hand's integrity and ability, he was agreeably disappointed. Connor worked hard, and actually learned fast. At the end of the week he was engaged permanently, and soon was the best workman in the shop.

He was a great talker, but not fond of drink or wasting money. As his wages grew, he hoarded every penny, and wore the same shabby clothes in which he had made his first appearance.

"Beer costs money," he said one day, "and ivery cint I spind puts off the bringing Nora and Jamesy over; and as for clothes, them I have must do me. Better no coat to my back than no wife and boy by my fireside; and anyhow, it 's slow work saving."

It was slow work, but he kept at it all the same. Other men, thoughtless and full of fun, tried to make him drink; made a jest of his saving habits, coaxed him to accompany them to places of amusement, or to share in their Sunday frolics.

All in vain. Connor liked beer, liked fun, liked companionship; but he would not delay that long-looked-for bringing of Nora over, and was not "mane enough" to accept favor of others. He kept his way, a martyr to his one great wish, living on little, working at night on any extra job that he could earn a few shillings by, running errands in his noon-tide hours of rest, and talking to any one who would listen to him of his one great hope, and of Nora and of little Jamesy.

At first, the men who prided themselves on being all Americans, and on turning out the best work in the city, made a sort of butt of Connor, whose "wild Irish" ways and verdancy were indeed often laughable. But he won their hearts at last; and when, one day, mounting a work-bench, he shook his little bundle, wrapped in a red kerchief, before their eyes, and shouted, "Look, boys; I 've got the whole at last! I 'm going to bring Nora and Jamesy over at last! Whorooo!! I 've got it!!!" all felt sympathy in his joy, and each grasped his great hand in cordial congratulations, and one proposed to treat all round, and drink a good voyage to Nora.

They parted in a merry mood, most of the men going to comfortable homes. But poor Connor's resting-place was a poor lodging-house, where he shared a crazy garret with four other men; and in the joy of his heart, the poor fellow exhibited his handkerchief, with his hard-earned savings tied up in a wad in the middle, before he put it under his pillow and fell asleep.

When he awakened in the morning, he found his treasure gone; some villain, more contemptible than most bad men, had robbed him.

At first Connor could not even believe it lost. He searched every corner ot the room, shook his quilt and blankets, and begged those about him "to quit joking, and give it back."

But at last he realized the truth—

"Is any man that bad that it's thaved from me?" he asked, in a breathless way. "Boys, is any man that bad?" And some one answered: "No doubt of it, Connor; it's sthole."

Then Connor put his head down on his hands and lifted up his voice and wept. It was one of those sights which men never forget. It seemed more than he could bear, to have Nora and his child "put," as he expressed it, "months away from him again."

But when he went to work that day, it seemed to all who saw him that he had picked up a new determination. His hands were never idle. His face seemed to say, "I'll have Nora with me yet."

At noon he scratched out a letter, blotted and very strangely scrawled, telling Nora what had happened; and those who observed him noticed that he had no meat with his dinner. Indeed, from that moment he lived on bread, potatoes, and cold water, and worked as few men ever worked before. It grew to be the talk of the shop, and, now that sympathy was excited, every one wanted to help Connor. Jobs were thrown in his way, kind words and friendly wishes helped him mightily; but no power could make him share the food or drink of any other workman. It seemed a sort of charity to him.

Still, he was helped along. A present from Mr. Bawne at pay-day, set Nora, as he said, "a week nearer," and this and that and the other added to the little hoard. It grew faster than the first, and Connor's burden was not so heavy. At last, before he hoped it, he was once more able to say, "I'm going to bring them over," and to show his handkerchief, in which, as before, he tied up his earnings; this time, however, only to his friends. Cautious among strangers, he hid the treasure, and kept his vest buttoned over it night and day until the tickets were bought and sent. Then every man, woman and child, capable of hearing or understanding, knew that Nora and her baby were coming; and so the days flew by, and brought at last a letter from his wife.

"She would start as he desired, and she was well and so was the boy, and might the Lord bring them safely to each other's arms, and bless them who had been so kind to him."

That was the substance of the epistle which Connor proudly assured his fellow-workmen Nora wrote herself. She had lived at service as a girl, with a certain good old lady, who had given her the items of an education, which Connor told upon his fingers. "The radin', that's one, and the writin', that's three, and, moreover, she knows all that a woman can." Then he looked up, with tears in his eyes, and asked,—"Do you wondher the time seems long between me an' her, boys?"

So it was. Nora at the dawn of day—Nora at noon—Nora at night—until the news came that the Stormy Petrel had come to port, and Connor, breathless and pale with excitement, flung his cap in the air and shouted.

It happened on a holiday afternoon, and half-a-dozen men were ready to go with Connor to the steamer and give his wife a greeting. Her little home was ready; Mr. Bawne's own servant had put it in order, and Connor took one peep at it before he started.

"She hadn't the like of that in the old counthry," he said, "but she'll know how to keep them tidy."

Then he led the way towards the dock where the steamer lay, and at a pace that made it hard for the rest to follow him. The spot was reached at last; a crowd of vehicles blockaded the street; a troop of emigrants came thronging up; fine cabin passengers were stepping into cabs, and drivers, porters, and all manner of employees were yelling and shouting in the usual manner. Nora would wait on board for her husband, he knew that.

The little group made their way into the vessel at last, and there, amid those who sat watching for coming friends, Connor searched for the two so dear to him; patiently at first, eagerly but patiently, but by-and-by growing anxious and excited.

"She would never go alone," he said; "she'd be lost entirely; I bade her wait, but I don't see her, boys; I think she's not in it."

"Why don't you see the captain?" asked one; and Connor jumped at the suggestion. In a few minutes he stood before a portly, rubicund man, who nodded to him kindly.

"I am looking for my wife, yer honor," said Connor, "and I can't find her."

"Perhaps she's gone ashore," said the captain.

"I bade her wait," said Connor.

"Women don't always do as they are bid, you know," said the captain.

"Nora would," said Connor;—"but maybe she was left behind. Maybe she did n't come. I somehow think she did n't."

At the name of Nora the captain started. In a moment he asked:

"What is your name?"

"Pat Connor," said the man.

"And your wife's name was Nora?"

"That's her name, and the boy with her is Jamesy, yer honor," said Connor.

The captain looked at Connor's friends; they looked at the captain. Then he said huskily: "Sit down, my man; I've got something to tell you."

"She's left behind," said Connor.

"She sailed with us," said the captain.

"Where is she?" asked Connor.

The captain made no answer.

"My man," he said, "we all have our trials; God sends them. Yes—Nora started with us."

Connor said nothing. He was looking at the captain, now, white to his lips.

"It's been a sickly season," said the captain; "we have had illness on board—the cholera. You know that."

"I did n't. I can't read; they kept it from me," said Connor.

"We did n't want to frighten him," said one, in a half whisper.

"You know how long we lay at quarantine?"

"The ship I came in did that," said Connor. "Did ye say Nora went ashore? Ought I to be looking for her, captain?"

"Many died, many children," went on the captain. "When we were half way here your boy was taken sick."

"Jamesy," gasped Connor.

"His mother watched him night and day," said the captain, "and we did all we could, but at last he died; only one of many. There were five buried that day. But it broke my heart to see the mother looking out upon the water. "It's his father I think of," said she; "he's longing to see poor Jamesy."

Connor groaned.

"Keep up if you can, my man," said the captain; "I wish any one else had it to tell rather than I. That night Nora was taken ill, also, very suddenly; she grew worse fast.

In the morning she called me to her. ' Tell Connor I died thinking of him,' she said, ' and tell him to meet me.' And my man, God help you, she never said anything more—in an hour she was gone."

Connor had risen. He stood up, trying to steady himself; looking at the captain with his eyes dry as two stones. Then he turned to his friends:

"I 've got my death, boys," he said, and then dropped to the deck like a log.

They raised him and bore him away. In an hour he was at home on the little bed which had been made ready for Nora, weary with her long voyage. There at last, he opened his eyes. Old Mr. Bawne bent over him; he had been summoned by the news, and the room was full of Connor's fellow workmen.

"Better, Connor?" asked the old man.

"A dale," said Connor. "It 's aisy now; I 'll be with her soon. And look ye, masther, I 've learnt one thing—God is good; He would n't let me bring Nora over to me, but he 's takin' me over to her and Jamesy over the river; do n't you see it, and her standin' on the other side to welcome me?"

And with these words Connor stretched out his arms. Perhaps he did see Nora—Heaven only knows—and so died.

Anonymous.

BREAK, BREAK, BREAK.

Break, break, break,
　　On thy cold gray stones, O Sea!
And I would that my tongue could utter
　　The thoughts that arise in me.

O well for the fisherman's boy,
　　That he shouts with his sister at play!
O well for the sailor-lad,
　　That he sings in his boat on the bay!

And the stately ships go on
　　To their haven under the hill;
But O for the touch of a vanished hand,
　　And the sound of a voice that is still.

Break, break, break,
   At the foot of thy crags, O Sea!
But the tender grace of a day that is dead
   Will never come back to me.

              Lord Tennyson.

THE EMPTY NEST.

A home in a quiet country place,
   Under the shadow of branches wide;
And a fair young mother with thoughtful face,
   Sewing a seam by the window side.

The sunshine stretches across the floor,
   The bright motes dance in its golden way,
And in and out, at the open door,
   The children run in their busy play.

Guiding her needle with careless skill,
   Her fingers fashion the garment white;
But weaving a fabric daintier still,
   Her swift thoughts follow the needle's flight.

Her heart lies hushed in her deep content,
   Her lips are humming an old love lay;
And still, with its music softly blent,
   She hears what the eager children say:

" We found it under the apple-tree,—
   A poor little empty yellowbird's nest;
See, it is round as a cup could be,
   And lined with down from the mother's breast.

" This is a leaf, all withered and dry,
   That once was a canopy overhead;
Does n't it almost make you cry
   To look at the dear little empty bed?

" All the birdies have flown away;
   But birds must fly or they would n't have wings;
And the mother knew they would go some day,
   When she used to cuddle the downy things.

" Do you think she is lonesome?   Why, there's a tear!
    And here is another—that makes two.
Why do you hug us, and look so queer?
    If *we* were birdies we would n't leave *you*."

Deep in the mother's listening heart
    Drops the prattle with sudden sting;
For lips may quiver, and tears may start,
    But *birds must fly or they would n't have wings.*
                        Emily Huntington Miller.

THE MOTHER'S DREAM.

I 'd a dream to-night
    As I fell asleep;
Oh! the touching sight
    Makes me still to weep:
Of my little lad,
Gone to leave me sad;
Ay, the child I had,
    But was not to keep.

As in heaven high,
    I my child did seek,
There, in train, came by
    Children fair and meek,
Each in lily white,
With a lamp alight;
Each was clear to sight,
    But they did not speak.

Then, a little sad,
    Came my child in turn,
But the lamp he had,
    Oh! it did not burn;
He, to clear my doubt,
Said, half turn'd about,
"Your tears put it out;
    Mother, never mourn."
                        W. Barnes.

EDWARD GRAY.

Sweet Emma Moreland of yonder town
  Met me walking on yonder way;
" And have you lost your heart?" she said;
  " And are you married yet, Edward Gray?"

Sweet Emma Moreland spoke to me:
  Bitterly weeping, I turned away;
"Sweet Emma Moreland, love no more
  Can touch the heart of Edward Gray.

" Ellen Adair she loved me well,
  Against her father's and mother's will:
To-day I sat for an hour and wept,
  By Ellen's grave, on the windy hill.

"Shy she was, and I thought her cold;
  Thought her proud, and fled over the sea;
Filled I was with folly and spite,
  When Ellen Adair was dying for me.

" Cruel, cruel the words I said!
  Cruelly came they back to-day:
' You 're too slight and fickle,' I said,
  ' To trouble the heart of Edward Gray. '

"There I put my face in the grass—
  Whispered, ' Listen to my despair:
I repent me of all I did;
  Speak a little, Ellen Adair!'

"Then I took a pencil and wrote
  On the mossy stone, as I lay,
' Here lies the body of Ellen Adair;
  And here the heart of Edward Gray!'

"Love may come, and love may go,
  And fly, like a bird, from tree to tree;
But I will love no more, no more,
  Till Ellen Adair come back to me.

"Bitterly wept I over the stone:
　　Bitterly weeping, I turned away;
There lies the body of Ellen Adair;
　　And there the heart of Edward Gray!"
Lord Tennyson.

PICTURES OF MEMORY.

Among the beautiful pictures
　　That hang on Memory's wall,
Is one of a dim old forest,
　　That seemeth best of all;
Not for its gnarled oaks olden,
　　Dark with the mistletoe;
Not for the violets golden
　　That sprinkle the vale below;
Not for the milk-white lilies
　　That lean from the fragrant ledge,
Coquetting all day with the sunbeams,
　　And stealing their golden edge;
Not for the vines on the upland,
　　Where the bright red berries rest,
Nor the pinks, nor the pale sweet cowslip,
　　It seemeth to me the best.

I once had a little brother,
　　With eyes that were dark and deep;
In the lap of that old dim forest
　　He lieth in peace asleep:

Light as the down of the thistle,
　　Free as the winds that blow
We roved there the beautiful summers,
　　The summers of long ago;
But his feet on the hills grew weary,
　　And, one of the autumn eves,
I made for my little brother
　　A bed of the yellow leaves.
Sweetly his pale arms folded
　　My neck in a meek embrace,

As the light of immortal beauty
   Silently covered his face;
And when the arrows of sunset
   Lodged in the tree-tops bright,
He fell, in his saint-like beauty,
   Asleep by the gates of light.
Therefore, of all the pictures
   That hang on Memory's wall,
The one of the dim old forest
   Seemeth the best of all.

              Alice Cary.

THE BANKS O' DOON.

Ye banks and braes o' bonnie Doon,
   How can ye bloom sae fresh and fair?
How can ye chant, ye little birds,
   And I sae weary, fu' o' care?
Thou 'lt break my heart, thou warbling bird,
   That wantons through the flowering thorn;
Thou minds me o' departed joys,
   Departed—never to return.

Aft hae I roved by bonnie Doon,
   To see the rose and woodbine twine;
And ilka bird sang o' its luve,
   And, fondly, sae did I o' mine.
Wi' lightsome heart I pou'd a rose,
   Fu' sweet upon its thorny tree;
And my fause luver stole my rose,
   But ah! he left the thorn wi' me.

              Robert Burns.

"ROCK OF AGES."

"Rock of Ages, cleft for me,"
  Thoughtlessly the maiden sung,
Fell the words unconsciously
  From her girlish, gleeful tongue;
Sung as little children sing,
  Sung as sing the birds in June;
Fell the words like light leaves sown
  On the current of the tune—
"Rock of Ages, cleft for me,
Let me hide myself in Thee."

Felt her soul no need to hide—
  Sweet the song as song could be
And she had no thought beside;
  All the words unheedingly
Fell from lips untouched by care,
  Dreaming not that each might be
On some other lips a prayer—
"Rock of Ages, cleft for me,
Let me hide myself in Thee."

"Rock of Ages, cleft for me—"
  'Twas a woman sung them now,
Pleadingly and prayerfully;
  Every word her heart did know;
Rose the song as storm-tossed bird
  Beats with weary wing the air;
Every note with sorrow stirred,
  Every syllable a prayer—
"Rock of Ages, cleft for me,
Let me hide myself in Thee."

"Rock of Ages, cleft for me—"
  Lips grown aged sung the hymn
Trustingly and tenderly,
  Voice grown weak and eyes grown dim—
"Let me hide myself in Thee."
  Trembling through the voice, and low,
Rose the sweet strain peacefully
  As a river in its flow;

Sung as only they can sing,
　　Who life's thorny paths have pressed;
Sung as only they can sing
　　Who behold the promised rest.

"Rock of Ages, cleft for me,"
　　Sung above a coffin-lid;
Underneath, all restfully
　　All life's cares and sorrows hid.
Never more, O storm-tossed soul,
　　Never more from wind or tide,
Never more from billow's roll
　　Wilt thou need thyself to hide.
Could the sightless, sunken eyes,
　　Closed beneath the soft gray hair,
Could the mute and stiffened lips,
　　Move again in pleading prayer,
Still, ay still the words would be,
"Let me hide myself in Thee."
　　　　　　　　　　Anonymous.

THE VOLUNTEER'S WIFE.

"An' sure I was tould to come to yer Honor,
　　To see if ye 'd write a few words to me Pat.
He 's gone for a soldier, is Misther O'Connor,
　　Wid a sthripe on his arm and a band on his hat.

"An' what 'll ye tell him?　It ought to be aisy
　　For sich as yer Honor to spake wid the pen,—
Jist say I 'm all right, and that Mavoorneen Daisy
　　(The baby, yer Honor) is betther again.

"For when he went off it 's so sick was the childer
　　She niver held up her blue eyes to his face;
And when I 'd be cryin' he 'd look but the wilder,
　　An' say, 'Would you wish for the counthry's disgrace?'

"So he left her in danger, and me sorely gratin',
　　To follow the flag wid an Irishman's joy;—

O, it's often I drame of the big drums a batin',
    An' a bullet gone straight to the heart of me boy.

"An' say will he send me a bit of his money,
    For the rint an' the docther's bill, due in a wake ;—
Well, surely, there's tears on yer eye-lashes, honey!
    Ah, faith, I've no right with such freedom to spake.

"You've overmuch trifling, I'll not give ye trouble,
    I'll find some one willin'— O, what can it be?
What's that in the newspaper folded up double?
    Yer Honor, don't hide it, but rade it to me.

"What, Patrick O'Connor! No, no, 'tis some other!
    Dead! dead! no, not him! 'Tis a wake scarce gone by.
Dead! dead! why, the kiss on the cheek of his mother,
    It hasn't had time yet, yer Honor, to dry.

"Don't tell me! It's not him! O God, am I crazy?
    Shot dead! O for love of sweet Heaven, say no.
O, what'll I do in the world wid poor Daisy!
    O, how will I live, an' O, where will I go!

"The room is so dark, I'm not seein' yer Honor,
    I think I'll go home—" And a sob, thick and dry,
Came sharp from the bosom of Mary O'Connor,
    But never a tear-drop welled up to her eye.

                    M. A. Dennison.

OUR FOLKS.

"Hi! Harry Holly! Halt,—and tell
    A fellow just a thing or two ;
You've had a furlough, been to see
    How all the folks in Jersey do.
It's months ago since I was there,—
    I, and a bullet from Fair Oaks ;
When you were home,— old comrade, say,
    Did you see any of our folks?

"You did? Shake hands,—O, ain't I glad;
　For if I do look grim and rough,
　I 've got some feelin'—
　　　　　　　　　People think
　A soldier's heart is mighty tough ;
But, Harry, when the bullets fly,
　And hot saltpeter flames and smokes,
While whole battalions lie afield,
　One 's apt to think about his folks.

"And so you saw them—when? and where?
　The old man—is he hearty yet?
And mother—does she fade at all?
　Or does she seem to pine and fret
For me? And Sis?—has she grown tall?
　And did you see her friend—you know
That Annie Moss—
　　　　　　(How this pipe chokes!)
Where did you see her?—tell me, Hal,
　A lot of news about our folks.

"You saw them in the church—you say;
　It 's likely, for they 're always there.
Not Sunday? no? A funeral? Who?
　Who, Harry? how you shake and stare!
All well, you say, and all were out;
　What ails you, Hal? Is this a hoax?
Why do n't you tell me, like a man,
　What is the matter with our folks?"

"I said all well, old comrade, true;
　　I say all well, for He knows best
Who takes the dear ones in His arms,
　Before the sun goes to the west.
The axe-man Death deals right and left,
　And flowers fall as well as oaks;
And so—
　　　　Fair Annie blooms no more!
And that's the matter with your folks.

"See, this long curl was kept for you;
　And this white blossom from her breast;
And here—your sister Bessie wrote
　A letter, telling all the rest.

Bear up, old friend."
                    Nobody speaks;
Only the old camp raven croaks,
    And soldiers whisper:
                    "Boys, be still;
There 's some bad news from Grainger's folks."

He turns his back—the only foe
    That ever saw it—on this grief,
And, as men will, keeps down the tears
    Kind Nature sends to Woe's relief.
Then answers he:
                    "Ah, Hal, I 'll try;
    But in my throat there 's something chokes,
Because, you see, I 've thought so long
    To count her in among our folks.

" I s'pose she must be happy now,
    But still I will keep thinking too,
I could have kept all trouble off,
    By being tender, kind, and true.
But maybe not.
                    She 's safe up there,
    And when the Hand deals other strokes,
She 'll stand by Heaven's gate, I know,
    And wait to welcome in our folks."
                                Ethel Lynn.

AULD ROBIN GRAY.

When the sheep are in the fauld, and the kye at hame,
And a' the warld to sleep are gane,
The waes o' my heart fa' in showers frae my ee,
When my gudeman lies sound by me.

Young Jamie loo'd me weel, and socht me for his bride;
But, saving a croun, he had naething else beside.
To mak that croun a pund, young Jamie gaed to sea;
And the croun and the pund were baith for me!

He hadna been awa a week but only twa,
When my mother she fell sick, and the cow was stown awa;
My father brak his arm, and young Jamie at the sea—
And auld Robin Gray cam' a-courtin' me.

My father cou'dna work, and my mother cou'dna spin;
I toiled day and nicht; but their bread I cou'dna win;
Auld Rob maintained them baith, and, wi' tears in his ee,
Said, "Jenny, for their sakes, oh, marry me!"

My heart it said nay, for I looked for Jamie back;
But the wind it blew high, and the ship it was a wrack;
The ship it was a wrack! Why didna Jamie dee?
Or, why do I live to say, Wae's me?

My father argued sair—my mother didna speak,
But she lookit in my face till my heart was like to break;
Sae they gied him my hand, though my heart was in the sea;
And auld Robin Gray was gudeman to me.

I hadna been a wife, a week but only four,
When, sitting sae mournfully at the door,
I saw my Jamie's wraith, for I cou'dna think it he,
Till he said, "I 'm come back for to marry thee!"

Oh sair, sair did we greet, and muckle did we say;
We took but ae kiss, and we tore ourselves away:
I wish I were dead, but I 'm no like to dee;
And why do I live to say, Wae's me?

I gang like a ghaist, and I carena to spin;
I daurna think on Jamie, for that wad be a sin;
But I 'll do my best a gude wife to be,
For auld Robin Gray is kind unto me.

Lady A. Lindsay.

JOHN ANDERSON, MY JO.

John Anderson, my jo, John,
  When we were first acquent,
Your locks were like the raven,
  Your bonnie brow was brent;
But now your brow is beld, John,
  Your locks are like the snaw;
But blessings on your frosty pow,
  John Anderson, my jo.

John Anderson, my jo, John,
  We clamb the hill thegither;
And mony a canty day, John,
  We 've had wi' ane anither.
Now we maun totter down, John,
  But hand in hand we 'll go;
And sleep thegither at the foot,
  John Anderson, my jo.
                    Robert Burns.

SOLEMNITY.

In the expression of solemnity three things are necessary:
First, Natural voice.
Second, Effusive utterance.
Third, Low pitch.

Here, as in pathetic reading, the natural voice and effusive utterance are used, and the same care should be taken to secure perfect *purity of tone* and a gentle *continuous emission of sound*.

Low pitch can be easily secured by striking the pitch of ordinary conversation, which is about the middle line of the voice, and descending on the musical scale three or four notes. The level of solemn expression will thus be reached, and with freedom from harshness of tone, united with an effusive utterance,.the conditions of solemn reading will be fully met.

SOLEMN SELECTIONS.

THE OLD CLOCK ON THE STAIRS.

Somewhat back from the village street
Stands the old-fashioned country-seat.
Across its antique portico
Tall poplar-trees their shadows throw,
And from its station in the hall
An ancient timepiece says to all,—
      " Forever—never!
      Never—forever!"

Half-way up the stairs it stands,
And points and beckons with its hands
From its case of massive oak,
Like a monk, who, under his cloak,

Crosses himself, and sighs, alas!
With sorrowful voice to all who pass,—
      " Forever—never!
        Never—forever!"

By day its voice is low and light;
But in the silent dead of night,
Distinct as a passing footstep's fall,
It echoes along the vacant hall,
Along the ceiling, along the floor,
And seems to say, at each chamber-door,
      " Forever—never!
        Never—forever!"

Through days of sorrow and of mirth,
Through days of death and days of birth,
Through every swift vicissitude
Of changeful time, unchanged it has stood,
And as if, like God, it all things saw,
It calmly repeats those words of awe,—
      " Forever—never!
        Never—forever!"

In that mansion used to be
Free-hearted Hospitality;
His great fires up the chimney roared;
The stranger feasted at his board;
But, like the skeleton at the feast,
That warning timepiece never ceased,
      " Forever—never!
        Never—forever!"

There groups of merry children played,
There youths and maidens dreaming strayed;
O precious hours! O golden prime!
And affluence of love and time!
Even as a miser counts his gold,
Those hours the ancient timepiece told,—
      " Forever—never!
        Never—forever!"

From that chamber, clothed in white,
The bride came forth on her wedding night;

There, in that silent room below,
The dead lay in his shroud of snow;
And in the hush that followed the prayer,
Was heard the old clock on the stair,—
      " Forever—never!
        Never—forever!"

All are scattered now and fled,
Some are married, some are dead;
And when I ask, with throbs of pain,
" Ah! when shall they all meet again?"
As in the days long since gone by,
The ancient timepiece makes reply,—
      " Forever—never!
        Never—forever!"

Never here, forever there,
Where all parting, pain and care,
And death and time shall disappear,—
Forever there, but never here!
The horologe of eternity
Sayeth this incessantly,—
      " Forever—never!
        Never—forever!"
               Henry Wadsworth Longfellow.

THANATOPSIS.

To him who, in the love of Nature, holds
Communion with her visible forms, she speaks
A various language: for his gayer hours
She has a voice of gladness, and a smile
And eloquence of beauty ; and she glides
Into his darker musings with a mild
And gentle sympathy, that steals away
Their sharpness, ere he is aware. When thoughts
Of the last bitter hour come like a blight
Over thy spirit, and sad images
Of the stern agony, and shroud, and pall,
And breathless darkness, and the narrow house

Make thee to shudder, and grow sick at heart,
Go forth under the open sky, and list
To Nature's teachings, while from all around—
Earth and her waters, and the depths of air—
Comes a still voice,—Yet a few days and thee
The all-beholding sun shall see no more
In all his course; nor yet in the cold ground,
Where thy pale form was laid, with many tears,
Nor in the embrace of ocean, shall exist
Thy image. Earth, that nourished thee, shall claim
Thy growth, to be resolved to earth again ;
And, lost each human trace, surrendering up
Thine individual being, shalt thou go
To mix forever with the elements ;
To be a brother to the insensible rock,
And to the sluggish clod, which the rude swain
Turns with his share, and treads upon. The oak
Shall send his roots abroad, and pierce thy mould.

Yet, not to thine eternal resting-place
Shalt thou retire alone,—nor couldst thou wish
Couch more magnificent. Thou shalt lie down
With patriarchs of the infant world,—with kings,
The powerful of the earth,—the wise, the good,
Fair forms, and hoary seers of ages past,
All in one mighty sepulchre. The hills,
Rock-ribbed, and ancient as the sun ; the vales
Stretching in pensive quietness between;
The venerable woods; rivers that move
In majesty, and the complaining brooks,
That make the meadows green; and, poured round all,
Old ocean's gray and melancholy waste,—
Are but the solemn decorations all
Of the great tomb of man! The golden sun,
The planets, all the infinite host of heaven,
Are shining on the sad abodes of death,
Through the still lapse of ages. All that tread
The globe are but a handful to the tribes
That slumber in its bosom. Take the wings
Of morning, traverse Barca's desert sands,
Or lose thyself in the continuous woods
Where rolls the Oregon, and hears no sound

Save his own dashings,—yet the dead are there!
And millions in those solitudes, since first
The flight of years began, have laid them down
In their last sleep,—the dead reign there alone!
So shalt thou rest; and what if thou withdraw
In silence from the living, and no friend
Take note of thy departure?   All that breathe
Will share thy destiny.   The gay will laugh
When thou art gone, the solemn brood of care
Plod on, and each one, as before, will chase
His favorite phantom; yet all these shall leave
Their mirth and their employments, and shall come
And make their bed with thee.   As the long train
Of ages glide away, the sons of men—
The youth in life's green spring, and he who goes
In the full strength of years, matron and maid,
And the sweet babe, and the gray-headed man—
Shall, one by one, be gathered to thy side
By those who in their turn shall follow them.

So live, that when thy summons comes to join
The innumerable caravan that moves
To the pale realms of shade, where each shall take
His chamber in the silent halls of death,
Thou go not, like the quarry-slave at night,
Scourged to his dungeon, but, sustained and soothed
By an unfaltering trust, approach thy grave
Like one who wraps the drapery of his couch
About him, and lies down to pleasant dreams.

William Cullen Bryant.

THE RAINY DAY.

The day is cold, and dark, and dreary;
It rains, and the wind is never weary;
The vine still clings to the mouldering wall,
But at every gust the dead leaves fall,
    And the day is dark and dreary.

My life is cold, and dark, and dreary;
It rains, and the wind is never weary;
My thoughts still cling to the mouldering Past,
But the hopes of youth fall thick in the blast,
 And the days are dark and dreary.

Be still, sad heart! and cease repining;
Behind the clouds is the sun still shining;
Thy fate is the common fate of all,
Into each life some rain must fall,
 Some days must be dark and dreary.
     Henry Wadsworth Longfellow.

THE BLUE AND THE GRAY.

[The women of Columbus, Mississippi, animated by nobler sentiments than are many of their sisters, have shown themselves impartial in their offerings made to the memory of the dead. They strewed flowers alike on the graves of the Confederate and of the National soldiers.]

By the flow of the inland river,
 Whence the fleets of iron have fled,
Where the blades of the grave-grass quiver,
 Asleep are the ranks of the dead;—
  Under the sod and the dew,
   Waiting the judgment day;—
  Under the one, the Blue;
   Under the other, the Gray.

These in the robings of glory,
 Those in the gloom of defeat,
All with the battle-blood gory,
 In the dusk of eternity meet;—
  Under the sod and the dew,
   Waiting the judgment day;—
  Under the laurel, the Blue;
   Under the willow, the Gray.

From the silence of sorrowful hours
 The desolate mourners go,
Lovingly laden with flowers
 Alike for the friend and the foe;—

Under the sod and the dew,
　Waiting the judgment day;—
Under the roses, the Blue;
　Under the lilies, the Gray.

So with an equal splendor
　The morning sun-rays fall,
With a touch impartially tender,
　On the blossoms blooming for all;—
　　Under the sod and the dew,
　　　Waiting the judgment day;—
　　'Broidered with gold, the Blue;
　　　Mellowed with gold, the Gray.

So, when the summer calleth,
　On forest and field of grain,
With an equal murmur falleth
　The cooling drip of the rain;—
　　Under the sod and the dew,
　　　Waiting the judgment day;—
　　Wet with the rain, the Blue;
　　　Wet with the rain, the Gray.

Sadly, but not with upbraiding,
　The generous deed was done;
In the storm of the years that are fading,
　No braver battle was won;—
　　Under the sod and the dew,
　　　Waiting the judgment day;—
　　Under the blossoms, the Blue;
　　　Under the garlands, the Gray.

No more shall the war-cry sever,
　Or the winding rivers be red;
They banish our anger forever
　When they laurel the graves of our dead!
　　Under the sod and the dew,
　　　Waiting the judgment day;—
　　Love and tears for the Blue;
　　　Tears and love for the Gray.
　　　　　　　　　　F. M. Finch.

THE DEATH OF THE FLOWERS.

The melancholy days are come, the saddest of the year,
Of wailing winds, and naked woods, and meadows brown
    and sear.
Heaped in the hollows of the grove the withered leaves lie
    dead;
They rustle to the eddying gust and to the rabbit's tread.
The robin and the wren are flown, and from the shrubs the
    jay,
And from the wood-top calls the crow through all the gloomy
    day.

Where are the flowers, the fair young flowers, that lately
    sprung and stood
In brighter light and softer airs, a beauteous sisterhood?
Alas! they all are in their graves; the gentle race of flowers
Are lying in their lowly beds, with the fair and good of ours.
The rain is falling where they lie; but the cold November rain
Calls not from out the gloomy earth the lovely ones again.

The wind-flower and the violet, they perished long ago,
And the brier-rose and the orchis died amid the summer's
    glow;
But on the hill the golden-rod, and the aster in the wood,
And the yellow sunflower by the brook in autumn beauty
    stood,
Till fell the frost from the clear cold heaven, as falls the
    plague on men,
And the brightness of their smile was gone from upland,
    glade, and glen.

And now, when comes the calm mild day, as still such days
    will come,
To call the squirrel and the bee from out their winter home;
When the sound of dropping nuts is heard, though all the
    trees are still,
And twinkle in the smoky light the waters of the rill,
The south-wind searches for the flowers whose fragrance late
    he bore,
And sighs to find them in the wood and by the stream no
    more.

And then I think of one who in her youthful beauty died,
The fair meek blossom that grew up and faded by my side.
In the cold moist earth we laid her, when the forests cast the
leaf,
And we wept that one so lovely should have a life so brief;
Yet not unmeet it was that one, like that young friend of
ours,
So gentle and so beautiful, should perish with the flowers.

William Cullen Bryant.

CARCASSONNE.

How old I am! I'm eighty year!
  I've worked both hard and long;
Yet, patient as my life has been,
One dearest sight I have not seen,—
  It almost seems a wrong:
A dream I had when life was new—
Alas, our dreams!   They come not true;
I thought to see fair Carcassonne!
I have not seen fair Carcassonne!

One sees it dimly from the height
  Beyond the mountain blue:
Fain would I walk five weary leagues—
I do not mind the road's fatigues—
  Through morn and evening dew;
But bitter frosts would fall at night,
And on the grapes that yellow blight;
I could not go to Carcassonne,
I never went to Carcassonne.

Our Vicar's right; he preaches loud,
  And bids us to beware!
He says: "O, guard the weakest part,
And most the traitor in the heart,
  Against ambition's snare!"
Perhaps in autumn I can find
Two sunny days with gentle wind;
I then could go to Carcassonne,
I still could go to Carcassonne.

They say it is as gay all time,
　　As holidays at home;
The gentles ride in gay attire,
And in the sun each gilded spire
　　Shoots up like those of Rome!
The Bishop the procession leads,
The generals curb their prancing steeds;
Alas! I know not Carcassonne!
Alas! I saw not Carcassonne!

My God and Father! pardon me,
　　If this, my wish, offends;
One sees some hope more high than he,
In age, as in his infancy,
　　To which his heart ascends.
My wife, my son have seen Narbonne,
My grandson went to Perpignan;
But I have not seen Carcassonne,
I never have seen Carcassonne.

Thus sighed a peasant, bent with age,
　　Half dreaming in his chair:
I said, "My friend, come go with me,
To-morrow, then, your eyes shall see
　　Those sights that seem so fair."
That night there came for passing soul,
The church bell's low and solemn toll!
He never saw gay Carcassonne!
Who has not known a Carcassonne?
　　　　　　　　　　M. E. W. Sherwood.

―――――――

FUNERAL HYMN.

How still and peaceful is the grave,
　　Where,—life's vain tumults past—
The appointed house, by Heaven's decree,
　　Receives us all at last!

The wicked there from troubling cease,—
　　Their passions rage no more;

And there the weary pilgrim rests
  From all the toils he bore.

All, leveled by the hands of death,
  Lie sleeping in the tomb,
Till God in judgment call them forth
  To meet their final doom.

                James Montgomery.

SERENITY, BEAUTY, LOVE.

The requirements are:

First—Natural voice.

Second—Effusive utterance.

Third—High pitch.

The pleasant effect produced by this combination was called by the ancients, the "Silvery tone." The quietude and delicacy of this class of selections demand especial care in securing a pure, musical and effusive quality of voice. The more pure, gentle and continuous the tones can be made, the more effective and pleasant will be the results of the reading.

To secure high pitch, let the voice ascend the musical scale three or four notes, beginning with the pitch of ordinary conversation.

SELECTIONS OF SERENITY, BEAUTY, LOVE.

ENDYMION.

The rising moon has hid the stars;
Her level rays, like golden bars,
    Lie on the landscape green,
        With shadows brown between.

And silver white the river gleams,
As if Diana, in her dreams,
        Had dropt her silver bow
        Upon the meadows low.

On such a tranquil night as this,
She woke Endymion with a kiss,
        When sleeping in the grove,
        He dreamed not of her love.

Like Dian's kiss, unasked, unsought,
Love gives itself, but is not bought;
 Nor voice, nor sound betrays
 Its deep, impassioned gaze.

It comes,—the beautiful, the free,
The crown of all humanity,—
 In silence and alone
 To seek the elected one.

It lifts the boughs, whose shadows deep,
Are Life's oblivion, the soul's sleep,
 And kisses the closed eyes
 Of him, who slumbering lies.

O weary hearts! O slumbering eyes!
O drooping souls, whose destinies
 Are fraught with fear and pain,
 Ye shall be loved again!

No one is so accursed by fate,
No one so utterly desolate,
 But some heart, though unknown,
 Responds unto his own.

Responds,—as if with unseen wings,
An angel touched its quivering strings;
 And whispers, in its song,
 " Where hast thou stayed so long!"
    Henry Wadsworth Longfellow.

THE BELLS OF SHANDON.

With deep affection
And recollection
I often think of
 Those Shandon bells,
Whose sounds so wild would,
In the days of childhood,
Fling round my cradle
 Their magic spells.

On this I ponder
Where'er I wander,
And thus grow fonder,
 Sweet Cork, of thee,—
With thy bells of Shandon,
That sound so grand on
The pleasant waters
 Of the river Lee.

I 've heard bells chiming
Full many a clime in,
Tolling sublime in
 Cathedral shrine,
While at a glibe rate
Brass tongues would vibrate;
But all their music
 Spoke naught like thine.

For memory, dwelling
On each proud swelling
Of thy belfry, knelling
 Its bold notes free,
Made the bells of Shandon
Sound far more grand on
The pleasant waters
 Of the river Lee.

I 've heard bells tolling
Old Adrian's Mole in,
Their thunder rolling
 From the Vatican,—
And cymbals glorious
Swinging uproarious
In the gorgeous turrets
 Of Notre Dame!

But thy sounds were sweeter
Than the dome of Peter
Flings o'er the Tiber,
 Pealing solemnly.
Oh! the bells of Shandon
Sound far more grand on
The pleasant waters
 Of the river Lee.

There 's a bell in Moscow;
While on tower and kiosk O
In St. Sophia
   The Turkman gets,
And loud in air
Calls men to prayer,
From the tapering summit
   Of tall minarets.

Such empty phantom
I freely grant them;
But there 's an anthem
   More dear to me—
'Tis the bells of Shandon,
That sound so grand on
The pleasant waters
   Of the river Lee.
          Francis Mahony.

MARY DONNELLY.

O lovely Mary Donnelly, it 's you I love the best!
If fifty girls were around you, I 'd hardly see the rest;
Be what it may the time of day, the place be where it will,
Sweet looks of Mary Donnelly, they bloom before me still.

Her eyes like mountain water that 's flowing on a rock,
How clear they are! how dark they are! and they give me
    many a shock;
Red rowans warm in sunshine, and wetted with a shower,
Could ne 'er express the charming lip that has me in its power.

Her nose is straight and handsome, her eyebrows lifted up,
Her chin is very neat and pert, and smooth like a china cup;
Her hair 's the brag of Ireland, so weighty and so fine,—
It 's rolling down upon her neck, and gathered in a twine.

The dance o' last Whit-Monday night exceeded all before;
No pretty girl for miles around was missing from the floor;
But Mary kept the belt of love, and O, but she was gay;
She danced a jig, she sung a song, and took my heart away!

When she stood up for dancing, her steps were so complete,
The music nearly killed itself, to listen to her feet;
The fiddler mourned his blindness, he heard her so much
    praised,
But blessed himself he was n't deaf when once her voice she
    raised.

And evermore I 'm whistling or lilting what you sung;
Your smile is always in my heart, your name beside my
    tongue.
But you 've as many sweethearts as you 'd count on both your
    hands,
And for myself, there's not a thumb or little finger stands.

O, you 're the flower of womankind, in country or in town;
The higher I exalt you, the lower I 'm cast down.
If some great lord should come this way and see your beauty
    bright,
And you to be his lady, I 'd own it was but right.

O, might we live together in lofty palace hall,
Where joyful music rises, and where scarlet curtains fall;
O, might we live together in a cottage mean and small,
With sods of grass the only roof, and mud the only wall!

O lovely Mary Donnelly, your beauty 's my distress;
It 's far too beauteous to be mine, but I 'll never wish it less;
The proudest place would fit your face, and I am poor and
    low,
But blessings be about you, dear, wherever you may go!
William Allingham.

EVANGELINE ON THE PRAIRIE.

Beautiful was the night.   Behind the black wall of the forest,
Tipping its summit with silver, arose the moon. On the
    river
Fell here and there through the branches a tremulous gleam
    of the moonlight,
Like the sweet thoughts of love on a darkened and devious
    spirit.

Nearer and round about her, the manifold flowers of the garden
Poured out their souls in odors, that were their prayers and confessions
Unto the night, as it went its way, like a silent Carthusian.
Fuller of fragrance than they, and as heavy with shadows and night-dews,
Hung the heart of the maiden. The calm and the magical moonlight
Seemed to inundate her soul with indefinable longings,
As, through the garden gate, and beneath the shade of the oak-trees,
Passed she along the path to the edge of the measureless prairie.
Silent it lay, with a silvery haze upon it, and fire-flies
Gleaming and floating away in mingled and infinite numbers.
Over her head the stars, the thoughts of God in the heavens,
Shone on the eyes of man, who had ceased to marvel and worship,
Save when a blazing comet was seen on the walls of that temple,
As if a hand had appeared and written upon them "Upharsin."
And the soul of the maiden, between the stars and the fire-flies,
Wandered alone, and she cried, "O Gabriel! O, my beloved!
Art thou so near unto me, and yet I cannot behold thee?
Art thou so near unto me, and yet thy voice does not reach me?
Ah! how often thy feet have trod this path to the prairie!
Ah! how often thine eyes have looked on the woodlands around me!
Ah! how often beneath this oak, returning from labor,
Thou hast lain down to rest, and to dream of me in thy slumbers.
When shall these eyes behold, these arms be folded about thee?"
Loud and sudden and near the note of a whip-poor-will sounded,
Like a flute in the woods; and anon, through the neighboring thickets,
Farther and farther away it floated and dropped into silence.

"Patience!" whispered the oaks from oracular caverns of
　darkness;
And, from the moonlit meadow, a sigh responded, "To-
　morrow!"

Henry Wadsworth Longfellow.

BRUSHWOOD.

On a weary slope of Apennine,
At sober dusk of day's decline,
Out of the solemn solitude
Of Vallombrosa's antique wood,
A withered woman, tanned and bent,
Bearing her bundled brushwood went,
Poising it on her palsied head,
As if in penance for prayers unsaid.

Her dull cheeks channeled were with tears,
Shed in the storms of eighty years;
Her wild hair fell in gusty flow,
White as the foamy brook below:
Still toiled she with her load alone,
With feeble feet, but steadfast will,
To gain her little home, that shone
Like a dreary lantern on the hill.

How far, how very far it seemed,
To where that starry taper gleamed,
Placed by her grandchild on the sill
Of the cottage window on the hill!
Many a parent heart before,
Laden till it could bear no more,
Has seen a heavenward light that smiled,
And knew it placed there by a child;—
A long-gone child, whose anxious face
Gazed toward them down the deeps of space,
Longing for the loved to come
To the quiet of that home.

Steeper and rougher grew the road,
Harder and heavier grew the load;
Her heart beat like a weight of stone
Against her breast.   A sigh and moan
Mingled with prayer escaped her lips
Of sorrow, o'er sorrowing night's eclipse.
"Of all who pass me by," she said,
"There is never one to lend me aid;
Could I but gain yon wayside shrine,
There would I rest this load of mine,
And tell my sacred rosary through,
And try what patient prayer would do."

Again she heard the toiling tread
Of one who climbed that way,—and said,
"I will be bold, though I should see
A monk or priest, or it should be
The awful abbot, at whose nod
The frighted people toil and plod:
I'll ask his aid to yonder place,
Where I may breathe a little space,
And so regain my home."   He came,
And halting by the ancient dame,
Heard her brief story and request,
Which moved the pity in his breast;
And so he straightway took her load,
Toiling beside her up the road,
Until, with heart that overflowed,
She begged him lay her bundled sticks
Close at the feet of the crucifix.

So down he set her brushwood freight
Against the wayside cross, and straight
She bowed her palsied head to greet
And kiss the sculptured Saviour's feet;
And then and there she told her grief,
In broken sentences and brief.
And now the memory o'er her came
Of days blown out, like a taper flame,
Never to be relighted, when,
From many a summer hill and glen,
She culled the loveliest blooms to shine

About the feet of this same shrine;
But now, where once her flowers were gay,
Naught but the barren brushwood lay!
She wept a little at the thought,
And prayers and tears a quiet brought,
Until anon, relieved of pain,
She rose to take her load again.
But lo! the bundle of dead wood
Had burst to blossom! and now stood
Dawning upon her marveling sight,
Filling the air with odorous light!

Then spake her traveler-friend: " Dear Soul,
Thy perfect faith hath made thee whole!
I am the Burthen-Bearer,—I
Will never pass the o'erladen by.
My feet are on the mountain steep;
They wind through valleys dark and deep;
They print the hot dust of the plain,
And walk the billows of the main.
Wherever is a load to bear,
My willing shoulder still is there!
Thy toil is done!" He took her hand,
And led her through a May-time land;
Where round her pathway seemed to wave
Each votive flower she ever gave
To make her favorite altar bright,
As if the angels, at their blight,
Had borne them to the fields of blue,
Where, planted 'mid eternal dew,
They bloom, as witnesses arrayed
Of one on earth who toiled and prayed.

Thomas Buchanan Read.

A PETITION TO TIME.

Touch us gently, Time!
  Let us glide adown thy stream
Gently,—as we sometimes glide
  Through a quiet dream!

Humble voyagers are we,
　　Husband, wife, and children three—
(One is lost,—an angel fled
　　To the azure overhead!)

Touch us gently, Time!
　　We 've not proud nor soaring wings:
Our ambition, *our* content,
　　Lies in simple things.
Humble voyagers are we,
　　O'er Life's dim unsounded sea,
Seeking only some calm clime;
　　Touch us *gently*, gentle Time!
　　　　　　　　　　Bryan Waller Procter.

ANNABEL LEE.

It was many and many a year ago,
　　In a kingdom by the sea,
That a maiden lived, whom you may know
　　By the name of Annabel Lee;
And this maiden, she lived with no other thought
　　Than to love, and be loved by me.

I was a child and she was a child,
　　In this kingdom by the sea;
But we loved with a love that was more than love,
　　I and my Annabel Lee,
With a love that the wingéd seraphs of heaven
　.Coveted her and me.

And this was the reason that long ago,
　　In this kingdom by the sea,
A wind blew out of a cloud, chilling
　　My beautiful Annabel Lee;
So that her high-born kinsmen came,
　　And bore her away from me,
To shut her up in a sepulcher,
　　In this kingdom by the sea.

The angels, not so happy in heaven,
   Went envying her and me.
Yes! that was the reason (as all men know)
   In this kingdom by the sea,
That the wind came out of the cloud by night,
   Chilling and killing my Annabel Lee.

But our love it was stronger by far than the love
   Of those who were older than we,
   Of many far wiser than we;
And neither the angels in heaven above,
   Nor the demons down under the sea,
Can ever dissever my soul from the soul
   Of the beautiful Annabel Lee.

For the moon never beams without bringing me dreams
   Of the beautiful Annabel Lee,
And the stars never rise but I feel the bright eyes
   Of the beautiful Annabel Lee.
And so, all the night-tide I lie down by the side
Of my darling, my darling, my life, and my bride,
   In her sepulcher there by the sea,
   In her tomb by the sounding sea.
                 Edgar Allan Poe.

SANDALPHON.

Have you read in the Talmud of old,
In the Legends the Rabbins have told
   Of the limitless realms of the air,
Have you read it,—the marvelous story
Of Sandalphon, the Angel of Glory,
   Sandalphon, the Angel of Prayer?

How, erect, at the outermost gates
Of the City Celestial he waits,
   With his feet on the ladder of light,
That, crowded with angels unnumbered,
By Jacob was seen, as he slumbered
   Alone in the desert at night?

The Angels of Wind and of Fire
Chant only one hymn, and expire
  With the song's irresistible stress;
Expire in their rapture and wonder,
As harp-strings are broken asunder
  By music they throb to express.

But serene in the rapturous throng,
Unmoved by the rush of the song,
  With eyes unimpassioned and slow,
Among the dead angels, the deathless
Sandalphon stands, listening breathless
  To sounds that ascend from below;—

From the spirits on earth that adore,
From the souls that entreat and implore
  In the fervor and passion of prayer;
From the hearts that are broken with losses,
And weary with dragging the crosses
  Too heavy for mortals to bear.

And he gathers the prayers as he stands,
And they change into flowers in his hands,
  Into garlands of purple and red;
And beneath the great arch of the portal,
Through the streets of the City Immortal
  Is wafted the fragrance they shed.

It is but a legend, I know,—
A fable, a phantom, a show,
  Of the ancient Rabbinical lore;
Yet the old mediæval tradition,
The beautiful, strange superstition,
  But haunts me and holds me the more.

When I look from my window at night,
And the welkin above is all white,
  All throbbing and panting with stars,
Among them majestic is standing
Sandalphon the angel, expanding
  His pinions in nebulous bars.

And the legend, I feel, is a part
Of the hunger and thirst of the heart,
   The frenzy and fire of the brain,
That grasps at the fruitage forbidden,
The golden pomegranates of Eden,
   To quiet its fever and pain.
                    Henry Wadsworth Longfellow.

WHEN THE KYE COME HAME.

Come, all ye jolly shepherds,
   That whistle through the glen!
I 'll tell ye o' a secret
   That courtiers dinna ken:
What is the greatest bliss
   That the tongue o' man can name?
'Tis to woo a bonnie lassie
   When the kye come hame.

> *When the kye come hame,*
> *When the kye come hame,—*
> *'Tween the gloomin' an' the mirk,*
> *When the kye come hame.*

'Tis not beneath the burgonet,
   Nor yet beneath the crown;
'Tis not on couch o' velvet,
   Nor yet in bed o' down:
'Tis beneath the spreading birk,
   In the glen without the name,
Wi' a bonnie, bonnie lassie,
   When the kye come hame.

There the blackbird bigs his nest,
   For the mate he lo'es to see,
And on the tapmost bough
   O, a happy bird is he!
There he pours his melting ditty,
   And love is a' the theme;
And he 'll woo his bonnie lassie,
   When the kye come hame.

When the blewart bears a pearl,
 And the daisy turns a pea,
And the bonnie lucken gowan
 Has fauldit up his ee,
Then the lavrock, frae the blue lift,
 Draps down and thinks nae shame
To woo his bonnie lassie,
 When the kye come hame.

See yonder pawky shepherd,
 That lingers on the hill;
His yowes are in the fauld,
 And his lambs are lying still;
Yet he dinna gang to bed,
 For his heart is in a flame,
To meet his bonnie lassie
 When the kye come hame.

When the little wee bit heart
 Rises high in the breast,
And the little wee bit starn
 Rises red in the east,
O, there 's a joy sae dear
 That the heart can hardly frame!
Wi' a bonnie, bonnie lassie,
 When the kye come hame.

Then since all Nature joins
 In this love without alloy,
O, wha wad prove a traitor
 To Nature's dearest joy?
Or wha wad choose a crown,
 Wi' its perils an' its fame,
And miss his bonnie lassie,
 When the kye come hame?

James Hogg.

GRAND, SUBLIME AND REVERENTIAL STYLES.

OROTUND VOICE.

The Orotund voice, or the voice that is used in the expression of impassioned selections, needs now to be specially considered, as we are about to treat of various classes of composition that depend upon that voice for their appropriate interpretation.

What is the Orotund voice, and wherein does it differ from the natural or conversational voice? These questions are pertinent to the present discussion.

The Natural and Orotund voices are manufactured in the same way, and differ only in their intensity and volume of sound. · If a drum-head be tapped by the finger, a feeble report is heard; but if you beat the drum with great force, a very much louder report follows each blow, and a consequent resonance is heard inside as the sound passes from one head of the drum to the other. So with these voices. In the case of the Natural voice, the sound made in the glottis, as we talk, is not sufficiently loud to produce any resonance, except a slight one in the head; but when by the action of the abdominal muscles, the air in the lungs is thrown into the glottis with great force, a loud explosion of sound is heard, and a consequent resonance takes place in the cavities of the body, especially in the chest; hence the term, chest tone.

The most direct answer that we can make to the inquiry, what is the Orotund voice and wherein does it differ from the Natural voice, is this: The Orotund voice is that full, deep and resonant sound heard in all impassioned sublimity, oratory and fierce emotion, and it differs specifically from the Natural voice in that its depth, fullness and roundness arise chiefly from resonance in the cavities of the body.

The use of the Orotund voice in impassioned styles is so common a thing in ordinary life that the mention of a single example may serve to dissipate the absurd notion that elocutionary rules are arbitrary and conventional. For example, when the boy loses a finger he does not talk, he roars; he has so much feeling to get rid of that he cannot find vent in the Natural voice, and is forced by an irresistible impulse to use a larger voice in order that he may find relief. You can *read* an essay, but you must *speak* an oration. The emotion that fills the orator's soul as he denounces an enemy, or excites his countrymen to heroic deeds, must find an outlet in the full, strong and ample tones of the Orotund.

There are three kinds of Orotund voice, Effusive, Expulsive and Explosive, each of which will receive a separate consideration.

EFFUSIVE OROTUND.

This kind of Orotund is used in the rendition of all *grand*, *sublime*, and *reverential* styles. It is the appropriate voice of prayer, of all the prayer services of the church, of nearly all hymns—since they are but prayers in verse—of the grand passages of the Prophets and Psalms, as well as the sublime utterances of the Revelation. It is also the appropriate voice for the expression of all emotions that are excited by the grandeur, vastness, or splendor of natural objects. The prevailing pitch of voice is low, and in profound awe, despair and horror, we descend to the lowest pitch.

Care should be taken to avoid all harshness of tone, as impure qualities of voice are more readily detected in the full, long-drawn notes of the Effusive Orotund than in any other style of reading or speaking. A deep, full, sonorous quality of voice, free from all false intonations, sudden transitions, or conversational inflections, should be cultivated for the proper expression of this class of selections.

GRAND, SUBLIME AND REVERENTIAL SELECTIONS.

HYMN TO MONT BLANC.

Hast thou a charm to stay the morning-star
In his steep course? so long he seems to pause
On thy bald, awful head, O sovereign Blanc!
The Arvé and Arveiron at thy base
Rave ceaselessly; but thou, most awful Form!
Risest from forth thy silent sea of pines,
How silently!   Around thee and above
Deep is the air and dark, substantial black—
An ebon mass: methinks thou piercest it,
As with a wedge!   But when I look again,
It is thine own calm home, thy crystal shrine,
Thy habitation from eternity!
O dread and silent Mount! I gazed upon thee,
Till thou, still present to the bodily sense,
Didst vanish from my thought: entranced in prayer,
I worshiped the Invisible alone.

Yet, like some sweet beguiling melody,
So sweet we know not we are listening to it,
Thou, the meanwhile, wast blending with my thought—
Yea, with my life and life's own secret joy:
Till the dilating Soul, enrapt, transfused,
Into the mighty vision passing, there,
As in her natural form, swelled vast to Heaven!

Awake, my soul! not only passive praise
Thou owest! not alone these swelling tears,
Mute thanks, and secret ecstasy!   Awake,
Voice of sweet song!   Awake, my heart, awake!
Green vales and icy cliffs, all join my Hymn.

Thou first and chief, sole Sovereign of the Vale!
O, struggling with the darkness all the night,
And visited all night by troops of stars,
Or when they climb the sky or when they sink:

Companion of the morning-star at dawn,
Thyself earth's rosy star, and of the dawn
Co-herald: wake, O wake, and utter praise!
Who sank thy sunless pillars deep in earth?
Who filled thy countenance with rosy light?
Who made thee parent of perpetual streams?

And you, ye five wild torrents fiercely glad!
Who called you forth from night and utter death,
From dark and icy caverns called you forth,
Down those precipitous, black, jagged rocks,
Forever shattered and the same for ever?
Who gave you your invulnerable life,
Your strength, your speed, your fury, and your joy,
Unceasing thunder and eternal foam?
And who commanded (and the silence came),
Here let the billows stiffen, and have rest?

Ye ice-falls! ye that from the mountain's brow
Adown enormous ravines slope amain—
Torrents, methinks, that heard a mighty voice,
And stopped at once amid their maddest plunge!
Motionless torrents! silent cataracts!
Who made you glorious as the gates of heaven
Beneath the keen full moon? Who bade the sun
Clothe you with rainbows? Who, with living flowers
Of loveliest blue, spread garlands at your feet?—
God! let the torrents, like a shout of nations,
Answer! and let the ice-plains echo, God!
God! sing, ye meadow-streams, with gladsome voice!
Ye pine-groves, with your soft and soul-like sounds!
And they, too, have a voice, yon piles of snow,
And in their perilous fall shall thunder, God!

Ye living flowers that skirt the eternal frost!
Ye wild goats sporting round the eagle's nest!
Ye eagles, playmates of the mountain-storm!
Ye lightnings, the dread arrows of the clouds!
Ye signs and wonders of the elements!
Utter forth God, and fill the hills with praise!

Thou, too, hoar Mount! with thy sky-pointing peaks,
Oft from whose feet the avalanche, unheard,

Shoots downward, glittering through the pure serene,
Into the depth of clouds that veil thy breast—
Thou, too, again, stupendous Mountain! thou
That as I raise my head, awhile bowed low
In adoration, upward from thy base
Slow traveling with dim eyes suffused with tears,
Solemnly seemest, like a vapory cloud,
To rise before me—Rise, O ever rise!
Rise like a cloud of incense, from the earth!
Thou kingly Spirit throned among the hills,
Thou dread ambassador from earth to heaven,
Great Hierarch! tell thou the silent sky,
And tell the stars, and tell yon rising sun,
Earth, with her thousand voices, praises God.

Samuel Taylor Coleridge.

THE BURIAL OF MOSES.

"And he buried him in a valley in the land of Moab, over against Beth-peor, but no man knoweth of his sepulcher unto this day." Deut. xxxiv. 6.

By Nebo's lonely mountain,
  On this side Jordan's wave,
In a vale in the land of Moab,
  There lies a lonely grave;
But no man dug that sepulcher,
  And no man saw it e'er,
For the angels of God upturned the sod,
  And laid the dead man there.

That was the grandest funeral
  That ever passed on earth;
But no man heard the tramping,
  Or saw the train go forth;
Noiselessly as the daylight
  Comes when the night is done,
And the crimson streak on ocean's cheek
  Grows into the great sun,—

Noiselessly as the springtime
  Her crown of verdure weaves,
And all the trees on all the hills
  Open their thousand leaves,—
So, without sound of music,
  Or voice of them that wept,
Silently down from the mountain crown
  The great procession swept.

Perchance the bald old eagle,
  On gray Beth-peor's height,
Out of his rocky eyrie,
  Looked on the wondrous sight.
Perchance the lion, stalking,
  Still shuns the hallowed spot;
For beast and bird have seen and heard
  That which man knoweth not.

Lo! when the warrior dieth,
  His comrades in the war,
With arms reversed, and muffled drum,
  Follow the funeral car.
They show the banners taken,
  They tell his battles won,
And after him lead his masterless steed,
  While peals the minute gun.

Amid the noblest of the land
  Men lay the sage to rest,
And give the bard an honored place
  With costly marble dressed.
In the great minster transept,
  Where lights like glories fall,
And the sweet choir sings, and the organ rings,
  Along the emblazoned wall.

This was the bravest warrior
  That ever buckled sword;
This the most gifted poet
  That ever breathed a word;
And never earth's philosopher
  Traced, with his golden pen,
On the deathless page, truths half so sage,
  As he wrote down for men.

And had he not high honor,
  The hillside for his pall;
To lie in state while angels wait
  With stars for tapers tall;
And the dark rock pines, like tossing plumes,
  Over his bier to wave;
And God's own hand, in that lonely land,
  To lay him in the grave?—

In that deep grave, without a name,
  Whence his uncoffined clay
Shall break again— most wondrous thought!—
  Before the judgment day,
And stand with glory wrapped around
  On the hills he never trod,
And speak of the strife that won our life
  With the Incarnate Son of God.

O, lonely tomb in Moab's land,
  O, dark Beth-peor's hill,
Speak to these curious hearts of ours,
  And teach them to be still.
God hath His mysteries of Grace—
  Ways that we cannot tell;
He hides them deep, like the secret sleep
  Of him he loved so well.

Mrs. Cecil Francis Alexander.

APOSTROPHE TO THE OCEAN.

There is a pleasure in the pathless woods,
  There is a rapture on the lonely shore,
There is society, where none intrudes,
  By the deep sea, and music in its roar.
  I love not man the less, but Nature more,
From these our interviews, in which I steal
  From all I may be, or have been before,
To mingle with the universe and feel
What I can ne'er express, yet cannot all conceal.

Roll on, thou deep and dark blue Ocean—roll!
　　Ten thousand fleets sweep over thee in vain,
Man marks the earth with ruin—his control
　　Stops with the shore;—upon the watery plain
　　The wrecks are all thy deed, nor doth remain
A shadow of man's ravage, save his own,
　　When for a moment, like a drop of rain,
He sinks into thy depths with bubbling groan,
Without a grave, unknelled, uncoffined, and unknown.

The armaments which thunderstrike the walls
　　Of rock-built cities, bidding nations quake,
And monarchs tremble in their capitals;
　　The oak leviathans, whose huge ribs make
　　Their clay creator the vain title take
Of lord of thee, and arbiter of war,—
　　These are thy toys, and, as the snowy flake,
They melt into thy yeast of waves, which mar
Alike the Armada's pride, or spoils of Trafalgar.

Thy shores are empires, changed in all save thee—
　　Assyria, Greece, Rome, Carthage,—what are they?
Thy waters wasted them while they were free,
　　And many a tyrant since; their shores obey
　　The stranger, slave, or savage; their decay
Has dried up realms to deserts:—not so thou,
　　Unchangeable, save to thy wild waves' play—
Time writes no wrinkle on thine azure brow—
Such as creation's dawn beheld, thou rollest now.

Thou glorious mirror, where the Almighty's form
　　Glasses itself in tempests; in all time,
Calm or convulsed—in breeze or gale or storm,
　　Icing the pole, or in the torrid clime
　　Dark heaving;—boundless, endless, and sublime—
The image of Eternity—the throne
　　Of the Invisible; even from out thy slime
The monsters of the deep are made; each zone
Obeys thee: thou goest forth, dread, fathomless, alone.

And I have loved thee, Ocean! and my joy
　　Of youthful sports was on thy breast to be

Borne, like thy bubbles, onward: from a boy
   I wantoned with thy breakers—they to me
   Were a delight; and if the freshening sea
Made them a terror,—'t was a pleasing fear;
   For I was, as it were, a child of thee,
And trusted to thy billows far and near,
And laid my hand upon thy mane—as I do here.
                                   Lord Byron.

THE LOST CHORD.

Seated one day at the organ,
   I was weary and ill at ease,
And my fingers wandered idly
   Over the noisy keys.

I do not know what I was playing,
   Or what I was dreaming then;
But I struck one chord of music,
   Like the sound of a great Amen.

It flooded the crimson twilight,
   Like the close of an Angel's Psalm,
And it lay on my fevered spirit
   With a touch of infinite calm.

It quieted pain and sorrow,
   Like love overcoming strife;
It seemed the harmonious echo
   From our discordant life.

It linked all perplexéd meanings
   Into one perfect peace,
And trembled away into silence
   As if it were loth to cease.

I have sought, but I seek it vainly,
   That one lost chord divine,
That came from the soul of the Organ,
   And entered into mine.

It may be that Death's bright angel
 Will speak in that chord again;
It may be that only in Heaven
 I shall hear that grand Amen.
     Adelaide A. Proctor.

HYMN TO THE NIGHT.

I heard the trailing garments of the Night
 Sweep through her marble halls!
I saw her sable skirts all fringed with light
 From the celestial walls!

I felt her presence, by its spell of might,
 Stoop o'er me from above;
The calm, majestic presence of the Night,
 As of the one I love.

I heard the sounds of sorrow and delight,
 The manifold, soft chimes,
That fill the haunted chambers of the Night,
 Like some old poet's rhymes.

From the cool cisterns of the midnight air
 My spirit drank repose;
The fountain of perpetual peace flows there,—
 From those deep cisterns flows.

O holy Night! from thee I learn to bear
 What man has borne before!
Thou layest thy finger on the lips of Care,
 And they complain no more.

Peace! Peace! Orestes-like I breathe this prayer!
 Descend with broad-winged flight,
The welcome, the thrice-prayed for, the most fair,
 The best-beloved Night!
     Henry Wadsworth Longfellow.

THE BARDS.

When the sweet day in silence hath departed,
　And twilight comes with dewy, downcast eyes,
The glowing spirits of the mighty-hearted
　Like stars around me rise.

Spirits whose voices pour an endless measure,
　Exhaustless as the choral founts of night,
Until my trembling soul, oppressed with pleasure,
　Throbs in a flood of light.

Old Homer's song in mighty undulations
　Comes surging ceaseless up the oblivious main:—
I hear the rivers from succeeding nations
　Go answering down again.

Hear Virgil's strain through pleasant pastures strolling,
　And Tasso's sweeping round through Palestine,
And Dante's deep and solemn river rolling
　Through groves of midnight pine.

I hear the iron Norseman's numbers ringing
　Through frozen Norway like a herald's horn;
And like a lark, hear glorious Chaucer singing
　Away in England's morn.

In Rhenish halls, still hear the pilgrim lover
　Chant his wild story to the wailing strings,
Till the young maiden's eyes are brimming over
　Like the full cup she brings.

And hear from Scottish hills the souls unquiet
　Pouring in torrents their perpetual lays,
As their impetuous mountain runnels riot
　In the long rainy days;

The world-wide Shakspeare—the imperial Spenser:
　Whose shafts of song o'ertop the angels' seats,—
While, delicate as from a silver censer,
　Float the sweet dreams of Keats!

Nor these alone—for through the growing present,
    Westward the starry path of Poesy lies—
Her glorious spirit, like the evening crescent,
    Comes rounding up the skies.

                    Thomas Buchanan Read.

RECESSIONAL.

God of our fathers, known of old—
    Lord of our far-flung battle-line—
Beneath whose awful hand we hold
    Dominion over palm and pine—
Lord God of Hosts, be with us yet,
Lest we forget—lest we forget!

The tumult and the shouting dies—
    The captains and the kings depart—
Still stands Thine ancient sacrifice,
    An humble and a contrite heart.
Lord God of Hosts, be with us yet,
Lest we forget—lest we forget!

Far-called our navies melt away—
    On dune and headland sinks the fire—
Lo, all our pomp of yesterday
    Is one with Nineveh and Tyre!
Judge of the Nations, spare us yet,
Lest we forget—lest we forget!

If, drunk with sight of power, we loose
    Wild tongues that have not Thee in awe—
Such boasting as the Gentiles use,
    Or lesser breeds without the Law—
Lord God of Hosts, be with us yet,
Lest we forget—lest we forget!

For heathen heart that puts her trust
    In reeking tube and iron shard—
All valiant dust that builds on dust,
    And guarding calls not Thee to guard—
For frantic boast and foolish word,
Thy mercy on Thy people, Lord!
    Amen.

                    Rudyard Kipling.

ORATORICAL STYLES.

EXPULSIVE OROTUND.

This form of the Orotund is used in the expression of all oratorical styles. The air instead of flowing from the mouth in a continuous stream as in the Effusive Orotund, is gathered up in a tense, compact volume and thrown into the glottis, whence it issues in the form of a short shout.

The key to the effective and easy expression of all oratorical styles requires a separate impulsion of air for each tone or word that is uttered. The tones of the orator thus formed resemble the firm resonant strokes of a bell, or the compact and solid blows of a hammer on an anvil. Flabbiness of tone, which destroys all vigor of expression, and imperfect vocalization, producing huskiness, would be speedily overcome if the tones were made firm by energetic expulsion of the air in the pronunciation of each word. Daily practice on the vowels and numerals, securing a sturdy and resonant tone in the enunciation of each word, is the most direct and simple way to acquire this form of expression.

Two essential points of advantage are gained by the adoption of these suggestions: First, economy of breath; second, distinctness of utterance. The tones being made in such a firm and compact manner, it is apparent that the liability of air escaping unvocalized is diminished, and what is used is put in such form as to secure the greatest amount of sound with the least possible expenditure of breath. In short, the speaker is working at his best with the least possible outlay of physical exertion.

Indistinctness is practically impossible, as each word is made by a separate impulsion of breath, and hence the speaker must be distinct in his utterance, if he pronounces individual words distinctly.

ORATORICAL SELECTIONS.

SOUTH CAROLINA.

If there be one State in the Union, Mr. President,—and I say it not in a boastful spirit,—that may challenge comparison with any other for a uniform, zealous, ardent, uncalculating devotion to the Union, that State is South Carolina.

Sir, from the very commencement of the Revolution, up to this hour, there is no sacrifice, however great, she has not cheerfully made; no service she has hesitated to perform. She has adhered to you in your prosperity; but in your adversity, she has clung to you with more than filial affection.

No matter what was the condition of her domestic affairs; though deprived of her resources, divided by parties, or surrounded with difficulties, the call of the country has been to her as the voice of God. Domestic discord ceased at the sound;—every man became at once reconciled to his brethren; and the sons of Carolina were all seen crowding together to the temple, bringing their gift to the altar of their common country.

What, sir, was the conduct of the South during the Revolution? Sir, I honor New England for her conduct in that glorious struggle. But great as is the praise which belongs to her, I think at least equal honor is due to the South. They espoused the quarrel of their brethren with a generous zeal, which did not suffer them to stop to calculate their interests in the dispute.

Favorites of the mother country, possessed of neither ships nor seamen, to create a commercial relationship, they might have found in their situation a guarantee that their trade would be forever fostered and protected by Great Britain. But, trampling on all consideration, either of interest or of safety, they rushed into the conflict; and fighting for principle, periled all in the sacred cause of freedom.

Never were there exhibited in the history of the world, higher examples of noble daring, dreadful suffering, and heroic endurance than by the Whigs of Carolina during the Revolution. The whole State, from the mountains to the sea, was overrun by an overwhelming force of the enemy. The fruits of industry perished on the spot where they were produced, or were consumed by the foe. The "plains of Carolina" drank up the most precious blood of her citizens. Black and smoking ruins marked the places which had been the habitations of her children!

Driven from their homes into the gloomy and almost impenetrable swamps,—even there the spirit of liberty survived; and South Carolina, sustained by the example of her Sumpters and her Marions, proved by her conduct that, though her soil might be overrun, the spirit of her people was invincible!

Robert Young Hayne.

NEW ENGLAND.

The gentleman from South Carolina taunts us with counting the costs of that war in which the liberties and honor of the country, and the interests of the North, as he asserts, were forced to go elsewhere for their defense. Will he sit down with me and count the cost now? Will he reckon up how much of treasure the State of South Carolina expended in that war, and how much the State of Massachusetts?—how much of the blood of either State was poured out on sea or land? I challenge the gentleman to the test of patriotism, which the army rolls, the navy lists, and the treasury books afford.

Sir, they who revile us for our opposition to the last war have looked only to the surface of things. They little know the extremities of suffering which the people of Massachusetts bore at that period, out of attachment to the Union,—their families beggared, their fathers and sons bleeding in camps, or pining in foreign prisons. They forget that not a field was marshaled on this side of the mountains in which the men of Massachusetts did not play their part, as became their sires, and their "blood fetched from mettle of war proof." They battled and bled, wherever battle was fought or blood drawn.

Nor only by land. I ask the gentleman, Who fought your naval battles in the last war? Who led you on to victory after victory, on the ocean and the lakes? Whose was the triumphant prowess before which the Red Cross of England paled with unwonted shames? Were they not men of New England? Were these not foremost in those maritime encounters which humbled the pride and power of Great Britain?

I appeal to my colleague before me from our common county of brave old Essex,—I appeal to my respected colleagues from the shores of the Old Colony. Was there a village or a hamlet on Massachusetts Bay which did not gather its hardy seamen to man the gun-decks of your ships of war? Did they not rally to the battle as men flock to a feast?

In conclusion, I beseech the House to pardon me, if I may have kindled, on this subject, into something of unseemly ardor. I cannot sit tamely by in humble, acquiescent silence when reflections, which I know to be unjust, are cast on the faith and honor of Massachusetts.

Had I suffered them to pass without admonition, I should have deemed that the disembodied spirits of her departed children, from their ashes mingled with the dust of every stricken field of the Revolution,—from their bones moldering to the consecrated earth of Bunker's Hill, of Saratoga, of Monmouth, would start up in visible shape before me to cry shame on me, their recreant countryman.

Sir, I have roamed through the world to find hearts nowhere warmer than hers; soldiers nowhere braver; patriots nowhere purer; wives and mothers nowhere truer; maidens nowhere lovelier; green valleys and bright rivers nowhere greener or brighter; and I will not be silent when I hear her patriotism or her truth questioned with so much as a whisper of detraction. Living, I will defend her; dying, I would pause in my last expiring breath to utter a prayer of fond remembrance for my native New England.

Caleb Cushing.

LORD PLUNKET ON THE IRISH PARLIAMENT.

Sir—I, in the most express terms, deny the *competency* of Parliament to abolish the Legislature of Ireland. I warn you, do not dare to lay your hand on the Constitution—I tell you that if, circumstanced as you are, you pass an act which surrenders the government of Ireland to the English Parliament, it will be a nullity, and that no man in Ireland will be bound to obey it. I make the assertion deliberately—I repeat it, and I call on any man who hears me to take down my words;—you have not been elected for this purpose—you are appointed to make *laws*, and not *legislatures*—you are appointed to *act under* the Constitution, not to *alter* it—you are appointed to *exercise* the functions of legislators, and *not to transfer them*—and if you do so, your act is a *dissolution* of the government—you resolve society into its original elements, and no man in the land is bound to obey you.

Sir, I state doctrines which are not merely founded in the immutable laws of justice and of truth. I state not merely the opinions of the ablest men who have written on the science of government; but I state the practice of our Constitution, as settled at the era of the Revolution, and I state the doctrine under which the House of Hanover derives its title to the throne. Has the King a right to transfer his crown? Is he competent to annex it to the crown of Spain, or of any other country? No—but he may abdicate it; and every man who knows the Constitution knows the consequence—the right reverts to the next in succession—if they all abdicate, it reverts to the people. The man who questions this doctrine, in the same breath must arraign the sovereign on the throne as an usurper. Are you competent to transfer your legislative rights to the French council of five hundred? Are you competent to transfer them to the British Parliament? I answer, No. When you transfer you abdicate, and the great original trust reverts to the people from whom it issued. Yourselves you may extinguish, but Parliament you cannot extinguish—it is enthroned in the hearts of the people—it is enshrined in the sanctuary of the Constitution; it is immortal as the island which it protects. As well might the frantic suicide hope that the act which destroys his miserable body should extinguish his eternal soul. Again, I therefore warn you, do not dare to lay your hands on the Constitution; it is above your power. Sir, I do not say that the Parliament and the people, by mutual consent and co-operation, may not change the form of the Constitution. Whenever such a case arises, it must be decided on its own merits—but that is not this case. If government considers this a season peculiarly fitted for *experiments* on the Constitution, they may call on the people. I ask you, Are you ready to do so? Are you ready to abide the event of such an appeal? What is it you must, in that event, submit to the people? Not this particular project; for if you dissolve the present form of government, they become free to choose any other—you fling them to the fury of the tempest; you must call on them to unhouse themselves of the established Constitution, and to fashion to themselves another. I ask again, Is this the time for an experiment of that nature?

Thank God, the people have manifested no such wish— so far as they have spoken, their voice is decidedly against this daring innovation. You know that no voice has been uttered in its favor, and you cannot be infatuated enough to take confidence from the silence which prevails in some parts of the kingdom; if you know how to appreciate that silence, it is more formidable than the most clamorous opposition— you may be rived and shivered by the lightning, before you hear the peal of the thunder! But, sir, we are told we should discuss this question with calmness and composure. I am called on to surrender my birthright and my honor, and I am told I should be calm, composed.

National pride! Independence of our country! These, we are told by the Minister, are only vulgar topics, fitted for the meridian of the mob, but unworthy to be mentioned in such an enlightened assembly as this; they are trinkets and gewgaws fit to catch the fancy of childish and unthinking people like you, sir, or like your predecessor in that chair, but utterly unworthy the consideration of this House, or of the matured understanding of the noble lord who conde-scends to instruct it! Gracious God! we see a PERRY reascending from the tomb, and raising his awful voice to warn us against the surrender of our freedom; and we see that the proud and virtuous feelings which warmed the breast of that aged and venerable man, are only calculated to excite the contempt of this young philosopher, who has been transplanted from the nursery to the cabinet, to outrage the feelings and understanding of the country.

Lord Plunket.

DANIEL O'CONNELL ON REPEAL OF THE UNION.

Probably the largest political gathering in the history of the world was held on the Hill of Tara, August 15, 1843. It is estimated that not less than a quarter of a million persons were present. They came from all parts of Ireland, under the guidance of their parish priests, to hear the great orator.

We are standing upon Tara of the Kings; the spot where the monarchs of Ireland were elected, and where the chieftains of Ireland bound themselves, by the most solemn pledges of honor, to protect their native land against the Dane and every stranger. This was emphatically the spot from which emanated every social power and legal authority by which the force of the entire country was concentrated for the purposes of national defense.

On this spot I have a most important duty to perform. I here protest, in the name of my country and in the name of my God, against the unfounded and unjust Union. My proposition to Ireland is that the Union is not binding on her people. It is void in conscience and in principle, and as a matter of constitutional law I attest these facts. Yes, I attest by everything that is sacred, without being profane, the truth of my assertions. There is no real union between the two countries, and my proposition is that there was no authority given to any one to pass the Act of Union. Neither the English nor the Irish Legislature was competent to pass that Act, and I arraign it on these grounds. One authority alone could make that Act binding, and that was the voice of the people of Ireland. The Irish Parliament was elected to make laws, and not to make legislatures; and, therefore, it had no right to assume the authority to pass the Act of Union. The Irish Parliament was elected by the Irish people as their trustees; the people were their masters, and the members were their servants, and had no right to transfer the property to any other power on earth. If the Irish Parliament had transferred its power of legislation to the French Chamber, would any man assert that the Act was valid? Would any man be mad enough to assert it? Would any man be insane enough to assert it, and would the insanity of the assertion be mitigated by sending any number of members to the French Chamber? Everybody must admit that it would not. What care I for France?—and I care as little for England as for France, for both countries are foreign to me. The very highest authority in England has proclaimed us to be aliens in blood, in religion, and in language. To show the invalidity of the Union, I will only quote the declaration of Lord Plunket in the Irish Parliament, who told them that they had no authority to transfer the legislation of the country to other hands. As well, said he, might a maniac imagine that the blow by which he destroys his wretched body annihilates his immortal soul, as you imagine that you can annihilate the soul of Ireland— her constitutional rights.

I therefore proclaim the nullity of the Union. In the face of Europe I proclaim its nullity. In the face of France and of Spain, I proclaim its nullity; and I proclaim its nullity in the face of the liberated States of America. I go farther, and proclaim its nullity on the grounds of the iniquitous means by which it was carried. It was effected by the most flagrant fraud. A rebellion was provoked by the Government of the day, in order that they might have a pretext for crushing the liberties of Ireland. There was this addition to the fraud, that at the time of the Union, Ireland had no legal protection. The Habeas Corpus Act was suspended, and the lives and liberties of the people were at the mercy of courtsmartial. You remember the shrieks of those who suffered under martial law. The next fraud was that the Irish people were not allowed to meet to remonstrate against it. In King's County the High Sheriff called the people together in the courthouse, and Colonel Connor, of the North Cork Militia, supported by artillery and a troop of horse, entered the courthouse at the head of two hundred of his regiment, and turned out the sheriff, magistrates, grand jurors, and freeholders assembled to petition against the enactment of the Union. In Tipperary a similar scene took place. A meeting convened by the High Sheriff was dispersed at the point of the bayonet. Thus public sentiment was stifled; and if there was a compact, as is alleged, it is void on account of the fraud and force by which it was carried.

My next impeachment against the Union is the gross corruption with which it was carried. No less than £1,275,000 was spent upon the rotten boroughs, and £2,000,000 was given in direct bribery. There was not one office that was not made instrumental to the carrying of the measure. Six to seven judges were raised to the Bench for the votes they gave in its support; and no less than twelve bishops were elevated to the Episcopal Bench for having taken the side of the Union; for corruption then spared nothing to effect its purpose—corruption was never carried so far; and if this is to be binding on the Irish nation, there is no use in honesty at all.

My next impeachment of the Union is its destructive and deleterious effect upon the industry and prosperity of the country. The county of Meath was once studded with noble residences. What is it now? You remember the once prosperous linen-weavers of Meath. There is scarcely a penny paid to them now. In short, the Union struck down the manufactures of Ireland. The Commissioners of the Poor Law prove that 120,000 persons in Ireland are in a state of destitution during the greater part of each year. How is it that in one of the most fertile countries in the world this should occur? But the Union is more a nullity on ecclesiastical grounds; for why should the great majority of the people of Ireland pay for the support of a religion which they do not believe to be true? The Union was carried by the most abominable corruption and bribery, by financial robbery on an extensive scale, which makes it the more heinous and oppressive; and the result is that Ireland is saddled with an unjust debt, her commerce is taken from her, her trade is destroyed, and a large number of her people are thus reduced to misery and distress.

On the 2nd of January last I called this the Repeal year, and I was laughed at for doing so. Are they laughing now? No; it is now my turn to laugh; and I will now say that in twelve months more we will have our Parliament again on College Green. The Queen has the undoubted prerogative at any time to order her Ministers to issue writs, which, being signed by the Lord Chancellor, the Irish Parliament would at once be convened without the necessity of applying to the English Legislature to repeal what they appear to consider a valid Act of Union. And if Sugden would not sign the writ, an Irish Chancellor would soon be found who would do so. And if we have our Parliament again in Dublin, is there, I would ask, a coward amongst you who would not rather die than allow it to be taken away by an Act of Union? Let every man who would not allow the Act of Union to pass hold up his hand. When the Irish Parliament is again assembled, I will defy any power on earth to take it from us again. Your shouts are almost enough to call to life those who rest in the grave. I can almost fancy the spirits of the mighty dead hovering over you, and the ancient kings and chiefs of Ireland, from the clouds, listening to the shouts sent up from Tara for Irish liberty. Your cheers will penetrate to the extremity of civilization. Our movement is the admiration of the world, for no other country can show so much force with so much propriety of conduct. No other country can show a people assembled for the highest national purposes that can actuate man; can show hundreds of thousands able in strength to carry any battle that ever was fought, and yet separating with the tranquillity of schoolboys. You have stood by me long—stand by me a little longer, and Ireland will be again a nation.

Daniel O'Connell.

ERSKINE ON THE FREEDOM OF THE PRESS.

I say without reserve, speaking merely in the abstract, and not meaning to decide upon the merits of Mr. Hastings's cause, that an impeachment for an error in judgment is contrary to the whole spirit of English criminal justice, which, though not binding on the House of Commons, ought to be a guide to its proceedings. I say that the extraordinary jurisdiction of impeachment ought never to be assumed to expose error, or to scourge misfortune, but to hold up a terrible example to corruption and willful abuse of authority, by extra legal pains.

Now, is it possible for any human being to believe that a man, having no other intention than to vilify the House of Commons (as this information charges), should yet keep his mind thus fixed and settled as the needle to the pole, upon the serious merits of Mr. Hastings's defense, without ever straying into matter even questionable, except in the two or three selected parts out of two or three hundred pages? This is a forbearance which could not have existed if calumny and detraction had been the malignant objects which led him to the inquiry and publication. The whole fallacy, therefore, arises from holding up to view a few detached passages, and carefully concealing the general tenor of the book.

It now remains to remind you that another consideration has been strongly pressed upon you, and, no doubt, will be insisted on in reply. You will be told that the matters which I have been justifying as legal, and even meritorious, have therefore not been made the subject of complaint; and that whatever intrinsic merit parts of the book may be supposed or even admitted to possess, such merit can afford no justification to the selected passages, some of which, even with the context, carry the meaning charged by the information, and which are indecent animadversions on authority. To this I would answer (still protesting as I do against the application of any one of the innuendoes), that if you are firmly persuaded of the singleness and purity of the author's intentions, you are not bound to subject him to infamy, because, in the zealous career of a just and animated composition, he happens to have tripped with his pen into an intemperate expression in one or two instances of a long work. If this severe duty were binding on your consciences, the liberty of the press would be an empty sound, and no man could venture to write on any subject, however pure his purpose, without an attorney at one elbow and a counsel at the other.

From minds thus subdued by the terrors of punishment there could issue no works of genius to expand the empire of human reason, nor any masterly compositions on the general nature of government, by the help of which the great commonwealths of mankind have founded their establishments; much less any of those useful applications of them to critical conjunctures by which, from time to time, our own Constitution, by the exertion of patriot citizens, has been brought back to its standard. Under such terrors, all the great lights of science and civilization must be extinguished; for men cannot communicate their free thoughts to one another with a lash held over their heads. It is the nature of everything that is great and useful, both in the animate and inanimate world, to be wild and irregular; and we must be contented to take them with the alloys which belong to them, or live without them. Genius breaks from the fetters of criticism; but its wanderings are sanctioned by its majesty and wisdom when it advances in its path. Subject it to the critic, and you tame it into dullness. Mighty rivers break down their banks in the winter, sweeping away to death the flocks which are fattened on the soil that they fertilize in the summer; the few may be saved by embankments from drowning, but the flock must perish of hunger. Tempests occasionally shake our dwellings and dissipate our commerce, but they scourge before them the lazy elements which, without them, would stagnate into pestilence. In like manner Liberty herself, the last and best gift of God to His creatures, must be taken just as she is; you might pare her down into bashful regularity, and shape her into a perfect model of severe, scrupulous law, but she would then be Liberty no longer; and you must be content to die under the lash of this inexorable justice which you had exchanged for the banners of Freedom.

Upon the principle on which the Attorney-General prays sentence upon my client—God have mercy upon us! Instead of standing before him in judgment with the hopes and consolations of Christians, we must call upon the mountains to cover us; for which of us can present, for omniscient examination, a pure, unspotted, and faultless course? But I humbly expect that the benevolent Author of our being will judge us as I have been pointing out for your example. Holding up the great volume of our lives in His hands, and regarding the general scope of them—if He discovers benevolence, charity and good-will to man beating in the heart, where He alone can look; if He finds that our conduct, though often forced out of the path by our infirmities, has been in general well directed, His all-searching eye will assuredly never pursue us into those little corners of our lives, much less will His justice select them for punishment without the general context of our existence, by which faults may be sometimes found to have grown out of virtues, and very many of our heaviest offenses to have been grafted by human imperfection upon the best and kindest of our affections. No, gentlemen, believe me, this is not the course of divine justice, or there is no truth in the gospels of heaven. If the general tenor of a man's conduct be such as I have represented it, he may walk through the shadow of death, with all his faults about him, with as much cheerfulness as in the common paths of life; because he knows that, instead of a stern accuser to expose before the Author of his nature those frail passages which, like the scored matter in the book before you, checker the volume of the brightest and best spent life, His mercy will obscure them from the eye of His purity, and our repentance will blot them out forever.

Lord Erskine.

LORD MACAULAY ON THE REFORM BILL.

I well remember a certain evening in the month of May, 1827. I had not then the honor of a seat in this House, but I was an attentive observer of its proceedings. The right honorable Baronet opposite, of whom personally I desire to speak with that high respect which I feel for his talents and his character, but of whose public conduct I must speak with the sincerity required by my public duty, was then, as he is now, out of office. He had just resigned the seals of the Home Department, because he conceived that the recent ministerial arrangements had been too favorable to the Catholic claims. He rose to ask whether it was the intention of the new Cabinet to repeal the Test and Corporation Acts, and to reform the Parliament. He bound up, I well remember, those two questions together; and he declared that, if the Ministers should either attempt to repeal the Test and Corporation Acts, or bring forward a measure of Parliamentary reform, he should think it his duty to oppose them to the utmost. Since that declaration was made, four years have elapsed; and what is now the state of the three questions which then chiefly agitated the minds of men? What is become of the Test and Corporation Acts? They are repealed. By whom? By the right honorable Baronet. What has become of the Catholic disabilities? They are removed. By whom? By the right honorable Baronet. The question of Parliamentary reform is still behind. But signs, of which it is impossible to misconceive the import, do most clearly indicate that, unless that question also be speedily settled, property, and order, and all the institutions of this great monarchy will be exposed to fearful peril. Is it possible that gentlemen long versed in high political affairs cannot read these signs? Is it possible that they can really believe that the representative system of England, such as it now is, will last till the year 1860? If not, for what would they have us wait? Would they have us wait merely that we may show to all the world how little we have profited by our own recent experience? Would they have us wait that we may once again hit the exact point where we can neither refuse with authority, nor concede with grace? Would they have us wait that the numbers of the discontented party may become larger, its demands higher, its feelings more acrimonious, its organization more complete? Would they have us wait till the whole tragi-comedy of 1827 has been acted over again; till they have been brought into office by a cry of "No Reform," to be reformers, as they were once before brought into office by a cry of "No Popery," to be emancipators? Have they obliterated from their minds the transactions of that year? And have they forgotten all the transactions of the succeeding year? Have they forgotten how the spirit of liberty in Ireland, debarred from its natural outlet, found a vent by forbidden passages? Have they forgotten how we were forced to indulge the Catholics in all the license of rebels, merely because we chose to withhold from them the liberties of subjects? Do they wait for associations more formidable than that of the Corn Exchange, for contributions larger than the Rent, for agitators more violent than those who, three years ago, divided with the King and the Parliament the sovereignty of Ireland? Do they wait for that last and most dreadful paroxysm of popular rage, for that last and most cruel test of military fidelity? Let them wait, if their past experience shall induce them to think that any high honor or any exquisite pleasure is to be obtained by a policy like this. Let them wait, if this strange and fearful infatuation be indeed upon them, that they should not see with their eyes, or hear with their ears, or understand with their heart. But let us know our interest and our duty better. Turn where we may, within, around, the voice of great events is proclaiming to us: Reform, that you may preserve. Now, therefore, while everything at home and abroad forebodes ruin to those who persist in a hopeless struggle against the spirit of the age; now, while the crash of the proudest throne of the Continent is still resounding in our ears; now, while the roof of a British palace affords an ignominious shelter to the exiled heir of forty kings; now, while we see on every side ancient institutions subverted, and great societies dissolved; now, while the heart of England is still sound; now, while old feelings and old associations retain a power and a charm which may too soon pass away; now, in this, your accepted time; now, in this, your day of salvation, take counsel, not of prejudice, not of party spirit, not of the ignominious pride of a fatal consistency, but of history, of reason, of the ages which are past, of the signs of this most portentous time. Pronounce in a manner worthy of the expectation with which this great debate has been anticipated, and of the long remembrance which it will leave behind. Renew the youth of the state. Save property, divided against itself. Save the multitude, endangered by its own ungovernable passions. Save the aristocracy, endangered by its own unpopular power. Save the greatest, and fairest, and most highly civilized community that ever existed, from calamities which may in a few days sweep away all the rich heritage of so many ages of wisdom and glory. The danger is terrible. The time is short. If this bill should be rejected, I pray to God that none of those who concur in rejecting it may ever remember their votes with unavailing remorse, amidst the wreck of laws, the confusion of ranks, the spoliation of property, and the dissolution of social order.

Lord Macaulay.

THE MARTYRDOM OF JOAN OF ARC.

At the time of Joan of Arc's appearance in history, France had become a province of England, the great city of Orleans had been for a year in a state of siege, the people were suffering incredible hardships, and the Dauphin, who had not yet been crowned, was about to give up the struggle in despair. The young peasant girl from Domrémy, who seemed the very embodiment of patriotic fervor, made her way to the court, rekindled the national pride, and proceeding to Orleans at the head of the French troops, raised the siege and entered in triumph. After other victories, she conducted the king to Rheims, where he was solemnly crowned. Then, feeling that her mission was ended, she begged to be allowed to return to her native village. But in vain. Her services were still demanded, and she was obliged to enter upon more than one military plan which she did not approve. Many misfortunes followed, till at last she was captured by the Burgundians, who basely surrendered her to the English.

Her trial was conducted by the Bishop of Beauvais, a Frenchman who was sold to English interests, and who hoped, by favor of the English leaders, to reach the highest preferment. From beginning to end the proceedings were barbarously cruel and unjust. Finally, the innocent young Maid of Orleans was condemned as a witch, and sentenced to be burned at the stake.

On the Wednesday after Trinity Sunday in 1431, being then about nineteen years of age, the Maid of Arc underwent her martyrdom. She was conducted before midday, guarded by eight hundred spearmen, to a platform of prodigious height, constructed of wooden billets supported by occasional walls of lath and plaster, and traversed by hollow spaces in every direction for the creation of air-currents. "Ten thousand men," says M. Michelet himself, "ten thousand men wept;" and of these ten thousand, the majority were political enemies knitted together by cords of superstition. What else was it but her constancy, united with her angelic gentleness, that drove the fanatic English soldier— who had sworn to throw a faggot on her scaffold—suddenly to turn away, a penitent for life, saying everywhere that he had seen a dove rising upon wings to heaven from the ashes where she had stood? What else drove the executioner to kneel at every shrine for pardon to *his* share in the tragedy? And if all this were insufficient, then I cite the closing act of her life, as valid on her behalf, were all other testimonies against her. The executioner had been directed to apply his torch from below. He did so. The fiery smoke rose upwards in billowing volumes. A Dominican monk was then standing almost at her side. Wrapped up in his sublime office, he saw not the danger, but still persisted in his prayers. Even then, when the last enemy was racing up the fiery stairs to seize her, even at that moment did this noblest of girls think only for *him*, the one friend that would not forsake her, and not for herself; bidding him with her last breath to care for his own preservation, but to leave *her* to God. That girl, whose latest breath ascended in this sublime expression of self-oblivion, did not utter the word *recant* either with her lips or in her heart. No; she did not, though one should rise from the dead to swear it.

*   *   *   *   *

Bishop of Beauvais! thy victim died in fire upon a scaffold, —thou upon a down bed. But for the departing minutes of life, both are oftentimes alike. At the farewell crisis, when the gates of death are opening and flesh is resting from its struggles, oftentimes the tortured and torturer have the same truce from carnal torment; both sink together into sleep; together both, sometimes, kindle into dreams. When the mortal mists were gathering fast upon you two, bishop and shepherd girl—when the pavilions of life were closing up their shadowy curtains about you—let us try, through the gigantic glooms, to decipher the flying features of your separate visions.

The shepherd girl that had delivered France—she, from

her dungeon, she, from her baiting at the stake, she, from her duel with fire, as she entered her last dream—saw Domrémy, saw the fountain of Domrémy, saw the pomp of forests in which her childhood had wandered. The Easter festival, which man had denied to her languishing heart—that resurrection of springtime, which the darkness of dungeons had intercepted from *her*, hungering after the glorious liberty of forests—were by God given back into her hands, as jewels that had been stolen from her by robbers. With those, perhaps (for the minutes of dreams can stretch into ages), was given back to her by God the bliss of childhood. By special privilege, for *her* might be created, in this farewell dream, a second childhood, innocent as the first; but not, like *that*, sad with the gloom of a fearful mission in the rear. The mission had now been fulfilled. The storm was weathered, the skirts even of that mighty storm were drawing off. The blood that she was to reckon for had been exacted; the tears that she was to shed in secret had been paid to the last. The hatred to herself in all eyes had been faced steadily, had been suffered, had been survived. And in her last fight upon the scaffold she had triumphed gloriously; victoriously she had tasted the stings of death. For all, except this comfort from her farewell dream, she had died—died, amidst the tears of ten thousand enemies—died, amidst the drums and trumpets of armies—died, amidst peals redoubling upon peals, volleys upon volleys, from the saluting clarions of martyrs.

Bishop of Beauvais! you also, entering your final dream, saw Domrémy. That fountain, of which the witnesses spoke so much, showed itself to your eyes in pure morning dews; but neither dews, nor the holy dawn could cleanse away the bright spots of innocent blood upon its surface. By the fountain, Bishop, you saw a woman seated, that hid her face. But as *you* draw near, the woman raises her wasted features. Would Domrémy know them again for the features of her child? Ah, but *you* know them, bishop, well! Oh, mercy! what a groan was *that* which the servants, waiting outside the bishop's dream at his bedside, heard from his laboring heart, as at this moment he turned away from the fountain and the woman, seeking rest in the forests afar off. Yet not *so* to escape the woman, whom once again he must behold before he dies. In the forests to which he prays for pity, will he find a respite? What a tumult, what a gathering of feet is there! In glades, where only wild deer should run, armies and nations are assembling; towering in the fluctuating crowd are phantoms that belong to departed hours. There is the Bishop of Beauvais, clinging to the shelter of thickets. What building is that which hands so rapid are raising? Is it a martyr's scaffold? Will they burn the child of Domrémy a second time? No: it is a tribunal that rises to the clouds; and two nations stand around it, waiting for a trial. Shall my Lord of Beauvais sit again upon the judgment seat, and again number the hours for the innocent? Ah! no: he is the prisoner at the bar. Already all is waiting: the mighty audience is gathered, the Court is hurrying to their seats, the witnesses are arrayed, the trumpets are sounding, the judge is taking his place. Oh! but this is sudden. My lord, have you no counsel? "Counsel I have none: in heaven above, or on earth beneath, counselor there is none now that would take a brief from *me:* all are silent." Is it, indeed, come to this? Alas, the time is short, the tumult is wondrous, the crowd stretches away into infinity, but yet I will search in it for somebody to take your brief: I know of somebody that will be your counsel. Who is this that cometh from Domrémy? Who is she in bloody coronation robes from Rheims? Who is she that cometh with blackened flesh from walking the furnaces of Rouen? This is she, the shepherd girl, counselor that had none for herself, whom I choose, bishop, for yours. She it is, I engage, that shall take my lord's brief. She it is, bishop, that would plead for you; yes, bishop, SHE—when heaven and earth are silent.

Thomas De Quincey.

THE APOSTROPHE TO THE VOLUNTEERS.

This oration was delivered at the time of the threatened invasion of England by France, under Napoleon. E. Paxton Hood, Robert Hall's biographer, writes as follows:

"At the time these words were pronounced, the entire country might be said to be waiting breathless with anxiety. About this time it was that Napoleon struck the famous medal, "London taken, 1804." His armies were spread all along the heights of Boulogne, waiting for the fleet which was to land them on our shores. * * * Ours was the only unconquered piece of territory worth conquering in Europe. It was, perhaps, the last great gasp of patriotism our country ever felt. Another such occasion has never occurred · we pray that it never may!"

From the most fixed principles of human nature, as well as from the examples of all history, we may be certain the conquest of this country, should it be permitted to take place, will not terminate in any ordinary catastrophe, in any much less calamitous than utter extermination. Our present elevation will be the exact measure of our future depression, as it will measure the fears and jealousies of those who subdue us. While the smallest vestige remains of our former greatness, while any trace or memorial exists of our having been once a flourishing and independent empire, while the nation breathes, they will be afraid of its recovering its strength, and never think themselves secure of their conquest till our navy is consumed, our wealth dissipated, our commerce extinguished, every liberal institution abolished, our nobles extirpated; whatever in rank, character, and talents gives distinction in society, called out and destroyed, and the refuse which remains swept together into a putrefying heap by the besom of destruction. The enemy will not need to proclaim his triumph; it will be felt in the most expressive silence of extended desolation.

To form an adequate idea of the duties of this crisis, it will be necessary to raise your minds to a level with your station, to extend your views to a distant futurity, and to consequences the most certain, though most remote. By a series of criminal enterprises, by the successes of guilty ambition, the liberties of Europe have been gradually extinguished: the subjugation of Holland, Switzerland, and the free towns of Germany, has completed that catastrophe; and we are the only people in the Eastern hemisphere, who are in the possession of equal laws and a free constitution. Freedom, driven from every spot on the Continent, has sought an asylum in a country which she always chose for her favorite abode; but she is pursued even here, and threatened with destruction. The inundation of lawless power, after covering the whole earth, threatens to follow us here; and we are most exactly, most critically placed, in the only aperture where it can be successfully repelled, in the Thermopylæ of the universe. As far as the interests of freedom are concerned, the most important by far of sublunary interests, you, my countrymen, stand in the capacity of the federal representatives of the human race; for with you it is to determine (under God) in what condition the latest posterity shall be born: their fortunes are entrusted to your care, and on your conduct at this moment depends the color and complexion of their destiny. If liberty, after being extinguished on the Continent, is suffered to expire here, whence is it ever to emerge in the midst of that thick night that will invest it? It remains with you, then, to decide whether that freedom, at whose voice the kingdoms of Europe awoke from the sleep of ages, to run a career of virtuous emulation in everything great and good; the freedom which dispelled the mists of superstition, and invited the nations to behold their God; whose magic touch kindled the rays of genius, the enthusiasm of poetry, and the flame of eloquence; the freedom which poured into our lap opulence and arts, and embellished life with innumerable institutions and improvements, till it became a theater of wonders; it is for you to decide whether this freedom shall yet survive, or be covered with a funeral pall and wrapt in eternal gloom. It is not necessary to await your determination. In the solicitude you feel to prove yourselves worthy of such a trust, every thought of what is afflicting in warfare, every apprehension of danger must vanish, and you are impatient to mingle in the battle of the civilized world.

While you have everything to fear from the success of the enemy, you have every means of preventing that success, so that it is next to impossible for victory not to crown your exertions. The extent of your resources, under God, is equal to the justice of your cause. But should Providence determine otherwise, should you fall in this struggle, should the nation fall, you will have the satisfaction—the purest allotted to man—of having performed your part; your names will be enrolled with the most illustrious dead, while posterity, to the end of time, as often as they revolve the events of this period, will turn to you a reverential eye. I cannot but imagine that virtuous heroes, legislators, and patriots, of every age and country, are bending from their elevated seats to witness this contest, as if they were incapable, till it be brought to a favorable issue, of enjoying their eternal repose. Enjoy that repose, illustrious immortals! Your mantle fell when you ascended; and thousands inflamed with your spirits, and impatient to tread in your steps, are ready *to swear by Him that sitteth upon the throne, and liveth for ever and ever*, they will protect freedom in her last asylum, and never desert that cause which you sustained by your labors, and cemented with your blood. And Thou, sole

Ruler among the children of men, to whom the shields of the
earth belong, *gird on Thy sword, Thou most mighty:* go forth
with our hosts in the day of battle! Impart, in addition to
their hereditary valor, that confidence of success which
springs from Thy presence! Pour into their hearts the spirit
of departed heroes! Inspire them with Thine own; and,
while led by Thine hand, and fighting under Thy banners,
open Thou their eyes to behold in every valley, and in every
plain, what the prophet beheld by the same illumination—
chariots of fire, and horses of fire! *'Then shall the strong
man be as a tow, and the maker of it as a spark; and they
shall both burn together, and none shall quench them.'*

*   *   *   *   *   *

Robert Hall.

EULOGY ON CHARLES SUMNER.

At the opening of the session in the Fall of 1872, Mr.
Sumner introduced two measures which, as he thought,
should complete the record of his political life. One was
his Civil Rights Bill, and the other, a resolution providing
that the names of the battles won over fellow-citizens in the
war of the Rebellion, should be removed from the regimental
colors of the army, and from the army register. This
resolution called forth a new storm against him. It was
denounced as an insult to the heroic soldiers of the Union,
and a degradation of their victories and well-earned
laurels. It was condemned as an unpatriotic act.

Charles Sumner insult the soldiers who had spilled their
blood in a war for human rights! Charles Sumner degrade
victories and depreciate laurels won for the cause of universal freedom! How strange an imputation!

Let the dead man have a hearing. This was his thought:
No civilized nation, from the republics of antiquity down to
our days, ever thought it wise or patriotic to preserve in
conspicuous and durable form the mementoes of victories
won over fellow-citizens in civil war. Why not?

Because every citizen should feel himself with all others
as the child of a common country, and not as a defeated foe.
All civilized governments of our days have instinctively followed the same dictate of wisdom and patriotism. The
Irishman, when fighting for old England at Waterloo, was

not to behold on the red cross floating above him the name of the Boyne. The Scotch Highlander, when standing in the trenches of Sebastopol, was not by the colors of his regiment to be reminded of Culloden. No French soldier at Austerlitz or Solferino had to read upon the tri-color any reminiscence of the Vendée. No Hungarian at Sadowa was taunted by any Austrian banner with the surrender of Villagos. No German regiment, from Saxony or Hanover, charging under the iron hail of Gravelotte, was made to remember by words written on a Prussian standard that the black eagle had conquered them at Koniggratz and Langensalza. Should the son of South Carolina, when at some future day defending the Republic against some foreign foe, be reminded by an inscription on the colors floating over him, that under this flag the gun was fired that killed his father at Gettysburg? Should this great and enlightened Republic, proud of standing in the front of human progress, be less wise, less large-hearted, than the ancients were two thousand years ago, and the kingly governments of Europe are to-day? Let the battle-flags of the brave volunteers, which they brought home from the war with the glorious record of their victories, be preserved intact as a proud ornament of our statehouses and armories. But let the colors of the army, under which the sons of all the States are to meet and mingle in common patriotism, speak of nothing but union,—not a union of conquerors and conquered, but a union which is the mother of all, equally tender to all, knowing of nothing but equality, peace and love among her children.

Such were the sentiments which inspired that resolution. Such were the sentiments which called forth a storm of obloquy. Such were the sentiments for which the Legislature of Massachusetts passed a solemn resolution of censure upon Charles Sumner,—Massachusetts, his own Massachusetts, whom he loved so ardently with a filial love,—of whom he was so proud, who had honored him so much in days gone by, and whom he had so long and so faithfully labored to serve and to honor!

How thankful I am, how thankful every human soul in Massachusetts, how thankful every American must be, that he did not die then! How thankful that he was spared to see the day when the heart of Massachusetts came back to him full of the old love and confidence, assuring him that he would again be her chosen son for her representative seat in the House of States;—when the lawgivers of the old commonwealth, obeying an irresistible impulse of justice, wiped away from the records of the Legislature, and from the fair name of the State, that resolution of censure which had stung him so deeply.

Now we have laid him into his grave, in the motherly soil of Massachusetts, which was so dear to him. He is at rest now, the stalwart, brave old champion, whose face and bearing were so austere, and whose heart was so full of tenderness; who began his career with a pathetic plea for universal peace and charity, and whose whole life was an arduous, incessant, never-resting struggle, which left him all covered with scars. And we can do nothing for him but commemorate his lofty ideals of liberty and equality, and justice, and reconciliation, and purity, and the earnestness and courage and touching fidelity with which he fought for them; so genuine in his sincerity, so single-minded in his zeal, so heroic in his devotion.

Carl Schurz.

IDOLS.

It is a grave thing when a State puts a man among her jewels, the glitter of whose fame makes doubtful acts look heroic. The honors we grant mark how high we stand, and they educate the future. The men we honor and the maxims we lay down in measuring our favorites, show the level and morals of the time. A name has been in every one's mouth of late, and men have exhausted language in trying to express their admiration and their respect. The courts have covered the grave of Mr. Choate with eulogy. Let us see what is their idea of a great lawyer. We are told that "he worked hard," "he never neglected his client," "he flung over the discussions of the forum the grace of a rare scholarship," "no pressure or emergency ever stirred him to an unkind word." A ripe scholar, a profound lawyer, a faithful servant of his client, a gentleman. This is a good record surely. May he sleep in peace. What he earned, God grant he may have. But the bar that seeks to claim for such a one a place among great jurists must itself be weak indeed. Not one high moral trait specified; not one patriotic act mentioned; not one patriotic service even claimed. Look at Mr. Webster's idea of what a lawyer should be in order to be called great, in the sketch he drew of Jeremiah Mason, and notice what stress he lays upon the religious and moral elevation, and the glorious and high purposes which crown his life. Nothing of this now; nothing but incessant eulogy. But not a word of one effort to lift the yoke of cruel or unequal legislation from the neck of its victim; not one attempt to make the code of his country wiser, purer, better; not one effort to bless his times or breathe a higher moral purpose into the community. Not one blow struck for right or for liberty, while the battle of the giants was going on about him; not one patriotic act to stir the hearts of his idolaters; not one public act of any kind whatever about whose merit friend or foe could even quarrel, unless when he scouted our great charter as a glittering generality, or jeered at the philanthropy which tried to practice the sermon on the mount.

When Cordus, the Roman senator, whom Tiberius murdered, was addressing his fellows he began: "Fathers, they accuse me of illegal words; plain proof that there are no illegal deeds with which to charge me." So with those eulogies. Words, nothing but words; plain proof that there were no deeds to praise. Yet this is the model which Massachusetts offers to the Pantheon of the great jurists of the world!

Suppose we stood in that lofty temple of jurisprudence,—on either side of us the statues of the great lawyers of every age and clime,—and let us see what part New England—Puritan, educated, free New England—would bear in the pageant.

Rome points to a colossal figure and says, "That is Papinian, who, when the Emperor Caracella murdered his own brother, and ordered the lawyer to defend the deed, went cheerfully to death, rather than sully his lips with the atrocious plea; and that is Ulpian, who, aiding his prince to put the army below the law, was massacred at the foot of a weak but virtuous throne."

And France stretches forth her grateful hands, crying, "That is D'Aguesseau, worthy, when he went to face an enraged king, of the farewell his wife addressed him: 'Go, forget that you have a wife and children to ruin, and remember only that you have France to save.'"

England says: "That is Coke, who flung the laurels of eighty years in the face of the first Stuart, in defense of the people. This is Selden, on every book of whose library you saw written the motto of which he lived worthy, 'Before everything, liberty!' That is Mansfield, silver-tongued, who proclaimed, 'Slaves cannot breathe in England; if their lungs receive our air, that moment they are free.'

"This is Romily, who spent life trying to make law synonymous with justice, and succeeded in making life and property safer in every city of the empire. And that is Erskine, whose eloquence, spite of Lord Eldon and George the Third, made it safe to speak and to print."

Then New England shouts, "This is Choate, who made it safe to murder, and of whose health thieves asked before they began to steal!"

Wendell Phillips.

TOUSSAINT L'OUVERTURE.

Some doubt the courage of the negro. Go to Hayti and stand on those fifty thousand graves of the best soldiers France ever had, and ask them what they think of the negro's sword. And if that does not satisfy you, go to France, to the splendid mausoleum of the Counts of Rochambeau, and to the eight thousand graves of Frenchmen who skulked home under the English flag, and ask them. And if that does not satisfy you, come home, and if it had been October, 1859, you might have come by way of quaking Virginia, and asked her what she thought of negro courage.

You may also remember this,—that we Saxons were slaves about four hundred years, sold with the land, and our fathers never raised a finger to end that slavery. They waited till Christianity and civilization, till commerce and the discovery of America melted away their chains. Every race has been, some time or other, in chains. But there never was a race that, weakened and degraded by such chattel slavery, unaided, tore off its own fetters, forged them into swords, and won its liberty on the battle-field, but one, and that was the black race of St. Domingo.

So much for the courage of the negro. Now look at his endurance. In 1805 he said to the white men, "This island is ours; not a white foot shall touch it." Side by side with him stood the South American republics, planted by the best blood of the countrymen of Lope de Vega and Cervantes. They topple over so often that you could no more daguerreotype their crumbling fragments than you could the waves of the ocean. And yet, at their side, the negro has kept his island sacredly to himself. Burn over New York to-night, fill up her canals, sink every ship, destroy her railroads, blot out every remnant of education from her sons; let her be ignorant and penniless, with nothing but her hands to begin the world again,—how much could she do in sixty years? And Europe, too, would lend you money, but she will not lend Hayti a dollar. Hayti, from the ruins of her colonial dependence, is become a civilized state, the seventh nation in the catalogue of commerce with this country, inferior in morals and education to none of the West Indian isles. Toussaint L'Ouverture made her what she is. Toussaint was indisputably their chief. Courage, purpose, endurance,— these are the tests. He did plant a state so deep that all the world has not been able to root it up.

Now, blue-eyed Saxon, proud of your race, go back with me to the commencement of the century, and select what statesman you please. Let him be either American or European; let him have a brain the result of six generations of culture; let him have the ripest training of university routine; let him add to it the better education of practical life; crown his temples with the silver of seventy years, and show me the man of Saxon lineage for whom his most sanguine admirer will wreathe a laurel rich as embittered foes have placed on the brow of this negro.

I would call him Napoleon, but Napoleon made his way to empire over broken oaths and through a sea of blood. This man never broke his word. I would call him Cromwell, but Cromwell was only a soldier, and the state he founded went down with him into his grave. I would call him Washington, but the great Virginian held slaves. This man risked his empire rather than permit the slave-trade in the humblest village of his dominions.

You think me a fanatic to-night, for you read history not with your eyes, but with your prejudices. But fifty years hence, when Truth gets a hearing, the Muse of History will put Phocion for the Greek, and Brutus for the Roman, Hampden for England, Lafayette for France, choose Washington as the bright, consummate flower of our earlier civilization, and John Brown the ripe fruit of our noon-day; then, dipping her pen in the sunlight, will write in the clear blue, above them all, the name of the soldier, the statesman, the martyr, Toussaint L'Ouverture.

Wendell Phillips.

IMPEACHMENT OF WARREN HASTINGS.

My Lords, you have now heard the principles on which Mr. Hastings governs the part of Asia subjected to the British empire. Here he has declared his opinion, that he is a despotic prince; that he is to use arbitrary power; and, of course, all his acts are covered with that shield. "I know," says he, "the Constitution of Asia only from its practice." Will your Lordships submit to hear the corrupt practices of mankind made the principles of Government?

He have arbitrary power! My Lords, the East India Company have not arbitrary power to give him; the King has no arbitrary power to give him; your Lordships have not; nor the Commons; nor the whole Legislature. We have no arbitrary power to give, because arbitrary power is a thing which neither any man can hold nor any man can give. No man can lawfully govern himself according to his own will, much less can one person be governed by the will of another. We are all born in subjection, all born equally, high and low, governors and governed, in subjection to one great, immutable, pre-existent law, prior to all our devices, and prior to all our contrivances, paramount to all our ideas and all our sensations, antecedent to our very existence, by which we are knit and connected in the eternal frame of the universe, out of which we cannot stir.

This great law does not arise from our conventions or compacts; on the contrary, it gives to our conventions and compacts all the force and sanction they can have;—it does not arise from our vain institutions. Every good gift is of God; all power is of God;—and He, who has given the power, and from whom alone it originates, will never suffer the exercise of it to be practiced upon any less solid foundation than the power itself. If, then, all dominion of man over man is the effect of the divine disposition, it is bound by the eternal laws of Him that gave it, with which no human authority can dispense; neither he that exercises it, nor even those who are subject to it: and if they were mad enough to make an express compact that should release their magistrate from his duty, and should declare their lives, liberties, and properties dependent upon, not rules and laws, but his mere capricious will, that covenant would be void.

This arbitrary power is not to be had by conquest. Nor can any sovereign have it by succession; for no man can succeed to fraud, rapine, and violence. Those who give and those who receive arbitrary power are alike criminal; and there is no man but is bound to resist it to the best of his power, wherever it shall show its face to the world.

Law and arbitrary power are in eternal enmity. Name me a magistrate, and I will name property; name me power, and I will name protection. It is a contradiction in terms; it is blasphemy in religion, it is wickedness in politics, to say that any man can have arbitrary power. In every patent of office the duty is included. For what else does a magistrate exist? To suppose for power, is an absurdity in idea. Judges are guided and governed by the eternal laws of justice, to which we are all subject. We may bite our chains, if we will; but we shall be made to know ourselves, and be taught that man is born to be governed by *law;* and he that will substitute *will* in the place of it, is an enemy to God.

My Lords, I do not mean to go further than just to remind your Lordships of this,—that Mr. Hastings's government was one whole system of oppression, of robbery of individuals, of spoliation of the public, and of supersession of the whole system of the English government, in order to vest in the worst of the natives all the power that could possibly exist in any government; in order to defeat the ends which all governments ought, in common, to have in view. In the name of the Commons of England, I charge all this villainy upon Warren Hastings, in this last moment of my application to you.

Therefore, it is with confidence that, ordered by the Commons of Great Britain, I impeach Warren Hastings of high crimes and misdemeanors.

I impeach him in the name of the Commons of Great Britain in Parliament assembled, whose parliamentary trust he has abused.

I impeach him in the name of the Commons of Great Britain, whose national character he has dishonored.

I impeach him in the name of the people of India, whose laws, rights, and liberties he has subverted.

I impeach him in the name of the people of India, whose property he has destroyed, whose country he has laid waste and desolate.

I impeach him in the name of human nature itself, which he has cruelly outraged, injured, and oppressed, in both sexes. And I impeach him in the name and by the virtue of those eternal laws of justice, which ought equally to pervade every age, condition, rank, and situation, in the world.

Edmund Burke.

CHARACTER OF WASHINGTON.

There are but three individuals upon whom mankind, with some approach to general consent, have bestowed the epithet of "the Great." Shall we compare our Washington for a moment with each of them? Shall we compare him with Peter the Great of Russia, who flourished in the beginning of the century, and hewed that political colossus of the North into form and symmetry? A sovereign of vast, though often most ill-directed energy; a fearless, and, on some occasions, a beneficent reformer; a consummate organizer, who, with a kind of rough tact, truly felt the pulses of national life in the Titanic frame which he called into being; pursuing a few grand ideas, though often by eccentric methods bordering on madness, but with a resolution which no labors could weary and no dangers appall, and forcing them with an iron will upon an unsympathizing and apathetic people. These are his titles to the epithet of "Great;" but with them all he was an unmitigated tyrant,—the murderer, perhaps the torturer, of his own son; a man who united the wisdom of a philosopher and the policy of a great prince with the tastes of a satyr, the manners of a barbarian, and the passions of a fiend; guilty of crimes so hideous and revolting, that if I attempted to describe them I should drive you shrieking from this hall. You surely would not permit me to place the name of Washington in comparison with his.

Or shall we compare him with Frederick the Second of Prussia, to whom complacent public opinion has also accorded the epithet of "Great." He was no doubt a military and a civil genius of the first order; by the energy of his character he built up a kingdom scarcely known by that title when he came to the throne, into a first-rate power; the fearless soldier, the profound strategist, the heroic chief; nor less a master of political combination, a zealous promoter of the material prosperity of his subjects, who doubled the population of his little kingdom, and increased all the resources in more than the same proportion, notwithstanding the wars in which he was continually involved; but at the same time a pedant, ostentatious, of superficial literary attainments, a wretched poetaster, a dupe of the insipid adulation of godless foreign wits, who flattered him to his face and ridiculed him behind his back; a German sovereign who yet preferred to write and speak poor broken French, in which Voltaire said there was not a sentence which you would not know to be the language of a foreigner; a prince raised by Providence in the bitter school of adversity to an absolute throne, entertaining the most exalted ideas of the kingly prerogative, drawing everything, even the administration of justice, into an arbitrary centralization, who had yet trained his undevout heart to believe that blind chance or blind destiny occupies the throne of the universe; that the heavens and the earth could do without a God, though the paltry electorate of Brandenburgh could not do without a king; and that while it was impossible for him to hold the scattered provinces of his little realm together without a daily outgoing of civil, military and judicial power, moved by one intellect and one will, could yet believe that the systems and systems which compose the universe, beyond the power of human speech to enumerate, or human thought to conceive, are thrown out into one vast anarchy, wheeling and hurtling through the regions of space without a lawgiver and a head; who, so thinking and so believing while he lived, when he came to die, in order to mark more emphatically his contempt for the species to which he belonged, instead of allowing his "poor old carcass," as he himself called it, to be laid by the side of his kindred, ordered that it should be buried with his favorite dogs at Potsdam!

Or shall we compare Washington with the third greatness of his age, the illustrious captain of the last generation in

France; that portentous blazing star which began to flame in the eastern sky as our benignant luminary was sinking in the west, amidst the golden clouds of a nation's blessings? I have no wish to trample on the memory of Napoleon the First, whom I regard by no means as the most ambitious of conquerors, the most arbitrary of despots, or the worst of men. The virtues and the feelings, like the talents, the opportunities, and the fortunes of this extraordinary man, are on too colossal a scale to be measured by ordinary standards of morality. The prevalent opinions in this country of his character and career have come to us through a British medium, discolored by a national prejudice and the deadly struggle of a generation; or by natural reaction have been founded on the panegyrics of grateful adherents and admiring subjects, who deem every Frenchman a partner in the glory of their chief. Posterity and impartial history will subdue the lights and relieve the shadows of the picture. They will accord to him a high, perhaps the highest, rank among the great masters of war, placing his name upon an equality with the three great captains of antiquity, if not above them; will point to his code as a noble monument of legislative wisdom; will dwell upon the creative vigor with which he brought order out of the chaos of the Revolution, retrieving the dilapidated finances and restoring the prostrate industry of France; will enumerate the harbors, the canals, the bridges, the public buildings, the Alpine roads, the libraries, the museums, and all the thousand works of industrious peace and productive art; will not withhold their admiration for the giant grasp of his genius and the imperial grandeur of his fortunes, nor deny a tribute of human sympathy to his calamitous decline and fall;—but the same impartial history will record more than one ineffaceable stain upon his character, and never, to the end of time, never on the page of historian, poet or philosopher; never till a taste for true moral greatness is eaten out of the hearts of men by a mean admiration of success and power; never in the exhortations of the prudent magistrate counseling his fellow-citizens for their good; never in the dark ages of national fortune, when anxious patriots explore the annals of the past for examples of public virtue; never in the admonition of the parent forming the minds of his children by lessons of fireside wisdom; never, O never, will the name of Napoleon, nor of any of the other of the famous conquerors of ancient and modern days, be placed upon a level with Washington's.

And while we on the 22d of February celebrate with solemn and joyous rites the great anniversary of our Washington, our fellow-citizens on the Hudson, on the Potomac, from the Southern plains to the Western lakes, are engaged in the same offices of gratitude and love. Nor we, nor they alone,—beyond the Ohio, beyond the Mississippi, along the stupendous trail of immigration from East to West, which, bursting into States as it moves westward, is already threading the Western prairies, swarming through the portals of the Rocky Mountains and winding down their slopes, the name and the memory of Washington on that gracious night will travel with the silver queen of heaven through sixty degrees of longitude, nor part company with her till she walks in her brightness through the golden gate of California, and passes serenely on to hold midnight court with her Australian stars. There and there only, in barbarous archipelagos, as yet untrodden by civilized man, the name of Washington is unknown; and there, too, when they swarm with enlightened millions, new honors shall be paid with ours to his memory.

Edward Everett.

EULOGY ON LAFAYETTE.

There have been those who have denied to Lafayette the name of a great man. What is greatness? Does goodness belong to greatness, and make an essential part of it? If it does, who, I would ask, of all the prominent names in history, has run through such a career with so little reproach, justly or unjustly bestowed? Are military courage and conduct the measure of greatness? Lafayette was intrusted by Washington with all kinds of service,—the laborious and complicated, which required skill and patience; the perilous, that demanded nerve; and we see him performing all with entire success and brilliant reputation. Is the readiness to meet vast responsibilities a proof of greatness? The memoirs of Mr. Jefferson show us that there was a moment, in 1789, when Lafayette took upon himself, as the head of the military force, the entire responsibility of laying down the basis of the Revolution. Is the cool and brave administration of gigantic power a mark of greatness? In all the whirlwind of the Revolution, and when, as commander-in-chief of the National Guard, an organized force of three millions of men, who, for any popular purpose, needed but a word, a look, to put them in motion, we behold him ever calm, collected, disinterested; as free from affectation as selfishness, clothed not less with humility than with power. Is the voluntary return, in advancing years, to the direction of affairs, at a moment like that, when, in 1815, the ponderous machinery of the French Empire was flying asunder,—stunning, rending, crushing thousands on every side,—a mark of greatness? Lastly, is it any proof of greatness to be able, at the age of seventy-three, to take the lead in a successful and bloodless revolution; to change the dynasty; to organize, exercise, and abdicate a military command of three and a half millions of men; to take up, to perform, and lay down the most momentous, delicate, and perilous duties, without passion, without hurry, without selfishness? Is it great to disregard the bribes of title, office, money; to live, to labor, and suffer for great public ends alone; to adhere to principle under all circumstances; to stand before Europe and America conspicuous, for sixty years, in the most responsible stations, the acknowledged admiration of all good men?

But it is more than time, fellow-citizens, that I commit the memory of this great and good man to your unprompted contemplation. On his arrival among you, ten years ago, when your civil fathers, your military, your children, your whole population, poured itself out, in one throng, to salute him; when your cannons proclaimed his advent with joyous salvos, and your acclamations were answered, from steeple to steeple, by festal bells,—with what delight did you not listen to his cordial and affectionate words—" I beg of you all, beloved citizens of Boston, to accept the respectful and warm thanks of a heart which has for nearly half a century been devoted to your illustrious city!"

That noble heart,—to which, if any object on earth was dear, that object was the country of his early choice, of his adoption, and his more than regal triumph,—that noble heart will beat no more for your welfare. Cold and still, it is already mingling with the dust. While he lived, you thronged with delight to his presence; you gazed with admiration on his placid features and venerable form, not wholly unshaken by the rude storms of his career; and now that he has departed, you have assembled in this cradle of the liberties for which, with your fathers, he risked his life, to pay the last honors to his memory. You have thrown open these conse-crated portals to admit the lengthened train, which has come to discharge the last public offices of respect to his name. You have hung these venerable arches, for the second time since their erection, with the sable badges of sorrow. You have thus associated the memory of Lafayette in those dis-tinguished honors which but a few years since you paid to your Adams and Jefferson.

There is not, throughout the world, a friend of liberty who has not dropped his head when he has heard that Lafay-ette is no more. Poland, Italy, Greece, Spain, Ireland, the South American republics—every country where man is struggling to recover his birthright,—have lost a benefactor, a patron in Lafayette. And what was it, fellow-citizens, which gave to our Lafayette his spotless fame? The love of liberty. What has consecrated his memory in the hearts of good men? The love of liberty. What nerved his youthful arm with strength, and inspired him, in the morning of his days, with sagacity and counsel? The living love of liberty. To what did he sacrifice power, and rank, and country, and freedom itself? To the horror of licentiousness,—to the sanctity of plighted faith,—to the love of liberty protected by law. Thus the great principle of your Revolutionary fathers, and of your Pilgrim sires, was the rule of his life— *the love of liberty protected by law.*

You have now assembled within these celebrated walls to perform the last duties of respect and love, on the birthday of your benefactor. The spirit of the departed is in high communion with the spirit of the place—the temple worthy of the new name which we now behold inscribed on its walls. Listen, Americans, to the lesson which seems borne to us on the very air we breathe, while we perform these dutiful rites! Ye winds, that wafted the Pilgrims to the land of promise, fan, in their children's hearts, the love of freedom! Blood, which our fathers shed, cry from the ground! Echoing arches of this renowned hall, whisper back the voices of other days! Glorious Washington, break the long silence of that votive canvas! Speak, speak, marble lips; teach us THE LOVE OF LIBERTY PROTECTED BY LAW.

Edward Everett.

GRATTAN'S REPLY TO MR. CORRY.

Has the gentleman *done?* Has he *completely* done? He was unparliamentary from the beginning to the end of his speech. There was scarce a word he uttered that was not a violation of the privileges of the House. But I did not call him to order,—why? because the limited talents of *some* men render it impossible for them to be severe *without* being unparliamentary. But before I sit down, I shall show him how to be severe and parliamentary at the same time.

On any other occasion I should think myself justifiable in treating with silent contempt anything which might fall from that honorable member; but there are times when the insignificance of the *accuser* is lost in the magnitude of the *accusation.* I know the difficulty the honorable gentleman labored under when he attacked me, conscious that, on a comparative view of our characters, public and private, there is nothing he could say which would injure me. The public would not believe the charge. I despise the falsehood. If such a charge were made by an honest man, I would answer it in the manner I shall do before I sit down. But I shall first reply to it when *not* made by an honest man.

The right honorable gentleman has called me " an unimpeached traitor." I ask why not "traitor," unqualified by any epithet? I will tell him: it was because he durst not. It was the act of a coward, who raises his arm to strike, but has not courage to give the blow. I will not call him villain, because it would be unparliamentary, and he is a privy counselor. I will not call him a fool, because he happens to be chancellor of the exchequer. But I say, he is one who has abused the privilege of Parliament and the freedom of debate, by uttering language which, if spoken out of the House, I should answer only with a *blow.* I care not how high his situation, how low his character, how contemptible his speech; whether a privy counselor or a parasite, my answer would be a blow.

He has charged me with being connected with the rebels. The charge is utterly, totally, and meanly false. Does the honorable gentleman rely on the report of the House of Lords for the foundation of his assertion? If he does, I can prove to the committee there was a physical impossibility of that report being true. But I scorn to answer any man for my conduct, whether he be a political coxcomb, or whether he brought himself into power by a false glare of courage or not.

I have returned,—not as the right honorable member has said, to raise another storm,—I have returned to discharge an honorable debt of gratitude to my country, that conferred a great reward for past services, which, I am proud to say, was not greater than my desert. I have returned to protect that Constitution of which I was the parent and founder, from the assassination of such men as the right honorable gentleman and his unworthy associates. They are corrupt, they are seditious, and they, at this very moment, are in a conspiracy against their country. I have returned to refute a libel, as false as it is malicious, given to the public under the appellation of a report of the committee of the Lords. Here I stand, ready for impeachment or trial. I dare accusation. I defy the honorable gentleman; I defy the government; I defy their whole phalanx; let them come forth. I tell the ministers, I will neither give quarter nor take it. I am here to lay the shattered remains of my constitution on the floor of this House, in defense of the liberties of my country.

Henry Grattan.

EULOGY ON WENDELL PHILLIPS.

In every strain of affectionate and discriminating admiration, the legislature, the pulpit and the press have spoken the praise of Wendell Phillips.

Sprung from the best New England parentage, at the age of sixteen he entered Harvard College. His classmates recall his manly pride and reserve, with the delightful conversation, the charming manner, and the affluence of kindly humor that was never lost. He sauntered and gently studied, not a devoted student, nor in the bent of his mind, nor in the special direction of sympathy, forecasting the reformer, but already the orator, and the easy master of the college platform.

After graduation he studied law, was admitted to the bar, and began practice in Boston. As he was sitting in his office one October afternoon waiting for his first client, the sound of unusual disturbance drew him to the street. There, within stone's throw of the scene of the Boston massacre, under the very shadow of Old South Church, he beheld a scene such as we of to-day can scarcely conceive—American women insulted for befriending their innocent sisters whose children were sold from their arms, and an American citizen assailed by a furious mob for maintaining that a man's right to liberty was inherent and inalienable. It was enough! As the jail doors closed upon Garrison to save his life, Garrison and his cause had won their most powerful ally. With the setting of that October sun vanished forever the career of prosperous ease which the genius and accomplishments of Phillips had seemed to foretell. His long-awaited client had come at last— scorned, scarred, wronged, degraded, and forsaken humanity.

When, two years later, at Alton, Illinois, Lovejoy was lynched for defending the right of innocent men and women to their personal freedom, it was with difficulty that Faneuil Hall was secured for a mass-meeting to denounce the appalling outrage; but when, in that meeting, after words of seemly protest had been uttered, a voice was heard, the voice of the high officer solemnly sworn to uphold the majesty of the law, declaring, in Faneuil Hall, amid a storm of howling applause, that an American put to death by a raging mob while defending his right of free speech died as the fool dieth, the Boston boy, all on fire, with Concord and Lexington tugging at his heart, unconsciously murmured, " Such a speech in Faneuil Hall must be answered in Faneuil Hall." " Why not answer it yourself?" whispered a neighbor. " Help me to the platform and I will," he answered; and pushing and struggling through the dense and threatening crowd, he reached the platform, was lifted upon it, and, advancing to speak, was greeted with a roar of hostile cries. But riding the whirlwind undismayed, as for many years thereafter he directed the same wild storm, he stood upon the platform in all the grace and beauty of imperial youth—the Greeks would ·have said, a God descended,—and in words which touched the mind and heart and conscience as with fire from heaven, recalling Boston to herself, he saved his native city and her cradle of liberty from the damning disgrace of stoning the first martyr in the great struggle for personal freedom. " Mr. Chairman," he said, " when I heard the gentleman lay down principles which placed the rioters, incendiaries, and murderers of Alton side by side with Otis and Hancock and Quincy and Adams, I thought those pictured lips would have broken into voice to rebuke the recreant American, the slanderer of the dead."

In all the annals of American speech there had been heard no such speech since Patrick Henry's electrical warning to George the Third. It was the greatest of oratorical triumphs when a supreme emotion, a sentiment which is to mould a people anew, lifts the orator to adequate expression. It transmitted, unextinguished, the torch of an eloquence that has roused nations, and changed the whole course of history. The mighty struggle indeed inspired universal eloquence; but, supreme over it all, was the eloquence of Phillips, as over the harmonious tumult of an orchestra, one clear voice, like a lark high poised in air, carries the melody.

He faced his audience with a tranquil mien and a beaming aspect that was never dimmed. He spoke, and in the measured cadences of his quiet voice there was intense feeling, but no declamation, no passionate appeal, no superficial and feigned emotion; it was simply colloquy, a gentleman conversing. Unconsciously, yet surely, the ear and heart were charmed. How was it done? Ah! how did Mozart do it? How Raphael? The secret of the rose's sweetness, the bird's ecstasy, the sunset's glory—this is the secret of genius and eloquence. What was seen, what was heard, was the form of noble manhood, the courteous and self-possessed tone, the flow of modulated and musical speech, sparkling with matchless richness of illustration, happy anecdote and historic parallel; with wit and pitiless invective, with stinging satire, with melodious pathos, with crackling epigram and limpid humor, like the bright ripples that play about the sure and steady prow of the resistless ship. The divine energy of his conviction utterly possessed him.

But he never flattered the mob, nor hung upon its neck, nor pandered to its passion, nor suffered its foaming hate or its exulting enthusiasm to touch the calm poise of his regnant soul. Those who were eager to insult and silence him when he pleaded for the negro, wept and shouted and rapturously crowned him when he paid homage to O'Connell. But the crowd did not follow him with huzzas. He moved in solitary majesty. And if, from his smooth speech, a lightning flash of satire or scorn struck a cherished lie, or an honored character, or a dogma of the party creed, and the crowd burst into a storm of furious dissent, he beat it into silence with uncompromising iteration. If it tried to drown his voice, he turned to the reporters and calmly said, "Howl on, I speak to thirty millions here."

Among her noblest sons his native city will ever cherish him, and gratefully recall the unbending Puritan soul that dwelt in a form so gracious and urbane. The plain house in which he lived, severely plain because the welfare of the suffering and the slave were preferred to book and picture and every fair device of art; the house to which the north star led the trembling fugitive; the radiant figure passing swiftly to and fro along these streets; the ceaseless charity untold, the strong sustaining heart of private friendship; the sacred domestic affection that must not here be named; the eloquence, which like the song of Orpheus, will fade from living memory as a doubtful tale; the great scene of his life in Faneuil Hall; the mighty struggle and the mighty triumph with which his name is forever blended; the consecration of a life hid with God in sympathy with man—these, all these, will live among your immortal traditions. And not among yours alone. As the years go by, and only the large outlines of lofty American characters and careers remain, the wide Republic will confess the benediction of a life like this, and gladly own that if, with perfect faith and hope assured, America would still stand and bid distant generations " Hail," the inspiration of her national life must be the sublime moral courage, the spotless purity, the unswerving integrity, the all-embracing humanity, the absolutely unselfish devotion of great powers to great public ends, which were the glory of Wendell Phillips.

George William Curtis.

ABRUPT AND STARTLING SELECTIONS.

EXPLOSIVE OROTUND.

Under this head come all *abrupt* and *startling emotions*, as fear, alarm, terror, hurry and commotion, anger, etc.

The chief peculiarity of this form of the Orotund is that the tones, as they issue from the glottis, resemble the successive reports of a pistol. In the case of the Expulsive Orotund, the form of utterance was a short shout. Here it has no prolongation whatsoever, but is a sudden, instantaneous burst of voice. Without this sharp, clear and pistol-like utterance, all pieces of anger and fierce emotion, as well as the fury and intensity of battle scenes, would be lost, and the words charged with fire and passion would fall from the the lips of the speaker lifeless and flat. On the other hand, if this explosive utterance were applied to oratory, it would crush out all the dignity of persuasive eloquence, and turn the prudent and manly utterance of the orator into angry diatribes.

The only style of oratory in which the voice assumes anything like an explosive form is that of fierce invective.

The prevailing pitch of the Explosive Orotund is *high*, and sometimes *very high*, and the movement of the voice quick or rapid.

SELECTIONS OF BOLD ADDRESS, ANGER, HURRY AND COMMOTION, ETC.

MARMION AND DOUGLAS.

The train from out the castle drew,
But Marmion stopped to bid adieu:—
   "Though something I might plain," he said,
"Of cold respect to stranger guest,

Sent hither by your king's behest,
  While in Tantallon's towers I stayed,
Part we in friendship from your land,
And noble Earl, receive my hand."—

But Douglas round him drew his cloak,
Folded his arms, and thus he spoke:—
"My manors, halls, and bowers shall still
Be open, at my sovereign's will,
To each one whom he lists, howe'er
Unmeet to be the owner's peer.
My castles are my king's alone
From turret to foundation-stone,—
The hand of Douglas is his own;
And never shall in friendly grasp
The hand of such as Marmion clasp."—

Burned Marmion's swarthy cheek like fire,
And shook his very frame for ire,
  And—"This to me!" he said,—
"An 't were not for thy hoary beard,
Such hand as Marmion's had not spared
  To cleave the Douglas' head!
And, first, I tell thee, haughty Peer,
He who does England's message here,
Although the meanest in her state,
May well, proud Angus, be thy mate:
And, Douglas, more I tell thee here,
  Even in thy pitch of pride,
Here in thy hold, thy vassals near,
(Nay, never look upon your lord,
And lay your hands upon your sword,)
  I tell thee, thou 'rt defied!
And if thou said'st I am not peer
To any lord in Scotland here,
Lowland or Highland, far or near,
  Lord Angus, thou hast lied!"—

On the Earl's cheek the flush of rage
O'ercame the ashen hue of age;
Fierce he broke forth,—"And dar'st thou then
To beard the lion in his den,
  The Douglas in his hall?

And hop'st thou hence unscathed to go?
No, by St. Bride of Bothwell, no!
Up drawbridge, grooms,—what, Warder, ho!
    Let the portcullis fall."—

Lord Marmion turned,—well was his need!—
And dashed the rowels in his steed,
Like arrow through the archway sprung;
The ponderous gate behind him rung:
To pass there was such scanty room,
The bars, descending, razed his plume.

The steed along the drawbridge flies,
Just as it trembled on the rise;
Not lighter does the swallow skim
Along the smooth lake's level brim;
And when Lord Marmion reached his band,
He halts, and turns with clenched hand,
And shout of loud defiance pours,
And shook his gauntlet at the towers.

                                   Sir Walter Scott.

BATTLE OF BEAL' AN DUINE.

No cymbal clash'd, no clarion rang,
    Still were the pipe and drum:
Save heavy tread, and armor's clang,
    The sullen march was dumb.
There breathed no wind their crests to shake,
    Or wave their flags abroad;
Scarce the frail aspen seem'd to quake,
    That shadowed o'er their road.

Their vaward scouts no tidings bring,
    Can rouse no lurking foe,
Nor spy a trace of living thing
    Save when they stirr'd the roe;
The host moves, like a deep-sea-wave;
Where rise no rocks its pride to brave,
    High-swelling, dark, and slow.

The lake is pass'd, and now they gain,
A narrow and a broken plain,
Before the Trosach's rugged jaws;
And here the horse and spearmen pause,
While to explore the dangerous glen,
Dive through the pass the archer-men.

At once there rose so wild a yell
Within that dark and narrow dell,
As all the fiends, from heaven that fell,
Had peal'd the banner-cry of hell!
Forth from the pass in tumult driven,
Like chaff before the wind of heaven,
    The archery appear:
For life! for life! their flight they ply—
And shriek, and shout, and battle-cry,
And plaids and bonnets waving high,
And broadswords flashing to the sky,
    Are maddening in the rear.
Onward they drive in dreadful race,
    Pursuers and pursued;
Before that tide of flight and chase,
How shall it keep its rooted place,
    The spearmen's twilight-wood?

—" Down, down," cried Mar, "your lances down!
    Bear back both friend and foe!"
Like reeds before the tempest's frown,
That serried grove of lances brown
    At once lay level'd low;
And closely shouldering side to side,
The bristling ranks the onset bide,—
—" We 'll quell the savage mountaineer,
    As their Tinchel cows the game!
They come as fleet as forest-deer
    We'll drive them back as tame."—
Bearing before them, in their course,
The relics of the archer-force,
Like wave with crest of sparkling foam,
Right onward did Clan-Alpine come.
Above the tide each broadsword bright,
Was brandishing like beam of light
    Each targe was dark below;

And with the ocean's mighty swing,
When heaving to the tempest's wing,
  They hurl'd them on the foe.
I heard the lances' shivering crash,
As when the whirlwind rends the ash;
I heard the broadswords' deadly clang,
As if an hundred anvils rang!
But Moray wheel'd his rearward rank
Of horsemen on Clan-Alpine's flank,
  —"My banner-man, advance!
I see," he cried, " their column shake,—
Now, gallants! for your ladies' sake,
  Upon them with the lance!"

The horsemen dash'd among the rout,
  As deer break through the broom;
Their steeds are stout, their swords are out,
  They soon make lightsome room.
Clan-Alpine's best are backward borne,—
  Where, where was Roderick then!
One blast upon his bugle-horn
  Were worth a thousand men.
And refluent through the pass of fear
  The battle's tide was pour'd;
Vanished the Saxon's struggling spear,
  Vanished the mountain-sword.
As Bracklinn's chasm, so black and steep,
  Receives her roaring linn,
As the dark caverns of the deep
  Suck the wild whirlpool in,
So did the deep and darksome pass
Devour the battle's mingled mass;
None linger now upon the plain,
Save those who ne'er shall fight again.
                 Sir Walter Scott.

THE BURIAL MARCH OF DUNDEE.

On the heights of Killiecrankie
  Yester-morn our army lay;
Slowly rose the mist in columns
  From the river's broken way;

Hoarsely roared the swollen torrent,
  And the Pass was wrapped in gloom,
When the clansmen rose together
  From their lair amidst the broom.

Then we belted on our tartans,
  And our bonnets down we drew,
And we felt our broadswords' edges,
  And we proved them to be true;
And we prayed the prayer of soldiers,
  And we cried the gathering-cry,
And we clasped the hands of kinsmen,
  And we swore to do or die!
Then our leader rode before us
  On his war-horse black as night,—
Well the Cameronian rebels
  Knew that charger in the fight!—
And a cry of exultation
  From the bearded warriors rose;
For we loved the house of Claver'se,
  And we thought of good Montrose.
But he raised his hand for silence—
  " Soldiers! I have sworn a vow:
Ere the evening star shall glisten
  On Schehallion's lofty brow,
Either we shall rest in triumph,
  Or another of the Græmes
Shall have died in battle-harness
  For his Country and King James!
Think upon the Royal Martyr,—
  Think of what his race endure,—
Think of him whom butchers murdered
  On the field of Magus Nuir:—
By his sacred blood I charge ye,
  By the ruined hearth and shrine,—
By the blighted hopes of Scotland
  By your injuries and mine,—
Strike this day as if the anvil
  Lay beneath your blows the while,
Be they covenanting traitors
  Or the brood of false Argyle!
Strike! and drive the trembling rebels
  Backwards o'er the stormy Forth;

Let them tell their pale Convention
   How they fared within the North.
Let them tell that Highland honor
   Is not to be bought nor sold,
That we scorn their Prince's anger
   As we loath his foreign gold.
Strike! and when the fight is over,
   If ye look in vain for me,
Where the dead are lying thickest,
   Search for him that was Dundee!"

Loudly then the hills re-echoed
   With our answer to his call,
But a deeper echo sounded
   In the bosoms of us all.
For the lands of wide Breadalbane,
   Not a man who heard him speak
Would that day have left the battle.
   Flashing eye and burning cheek
Told the clansmen's fierce emotion,
   And they harder drew their breath.
For their souls were strong within them,
   Stronger than the grasp of death.
Soon we heard a challenge-trumpet
   Sounding in the Pass below,
And the distant tramp of horses,
   And the voices of the foe;
Down we crouched amid the bracken,
   Till the Lowland ranks drew near,
Panting like the hounds in summer,
   When they scent the stately deer.
From the dark defile emerging,
   Next we saw the squadrons come,
Leslie's foot and Leven's troopers
   Marching to the tuck of drum;
Through the scattered wood of birches,
   O'er the broken ground and heath,
Wound the long battalion slowly,
   Till they gained the plain beneath;
Then we bounded from our covert,—
   Judge how looked the Saxons then,
When they saw the rugged mountains
   Start to life with arméd men!

Like a tempest down the ridges
    Swept the hurricane of steel,
Rose the slogan of Macdonald,—
    Flashed the broadsword of Lochiel!
Vainly sped the withering volley
    'Mongst the foremost of our band,—
On we poured until we met them,
    Foot to foot, and hand to hand.
Horse and man went down like drift-wood
    When the floods are black at Yule,
And their carcasses are whirling
    In the Garry's deepest pool.
Horse and man went down before us,—
    Living foe there tarried none
On the field of Killiecrankie,
    When that stubborn fight was done!

And the evening star was shining
    On Schehallion's distant head,
When we wiped our bloody broadswords,
    And returned to count the dead.
There we found him gashed and gory,
    Stretched upon the cumbered plain,
As he told us where to seek him,
    In the thickest of the slain.
And a smile was on his visage,
    For within his dying ear
Pealed the joyful note of triumph,
    And the clansmen's clamorous cheer;
So, amidst the battle's thunder,
    Shot, and steel, and scorching flame,
In the glory of his manhood
    Passed the spirit of the Græme!

Open wide the vaults of Atholl,
    Where the bones of heroes rest,—
Open wide the hallowed portals
    To receive another guest!
Last of Scots, and last of freemen,—
    Last of all that dauntless race,
Who would rather die unsullied
    Than outlive the land's disgrace!
O thou lion-hearted warrior!

Reck not of the after-time;
　Honor may be deemed dishonor,
　　Loyalty be called a crime.
Sleep in peace with kindred ashes
　　Of the noble and the true,
Hands that never failed their country,
　　Hearts that never baseness knew.
Sleep!—and till the latest trumpet
　　Wakes the dead from earth and sea,
Scotland shall not boast a braver
　　Chieftain than our own Dundee!
　　　　　　W. Edmondstoune Aytoun.

MILES STANDISH'S ENCOUNTER WITH THE INDIANS.

After a three days' march he came to an Indian encampment
　　Pitched on the edge of a meadow, between the sea and the forest;
Women at work by the tents, and the warriors, horrid with war-paint,
Seated about a fire, and smoking and talking together;
Who, when they saw from afar the sudden approach of the white men,
Saw the flash of the sun on breastplate and saber and musket,
Straightway leaped to their feet, and two, from among them advancing,
Came to parley with Standish, and offer him furs as a present;
Friendship was in their looks, but in their hearts there was hatred.
Braves of the tribe were these, and brothers gigantic in stature,
Huge as Goliath of Gath, or the terrible Og, king of Bashan;
One was Pecksuot named, and the other was called Wattawamat.
Round their necks were suspended their knives in scabbards of wampum,

Two-edged, trenchant knives, with points as sharp as a
 needle.
Other arms had they none, for they were cunning and
 crafty.
"Welcome, English!" they said,—these words they had
 learned from the traders
Touching at times on the coast, to barter and chaffer for
 peltries.
Then in their native tongue they began to parley with
 Standish,
Through his guide and interpreter, Hobomok, friend of
 the white man,
Begging for blankets and knives, but mostly for muskets
 and powder,
Kept by the white man, they said, concealed, with the
 plague, in his cellars,
Ready to be let loose, and destroy his brother the red man!
But when Standish refused, and said he would give them
 the Bible,
Suddenly changing their tone, they began to boast and to
 bluster.
Then Wattawamat advanced with a stride in front of the
 other,
And, with a lofty demeanor, thus vauntingly spake to the
 Captain:
"Now Wattawamat can see, by the fiery eyes of the
 Captain,
Angry is he in his heart; but the heart of the brave Wat-
 tawamat
Is not afraid of the sight. He was not born of a woman,
But on a mountain, at night, from an oak-tree riven by
 lightning,
Forth he sprang at a bound, with all his weapons about him,
Shouting, 'Who is there here to fight with the brave Wat-
 tawamat?'"
Then he unsheathed his knife, and, whetting the blade on
 his left hand,
Held it aloft and displayed a woman's face on the handle,
Saying, with bitter expression and look of sinister meaning:
"I have another at home, with the face of a man on the
 handle;
By and by they shall marry; and there will be plenty of
 children!"

Then stood Pecksuot forth, self-vaunting, insulting
  Miles Standish:
While with his fingers he patted the knife that hung at his
  bosom,
Drawing it half from its sheath, and plunging it back, as
  he muttered,
"By and by it shall see; it shall eat; ah, ha! but shall
  speak not!
This is the mighty Captain the white men have sent to
  destroy us!
He is a little man; let him go and work with the women!"

  Meanwhile Standish had noted the faces and figures of
  Indians
Peeping and creeping about from bush to tree in the forest,
Feigning to look for game, with arrows set on their bow-
  strings,
Drawing about him still closer and closer the net of their
  ambush.
But undaunted he stood, and dissembled and treated them
  smoothly;
So the old chronicles say, that were writ in the days of
  the fathers.
But when he heard their defiance, the boast, the taunt,
  and the insult,
All the hot blood of his race, of Sir Hugh and of Thurs-
  ton de Standish,
Boiled and beat in his heart, and swelled in the veins of
  his temples.
Headlong he leaped on the boaster, and, snatching his
  knife from its scabbard,
Plunged it into his heart, and, reeling backward, the
  savage
Fell with his face to the sky, and a fiendlike fierceness
  upon it.
Straight there arose from the forest the awful sound of the
  war-whoop,
And like a flurry of snow on the whistling wind of Decem-
  ber,
Swift and sudden and keen came a flight of feathery
  arrows.
Then came a cloud of smoke, and out of the cloud came
  the lightning,

Out of the lightning thunder; and death unseen ran
 before it.
Frightened the savages fled for shelter in swamp and in
 thicket,
Hotly pursued and beset; but their sachem, the brave
 Wattawamat,
Fled not; he was dead. Unswerving and swift had a
 bullet
Passed through his brain, and he fell with both hands
 clutching the greensward,
Seeming in death to hold back from his foe the land of
 his fathers.
Thus the first battle was fought and won by the stalwart
 Miles Standish.

Henry Wadsworth Longfellow.

THE BATTLE OF IVRY.

Now glory to the Lord of Hosts, from whom all glories
 are!
And glory to our Sovereign Liege, King Henry of Navarre!
Now let there be the merry sound of music and the dance,
Through thy corn-fields green, and sunny vales, O pleas-
 ant land of France!
And thou, Rochelle, our own Rochelle, proud city of the
 waters,
Again let rapture light the eyes of all thy mourning
 daughters;
As thou wert constant in our ills, be joyous in our joy,
For cold and stiff and still are they who wrought thy
 walls annoy.
Hurrah! hurrah! a single field hath turned the chance of
 war.
Hurrah! hurrah! for Ivry and King Henry of Navarre!

Oh, how our hearts were beating, when, at the dawn of day,
We saw the army of the League drawn out in long array;
With all its priest-led citizens, and all its rebel peers,
And Appenzel's stout infantry, and Egmont's Flemish
 spears!

There rode the brood of false Lorraine, the curses of our
    land!
And dark Mayenne was in the midst, a truncheon in his
    hand;
And as we looked on them, we thought of Seine's empur-
    pled flood,
And good Coligni's hoary hair all dabbled with his blood;
And we cried unto the living God, who rules the fate of
    war,
To fight for His own holy Name, and Henry of Navarre.

The King has come to marshal us, in all his armor drest,
And he has bound a snow-white plume upon his gallant
    crest.
He looked upon his people, and a tear was in his eye;
He looked upon the traitors, and his glance was stern and
    high.
Right graciously, he smiled on us, as rolled from wing to
    wing,
Down all our line, in deafening shout, "God save our lord,
    the King!"
"And if my standard-bearer fall,—as fall full well he may,
For never saw I promise yet of such a bloody fray,—
Press where ye see my white plume shine, amid the ranks
    of war,
And be your oriflamme, to-day, the helmet of Navarre."

Hurrah! the foes are moving!   Hark to the mingled din
Of fife, and steed, and trump, and drum, and roaring
    culverin!
The fiery Duke is pricking fast across Saint André's plain,
With all the hireling chivalry of Guelders and Almayne.
Now, by the lips of those ye love, fair gentlemen of
    France,
Charge for the golden lilies now,—upon them with the
    lance!
A thousand spurs are striking deep, a thousand spears in
    rest,
A thousand knights are pressing close behind the snow-
    white crest,
And in they burst, and on they rushed, while, like a guid-
    ing star,
Amidst the thickest carnage blazed the helmet of Navarre.

Now, God be praised, the day is ours! Mayenne hath
  turned his rein,
D'Aumale hath cried for quarter—the Flemish Count is
  slain;
Their ranks are breaking like thin clouds before a Biscay
  gale;
The field is heaped with bleeding steeds, and flags, and
  cloven mail.
And then we thought on vengeance, and all along our van,
"Remember St. Bartholomew!" was passed from man to
  man;
But out spake gentle Henry then, "No Frenchman is my
  foe;
Down, down with every foreigner; but let your brethren
  go."
Oh! was there ever such a knight, in friendship or in war,
As our sovereign lord, King Henry, the soldier of Navarre!

Ho! maidens of Vienna! Ho! matrons of Lucerne!
Weep, weep, and rend your hair for those who never shall
  return;
Ho! Philip, send for charity thy Mexican pistoles,
That Antwerp monks may sing a mass for thy poor spear-
  men's souls!
Ho! gallant nobles of the League, look that your arms be
  bright!
Ho! burghers of St. Genevieve, keep watch and ward
  to-night!
For our God hath crushed the tyrant, our God hath raised
  the slave,
And mocked the counsel of the wise and the valor of the
  brave.
Then glory to His holy name, from whom all glories are;
And glory to our sovereign lord, King Henry of Navarre!
                                        Lord Macaulay.

THE CHARGE OF THE LIGHT BRIGADE.

Half a league, half a league,
  Half a league onward,
All in the valley of death
  Rode the six hundred.

"Forward, the Light Brigade!
Charge for the guns!" he said.
Into the valley of death
  Rode the six hundred.

"Forward, the Light Brigade!"
Was there a man dismayed?
Not though the soldiers knew
  Some one had blundered:
Theirs not to make reply,
Theirs not to reason why,
Theirs but to do and die:
Into the valley of death
  Rode the six hundred.

Cannon to right of them,
Cannon to left of them,
Cannon in front of them,
  Volleyed and thundered:
Stormed at with shot and shell,
Boldly they rode and well:
Into the jaws of death,
Into the mouth of hell,
  Rode the six hundred.

Flashed all their sabers bare,
Flashed as they turned in air,
Sab'ring the gunners there,
Charging an army, while
  All the world wondered:
Plunged in the battery smoke,
Right through the line they broke:
Cossack and Russian
Reeled from the saber-stroke,
  Shattered and sundered.
Then they rode back—but not,
  Not the six hundred.

Cannon to right of them,
Cannon to left of them,
Cannon behind them,
  Volleyed and thundered:
Stormed at with shot and shell,

While horse and hero fell,
They that had fought so well,
Came through the jaws of death,
Back from the mouth of hell,
All that was left of them,
    Left of six hundred.

When can their glory fade?
Oh, the wild charge they made!
    All the world wondered.
Honor the charge they made!
Honor the Light Brigade,
    Noble six hundred!

Lord Tennyson.

THE BATTLE OF FONTENOY.

MAY 11, 1745.

Thrice, at the huts of Fontenoy, the English column failed,
And, twice, the lines of Saint Antoine, the Dutch in vain
    assailed;
For town and slope were filled with fort and flanking
    battery,
And well they swept the English ranks, and Dutch auxil-
    iary.
As vainly, through De Barri's wood, the British soldiers
    burst,
The French artillery drove them back, diminished and
    dispersed.
The bloody Duke of Cumberland beheld with anxious eye,
And ordered up his last reserve, his latest chance to try.
On Fontenoy, on Fontenoy, how fast his generals ride!
And mustering come his chosen troops, like clouds at
    eventide.

Six thousand English veterans in stately column tread,—
Their cannon blaze in front and flank, Lord Hay is at
    their head;
Steady they step adown the slope—steady they climb the
    hill;
Steady they load—steady they fire, moving right onward
    still,

Betwixt the wood and Fontenoy, as through a furnace
  blast,
Through rampart, trench, and palisade, and bullets showering fast;
And on the open plain above they rose and kept their
  course,
With ready fire and grim resolve, that mocked at hostile
  force;
Past Fontenoy, past Fontenoy, while thinner grow their
  ranks,
They break, as broke the Zuyder Zee through Holland's
  ocean banks.

More idly than the summer flies, French tirailleurs rush
  round;
As stubble to the lava tide, French squadrons strew the
  ground;
Bombshell, and grape, and roundshot tore, still on they
  marched and fired—
Fast from each volley, grenadier and voltigeur retired.
"Push on my household cavalry;" King Louis madly
  cried;
To death they rush, but rude their shock—not unavenged
  they died.
On through the camp the column trod—King Louis turns
  his rein;
"Not yet, my liege," Saxe interposed, "the Irish troops
  remain;"
And Fontenoy, famed Fontenoy, had been a Waterloo,
Were not these exiles ready then,—fresh, vehement, and
  true.

"Lord Clare," he says, "you have your wish; there are
  your Saxon foes!"
The marshal almost smiled to see, so furiously he goes!
How fierce the look these exiles wear, who 're wont to be
  so gay,
The treasured wrongs of fifty years are in their hearts
  to-day—
The treaty broken, ere the ink wherewith 'twas writ could
  dry,
Their plundered homes, their ruined shrines, their women's
  parting cry,

Their priesthood hunted down like wolves, their country
 overthrown,—
Each looks, as if revenge for all were staked on him alone.
On Fontenoy, on Fontenoy, nor ever yet elsewhere,
Rushed on to fight a nobler band than those proud
 exiles were.

O'Brien's voice is hoarse with joy, as, halting, he com-
 mands,
"Fix bay'nets—Charge!" Like mountain-storm, rush on
 these fiery bands.
Thin is the English column now, and faint their volleys
 grow,
Yet, must'ring all the strength they have, they make a
 gallant show.
They dress their ranks upon the hill to face that battle
 wind—
Their bayonets the breakers' foam; like rocks, the men
 behind!
One volley crashes from their line, when, through the
 surging smoke,
With empty guns clutched in their hands, the headlong
 Irish broke.
On Fontenoy, on Fontenoy, hark to that fierce huzza!
"Revenge! remember Limerick! dash down the Sasse-
 nagh!"

Like lions leaping at a fold, when mad with hunger's pang,
Right up against the English line the Irish exiles sprang:
Bright was their steel, 'tis bloody now, their guns are
 filled with gore;
Through shattered ranks, and severed files, and trampled
 flags they tore;
The English strove with desperate strength, paused, ral-
 lied, staggered, fled—
The green hillside is matted close with dying and with
 dead;
Across the plain, and far away passed on that hideous
 wrack,
While cavalier and fantassin dash in upon their track.
On Fontenoy, on Fontenoy, like eagles in the sun,
With bloody plumes the Irish stand—the field is fought
 and won!

Thomas Davis.

HERVÉ RIEL.

On the sea and at the Hogue, sixteen hundred ninety-two,
   Did the English fight the French,—woe to France!
And the thirty-first of May, helter-skelter through the
     blue,
Like a crowd of frightened porpoises a shoal of sharks
     pursue,
   Came crowding ship on ship to Saint Malo on the Rance,
With the English fleet in view.

'Twas the squadron that escaped, with the victor in full
     chase,
   First and foremost of the drove, in his great ship,
      Damfreville;
     Close on him fled, great and small,
     Twenty-two good ships in all;
And they signaled to the place,
"Help the winners of a race!
     Get us guidance, give us harbor, take us quick,—or,
      quicker still,
     Here 's the English can and will!"

Then the pilots of the place put out brisk and leaped
     on board.
     "Why, what hope or chance have ships like these to
      pass?" laughed they;
"Rocks to starboard, rocks to port, all the passage
     scarred and scored,
Shall the Formidable here, with her twelve and eighty guns,
   Think to make the river-mouth by the single narrow way,
Trust to enter where 'tis ticklish for a craft of twenty
     tons,
     And with flow at full beside?
     Now 'tis slackest ebb of tide.
   Reach the mooring? Rather say,
While rock stands or water runs,
   Not a ship will leave the bay!"

Then was called a council straight;
Brief and bitter the debate:
"Here 's the English at our heels; would you have them
     take in tow

All that's left us of the fleet, linked together stern and
    bow,
For a prize to Plymouth Sound?
Better run the ships aground!"
   (Ended Damfreville his speech.)
"Not a minute more to wait!
  Let the captains all and each
  Shove ashore, then blow up, burn the vessels on the
    beach!
France must undergo her fate."
"Give the word!"   But no such word
Was ever spoke or heard;
  For up stood, for out stepped, for in struck amid all
    these,—
A captain? A lieutenant? A mate,—first, second, third?
   No such man of mark, and meet
   With his betters to compete!
   But a simple Breton sailor pressed by Tourville for
    the fleet,—
A poor coasting-pilot he, Hervé Riel the Croisickese.
And "What mockery or malice have we here?" cries
   Hervé Riel;
  "Are you mad, you Malouins? Are you cowards, fools
    or rogues?
Talk to me of rocks and shoals, me who took the sound-
   ings, tell
On my fingers every bank, every shallow, every swell
  'Twixt the offing here and Greve, where the river dis-
    embogues?
Are you bought by English gold? Is it love the lying's
   for?
   Morn and eve, night and day,
   Have I piloted your bay,
   Entered free and anchored fast at the foot of
    Solidor.
  Burn the fleet, and ruin France? That were worse than
   fifty Hogues!
   Sirs, they know I speak the truth! Sirs, believe me,
    there's a way!
Only let me lead the line,
  Have the biggest ship to steer,
  Get this Formidable clear,
Make the others follow mine.

And I lead them most and least by a passage I know well,
  Right to Solidor, past Greve,
    And there lay them safe and sound;
  And if one ship misbehave,—
    Keel so much as grate the ground,—
Why, I 've nothing but my life; here 's my head!'' cries
      Hervé Riel.

Not a minute more to wait.
''Steer us in, then, small and great!
  Take the helm, lead the line, save the squadron!''
      cried its chief.
Captains, give the sailor place!
  He is Admiral, in brief.
Still the north-wind, by God's grace.
See the noble fellow's face
As the big ship, with a bound,
Clears the entry like a hound,
Keeps the passage as its inch of way were the wide sea's
      profound!
  See, safe through shoal and rock,
  How they follow in a flock.
Not a ship that misbehaves, not a keel that grates the
      ground.
  Not a spar that comes to grief!
The peril, see, is past,
All are harbored to the last;
And just as Hervé Riel halloos ''Anchor!''—sure as fate,
Up the English come, too late.

So the storm subsides to calm;
  They see the green trees wave
  On the heights o'erlooking Greve;
Hearts that bled are stanched with balm.
''Just our rapture to enhance,
  Let the English rake the bay,
Gnash their teeth and glare askance
  As they cannonade away!
'Neath rampired Solidor pleasant riding on the Rance!''
How hope succeeds despair on each captain's counte-
      nance!
Outburst all with one accord,
  ''This is Paradise for Hell!

Let France, let France's King
    Thank the man that did the thing!''
What a shout and all one word,
    ''Hervé Riel!''
As he stepped in front once more,
    Not a symptom of surprise
    In the frank blue Breton eyes,
Just the same man as before.

Then said Damfreville, ''My friend,
I must speak out at the end,
    Though I find the speaking hard:
Praise is deeper than the lips;
You have saved the king his ships,
    You must name your own reward,
Faith, our sun was near eclipse!
Demand whate'er you will,
France remains your debtor still.
Ask to heart's content, and have! or my name 's not
    Damfreville.''

Then a beam of fun outbroke
On the bearded mouth that spoke,
As the honest heart laughed through
Those frank eyes of Breton blue;
''Since I needs must say my say,
    Since on board the duty 's done,
    And from Malo Roads to Croisic Point, what is it but a
        run?—
Since 'tis ask and have I may,—
    Since the others go ashore,—
Come! A good whole holiday!
    Leave to go and see my wife, whom I call the Belle
        Aurore!''
    That he asked, and that he got,—nothing more.

Name and deed alike are lost;
Not a pillar nor a post
    In his Croisic keeps alive the feat as it befell;
Not a head in white and black
On a single fishing-smack.
In memory of the man but for whom had gone to wrack—

All that France saved from the fight whence England
    bore the bell.
Go to Paris; rank on rank
  Search the heroes flung pell-mell
On the Louvre, face and flank;
  You shall look long enough ere you come to Hervé Riel.
So, for better or for worse,
Hervé Riel, accept my verse!
In my verse, Hervé Riel, do thou once more
Save the squadron, honor France, love thy wife, the Belle
    Aurore!

                         Robert Browning.

WARREN'S ADDRESS.

Stand! the ground 's your own, my braves!
Will ye give it up to slaves?
Will ye look for greener graves?
  Hope ye mercy still?
What 's the mercy despots feel?
Hear it in that battle-peal!
Read it on yon bristling steel!
  Ask it,—ye who will.

Fear ye foes who kill for hire?
Will ye to your *homes* retire?
Look behind you!—they 're afire!
  And, before you, see
Who have done it! From the vale
On they come!—and will ye quail?
Leaden rain and iron hail
  Let their welcome be!

In the God of battles trust!
Die we may,—and die we must:
But, O, where can dust to dust
  Be consigned so well,
As where heaven its dew shall shed
On the martyred patriot's bed,
And the rocks shall raise their head,
  Of his deeds to tell.

                        John Pierpont.

HOW THEY BROUGHT THE GOOD NEWS FROM GHENT TO AIX.

I sprang to the stirrup, and Joris and he;
I galloped, Dirck galloped, we galloped all three;
"Good speed!" cried the watch as the gate-bolts undrew,
"Speed!" echoed the wall to us galloping through.
Behind shut the postern, the lights sank to rest,
And into the midnight we galloped abreast.

Not a word to each other; we kept the great pace,—
Neck by neck, stride by stride, never changing our place;
I turned in my saddle and made its girths tight,
Then shortened each stirrup and set the pique right,
Rebuckled the cheek-strap, chained slacker the bit,
Nor galloped less steadily Roland a whit.

'Twas a moonset at starting; but while we drew near
Lokeren, the cocks crew and twilight dawned clear;
At Boom a great yellow star came out to see;
At Düffeld 'twas morning as plain as could be;
And from Mecheln church-steeple we heard the half-
      chime,—
So Joris broke silence with "Yet there is time!"

At Aerschot up leaped of a sudden the sun,
And against him the cattle stood black every one,
To stare through the mist at us galloping past;
And I saw my stout galloper Roland at last,
With resolute shoulders, each butting away
The haze, as some bluff river headland its spray;
And his low head and crest, just one sharp ear bent back
For my voice, and the other pricked out on his track;
And one eye's black intelligence,—ever that glance
O'er its white edge at me, his own master, askance;
And the thick heavy spume-flakes, which aye and anon
His fierce lips shook upward in galloping on.

By Hasselt Dirck groaned; and cried Joris, "Stay spur!
Your Roos galloped bravely, the fault 's not in her;
We 'll remember at Aix,"—for one heard the quick wheeze
Of her chest, saw the stretched neck, and staggering knees,

And sunk tail, and horrible heave of the flank,
As down on her haunches she shuddered and sank.
So we were left galloping, Joris and I,
Past Looz and past Tongres, no cloud in the sky;
The broad sun above laughed a pitiless laugh;
'Neath our feet broke the brittle, bright stubble like chaff;
Till over by Dalhem a dome-spire sprang white,
And "Gallop," gasped Joris, "for Aix is in sight!"

"How they'll greet us!"—and all in a moment his roan
Rolled neck and croup over, lay dead as a stone;
And there was my Roland to bear the whole weight
Of the news which alone could save Aix from her fate,
With his nostrils like pits full of blood to the brim,
And with circles of red for his eye-sockets' rim.

Then I cast loose my buff-coat, each holster let fall,
Shook off both my jack-boots, let go belt and all,
Stood up in the stirrup, leaned, patted his ear,
Called my Roland his pet name, my horse without peer,—
Clapped my hands, laughed and sung, any noise, bad or
    good,
Till at length into Aix Roland galloped and stood.

And all I remember is friends flocking round,
As I sate with his head 'twixt my knees on the ground;
And no voice but was praising this Roland of mine,
As I poured down his throat our last measure of wine,
Which (the burgesses voted by common consent)
Was no more than his due who brought good news from
    Ghent.

                                    Robert Browning.

MISCELLANEOUS.

The selections under this head are of varied emotion, and no satisfactory classification can be made unless each piece is analyzed; hence, it has been thought best to rely upon the suggestions already given as the best means for successful interpretation.

The student, after careful study of the leading styles of composition which have been considered, will have acquired such familiarity with the written forms of impassioned literature, that he will be prepared to analyze the spirit and temper of all selections involving a variety of emotions.

MISCELLANEOUS SELECTIONS.

KING ROBERT OF SICILY.

Robert of Sicily, brother of Pope Urbane
And Valmond, Emperor of Allemaine,
Appareled in magnificent attire,
With retinue of many a knight and squire,
On St. John's eve, at vespers, proudly sat
And heard the priests chant the Magnificat.
And as he listened, o'er and o'er again
Repeated, like a burden or refrain,
He caught the words, "*Deposuit potentes*
De sede et exaltavit humiles;"
And slowly lifting up his kingly head,
He to a learned clerk beside him said,

"What mean these words?" The clerk made answer meet,
"He has put down the mighty from their seat,
And has exalted them of low degree."
Thereat King Robert muttered scornfully,
" 'Tis well that such seditious words are sung

Only by priests and in the Latin tongue;
For unto priests and people be it known,
There is no power can push me from my throne!"
And leaning back, he yawned and fell asleep,
Lulled by the chant monotonous and deep.

When he awoke it was already night;
The church was empty, and there was no light,
Save where the lamps, that glimmered few and faint
Lighted a little space before some saint.
He started from his seat and gazed around,
But saw no living thing and heard no sound.
He groped towards the door, but it was locked;
He cried aloud, and listened, and then knocked,
And uttered awful threatenings and complaints,
And imprecations upon men and saints,
The sounds re-echoed from the roof and walls
As if dead priests were laughing in their stalls.

At length the sexton, hearing from without
The tumult of the knocking and the shout,
And thinking thieves were in the house of prayer,
Came with his lantern, asking, "Who is there?"
Half choked with rage, King Robert fiercely said,
"Open: 'tis I, the King! Art thou afraid?"
The frightened sexton, muttering, with a curse,
"This is some drunken vagabond, or worse!"
Turned the great key and flung the portal wide;
A man rushed by him at a single stride,
Haggard, half naked, without hat or cloak,
Who neither turned, nor looked at him, nor spoke,
But leaped into the blackness of the night
And vanished like a specter from his sight.

Robert of Sicily, brother of Pope Urbane
And Valmond, Emperor of Allemaine,
Despoiled of his magnificent attire,
Bareheaded, breathless, and besprent with mire,
With sense of wrong and outrage desperate,
Strode on and thundered at the palace gate;
Rushed through the court-yard, thrusting in his rage
To right and left each seneschal and page,
And hurried up the broad and sounding stair,

His white face ghastly in the torches' glare.
From hall to hall he passed with breathless speed;
Voices and cries he heard, but did not heed,
Until at last he reached the banquet room,
Blazing with light and breathing with perfume.

There on the dais sat another king,
Wearing his robes, his crown, his signet-ring,
King Robert's self in feature, form and height,
But all transfigured with angelic light!
It was an Angel; and his presence there
With a divine effulgence filled the air.

A moment speechless, motionless, amazed,
The throneless monarch on the Angel gazed,
Who met his look of anger and surprise
With the divine compassion of his eyes;
Then said, "Who art thou? and why com'st thou here?"
To which King Robert answered with a sneer,
"I am the King, and come to claim my own
From an impostor, who usurps my throne!"
And suddenly, at these audacious words,
Up sprang the angry guests, and drew their swords!
The Angel answered with unruffled brow,
"Nay, not the King, but the King's Jester, thou
Henceforth shalt wear the bells and scalloped cape,
And for thy counselor shalt lead an ape;
Thou shalt obey my servants when they call,
And wait upon my henchmen in the hall!"

Deaf to King Robert's threats and cries and prayers,
They thrust him from the hall and down the stairs;
A group of tittering pages ran before,
And as they opened wide the folding-door,
His heart failed, for he heard, with strange alarms,
The boisterous laughter of the men-at-arms,
And all the vaulted chamber roar and ring
With the mock plaudits of "Long live the King!"
Next morning, waking with the day's first beam,
He said within himself, "It was a dream!"
But the straw rustled as he turned his head,
There were the cap and bells beside his bed,
Around him rose the bare, discolored walls,

Close by, the steeds were champing in their stalls,
And in the corner, a revolting shape,
Shivering and chattering sat the wretched ape.
It was no dream; the world he loved so much
Had turned to dust and ashes at his touch!

Days came and went; and now returned again
To Sicily the old Saturnian reign;
Under the Angel's governance benign
The happy island danced with corn and wine,
And deep within the mountain's burning breast
Enceladus, the giant, was at rest.

Meanwhile King Robert yielded to his fate,
Sullen and silent and disconsolate.
Dressed in the motley garb that Jesters wear,
With look bewildered and a vacant stare,
Close shaven above the ears, as monks are shorn,
By courtiers mocked, by pages laughed to scorn,
His only friend the ape, his only food
What others left,—he still was unsubdued.
And when the Angel met him on his way,
And half in earnest, half in jest, would say,
Sternly, though tenderly, that he might feel
The velvet scabbard held a sword of steel,
"Art thou the King?" the passion of his woe
Burst from him in resistless overflow,
And, lifting high his forehead he would fling
The haughty answer back, "I am, I am the King!"

Almost three years were ended; when there came
Ambassadors of great repute and name
From Valmond, Emperor of Allemaine,
Unto King Robert, saying that Pope Urbane
By letter summoned them forthwith to come
On Holy Thursday to his city of Rome.
The Angel with great joy received his guests,
And gave them presents of embroidered vests,
And velvet mantles with rich ermine lined,
And rings and jewels of the rarest kind.
Then he departed with them o'er the sea
Into the lovely land of Italy,

Whose loveliness was more resplendent made
By the mere passing of that cavalcade,
With plumes, and cloaks, and housings, and the stir
Of jeweled bridle and of golden spur.

And lo! among the menials, in mock state,
Upon a piebald steed, with shambling gait,
His cloak of fox-tails flapping in the wind,
The solemn ape demurely perched behind,
King Robert rode, making huge merriment
In all the country towns through which they went.

The Pope received them with great pomp and blare
Of bannered trumpets, on Saint Peter's square,
Giving his benediction and embrace,
Fervent, and full of apostolic grace.

While with congratulations and with prayers
He entertained the Angel unawares,
Robert, the Jester, bursting through the crowd,
Into their presence rushed, and cried aloud,
"I am the King! Look and behold in me
Robert, your brother, King of Sicily!
This man who wears my semblance to your eyes,
Is an impostor in a king's disguise.
Do you not know me? does no voice within
Answer my cry, and say we are akin?"
The Pope in silence, but with troubled mien,
Gazed at the Angel's countenance serene;
The Emperor, laughing, said, "It is strange sport
To keep a madman for thy Fool at court!"
And the poor, baffled Jester in disgrace
Was hustled back among the populace.

In solemn state the Holy Week went by,
And Easter Sunday gleamed upon the sky;
The presence of the Angel, with its light,
Before the sun rose, made the city bright,
And with new fervor filled the hearts of men,
Who felt that Christ indeed had risen again.
Even the Jester on his bed of straw,
With haggard eyes the unwonted splendor saw;

He felt within a power unfelt before,
And, kneeling humbly on his chamber floor,
He heard the rushing garments of the Lord
Sweep through the silent air, ascending heavenward

And now the visit ending, and once more
Valmond returning to the Danube's shore,
Homeward the Angel journeyed, and again
The land was made resplendent with his train
Flashing along the towns of Italy
Unto Salerno, and from thence by sea.
And when once more within Palermo's wall,
And seated on the throne in his great hall,
He heard the Angelus from convent towers,
As if a better world conversed with ours,
He beckoned to King Robert to draw nigher,
And with a gesture bade the rest retire;
And when they were alone, the Angel said,
"Art thou the King?" Then, bowing down his head,
King Robert crossed both hands upon his breast,
And meekly answered him: "Thou knowest best!
My sins as scarlet are; let me go hence,
And in some cloister's school of penitence,
Across those stones, that pave the way to heaven,
Walk barefoot, till my guilty soul be shriven!"

The Angel smiled, and from his radiant face
A holy light illumined all the place,
And through the open window, loud and clear,
They heard the monks chant in the chapel near,
Above the stir and tumult of the street:
"He has put down the mighty from their seat,
And has exalted them of low degree!"
And through the chant a second melody
Rose like the throbbing of a single string:
"I am an Angel, and thou art the King!"

King Robert, who was standing near the throne,
Lifted his eyes, and lo! he was alone!
But all appareled as in days of old,
With ermined mantle and with cloth of gold;
And when his courtiers came, they found him there
Kneeling upon the floor, absorbed in silent prayer.

Henry Wadsworth Longfellow.

HORATIUS AT THE BRIDGE.

Lars Porsena of Clusium,
  By the nine gods he swore
That the great house of Tarquin
  Should suffer wrong no more.
By the nine gods he swore it,
  And named a trysting day,
And bade his messengers ride forth,
East and west and south and north,
  To summon his array.

East and west and south and north
  The messengers ride fast,
And tower and town and cottage
  Have heard the trumpet's blast.
The horsemen and the footmen
  Are pouring in amain
From many a stately market-place,
  From many a fruitful plain.

And now hath every city
  Sent up her tale of men;
The foot are fourscore thousand,
  The horse are thousands ten.
Before the gates of Sutrium
  Is met the great array,
A proud man was Lars Porsena
  Upon the trysting day.

But by the yellow Tiber
  Was tumult and affright:
From all the spacious champaign
  To Rome men took their flight.
A mile around the city,
  The throng stopped up the ways;
A fearful sight it was to see
  Through two long nights and days.

Now, from the rock Tarpeian,
  Could the wan burghers spy
The line of blazing villages
  Red in the midnight sky.

The Fathers of the City,
  They sat all night and day,
For every hour some horseman came
  With tidings of dismay.

They held a council standing
  Before the river-gate;
Short time was there, ye well may guess
  For musing or debate.
Outspake the Consul roundly:
  "The bridge must straight go down;
For since Janiculum is lost,
  Naught else can save the town."

Just then a scout came flying,
  All wild with haste and fear:
"To arms! to arms! Sir Consul;
  Lars Porsena is here."
On the low hills to westward
  The Consul fixed his eye,
And saw the swarthy storm of dust
  Rise fast along the sky.

And nearer, fast and nearer,
  Doth the red whirlwind come;
And louder still and still more loud,
From underneath that rolling cloud,
Is heard the trumpet's war-note proud
  The trampling and the hum.
And plainly and more plainly
  Now through the gloom appears,
Far to left and far to right,
In broken gleams of dark-blue light,
The long array of helmets bright,
  The long array of spears.

But the Consul's brow was sad,
  And the Consul's speech was low,
And darkly looked he at the wall,
  And darkly at the foe:
"Their van will be upon us
  Before the bridge goes down;
And if they once may win the bridge,
  What hope to save the town?"

Then outspake brave Horatius,
  The captain of the gate:
"To every man upon this earth
  Death cometh soon or late.
And how can man die better
  Than facing fearful odds
For the ashes of his fathers
  And the temples of his gods?

"Hew down the bridge, Sir Consul,
  With all the speed ye may;
I, with two more to help me,
  Will hold the foe in play,—
In yon strait path a thousand
  May well be stopped by three.
Now who will stand on either hand,
  And keep the bridge with me?"

Then outspake Spurius Lartius,—
  A Ramnian proud was he:
"Lo, I will stand at thy right hand,
  And keep the bridge with thee."
And outspake strong Herminius,—
  Of Titian blood was he:
"I will abide on thy left side,
  And keep the bridge with thee."

"Horatius," quoth the Consul,
  "As thou sayest, so let it be."
And straight against that great array,
  Forth went the dauntless Three.
Now, while the Three were tightening
  Their harness on their backs,
The Consul was the foremost man
  To take in hand an axe;
And Fathers mixed with Commons
  Seized hatchet, bar, and crow,
And smote upon the planks above,
  And loosed the props below.

Meanwhile the Tuscan army,
  Right glorious to behold,
Came flashing back the noonday light,
Rank behind rank, like surges bright

Of a broad sea of gold.
Four hundred trumpets sounded
  A peal of warlike glee,
As that great host, with measured tread,
And spears advanced, and ensigns spread,
Rolled slowly towards the bridge's head,
  Where stood the dauntless Three.

The three stood calm and silent,
  And looked upon the foes,
And a great shout of laughter
  From all the vanguard rose;
And forth three chiefs came spurring
  Before that mighty mass;
To earth they sprang, their swords they drew,
And lifted high their shields, and flew
  To win the narrow pass.

Aunus, from green Tifernum,
  Lord of the hill of vines;
And Seius, whose eight hundred slaves
  Sicken in Ilva's mines;
And Picus, long to Clusium
  Vassal in peace and war.

Stout Lartius hurled down Aunus
  Into the stream beneath;
Herminius struck at Seius,
  And clove him to the teeth;
At Picus brave Horatius
  Darted one fiery thrust,
And the proud Umbrian's gilded arms
  Clashed in the bloody dust.

But now no sound of laughter
  Was heard amongst the foes.
A wild and wrathful clamor
  From all the vanguard rose.
Six spears' lengths from the entrance
  Halted that mighty mass,
And for a space no man came forth
  To win the narrow pass.

But, hark! the cry is Astur;
 And lo! the ranks divide;
And the great lord of Luna
 Comes with his stately stride.
Upon his ample shoulders
 Clangs loud the fourfold shield,
And in his hand he shakes the brand
 Which none but he can wield.

He smiled on those bold Romans,
 A smile serene and high;
He eyed the flinching Tuscans,
 And scorn was in his eye.
Quoth he, "The she-wolf's litter
 Stand savagely at bay;
But will ye dare to follow,
 If Astur clears the way?"

Then, whirling up his broadsword
 With both hands to the height,
He rushed against Horatius,
 And smote with all his might;
With shield and blade Horatius
 Right deftly turned the blow,
The blow, though turned, came yet too nigh;
It missed his helm, but gashed his thigh.
The Tuscans raised a joyful cry
 To see the red blood flow.

He reeled, and on Herminius
 He leaned one breathing-space,
Then, like a wild-cat mad with wounds,
 Sprang right at Astur's face.
Through teeth and skull and helmet
 So fierce a thrust he sped,
The good sword stood a handbreadth out
 Behind the Tuscan's head.

And the great lord of Luna
 Fell at that deadly stroke,
As falls on Mount Avernus
 A thunder-smitten oak.

On Astur's throat Horatius
  Right firmly pressed his heel,
And thrice and four times tugged amain,
  Ere he wrenched out the steel.
"And see," he cried, "the welcome,
  Fair guests, that waits you here!
What noble Lucumo comes next
  To taste our Roman cheer?"

But meanwhile axe and lever
  Have manfully been plied,
And now the bridge hangs tottering
  Above the boiling tide.
"Come back, come back, Horatius!"
  Loud cried the Fathers all;
"Back, Lartius! back, Herminius!
  Back, ere the ruin fall!"

Back darted Spurius Lartius;
  Herminius darted back;
And, as they passed, beneath their feet
  They felt the timbers crack;
But when they turned their faces,
  And on the further shore
Saw brave Horatius stand alone,
  They would have crossed once more.
But, with a crash like thunder,
  Fell every loosened beam,
And, like a dam, the mighty wreck
  Lay right athwart the stream;
And a long shout of triumph
  Rose from the walls of Rome;
As to the highest turret-tops
  Was splashed the yellow foam.

Alone stood brave Horatius,
  But constant still in mind,—
Thrice thirty thousand foes before,
  And the broad flood behind.
"Down with him!" cried false Sextus,
  With a smile on his pale face;
"Now yield thee," cried Lars Porsena,
  "Now yield thee to our grace!"

Round turned he, as not deigning
    Those craven ranks to see;
Naught spake he to Lars Porsena,
    To Sextus naught spake he;
But he saw on Palatinus
    The white porch of his home;
And he spake to the noble river
    That rolls by the towers of Rome:

"O Tiber, Father Tiber!
    To whom the Romans pray,
A Roman's life, a Roman's arms,
    Take thou in charge this day!"
So he spake, and, speaking, sheathed
    The good sword by his side,
And, with his harness on his back,
    Plunged headlong in the tide.

No sound of joy or sorrow
    Was heard from either bank,
But friends and foes in dumb surprise,
With parted lips and straining eyes,
    Stood gazing where he sank;
And when above the surges
    They saw his crest appear,
All Rome sent forth a rapturous cry,
And even the ranks of Tuscany
    Could scarce forbear to cheer.

But fiercely ran the current,
    Swollen high by months of rain,
And fast his blood was flowing,
    And he was sore in pain,
And heavy with his armor,
    And spent with changing blows;
And oft they thought him sinking,
    But still again he rose.

And now he feels the bottom;—
    Now on dry earth he stands;
Now round him throng the Fathers
    To press his gory hands.

And now, with shouts and clapping,
    And noise of weeping loud,
He enters through the River Gate,
    Borne by the joyous crowd.

                              Lord Macaulay.

THE VAGABONDS.

We are two travelers, Roger and I.
    Roger's my dog:—come here, you scamp!
Jump for the gentlemen,—mind your eye!
    Over the table,—look out for the lamp!—
The rogue is growing a little old;
    Five years we've tramped through wind and weather,
And slept outdoors when nights were cold,
    And ate and drank—and starved together.

We've learned what comfort is, I tell you!
    A bed on the floor, a bit of rosin,
A fire to thaw our thumbs (poor fellow!
    The paw he holds up there's been frozen),
Plenty of catgut for my fiddle
    (This outdoor business is bad for the strings),
Then a few nice buckwheats hot from the griddle,
    And Roger and I set up for kings!

No, thank ye, sir,—I never drink;
    Roger and I are exceedingly moral,—
Are n't we, Roger?—see him wink!—
    Well, something hot then,—we won't quarrel.
He's thirsty, too,—see him nod his head?
    What a pity, sir, that dogs can't talk!
He understands every word that's said,—
    And he knows good milk from water-and-chalk.

The truth is, sir, now I reflect,
    I 've been so sadly given to grog,
I wonder I 've not lost the respect
    (Here 's to you, sir!) even of my dog.
But he sticks by through thick and thin;
    And this old coat, with its empty pockets,
And rags that smell of tobacco and gin,
    He 'll follow while he has eyes in his sockets.

There is n't another creature living
  Would do it, and prove, through every disaster,
So fond, so faithful, and so forgiving
  To such a miserable, thankless master!
No, sir!—see him wag his tail and grin!
  By George! it makes my old eyes water!—
That is, there 's something in this gin
  That chokes a fellow. But no matter!

We 'll have some music, if you 're willing,
  And Roger (hem! what a plague a cough is, sir!)
Shall march a little. Start, you villain!
  Stand straight! 'Bout face! Salute your officer!
Put up that paw! Dress! Take your rifle!
  (Some dogs have arms, you see!) Now hold your
Cap while the gentlemen give a trifle,
  To aid a poor old patriot soldier!

March! Halt! Now show how the rebel shakes,
  When he stands up to hear his sentence.
Now tell us how many drams it takes
  To honor a jolly new acquaintance.
Five yelps,—that 's five; he 's mighty knowing!
  The night 's before us, fill the glasses!—
Quick, sir! I 'm ill,—my brain is going!—
  Some brandy,—thank you,—there!—it passes!

Why not reform? That 's easily said;
  But I 've gone through such wretched treatment,
Sometimes forgetting the taste of bread,
  And scarce remembering what meat meant,
That my poor stomach 's past reform;
  And there are times when, mad with thinking,
I 'd sell out heaven for something warm
  To prop a horrible inward sinking.

Is there a way to forget to think?
  At your age, sir, home, fortune, friends,
A dear girl's love,—but I took to drink,—
  The same old story; you know how it ends.
If you could have seen these classic features,—
  You need n't laugh, sir; they were not then
Such a burning libel on God's creatures:
  I was one of your handsome men!

If you had seen her, so fair and young,
  Whose head was happy on this breast!
If you could have heard the songs I sung
  When the wine went round, you would n't have guessed
That ever I, sir, should be straying
  From door to door, with fiddle and dog,
Ragged and penniless, and playing
  To you to-night for a glass of grog!

She 's married since,—a parson's wife;
  'Twas better for her that we should part,—
Better the soberest, prosiest life
  Than a blasted home and a broken heart.
Have I seen her? Once; I was weak and spent
  On the dusty road, a carriage stopped;
But little she dreamed, as on she went,
  Who kissed the coin that her fingers dropped!

You 've set me talking, sir; I 'm sorry;
  It makes me wild to think of the change!
What do you care for a beggar's story?
  Is it amusing? you find it strange?
I had a mother so proud of me!
  'Twas well she died before— Do you know
If the happy spirits in heaven can see
  The ruin and wretchedness here below?

Another glass, and strong, to deaden
  This pain; then Roger and I will start.
I wonder, has he such a lumpish, leaden,
  Aching thing in place of a heart?
He is sad sometimes, and would weep if he could,
  No doubt, remembering things that were,—
A virtuous kennel, with plenty of food,
  And himself a sober, respectable cur.

I 'm better now; that glass was warming.
  You rascal! limber your lazy feet!
We must be fiddling and performing
  For supper and bed, or starve in the street.
Not a very gay life to lead, you think?
  But soon we shall go where lodgings are free,
And the sleepers need neither victuals nor drink;—
  The sooner the better for Roger and me!

                              J. T. Trowbridge.

SCENE FROM THE LITTLE MINISTER.

Within a squirrel's leap of the wood, an old woman was standing at the door of a mud house, listening for the approach of the trap that was to take her to the poor-house. It was Nanny Webster. She was not crying. She had redd up her house for the last time, and put on her black merino. Her mouth was wide open while she listened. If you had addressed her, you would have thought her polite and stupid. When she heard the dog-cart she screamed.

No neighbor was with her. If you think this hard, it is because you do not understand. Perhaps Nanny had never been very lovable except to one man, and him, it is said, she lost through her own vanity.

The door stood open, and Nanny was crouching against the opposite wall of the room, such a poor, dull kitchen, that you would have thought the furniture had still to be brought into it. The blanket and the piece of old carpet that was Nanny's coverlet were already packed in her box. The plate rack was empty. Only the round table and the two chairs, and the stools and some pans were being left behind.

"Well, Nanny," said Doctor McQueen, "I have come, and you see Mr. Dishart, the minister, is with me."

Nanny rose up bravely. She knew the doctor was good to her, and she wanted to thank him. "Thank you kindly, sirs," she said. "Please to take a chair." Both men sat down. The doctor thought it best they should depart at once, and so he rose.

"Oh, no, doctor," cried Nanny in alarm.

"But you are ready?"

"Ay," she said, "I have been ready this twa hours, but you micht wait a minute. Hendry Munn and Andrew Allardyce is coming yont the road, and they would see me."

"Wait, doctor," the minister said.

"Thank you kindly, sir," answered Nanny.

"But, Nanny," the doctor said, "you must remember what I told you about the poorhouse. It is a fine place, and you will be very happy in it."

"Ay, I 'll be happy in 't," Nanny faltered, "but, doctor, if I could just hae bidden on here though I wasna happy!"

"Think of the food you will get; broth nearly every day."

"It—it 'll be terrible enjoyable," Nanny said.

"And there will be pleasant company for you always," continued the doctor, "and a nice room to sit in. Why, after you have been there a week, you won't be the same woman."

"That 's it!" cried Nanny, with sudden passion. "Na, na; I 'll be a woman on the poor's rates. Oh, mither, mither, you little thocht that I would come to this!"

"Nanny, I am ashamed of you."

"I humbly speir your forgiveness, sir, and you micht bide just a wee yet. I 've been ready to gang this twa hours, but now that the machine is at the gate, I dinna ken how it is, but I 'm terrible sweir to come awa'. Oh, Mr. Dishart, it 's richt true what the doctor says about the—the place, but I canna just take it in. I 'm—I 'm gey auld."

"You will often get out to see your friends," said the minister.

"Na, na, na, dinna say that; I 'll gang, but you manna bid me ever come out, except in a hearse. Dinna let onybody in Thrums look on my face again."

"We must go," said the doctor firmly. "Put on your bonnet, Nanny."

She took the bonnet from her bed and put it on slowly.

"Are you sure there 's naebody looking?" she asked.

The doctor glanced at the minister, and he arose.

"Let us pray," he said; and the three went down on their knees.

It was not the custom of Auld Licht ministers to leave any house until they had offered up a prayer, and to us it always seemed that when the little minister prayed he was at the knees of God; but now Nanny was speaking too, and her words choked his. At first she only whispered, but soon what was eating her heart burst out painfully, and she did not know that the minister had stopped. They were such moans as these that brought him back to earth:

"I 'll ha'e to gang. . . . . I 'm a base woman no' to be mair thankfu' to them that is so good to me.

. . . . Oh, mither! . . . . I wish terrible they had come and ta'en me at nicht. . . . . It's a dog-cart, and I was praying it micht be a cart, so that they could cover me wi' straw."

"This is more than I can stand," the doctor cried.

Nanny rose frightened.

"I've tried you, sair," she said, "but, oh, I'm grateful, and I'm ready now."

They all advanced toward the door without another word, and Nanny even tried to smile. But in the middle of the floor something came over her, and she stood there. The minister took her hand, and it was cold. She looked from one to the other, her mouth opening and shutting.

"I canna help it," she said.

"It's cruel hard," muttered the doctor. "I knew this woman when she was a lassie."

The little minister stretched out his hands, "Have pity on her, O God!"

Nanny heard the words. "Oh, God," she cried, "you micht!"

God needs no minister to tell him what to do, but it was His will that the poorhouse should not have this woman. He made use of a strange instrument, no other than the Egyptian, who now opened the mud house door.

The gypsy had been passing the house, perhaps on her way to Thrums for gossip, and it was only curiosity, born suddenly of the minister's cry, that made her enter.

"This is no place for you," said he fiercely, when Nanny, too distraught to think, fell crying at the Egyptian's feet.

"They are taking me to the poorhouse. Dinna let them, dinna let them."

"How dare you!" cried the gypsy, stamping her foot; and they quaked like malefactors.

"You don't see ——" the minister began, but her indignation stopped him.

"You coward!" she said.

"This is all very well," said the doctor, "but a woman's sympathy ——"

"A woman! Ah, if I could be a man for only five minutes! You poor dear, I won't let them take you away. Go!" she said, looking triumphantly at both minister and doctor, and pointing grandly to the door.

"Is this an Egyptian, or is she a queen," the doctor said in a low voice to the minister. "Hoots, man, don't look so shame-faced. We are not criminals. Say something."

Then to the Egyptian the little minister said firmly, "You mean well, but you are doing this poor woman a cruelty in holding out hopes to her that cannot be realized. Sympathy is not meal and bedclothes, and these are what she needs."

"And you who live in luxury would send her to the poorhouse for them. I thought better of you."

"Tuts!" said the doctor, losing his patience. "Mr. Dishart gives more than any other man in Thrums to the poor, and he is not to be preached to by a gypsy. We are waiting for you, Nanny."

"Ay, I 'm coming. I 'll hae to gang, lassie. Dinna greet for me."

But the Egyptian said, "No, you are not going. It is these men who are going. Go, sirs, and leave us."

"And you will provide for Nanny?" asked the doctor, contemptuously.

"Yes."

"And where is the siller to come from?"

"That is my affair, and Nanny's. Begone, both of you. She shall never want again. See how the very mention of your going brings back life to her face."

"I won't begone," the doctor said roughly, "till I see the color of your siller."

"Oh! the money," said the Egyptian scornfully. She put her hand into her pocket confidently, as if used to well-filled purses, but could only draw out two silver pieces. "I had forgotten."

"I thought so," said the cynical doctor. "Come, Nanny."

"You presume to doubt me!" the Egyptian said, blocking his way to the door.

"How could I presume to believe you?" he answered. "You are a beggar by profession, and yet talk as if— Pooh, nonsense."

"I could live on terrible little," Nanny whispered.

"Seven shillings a week," rapped out the doctor.

"Is that all?" the Egyptian asked. "She shall have it."

"When?"

"At once. No, it is not possible to-night, but to-morrow I will bring five pounds; no, I will send it; no, you must come for it. You will meet me to-morrow about this hour at—say the Kaims of Cushie?"

"No, I won't. Even if I went to the Kaims I should not find you there."

"You are a cruel, hard man," the Egyptian said, beginning to lose hope. "But, see, look at this ring. Do you know its value?"

"Mercy on us!" Nanny cried; "I believe it's what they call a diamond."

"See, I will give it to you to hold in hostage. If I am not at the Kaims to get it back, you can keep it."

The doctor took the ring in his hand and examined it curiously.

"There is a quirk in this," he said at last, "that I do n't like. Take back your ring, lassie. Mr. Dishart, give Nanny your arm unless you trust this woman's word."

"You do trust me," the Egyptian said, with wet eyes.

"Yes," he said firmly, "I trust you;" and the words that had been so difficult to say were the right words—

J. M. Barrie.

CATILINE'S DEFIANCE.

Conscript Fathers:
I do not rise to waste the night in words;
Let that Plebeian talk, 'tis not *my* trade;
But *here* I stand for right,—let him show *proofs*,—
For Roman right, though none, it seems, dare stand
To take their share with me. Ay, cluster there!
Cling to your master, judges, Romans, *slaves!*
His charge is false;—I *dare* him to his proofs.
You have my answer. Let my actions speak!

But this I will avow, that I *have* scorned
And still *do* scorn, to hide my sense of wrong.
Who brands me on the forehead, breaks my sword,
Or lays the bloody scourge upon my back,
Wrongs me not half so much as he who shuts

The gates of honor on me,—turning out
The Roman from his birthright; and for what?
To fling your offices to every slave!
Vipers, that creep where man disdains to climb,
And, having wound their loathsome track to the top
Of this huge, moldering monument of Rome,
Hang hissing at the nobler man below.
  Come, consecrated Lictors, from your thrones;

                                    [*To the Senate.*

Fling down your scepters; take the rod and axe,
And make the murder as you make the law.

  Banished from Rome! What 's banished but set free
From daily contact of the things I loathe?
"Tried and convicted traitor!" Who says this?
Who 'll prove it, at his peril, on my head?
Banished! I thank you for 't. It breaks my chain!
I held some slack allegiance till this hour;
But *now* my sword 's my own. Smile on, my Lords!
I scorn to count what feelings, withered hopes,
Strong provocations, bitter, burning wrongs,
I have within my heart's hot cells shut up,
To leave you in your lazy dignities.
But here I stand and scoff you! here I fling
Hatred and full defiance in your face!
Your Consul 's merciful;—for this all thanks.
He *dares* not touch a hair of Catiline!

  "Traitor!" I go; but, I *return!* This—trial!
Here I devote your Senate! I 've had wrongs
To stir a fever in the blood of age,
Or make the infant's sinews strong as steel.
This day 's the birth of sorrow; this hour's work
Will breed proscriptions! Look to your hearths, my Lords!
For there, henceforth, shall sit, for household gods,
Shapes hot from Tartarus; all shames and crimes;
Wan Treachery, with his thirsty dagger drawn;
Suspicion, poisoning his brother's cup;
Naked Rebellion, with the torch and axe,
Making his wild sport of your blazing thrones;
Till Anarchy comes down on you like night,
And Massacre seals Rome's eternal grave.

I go; but not to leap the gulf alone.
I go; but when I come, 't will be the burst
Of ocean in the earthquake,—rolling back
In swift and mountainous ruin.   Fare you well!
You build my funeral-pile; but your best blood
Shall quench its flame!   Back, slaves!   [*To the Lictors.*
I will return.

George Croly.

GUINEVERE.

Queen Guinevere had fled the court, and sat
There in the holy house at Almesbury
Weeping, none with her save a little maid,
A novice: one low light betwixt them burn'd,
Blurr'd by the creeping mist, for all abroad,
Beneath a moon unseen albeit at full,
The white mist, like a face-cloth to the face,
Clung to the dead earth, and the land was still.

        And while the Queen sat brooding thus
And grew half-guilty in her thoughts again,
There rode an armed warrior to the doors.
A murmuring whisper thro' the nunnery ran,
Then on a sudden a cry, "The King!"   She sat
Stiff-stricken, listening; but when armed feet
Thro' the long gallery from the outer doors
Rang coming, prone from off her seat she fell,
And grovell'd with her face against the floor:
There, with her milk-white arms and shadowy hair,
She made her face a darkness from the King:
And in the darkness heard his armed feet
Pause by her; then came silence, then a voice,
Monotonous and hollow like a ghost's,
Denouncing judgment, but tho' changed, the King's:

"Liest thou here so low, the child of one
I honor'd, happy, dead before thy shame?
Yet think not that I come to urge thy crimes,
I did not come to curse thee, Guinevere,
I, whose vast pity almost makes me die
To see thee, laying there thy golden head,

My pride in happier summers, at my feet.
The wrath which forced my thoughts on that fierce law,
The doom of treason and the flaming death
(When first I learnt thee hidden here) is past.
The pang—which, while I weigh'd thy heart with one
Too wholly true to dream untruth in thee,
Made my tears burn—is also past, in part.
And all is past, the sin is sinn'd, and I,
Lo! I forgive thee, as Eternal God
Forgives: do thou for thine own soul the rest.
But how to take last leave of all I loved?
O golden hair, with which I used to play
Not knowing! O imperial-molded form,
And beauty such as woman never wore,
Until it came a kingdom's curse with thee—
I cannot touch thy lips, they are not mine,
But Lancelot's: nay, they never were the King's.
I cannot take thy hand; that, too, is flesh,
And in the flesh thou hast sinn'd; and mine own flesh,
Here looking down on thine polluted, cries,
'I loathe thee:' yet not less, O Guinevere,
For I was ever virgin save for thee,
My love thro' flesh hath wrought into my life
So far, that my doom is, I love thee still.
Let no man dream but that I love thee still.
Perchance, and so thou purify thy soul,
And so thou lean on our fair father Christ,
Hereafter in that world where all are pure
We two may meet before high God, and thou
Wilt spring to me, and claim me thine, and know
I am thine husband—not a smaller soul,
Nor Lancelot, nor another. Leave me that,
I charge thee, my last hope. Now must I hence.
Thro' the thick night I hear the trumpet blow:
They summon me, their King, to lead mine hosts
Far down to that great battle in the west,
Where I must strike against the man they call
My sister's son—and strike him dead, and meet myself
Death, or I know not what mysterious doom.
And thou remaining here wilt learn the event;
But hither shall I never come again,
Never lie by thy side; see thee no more—
Farewell!''

And while she grovell'd at his feet,
She felt the King's breath wander o'er her neck,
And in the darkness o'er her fallen head,
Perceived the waving of his hands that blest.

Then, listening till those armed steps were gone,
Rose the pale Queen, and in her anguish found
The casement.

Then she stretched out her arms and cried aloud:
                                "Gone—my lord!
Gone thro' my sin to slay and to be slain!
And he forgave me, and I could not speak.
Farewell? I should have answer'd his farewell.
His mercy choked me. Gone, my lord, the King,
My own true lord! how dare I call him mine?
The shadow of another cleaves to me,
And makes me one pollution: he, the King,
Call'd me polluted: shall I kill myself?
What help in that? I cannot kill my sin,
If soul be soul; nor can I kill my shame;
No, nor by living can I live it down.
The days will grow to weeks, the weeks to months,
The months will add themselves and make the years,
The years will roll into the centuries,
And mine will ever be a name of scorn.
I must not dwell on that defeat of fame.
Let the world be; that is but of the world.
What else? what hope? I think there was a hope,
Except he mock'd me when he spake of hope;
His hope he call'd it; but he never mocks,
For mockery is the fume of little hearts.
And blessed be the King, who hath forgiven
My wickedness to him, and let me hope
That in mine own heart I can live down sin
And be his mate hereafter in the heavens
Before high God. Ah, great and gentle lord,
Who wast, as is the conscience of a saint
Among his warring senses, to thy knights—
To whom my false voluptuous pride, that took
Full easily all impressions from below,
Would not look up, or half-despised the height
To which I would not or I could not climb—

I thought I could not breathe in that fine air
That pure severity of perfect light—
I wanted warmth and color which I found
In Lancelot—now I see thee what thou art;
Thou art the highest and most human, too,
Not Lancelot, nor another. Is there none
Will tell the King I love him tho' so late?
Now—ere he goes to the great battle? none:
Myself must tell him in that purer life,
But now it were too daring. Ah, my God,
What might I not have made of thy fair world,
Had I but loved thy highest creature here?
It was my duty to have loved the highest:
It surely was my profit had I known:
It would have been my pleasure had I seen.
We needs must love the highest when we see it,
Not Lancelot, nor another."

Lord Tennyson.

ECHO AND THE FERRY.

Ay, Oliver! I was but seven, and he was eleven;
He looked at me pouting and rosy. I blushed where I stood.
They had told us to play in the orchard (and I only seven!
A small guest at the farm); but he said, "Oh! a girl was
    no good!"
So he whistled and went, he went over the stile to the wood.
It was sad, it was sorrowful! Only a girl—only seven!
At home in the dark London smoke I had not found it out.
The pear-trees looked on in their white, and bluebirds
    flashed about,
And they, too, were angry as Oliver. Were they eleven?
I thought so. Yes, every one else was eleven—eleven!

So Oliver went, but the cowslips were tall at my feet,
And all the white orchard with fast-falling blossom was
    littered;
And under and over the branches those little birds twit-
    tered,
While hanging head downward they scolded because I
    was seven.

A pity—a very great pity. One should be eleven.
But soon I was happy, the smell of the world was so sweet,
And I saw a round hole in an apple-tree rosy and old.
Then I knew, for I peeped, and I felt it was right they
should scold.
Eggs small and eggs many. For gladness I broke into
laughter;
And then some one else—oh! how softly!—came after,
came after
  With laughter—with laughter came after.

And no one was near us to utter that sweet, mocking call,
That soon very tired sank low with a mystical fall.
But this was the country—perhaps it was close under
heaven;
Oh! nothing so likely; the voice might have come from
it even.
I knew about heaven. But this was the country, of this
Light, blossom, and piping, and flashing of wings not at all.
Not at all. No. But one little bird was an easy forgiver:
She peeped, she drew near as I moved from her domicile
small,
Then flashed down her hole like a dart—like a dart from
the quiver,
And I waded atween the long grasses, and felt it was bliss.

—So this was the country; clear dazzle of azure and shiver
And whisper of leaves, and a humming all over the tall
White branches, a humming of bees. And I came to the
wall—
A little, low wall—and looked over, and there was the river,
The lane that led on to the village, and then the sweet
river,
Clear shining and slow, she had far, far to go from her
snow;
But each rush gleamed a sword in the sunlight to guard
her long flow,
And she murmured, methought, with a speech very soft—
very low.
"The ways will be long, but the days will be long," quoth
the river,
"To me a long liver, long, long!" quoth the river—the
river.

I dreamed of the country that night, of the orchard, the
sky,
The voice that had mocked coming after and over and
under.
But at last—in a day or two, namely—Eleven and I
Were very fast friends, and to him I confided the wonder.
He said that was Echo. "Was Echo a wise kind of bee
That had learned how to laugh? Could it laugh in one's
ear and then fly,
And laugh again yonder?" "No; Echo"—he whispered
it low—
"Was a woman, they said, but a woman whom no one
could see
And no one could find; and he did not believe it, not he;
But he could not get near for the river that held us asunder.
Yet I that had money—a shilling, a whole silver shilling—
We might cross if I thought I would spend it." "Oh!
yes, I was willing"—
And we ran hand in hand; we ran down to the ferry, the
ferry,
And we heard how she mocked at the folk with a voice
clear and merry
When they called for the ferry; but, oh! she was very—
was very
Swift-footed. She spoke and was gone; and when Oliver
cried,
"Hie over! hie over! you man of the ferry—the ferry!"
By the still water's side she was heard far and wide—she
replied,
And she mocked in her voice sweet and merry, "You man
of the ferry,
You man of—you man of the ferry!"

"Hie over!" he shouted. The ferryman came at his call-
ing;
Across the clear reed-bordered river he ferried us fast.
Such a chase! Hand in hand, foot to foot, we ran on; it
surpassed
All measure her doubling—so close, then so far away fall-
ing,
Then gone, and no more. Oh! to see her but once unaware,
And the mouth that had mocked; but we might not (yet
sure she was there),

Nor behold her wild eyes, and her mystical countenance fair.

We sought in the wood, and we found the wood-wren in her stead;

In the field, and we found but the cuckoo that talked over-head;

By the brook, and we found the reed-sparrow deep-nested, in brown;

Not Echo, fair Echo! for Echo, sweet Echo! was flown.

So we came to the place where the dead people wait till God call.

The church was among them, gray moss over roof, over wall.

Very silent, so low. And we stood on a green, grassy mound

And looked in at the window, for Echo, perhaps, in her round

Might have come in to hide there. But, no; every oak-carven seat

Was empty. We saw the great Bible—old, old, very old,

And the parson's great Prayer-book beside it; we heard the slow beat

Of the pendulum swing in the tower; we saw the clear gold

Of a sunbeam float down to the aisle, and then waver and play

On the low chancel step and the railing; and Oliver said,

"Look, Katie! look, Katie! when Lettice came here to be wed

She stood where that sunbeam drops down, and all white was her gown;

And she stepped upon flowers they strewed for her." Then quoth small Seven:

"Shall I wear a white gown and have flowers to walk upon ever?"

All doubtful: "It takes a long time to grow up," quoth Eleven;

"You're so little, you know, and the church is so old, it can never

Last on till you're tall." And in whispers—because it was old

And holy, and fraught with strange meaning, half felt, but not told,

Full of old parsons' prayers, who were dead, of old days,
  of old folk,
Neither heard nor beheld, but about us—in whispers we
  spoke.
Then we went from it softly, and ran hand in hand to the
  strand,
While bleating of flocks and birds' piping made sweeter
  the land.
And Echo came back e'en as Oliver drew to the ferry.

Ay, here—it was here that we woke her, the Echo of old;
All life of that day seems an echo, and many times told.
Shall I cross by the ferry to-morrow, and come in my
  white
To that little low church? and will Oliver meet me anon?
Will it all seem an echo from childhood passed over—
  passed on?

Jean Ingelow.

THE VICTOR OF MARENGO.

Napoleon was sitting in his tent; before him lay a map
of Italy. He took four pins and stuck them up; measured, moved the pins, and measured again. "Now," said
he, "that is right; I will capture him there!"

"Who, sir?" said an officer.

"Milas, the old fox of Austria. He will retire from
Genoa, pass Turin, and fall back on Alexandria. I shall
cross the Po, meet him on the plains of Laconia, and conquer him there," and the finger of the child of destiny
pointed to Marengo.

Two months later the memorable campaign of 1800
began. The 20th of May saw Napoleon on the heights of
St. Bernard. The 22d, Larmes, with the army of Genoa,
held Padua. So far, all had been well with Napoleon.
He had compelled the Austrians to take the position he
desired; reduced the army from one hundred and twenty
thousand to forty thousand men; dispatched Murat to the
right, and June 14th moved forward to consummate his
masterly plan.

But God threatened to overthrow his scheme! A little rain had fallen in the Alps, and the Po could not be crossed in time. The battle was begun. Milas, pushed to the wall, resolved to cut his way out; and Napoleon reached the field to see Larmes beaten, Champeaux dead, Desaix still charging old Milas, with his Austrian phalanx at Marengo, till the consular guard gave way, and the well-planned victory was a terrible defeat. Just as the day was lost, Desaix, the boy General, sweeping across the field at the head of his cavalry, halted on the eminence where stood Napoleon. There was in the corps a drummer-boy, a gamin whom Desaix had picked up in the streets of Paris. He had followed the victorious eagle of France in the campaigns of Egypt and Germany. As the columns halted, Napoleon shouted to him: "Beat a retreat!"

The boy did not stir.

"Gamin, beat a retreat!"

The boy stopped, grasped his drumsticks, and said: "Sir, I do not know how to beat a retreat; Desaix never taught me that; but I can beat a charge,—oh! I can beat a charge that will make the dead fall into line. I beat that charge at the Pyramids; I beat that charge at Mount Tabor; I beat it again at the bridge of Lodi. May I beat it here?"

Napoleon turned to Desaix, and said: "We are beaten; what shall we do?"

"Do? Beat them! It is only three o'clock, and there is time enough to win a victory yet. Up! the charge! beat the old charge of Mount Tabor and Lodi!"

A moment later the corps, following the sword-gleam of Desaix, and keeping step with the furious roll of the gamin's drum, swept down on the host of Austrians. They drove the first line back on the second—both on the third, and there they died. Desaix fell at the first volley, but the line never faltered, and as the smoke cleared away, the gamin was seen in front of his line marching right on, and still beating the furious charge. Over the dead and wounded, over breastworks and fallen foe, over cannon belching forth their fire of death, he led the way to victory, and the fifteen days in Italy were ended. To-day men point to Marengo in wonder. They admire the power and foresight that so skillfully handled the battle, but they forget that a general only thirty years of age made a victory of a defeat. They forget that a gamin of Paris put to shame "the child of destiny."

Anonymous.

MAMMY'S LI'L' BOY.

Who all time dodgin' en de cott'n en de corn?
   Mammy's li'l' boy, mammy's li'l' boy!
Who all time stealin' ole massa's dinner-horn?
   Mammy's li'l' baby boy.

      Byo baby boy, oh bye,
      By-o li'l' boy!
      Oh, run ter es mammy
      En she tek 'im in 'er arms,
      Mammy's li'l' baby boy.

Who all time runnin' ole gobble roun' de yard?
   Mammy's li'l' boy, mammy's li'l' boy!
Who tek 'e stick 'n hit ole possum dog so hard?
   Mammy's li'l' baby boy.

      Byo baby boy, oh bye,
      By-o li'l' boy!
      Oh, run ter es mammy
      En climb up en 'er lap,
      Mammy's li'l' baby boy.

Who all time stumpin' es toe ergin er rock?
   Mammy's li'l' boy, mammy's li'l' boy!
Who all the time er-rippin' big hole en es frock?
   Mammy's li'l' baby boy.

      Byo baby boy, oh bye,
      By-o li'l' boy!
      Oh, run ter es mammy
      En she wipe es li'l' eyes,
      Mammy's li'l' baby boy.

Who all time er-losin' de shovel en de rake?
   Mammy's li'l' boy, mammy's li'l' boy!

Who all de time tryin' ter ride 'e lazy drake?
  Mammy's li'l' baby boy.

        Byo baby boy, oh bye,
        By-o li'l' boy!
        Oh, scoot fer yer mammy
        En she hide yer f'om yer ma,
        Mammy's li'l' baby boy.

Who all de time er-trottin' ter de kitchen fer er bite?
  Mammy's li'l' boy, mammy's li'l' boy!
Who mess 'esef wi' taters twell his clothes dey look er sight?
  Mammy's li'l' baby boy.

        Byo baby boy, oh bye,
        By-o li'l' boy!
        En 'e run ter es mammy
        Fer ter git 'im out er trouble,
        Mammy's li'l' baby boy.

Who all time er-frettin' en de middle er de day?
  Mammy's li'l' boy, mammy's li'l' boy!
Who all time er-gettin' so sleepy 'e can't play?
  Mammy's li'l' baby boy.

        Byo baby boy, oh bye,
        By-o li'l' boy!
        En 'e come ter es mammy
        Ter rock 'im en 'er arms,
        Mammy's li'l' baby boy.
        Shoo, shoo, shoo-shoo-shoo,
        Shoo, shoo, shoo!

        Shoo, shoo, shoo-shoo-shoo,
        Shoo, li'l' baby, shoo!
        Shoo, shoo, shoo-shoo-shoo,
        Shoo, shoo, shoo,
        Shoo . . . .

  Deir now, lay right down on mammy's bed en go 'long
back ter sleep,—shoo-shoo!
                                                H. S. Edwards.

RIENZI TO THE ROMANS.

Friends!
I come not here to talk.   Ye know too well
The story of our thraldom.   We are slaves!
The bright sun rises to his course, and lights
A race of slaves! he sets, and his last beam
Falls on a slave!   Not such as swept along
By the full tide of power, the conqueror leads
To crimson glory and undying fame,
But base, ignoble slaves!—slaves to a horde
Of petty tyrants, feudal despots; lords
Rich in some dozen paltry villages,
Strong in some hundred spearmen, only great
In that strange spell,—a name!   Each hour, dark fraud,
Or open rapine, or protected murder,
Cries out against them.   But this very day
An honest man, my neighbor,—there he stands,—
Was struck—struck like a dog—by one who wore
The badge of Ursini! because, forsooth,
He tossed not high his ready cap in air,
Nor lifted up his voice in servile shouts,
At sight of that great ruffian!   Be we men,
And suffer such dishonor? men, and wash not
The stain away in blood? such shames are common.
I have known deeper wrongs.   I that speak to ye—
I had a brother once, a gracious boy,
Full of all gentleness, of calmest hope,
Of sweet and quiet joy; there was the look
Of heaven upon his face which limners give
To the beloved disciple.   How I loved
That gracious boy! younger by fifteen years,
Brother at once and son!   He left my side,—
A summer bloom on his fair cheeks, a smile
Parting his innocent lips.   In one short hour
The pretty, harmless boy was slain!   I saw
The corse, the mangled corse, and then I cried
For vengeance!   Rouse, ye Romans!   Rouse, ye slaves!
Have ye brave sons?—Look in the next fierce brawl
To see them die!   Have ye fair daughters?—Look
To see them live, torn from your arms, disdained,
Dishonored; and, if ye dare call for justice,

Be answered by the lash! Yet this is Rome,
That sate on her seven hills, and from her throne
Of beauty ruled the world! Yet we are Romans.
Why, in that elder day to be a Roman
Was greater than a king! And once again—
Hear me, ye walls, that echoed to the tread
Of either Brutus!—once again I swear
The eternal city shall be free!

Mary Russell Mitford.

LOCHINVAR.

O, young Lochinvar is come out of the west,
Through all the wide Border his steed was the best;
And, save his good broadsword, he weapon had none,
He rode all unarmed, and he rode all alone.
So faithful in love, and so dauntless in war,
There never was knight like the young Lochinvar.

He stayed not for brake, and he stopped not for stone,
He swam the Eske River where ford there was none,
But, ere he alighted at Netherby gate,
The bride had consented, the gallant came late;
For a laggard in love, and a dastard in war,
Was to wed the fair Ellen of brave Lochinvar.

So boldly he entered the Netherby Hall,
Among bridesmen, and kinsmen, and brothers, and all.
Then spoke the bride's father, his hand on his sword,
(For the poor craven bridegroom said never a word),
"O, come ye in peace here, or come ye in war,
Or to dance at our bridal, young Lord Lochinvar?"

"I long wooed your daughter, my suit you denied;—
Love swells like the Solway, but ebbs like its tide,—
And now I am come, with this lost love of mine,
To lead but one measure, drink one cup of wine;
There are maidens in Scotland more lovely by far,
That would gladly be bride to the young Lochinvar."

The bride kissed the goblet; the knight took it up,
He quaffed off the wine, and threw down the cup.
She looked down to blush, and she looked up to sigh.
With a smile on her lips and a tear in her eye,
He took her soft hand, ere her mother could bar,—
"Now tread we a measure," said young Lochinvar.

So stately his form, so lovely her face,
That never a hall such a galliard did grace;
While her mother did fret, and her father did fume,
And the bridegroom stood dangling his bonnet and plume;
And the bridemaidens whispered, "'T were better by far
To have matched our fair cousin with young Lochinvar."

One touch to her hand, and one word in her ear,
When they reached the hall-door, and the charger stood
      near;
So light to the croupe the fair lady he swung,
So light to the saddle before her he sprung;
"She is won! we are gone! over bank, bush, and scaur;
They 'll have fleet steeds that follow," quoth young Loch-
      invar.

There was mounting 'mong Græmes of the Netherby clan;
Forsters, Fenwicks, and Musgraves, they rode and they
      ran:
There was racing and chasing on Cannobie lea,
But the lost bride of Netherby ne'er did they see.
So daring in love, and so dauntless in war;
Have ye e'er heard of gallant like young Lochinvar?
                                        Sir Walter Scott.

THE PICKET GUARD.

"All quiet along the Potomac," they say,
   "Except now and then a stray picket
Is shot, as he walks on his beat, to and fro,
   By a rifleman off in the thicket.

" 'Tis nothing—a private or two, now and then,
   Will not count in the news of the battle;

Not an officer lost—only one of the men,
  Moaning out, all alone, the death-rattle. "

All quiet along the Potomac to-night,
  Where the soldiers lie peacefully dreaming;
Their tents in the rays of the clear autumn moon,
  Or the light of the watchfires are gleaming.

A tremulous sigh, as the gentle night wind
  Through the forest-leaves softly is creeping;
While stars up above, with their glittering eyes,
  Keep guard—for the army is sleeping.

There 's only the sound of the lone sentry's tread
  As he tramps from the rock to the fountain,
And thinks of the two in the low trundle-bed
  Far away in the cot on the mountain.

His musket falls slack—his face, dark and grim,
  Grows gentle with memories tender,
As he mutters a prayer for the children asleep—
  For their mother—may Heaven defend her!

The moon seems to shine just as brightly as then,
  That night, when the love yet unspoken
Leaped up to his lips—when low-murmured vows
  Were pledged to be ever unbroken.

Then drawing his sleeve roughly over his eyes,
  He dashes off tears that are welling,
And gathers his gun closer up to its place
  As if to keep down the heart-swelling.

He passes the fountain, the blasted pine-tree—
  The footstep is lagging and weary;
Yet onward he goes through the broad belt of light
  Toward the shades of the forest so dreary.

Hark! was it the night-wind that rustled the leaves?
  Was it moonlight so wondrously flashing?
It looked like a rifle—"Ah! Mary, good-by!"
  And the life-blood is ebbing and plashing.

All quiet along the Potomac to-night,
  No sound save the rush of the river;
While soft falls the dew on the face of the dead,
  The picket 's off duty forever.

                  Mrs. Ethel Lynn Beers.

FOR A' THAT, AND A' THAT.

Is there, for honest poverty,
  That hangs his head, and a' that?
The coward-slave, we pass him by,
  And dare be poor, for a' that;
    For a' that, and a' that,
      Our toils obscure, and a' that;
    The rank is but the guinea's stamp;
      The man's the gowd for a' that.

What tho' on hamely fare we dine,
  Wear hodden-gray, and a' that;
Gie fools their silks, and knaves their wine,
  A man's a man, for a' that;
    For a' that, and a' that,
      Their tinsel show, and a' that;
    The honest man, tho' ne'er sae poor,
      Is king o' men for a' that.

Ye see yon birkie, ca'ed a lord,
  Wha struts, and stares, and a' that;
Tho' hundreds worship at his word,
  He 's but a coof for a' that;
    For a' that, and a' that,
      His riband, star, and a' that;
    The man of independent mind,
      He looks and laughs at a' that.

A king can mak a belted knight,
  A marquis, duke, and a' that;
But an honest man 's aboon his might,
  Guid faith, he maunna fa' that!

> For a' that, and a' that,
>> Their dignities, and a' that;
>> The pith o' sense, and pride o' worth,
>>> Are higher ranks than a' that.

> Then let us pray that come it may,
>> As come it will for a' that,
> That sense and worth, o'er a' the earth,
>> May bear the gree, and a' that;
>>> For a' that, and a' that,
>>>> It 's coming yet, for a' that;
>>> That man to man, the warld o'er,
>>>> Shall brothers be for a' that.

Robert Burns.

MAGDALENA, OR THE SPANISH DUEL.

> Near the city of Sevilla,
>> Years and years ago—
> Dwelt a lady in a villa,
>> Years and years ago;—
> And her hair was black as night,
> And her eyes were starry bright;
> Olives on her brow were blooming,
> Roses red her lips perfuming,
> And her step was light and airy
> As the tripping of a fairy;
> When she spoke, you thought, each minute,
> 'Twas the trilling of a linnet;
> When she sang, you heard a gush
> Of full-voiced sweetness like a thrush;
> And she struck from the guitar
> Ringing music, sweeter far
> Than the morning breezes make
> Through the lime-trees when they shake—
> Than the ocean murmuring o'er
> Pebbles on the foamy shore.
> Orphaned both of sire and mother,
>> Dwelt she in that lonely villa,
> Absent now her guardian brother
>> On a mission from Sevilla.

Skills it little now the telling
    How I wooed that maiden fair,
Tracked her to her lonely dwelling
    And obtained an entrance there.

Ah! that lady of the villa!
    And I loved her so,
Near the city of Sevilla,
    Years and years ago,
Ay de mi!—Like echoes falling
    Sweet and sad and low,
Voices come at night, recalling
    Years and years ago.
Once again I 'm sitting near thee,
    Beautiful and bright;
Once again I see and hear thee
    In the autumn night;
Once again I 'm whispering to thee
    Faltering words of love;
Once again with song I woo thee
    In the orange grove,
Growing near that lonely villa
    Where the waters flow
Down to the city of Sevilla—
    Years and years ago.

'Twas an autumn eve: the splendor
    Of the day was gone,
And the twilight, soft and tender,
    Stole so gently on
That the eye could scarce discover
How the shadows, spreading over,
    Like a veil of silver gray,
Toned the golden clouds, sun painted,
Till they paled, and paled, and fainted
    From the face of heaven away.
And a dim light rising slowly
    O'er the welkin spread,
Till the blue sky, calm and holy,
    Gleamed above our head;
And the thin moon, newly nascent,
    Shone in glory meek and sweet,
As Murillo paints her crescent
    Underneath Madonna's feet.

And we sat outside the villa
    Where the waters flow
Down to the city of Sevilla—
    Years and years ago.

There we sate—the mighty river
    Wound its serpent course along
Silent, dreamy Guadalquivir,
    Famed in many a song.
Silver gleaming 'mid the plain
Yellow with the golden grain,
Gliding down through deep, rich meadows,
    Where the sated cattle rove,
Stealing underneath the shadows
    Of the verdant olive grove;
With its plenitude of waters,
    Ever flowing calm and slow,
Loved by Andalusia's daughters,
    Sung by poets long ago.

Seated half within a bower
    Where the languid evening breeze
Shook out odors in a shower
    From oranges and citron trees,

Sang she from a romancero,
    How a Moorish chieftain bold
Fought a Spanish caballero
    By Sevilla's walls of old.

How they battled for a lady,
    Fairest of the maids of Spain—
How the Christian's lance, so steady,
    Pierced the Moslem through the brain.

Then she ceased—her black eyes moving,
    Flashed, as asked she with a smile,—
"Say, are maids as fair and loving—
    Men as faithful, in your isle?"

"British maids," I said, "are ever
    Counted fairest of the fair;
Like the swans on yonder river
    Moving with a stately air.

"Wooed not quickly, won not lightly—
  But when won, forever true;
Trial draws the bond more tightly,
  Time can ne'er the knot undo."

"And the men?"—"Ah! dearest lady,
  Are—quien sabe? who can say?
To make love they 're ever ready,
  When they can and where they may;

"Fixed as waves, as breezes steady
  In a changeful April day—
Como brisas, como rios,
  No se sabe, sabe Dios."

"Are they faithful?"—"Ah! quien sabe?
  Who can answer that they are?
While we may we should be happy."—
  Then I took up her guitar,
And I sang in sportive strain,
This song to an old air of Spain:

"QUIEN SABE."

I

"The breeze of the evening that cools the hot air,
  That kisses the orange and shakes out thy hair,
Is its freshness less welcome, less sweet its perfume,
  That you know not the region from whence it is come?
Whence the wind blows, where the wind goes,
Hither and thither and whither—who knows?
                          Who knows?
Hither and thither—but whither—who knows?

II

"The river forever glides singing along,
  The rose on the bank bends a'down to its song;
And the flower, as it listens, unconsciously dips,
  Till the rising wave glistens and kisses its lips.
But why the wave rises and kisses the rose,
And why the rose stoops for those kisses—who knows?
                          Who knows?
And away flows the river—but whither—who knows?

III

"Let *me* be the breeze, love, that wanders along
  The river that ever rejoices in song;
Be *thou* to my fancy the orange in bloom,
  The rose by the river that gives its perfume.
Would the fruit be so golden, so fragrant the rose,
If no breeze and no wave were to kiss them? — who
    knows?
                          Who knows?
If no breeze and no wave were to kiss them? — who
    knows?"

    As I sang, the lady listened,
        Silent save one gentle sigh;
    When I ceased, a tear-drop glistened
        On the dark fringe of her eye.

    Then my heart reproved the feeling
        Of that false and heartless strain,
    Which I sang in words concealing
        What my heart would hide in vain.

    Up I sprang.   What words were uttered
        Bootless now to think or tell—
    Tongues speak wild when hearts are fluttered
        By the mighty master-spell.

    Love, avowed with sudden boldness,
        Heard with flushings that reveal,
    Spite of woman's studied coldness,
        Thoughts the heart cannot conceal.

    Words half-vague and passion-broken,
        Meaningless, yet meaning all
    That the lips have left unspoken,
        That we never may recall.

  "Magdalena, dearest, hear me,"
        Sighed I, as I seized her hand—
  "Hola! Senor," very near me,
        Cries a voice of stern command.

And a stalwart caballero
    Comes upon me with a stride,
On his head a slouched sombrero,
    A toledo by his side.

From his breast he flung his capa,
    With a stately Spanish air—

"Will your worship have the goodness
    To release that lady's hand?"—
"Senor," I replied, "this rudeness
    I am not prepared to stand.

"Magdalena, say"—the maiden
    With a cry of wild surprise,
As with secret sorrow laden,
    Fainting sank before my eyes.

Then the Spanish caballero
    Bowed with haughty courtesy,
Solemn as a tragic hero,
    And announced himself to me.

    "Senor, I am Don Camillo
    Guzman Miguel Pedrillo
    De Xymenes y Ribera
    Y Santallos y Herrera
    Y de Rivas y Mendoza
    Y Quintana y de Rosa
    Y Zorrilla y—"

        "No more, sir,
'Tis as good as twenty score, sir,"
    Said I to him, with a frown;
"Mucha bulla para nada,
    No palabras, draw your 'spada;"
"If you 're up for a duello
You will find I 'm just your fellow—
    Senor, I am PETER BROWN!"

By the river's bank that night,
    Foot to foot in strife,
Fought we in the dubious light,
    A fight of death or life.

Don Camillo slashed my shoulder;
With the pain I grew the bolder,
    Close, and closer still I pressed;
Fortune favored me at last.
I broke his guard, my weapon passed
    Through the caballero's breast—
Down to the earth went Don Camillo
Guzman Miguel Pedrillo
De Xymenes y Ribera
Y Santallos y Herrera
Y de Rivas y Mendoza
Y Quintana y de Rosa
Y Zorilla y—one groan,
And he lay motionless as stone.
The man of many names went down,
Pierced by the sword of PETER BROWN.

Oft when autumn eve is closing,
    Pensive, puffing a cigar
In my chamber lone reposing,
Musing half, and half a-dozing,
    Comes a vision from afar
Of that lady of the villa
In her satin, fringed mantilla,
And that haughty caballero
With his capa and sombrero,
Vainly in my mind revolving
    That long, jointed, endless name;—
'Tis a riddle past my solving,
    Who he was, or whence he came.
Was he that brother home returned?
Was he some former lover spurned?
Or some family *fiancé*
That the lady did not fancy?
Was he any one of those?
Sabe Dios. Ah! God knows.

Sadly smoking my manilla,
    Much I long to know
How fares the lady of the villa
    That once charmed me so,
When I visited Sevilla
    Years and years ago.

Has she married a Hidalgo?
Gone the way that ladies all go
In those drowsy Spanish cities,
Wasting life—a thousand pities—
Waking up for a fiesta
From an afternoon siesta,
To "Giralda" now repairing,
Or the Plaza for an airing;
At the shaded *reja* flirting,
At a bull-fight now disporting;
Does she walk at evenings ever
Through the gardens by the river?
Guarded by an old duenna
Fierce and sharp as a hyena,
With her goggles and her fan
Warning off each rakish man?
Is she dead, or is she living?
Is she for my absence grieving?
Is she wretched, is she happy?
Widow, wife, or maid?   Quien sabe?
Does she smile, or does she frown,
When she thinks of—PETER BROWN.

J. F. Waller.

THE THREE BELLS.

This poem refers to the well-known rescue of the crew of an American vessel sinking in mid-ocean, by Captain Leighton, of the English ship Three Bells. Unable to take them off, in the night and the storm, he stayed by them until morning, shouting to them from time to time through his trumpet, "Never fear, hold on; I 'll stand by you!"

Beneath the low-hung night cloud
    That raked her splintering mast,
The good ship settled slowly,
    The cruel leak gained fast.

Over the awful ocean
    Her signal guns pealed out;
Dear God! was that thy answer,
    From the horror round about?

A voice came down the wild wind,—
  "Ho! ship ahoy!" its cry;
"Our stout Three Bells of Glasgow
  Shall stand till daylight by!"

Hour after hour crept slowly,
  Yet on the heaving swells
Tossed up and down the ship-lights,—
  The lights of the Three Bells.

And ship to ship made signals;
  Man answered back to man;
While oft, to cheer and hearten,
  The Three Bells nearer ran.

And the captain from her taffrail
  Sent down his hopeful cry;
"Take heart! hold on!" he shouted,
  "The Three Bells shall stand by!"

All night across the waters
  The tossing lights shone clear;
All night from reeling taffrail
  The Three Bells sent her cheer.

And when the dreary watches
  Of storm and darkness passed,
Just as the wreck lurched under,
  All souls were saved at last.

Sail on, Three Bells, forever,
  In grateful memory sail!
Ring on, Three Bells of rescue,
  Above the wave and gale!

Type of the Love eternal,
  Repeat the Master's cry,
As tossing through our darkness
  The lights of God draw nigh!
                    John G. Whittier.

THE LAUNCHING OF THE SHIP.

"Build me straight, O worthy Master!
   Stanch and strong, a goodly vessel,
That shall laugh at all disaster,
   And with wave and whirlwind wrestle!"

Day by day the vessel grew,
With timbers fashioned strong and true,
Stemson and keelson and sternson knee,
Till, framed with perfect symmetry,
A skeleton ship rose up to view!
And around the bows and along the side
The heavy hammers and mallets plied,
Till after many a week, at length,
Wonderful for form and strength,
Sublime in its enormous bulk,
Loomed aloft the shadowy hulk!
And around it columns of smoke, upwreathing,
Rose from the boiling, bubbling, seething
   Caldron, that glowed,
   And overflowed
With the black tar, heated for the sheathing.
And amid the clamors
Of clattering hammers,
He who listened heard now and then
The song of the Master and his men:

"Build me straight, O worthy Master,
   Stanch and strong, a goodly vessel,
That shall laugh at all disaster,
   And with wave and whirlwind wrestle!"

All is finished! and at length
   Has come the bridal day
Of beauty and of strength.
To-day the vessel shall be launched!
With fleecy clouds the sky is blanched,
   And o'er the bay,
Slowly, in all his splendors dight,
The great Sun rises to behold the sight.

The Ocean old,
Centuries old,
Strong as youth, and as uncontrolled,
Paces restless to and fro,
Up and down the sands of gold.
His beating heart is not at rest;
And far and wide,
With ceaseless flow,
His beard of snow
Heaves with the heaving of his breast.

He waits impatient for his bride.
There she stands,
With her foot upon the sands!
Decked with flags and streamers gay,
In honor of her marriage day,
Her snow-white signals, fluttering, blending,
Round her like a veil descending,
Ready to be
The bride of the gray old Sea.

Then the Master,
With a gesture of command,
Waved his hand:
And at the word,
Loud and sudden there was heard
All around them and below,
The sound of hammers, blow on blow,
Knocking away the shores and spurs.
And see! she stirs!
She starts—she moves—she seems to feel
The thrill of life along her keel,
And, spurning with her foot the ground,
With one exulting, joyous bound,
She leaps into the ocean's arms!
And lo! from the assembled crowd
There rose a shout, prolonged and loud,
That to the ocean seemed to say,
"Take her, O bridegroom, old and gray,
Take her to thy protecting arms,
With all her youth and all her charms!"

How beautiful she is! how fair
  She lies within those arms, that press
  Her form with many a soft caress
Of tenderness and watchful care!
  Sail forth into the sea, O, ship!
Through wind and wave, right onward steer!
  The moistened eye, the trembling lip,
Are not the signs of doubt or fear.

Sail forth into the sea of life,
Oh, gentle, loving, trusting wife,
And safe from all adversity,
Upon the bosom of that sea
Thy comings and thy goings be!
For gentleness, and love, and trust,
Prevail o'er angry wave and gust;
And in the wreck of noble lives
Something immortal still survives!

Thou, too, sail on, O ship of State!
Sail on, O Union, strong and great!
  Humanity, with all its fears,
  With all its hopes of future years,
Is hanging breathless on thy fate!
We know what Master laid thy keel,
What workman wrought thy ribs of steel,
  Who made each mast, and sail, and rope,
What anvils rang, what hammers beat,
In what a forge, and what a heat,
  Were shaped the anchors of thy hope.

Fear not each sudden sound and shock;
'Tis of the wave, and not the rock;
'Tis but the flapping of the sail,
And not a rent made by the gale;
In spite of rock and tempest roar,
In spite of false lights on the shore,
Sail on, nor fear to breast the sea!
Our hearts, our hopes, are all with thee;
  Our hearts, our hopes, our prayers, our tears,
  Our faith triumphant o'er our fears,
Are all with thee—are all with thee!
                Henry Wadsworth Longfellow.

BETSY AND I ARE OUT.

Draw up the papers, lawyer, and make 'em good and stout,
For things at home are cross-ways, and Betsy and I are
    out,—
We who have worked together so long as man and wife
Must pull in single harness the rest of our nat'ral life.

"What is the matter," says you? "I swan! it's hard to
    tell!
Most of the years behind us we've passed by very well;
I have no other woman—she has no other man;
Only we've lived together as long as ever we can.

So I have talked with Betsy, and Betsy has talked with me;
And we've agreed together that we can never agree;
Not that we've catched each other in any terrible crime;
We've been a gatherin' this for years, a little at a time.

There was a stock of temper we both had, for a start;
Although we ne'er suspected 't would take us two apart;
I had my various failings, bred in the flesh and bone,
And Betsy, like all good women, had a temper of her own.

The first thing, I remember, whereon we disagreed,
Was somethin' concerning heaven—a difference in our
    creed;
We arg'ed the thing at breakfast—we arg'ed the thing at
    tea—
And the more we arg'ed the question, the more we
    could n't agree.

And the next that I remember was when we lost a cow;
She had kicked the bucket, for certain—the question was
    only—How?
I held my opinion, and Betsy another had;
And when we were done a talkin', we both of us was
    mad.

And the next that I remember, it started in a joke;
But for full a week it lasted and neither of us spoke.
And the next was when I fretted because she broke a bowl;
And she said I was mean and stingy, and had n't any soul.

And so the thing kept workin', and all the self-same way;
Always somethin' to arg'e and somethin' sharp to say,—
And down on us came the neighbors, a couple o' dozen
    strong,
And lent their kindest sarvice to help the thing along.

And there have been days together—and many a weary
    week—
When both of us were cross and spunky, and both too
    proud to speak;
And I have been thinkin' and thinkin', the whole of the
    summer and fall,
If I can't live kind with a woman, why, then I won't at all.

And so I 've talked with Betsy, and Betsy has talked with
    me;
And we have agreed together that we can never agree;
And what is hers shall be hers, and what is mine shall be
    mine;
And I 'll put it in the agreement and take it to her to sign.

Write on the paper, lawyer—the very first paragraph—
Of all the farm and live stock, she shall have her half;
For she has helped to earn it, through many a weary day,
And it 's nothin' more than justice that Betsy has her pay.

Give her the house and homestead; a man can thrive and
    roam,
But women are wretched critters, unless they have a home.
And I have always determined, and never failed to say,
That Betsy never should want a home, if I was taken away.

There 's a little hard money besides, that 's drawin' tol'ra-
    ble pay,
A couple of hundred dollars laid by for a rainy day,—
Safe in the hands of good men, and easy to get at;
Put in another clause there, and give her all of that.

I see that you are smiling, sir, at my givin' her so much;
Yes, divorce is cheap, sir, but I take no stock in such;
True and fair I married her, when she was blithe and
    young,
And Betsy was always good to me, exceptin' with her
    tongue.

When I was young as you, sir, and not so smart, perhaps,
For me she mittened a lawyer, and several other chaps;
And all of 'em was flustered, and fairly taken down,
And for a time I was counted the luckiest man in town.

Once, when I had a fever—I won't forget it soon—
I was hot as a basted turkey and crazy as a loon—
Never an hour went by me when she was out of sight;
She nursed me true and tender, and stuck to me day and
    night.

And if ever a house was tidy, and ever a kitchen clean,
Her house and kitchen was tidy as any I ever seen;
And I do n't complain of Betsy or any of her acts,
Exceptin' when we 've quarreled, and told each other
    facts.

So draw up the paper, lawyer, and I'll go home to-night,
And read the agreement to her and see if it 's all right;
And then in the mornin' I 'll sell to a tradin' man I know—
And kiss the child that was left to us, and out in the
    world I 'll go.

And one thing put in the paper, that first to me did n't
    occur;
That when I am dead at last she will bring me back to her,
And lay me under the maple we planted years ago,
When she and I was happy, before we quarreled so.

And when she dies, I wish that she would be laid by me;
And lyin' together in silence, perhaps we 'll then agree;
And if ever we meet in heaven, I would n't think it queer
If we loved each other the better because we 've quarreled
    here.

                                        Will M. Carleton.

_____

ABOU BEN ADHEM.

Abou Ben Adhem (may his tribe increase!)
Awoke one night from a deep dream of peace,
And saw within the moonlight in his room,
Making it rich and like a lily in bloom,
An angel writing in a book of gold;

Exceeding peace had made Ben Adhem bold,
And to the presence in the room he said,
"What writest thou?"—The vision raised its head,
And, with a look made of all sweet accord,
Answered, "The names of those who love the Lord."

"And is mine one?" said Abou. "Nay, not so,"
Replied the angel.—Abou spoke more low,
But cheerily still; and said, "I pray thee, then,
Write me as one that loves his fellow-men."

The angel wrote and vanished. The next night
It came again, with a great wakening light,
And showed the names whom love of God had blessed,
And, lo! Ben Adhem's name led all the rest!

Leigh Hunt.

THE WRECK OF THE HESPERUS.

It was the schooner Hesperus
  That sailed the wintry sea;
And the skipper had taken his little daughter,
  To bear him company.

Blue were her eyes as the fairy flax,
  Her cheeks like the dawn of day,
And her bosom white as the hawthorn buds
  That ope in the month of May.

The skipper he stood beside the helm,
  His pipe was in his mouth,
And he watched how the veering flaw did blow
  The smoke now west, now south.

Then up and spake an old sailor,
  Had sailed the Spanish main,
"I pray thee, put into yonder port,
  For I fear a hurricane.

"Last night the moon had a golden ring,
  And to-night no moon we see!"
The skipper, he blew a whiff from his pipe,
  And a scornful laugh laughed he.

Colder and louder blew the wind,
  A gale from the northeast;
The snow fell hissing in the brine,
  And the billows frothed like yeast.

Down came the storm, and smote amain
  The vessel in its strength;
She shuddered and paused, like a frightened steed,
  Then leaped her cable's length.

"Come hither! come hither! my little daughter,
  And do not tremble so;
For I can weather the roughest gale,
  That ever wind did blow."

He wrapped her warm in his seaman's coat
  Against the stinging blast;
He cut a rope from a broken spar,
  And bound her to the mast.

"O father! I hear the church-bells ring,
  O say, what may it be?"
"'Tis a fog-bell on a rock-bound coast!"—
  And he steered for the open sea.

"O father! I hear the sound of guns,
  O say, what may it be?"
"Some ship in distress, that cannot live
  In such an angry sea!"

"O father! I see a gleaming light,
  O say, what may it be?"
But the father answered never a word,
  A frozen corpse was he.

Lashed to the helm, all stiff and stark,
  With his face turned to the skies,
The lantern gleamed through the gleaming snow
  On his fixed and glassy eyes.

Then the maiden clasped her hands and prayed
  That savéd she might be;
And she thought of Christ, who stilled the wave,
  On the Lake of Galilee.

And fast through the midnight dark and drear,
  Through the whistling sleet and snow,
Like a sheeted ghost, the vessel swept
  Towards the reef of Norman's Woe.

And ever the fitful gusts between
  A sound came from the land;
It was the sound of the trampling surf
  On the rocks and the hard sea-sand.

The breakers were right beneath her bows,
  She drifted a dreary wreck,
And a whooping billow swept the crew
  Like icicles from her deck.

She struck where the white and fleecy waves
  Looked soft as carded wool,
But the cruel rocks, they gored her side
  Like the horns of an angry bull.

Her rattling shrouds, all sheathed in ice,
  With the masts went by the board;
Like a vessel of glass, she stove and sank,
  Ho! ho! the breakers roared!

At daybreak, on the bleak sea-beach,
  A fisherman stood aghast,
To see the form of a maiden fair
  Lashed close to a drifting mast.

The salt sea was frozen on her breast;
  The salt tears in her eyes;
And he saw her hair, like the brown sea-weed,
  On the billows fall and rise.

Such was the wreck of the Hesperus,
  In the midnight and the snow!
Christ save us all from a death like this,
  On the reef of Norman's Woe!
            Henry Wadsworth Longfellow.

AMY ROBSART AND RICHARD VARNEY.

FROM "KENILWORTH."

Dudley, Earl of Leicester, the favorite of Queen Elizabeth, having recently married Amy Robsart, has concealed her at Cumnor Place, fearing that, if his marriage is made public, he may lose court favor. The Queen, who has been led to believe that Amy is the wife of the Earl's unprincipled servant Varney, orders her to be present at the approaching festivities at Kenilworth Castle. Influenced by the designing Varney, Leicester writes a letter to Amy, conjuring her, for reasons nearly concerning his own life and honor, to come to Kenilworth as the supposed wife of his servant. Varney himself is the bearer of the letter. He enters the apartments of the Countess, his dress in disorder from hasty riding through a dark night and foul ways.

"You bring news from my lord, Master Varney—Gracious Heaven! is he ill?"

"No, madam, thank Heaven! Compose yourself, and permit me to take breath ere I communicate my tidings."

"No breath, sir; I know your theatrical arts. Since your breath hath sufficed to bring you hither, it may suffice to tell your tale, at least briefly, and in the gross."

"Madam, we are not alone, and my lord's message was for your ear only."

"Leave us, Janet, and Master Foster, but remain in the next apartment, and within call."

Foster and his daughter retired, agreeably to the Lady Leicester's commands, into the next apartment.

All was as still as death, and the voices of those who spoke in the inner chamber were, if they spoke at all, carefully subdued to a tone which could not be heard in the next. At once, however, they were heard to speak fast, thick, and hastily.

"Undo the door, sir, I command you! Undo the door! I will have no other reply! What ho! without there! Janet, alarm the house! Foster, break open the door—I am detained here by a traitor! Use axe and lever, Master Foster—I will be your warrant!"

"It shall not need, madam; if you please to expose my lord's important concerns and your own to the general ear, I will not be your hindrance."

Janet, as soon as the door was open, ran to her mistress; and more slowly, yet with more haste than he was wont, Anthony Foster went to Richard Varney.

"What in the name of Satan, have you done to her?" said Foster to his friend.

"Who, I—nothing, nothing but communicated to her her lord's commands, which, if the lady list not to obey, she knows better how to answer it than I may pretend to do."

"Now, by Heaven, Janet, the false traitor lies in his throat! He must needs lie, for he speaks to the dishonor of my noble lord; he must needs lie doubly, for he speaks to gain ends of his own, equally execrable and unattainable."

"You have misapprehended me, lady; let this matter rest till your passion be abated, and I will explain all."

"Thou shalt never have an opportunity to do so," said the Countess. "Look at him, Janet. He is fairly dressed, hath the outside of a gentleman, and hither he came to persuade me it was my lord's pleasure—nay, more, my wedded lord's command, that I should go with him to Kenilworth, and before the Queen and nobles, and in presence of my own wedded lord, that I should acknowledge him—*him* there, that very cloak-brushing, shoe-cleaning fellow—*him* there, my lord's lackey, for my liege lord and husband; furnishing against myself, great God! whenever I was to vindicate my right and my rank, such weapons as would hew my just claim from the root, and destroy my character to be regarded as an honorable matron of the English nobility!"

"You hear her, Foster, and you, young maiden, hear this lady; you hear that her heat only objects to me the course which our good lord, for the purpose to keep certain matters secret, suggests in the very letter which she holds in her hands."

"Never will I believe that the noble Dudley gave countenance to so dastardly, so dishonorable a plan. Thus I tread on his infamy, if indeed it be, and thus destroy its remembrance forever!"

So saying, she tore in pieces Leicester's letter, and stamped, in the extremity of impatience, as if she would have annihilated the minute fragments into which she had rent it.

"Bear witness, she hath torn my lord's letter, in order to burden me with the scheme of his devising; and although it promises naught but danger and trouble to me, she would lay it to my charge, as if it had any purpose of mine own in it."

"Thou liest, thou treacherous slave! Thou liest! Let me go, Janet. Were it the last word I have to speak, he lies; he had his own foul ends, and broader he would have displayed them, had my passion permitted me to preserve the silence which at first encouraged him to unfold his vile projects."

"Madam, I entreat you to believe yourself mistaken."

"As soon will I believe light darkness. Have I drank of oblivion? Do I not remember former passages, which, known to Leicester, had given thee the preferment of a gallows, instead of the honor of this intimacy? I would I were a man but for five minutes! It were space enough to make a craven like thee confess his villainy. But go! begone! Tell thy master, that when I take the foul course to which such scandalous deceits as thou hast recommended on his behalf must necessarily lead me, I will give him a rival something worthy of the name. He shall not be supplanted by an ignominious lackey, whose best fortune is to catch a gift of his master's last suit of clothes ere it is threadbare. Go! begone, sir! I scorn thee so much, that I am ashamed to have been angry with thee." *Sir Walter Scott.*

THE COUNTESS AMY AND HER HUSBAND.

FROM "KENILWORTH."

Amy Robsart was confined in a room in one of the towers, while Queen Elizabeth, attended by court-ladies and gentlemen, went on a hunting expedition. When they returned, Lord Leicester determined to see Amy. Disguised as a servant of Varney, who had free access to Amy's room under the character of her husband, Lord Leicester passed the sentinel in safety, and entered the room.

"Dudley!" she exclaimed, "Dudley! and art thou come at last?" And with the speed of lightning she flew to her husband, hung round his neck, and, unheeding the presence of Varney, overwhelmed him with caresses, while she bathed his face in a flood of tears; muttering, at the same time, but in broken and disjointed monosyllables, the fondest expressions which Love teaches his votaries.

He received and repaid her caresses with fondness mingled with melancholy, the last of which she seemed scarcely to observe, until the first transport of her own joy was over; when, looking anxiously in his face, she asked if he was ill.

"Not in my body, Amy," was his answer.

"Then I will be well, too.—O Dudley! I have been ill!—very ill, since we last met! I have been in sickness, in grief, and in danger. But thou art come, and all is joy and health, and safety!"

"Alas! Amy," said Leicester, "thou hast undone me!"

"I, my lord?" said Amy, her cheek at once losing its transient flush of joy—"how could I injure that which I love better than myself?"

"I would not upbraid you, Amy," replied the earl; "but are you not here contrary to my express commands —and does not your presence here endanger both yourself and me?"

"Does it, does it, indeed!" she exclaimed eagerly: "then why am I here a moment longer? Oh, if you knew by what fears I was urged to quit Cumnor Place!—but I will say nothing of myself—only that if it might be otherwise, I would not willingly return thither;—yet if it concern your safety——"

"We will think, Amy, of some other retreat," said Leicester; "you shall go to one of my northern castles, under the personage—it will be but needful, I trust, for a very few days—of Varney's wife."

"How, my lord of Leicester!" said the lady, disengaging herself from his embraces; "is it to your wife you give the dishonorable counsel to acknowledge herself the bride of another—and of all men, the bride of that Varney?"

"Madam, I speak it in earnest; Varney is my true and faithful servant, trusted in my deepest secrets. I had better lose my right hand than his service at this moment. You have no cause to scorn him as you do."

"I could assign one, my lord, and I see he shakes even under that assured look of his. But he that is necessary as your right hand to your safety, is free from any accusation of mine. May he be true to you; and that he may be true, trust him not too far. But it is enough to say, that I will not go with him unless by violence, nor would I acknowledge him as my husband, were all——"

"It is a temporary deception, madam, necessary for both our safeties, endangered by you through female caprice, or the premature desire to seize on a rank to which I gave you title, only under condition that our marriage, for a time, should continue secret. If my proposal disgust you, it is yourself has brought it on both of us. There is no other remedy—you must do what your own impatient folly hath rendered necessary—I command you."

"I cannot put your commands, my lord, in balance with those of honor and conscience. I will *not*, in this instance, obey you. You may achieve your own dishonor, to which these crooked policies naturally tend, but I will do naught that can blemish mine."

"My lord, my lady is too much prejudiced against me, unhappily, to listen to what I can offer; yet it may please her better than what she proposes. She has good interest with Master Edmund Tressilian, and could doubtless prevail on him to consent to be her companion to Lidcote Hall, and there she might remain in safety until time permitted the development of this mystery."

Leicester was silent, but stood looking eagerly on Amy, with eyes which seemed to glow as much with suspicion as displeasure.

The countess only said, "Would to God I were in my father's house! When I left it, I little thought I was leaving peace of mind and honor behind me."

Varney proceeded with a tone of deliberation, "Doubtless this will make it necessary to take strangers into my lord's counsels; but surely the countess will be warrant for the honor of Master Tressilian, and such of her father's family——"

"Peace, Varney," said Leicester; "by Heaven, I will strike my dagger into thee, if again thou namest Tressilian as a partner of my counsels!"

"And wherefore not?" said the countess; "unless they be counsels fitter for such as Varney, than for a man of stainless honor and integrity. My lord, my lord, bend no angry brows on me—it is the truth, and it is I who speak it. I once did Tressilian wrong for your sake. I will not do him the further injustice of being silent when his honor is brought into question. I can forbear," she said, looking at Varney, "to pull the mask off hypocrisy, but I will not permit virtue to be slandered in my hearing."

There was a dead pause. Leicester stood displeased, yet undetermined, and too conscious of the weakness of his cause; while Varney, with a deep and hypocritical affectation of sorrow, mingled with humility, bent his eyes on the ground.

It was then that the Countess Amy displayed, in the midst of distress and difficulty, the natural energy of character, which would have rendered her, had fate allowed, a distinguished ornament of the rank which she held.

She walked up to Leicester with a composed step, a dignified air, and looks in which strong affection essayed in vain to shake the firmness of conscious truth and rectitude of principle. "You have spoken your mind, my lord," she said, "in these difficulties with which, unhappily, I have found myself unable to comply. This gentleman—this person I should say—has hinted at another scheme, to which I object not, but as it displeases you. Will your lordship be pleased to hear what a young and timid woman, but your most affectionate wife, can suggest in the present extremity?"

Leicester was silent, but bent his head toward the countess, as an intimation that she was at liberty to proceed.

"There hath been but one cause for all these evils, my lord," she proceeded; "and it resolves itself into the mysterious duplicity with which you have been induced to surround yourself. Extricate yourself at once, my lord, from the tyranny of these disgraceful trammels. Take your ill-fated wife by the hand, lead her to the footstool of Elizabeth's throne; say, that 'in a moment of infatuation moved by supposed beauty, of which none perhaps can now trace even the remains, I gave my hand to this Amy Robsart.' You will then have done justice to me, my lord, and to your own honor; and should law or power require you to part from me, I will oppose no objection, since then I may with honor hide a grieved and broken heart in those shades from which your love withdrew me. Then—have but a little patience,—and Amy's life will not long darken your brighter prospects."

"I am not worthy of you, Amy, that could weigh aught which ambition has to give against such a heart as thine! I have a bitter penance to perform, in disentangling all the meshes of my own deceitful policy. And the queen—but let her take my head, as she has threatened!''

"Your head, my lord! because you use the freedom and liberty of an English subject in choosing a wife? For shame; it is this distrust of the queen's justice, this misapprehension of danger, which cannot but be imaginary, that, like scare-crows, have induced you to forsake the straightforward path, which, as it is the best, is also the safest.''

"Ah, Amy, thou little knowest! Fear not, thou shalt see Dudley bear himself worthy of his name. I must instantly communicate with some of those friends on whom I can best rely; for, as things stand, I may be made prisoner in my own castle.''

"O my good lord, make no faction in a peaceful state! There is no friend can help us so well as our own candid truth and honor. Bring but these to our assistance, and you are safe amidst a whole army of the envious and malignant. Leave these behind you, and all other defense will be fruitless. Truth, my noble lord, is well painted unarmed.''

"But Wisdom, Amy, is arrayed in panoply of proof. Argue not with me on the means I shall use to render my confession as safe as may be; it will be fraught with enough of danger, do what we will.—Varney, we must hence.—Farewell, Amy, whom I am to vindicate as mine own, at an expense and risk of which thou alone couldst be worthy! You shall soon hear further from me.''

He embraced her fervently, muffled himself as before, and accompanied Varney from the apartment.

Sir Walter Scott.

EXTRACT FROM *MORITURI SALUTAMUS.*

In mediæval Rome, I know not where,
There stood an image with its arm in air,
And on its lifted finger, shining clear,
A golden ring with the device, ''Strike here!''
Greatly the people wondered, though none guessed
The meaning that these words but half expressed,
Until a learned clerk, who at noonday
With downcast eyes was passing on his way,

Paused, and observed the spot, and marked it well,
Whereon the shadow of the finger fell,
And coming back at midnight, delved, and found
A secret stairway leading underground.

Down this he passed into a spacious hall,
Lit by a flaming jewel on the wall;
And opposite, in threatening attitude,
With bow and shaft a brazen statue stood;
Upon its forehead, like a coronet,
Were these mysterious words of menace set:
"That which I am, I am; my fatal aim
None can escape, not even yon luminous flame!"
Midway the hall was a fair table placed,
With cloth of gold, and golden cups enchased
With rubies, and the plates and knives were gold,
And gold the bread and viands manifold.
Around it, silent, motionless, and sad,
Were seated gallant knights in armor clad,
And ladies beautiful with plume and zone,
But they were stone, their hearts within were stone;
And the vast hall was filled in every part
With silent crowds, stony in face and heart.

Long at the scene, bewildered and amazed,
The trembling clerk in speechless wonder gazed;
Then from the table, by his greed made bold,
He seized a goblet and a knife of gold,
And suddenly from their seats the guests upsprang,
The vaulted ceilings with loud clamors rang,
The archer sped his arrow, at their call,
Shattering the lambent jewel on the wall,
And all was dark around and overhead;—
Stark on the floor the luckless clerk lay dead!

The writer of this legend then records
Its ghostly application in these words:
The image is the Adversary old,
Whose beckoning finger points to realms of gold;
Our lusts and passions are the downward stair
That leads the soul from a diviner air;
The archer, Death, the flaming jewel, Life
Terrestrial goods, the goblet and the knife,

The knights and ladies, all whose flesh and bone
By avarice have been hardened into stone;
The clerk, the scholar, whom the love of pelf
Tempts from his books and from his nobler self.

Henry Wadsworth Longfellow.

SHAMUS O'BRIEN.

Jist after the war, in the year '98,
As soon as the boys wor all scattered and bate,
'Twas the custom, whenever a pisant was got,
To hang him by thrial—barrin' sich as was shot.
There was thrial by jury goin' on by daylight,
And the martial-law hangin' the lavins by night.
It 's them was hard times for an honest gossoon:
If he missed in the judges—he 'd meet a dragoon;
An' whether the sodgers or judges gev sentence,
The divil a much time they allowed for repentance.
An' it 's many 's the fine boy was then on his keepin'
Wid small share iv restin' or atin' or sleepin',
An' because they loved Erin, an' scorned to sell it,
A prey for the bloodhound, a mark for the bullet—
Unsheltered by night, and unrested by day,
With the heath for their barrack, revenge for their pay;
An' the bravest an' hardiest boy iv them all
Was SHAMUS O'BRIEN, from the town iv Glingall.

His limbs were well set, an' his body was light,
An' the keen-fanged hound had not teeth half so white;
But his face was as pale as the face of the dead,
And his cheek never warmed with the blush of the red.

An' for all that he was n't an ugly young bye,
For the divil himself could n't blaze with his eye,
So droll an' so wicked, so dark and so bright,
Like a fire-flash that crosses the depth of the night!
An' he was the best mower that ever has been,
An' the illigantest hurler that ever was seen.
An' in fencin' he gave Patrick Mooney a cut,
An' in jumpin' he bate Tim Mulloney a fut;

An' for lightness of fut there was n't his peer,
For, begorra, he could almost outrun the red deer!
An' his dancin' was sich that the men used to stare,
An' the women turn crazy, he done it so quare;
An' begorra, the whole world gev in to him there.
An' it 's he was the boy that was hard to be caught,
An' it 's often he run, an' it 's often he fought,
An' it 's many the one can remember right well
The quare things he done: an' it 's often I heerd tell
How he frightened the magistrates in Caharbally,
An' 'scaped through the sodgers in Aherloe valley;
How he lathered the yeomen, himself agin four,
An' stretched the two strongest on old Galtimore.
But the fox must sleep sometimes, the wild deer must rest,
An' treachery prey on the blood iv the best;
Afther many a brave action of power and pride,
An' many a hard night on the mountain's bleak side,
An' a thousand great dangers and toils overpast,
In the darkness of night he was taken at last.

Now, SHAMUS, look back on the beautiful moon,
For the door of the prison must close on you soon,
An' take your last look at her dim lovely light,
That falls on the mountain and valley this night;
One look at the village, one look at the flood,
An' one at the sheltering, far-distant wood;
Farewell to the forest, farewell to the hill,
An' farewell to the friends that will think of you still;
Farewell to the pathern, the hurlin' an' wake,
And farewell to the girl that would die for your sake.
An' twelve sodgers brought him to Maryborough jail,
An' the turnkey resaved him, refusin' all bail.

Well, as soon as a few weeks was over and gone,
The terrible day iv the thrial kem on,
There was sich a crowd there was scarce room to stand,
An' sodgers on guard, an' dhragoons sword-in-hand;
An' the courthouse so full that the people were bothered,
An' attorneys an' criers on the point iv bein' smothered;
An' counselors almost gev over for dead,
An' the jury sittin' up in their box overhead;
An' the judge settled out so determined an' big
With his gown on his back, and an illegant new wig;

An' silence was called, an' the minute it was said
The court was as still as the heart of the dead,
An' they heard but the openin' of one prison lock,
An' SHAMUS O'BRIEN kem into the dock.

For one minute he turned his eye round on the throng,
An' he looked at the bars so firm and so strong,
An' he saw that he had not a hope nor a friend,
A chance to escape, nor a word to defend;
An' he folded his arms as he stood there alone,
As calm and as cold as a statue of stone;
And they read a big writin', a yard long at laste,
An' JIM did n't understand it nor mind it a taste,
An' the judge took a big pinch iv snuff, and he says,
"Are you guilty or not, JIM O'BRIEN, av you plase?"

An' all held their breath in the silence of dhread,
An' SHAMUS O'BRIEN made answer and said:
"My lord, if you ask me, if in my lifetime
I thought any treason, or did any crime
That should call to my cheek, as I stand alone here,
The hot blush of shame, or the coldness of fear,
Though I stood by the grave to receive my death-blow
Before GOD and the world I would answer you, No!
But if you would ask me, as I think it like,
If in the rebellion I carried a pike,
An' fought for ould Ireland from the first to the close,
An' shed the heart's blood of her bitterest foes,
I answer you, Yes; and I tell you again,
Though I stand here to perish, it 's my glory that then
In her cause I was willin' my veins should run dhry,
An' that now for her sake I am ready to die."

Then the silence was great, and the jury smiled bright,
An' the judge was n't sorry the job was made light;
By my sowl, it 's himself was the crabbed ould chap!
In a twinklin' he pulled on his ugly black cap.
Then SHAMUS' mother, in the crowd standin' by,
Called out to the judge with a pitiful cry:
"O judge! darlin', do n't, O, do n't say the word!
The crather is young, have mercy, my lord;
He was foolish, he did n't know what he was doin';
You do n't know him, my lord—O do n't give him to ruin!

He's the kindliest crathur, the tendherest-hearted;
Do n't part us forever, we that's so long parted.
Judge, mavourneen, forgive him, forgive him, my lord,
An' God will forgive you—O do n't say the word!"

That was the first minute that O'BRIEN was shaken,
When he saw that he was not quite forgot or forsaken;
An' down his pale cheeks, at the word of his mother,
The big tears wor runnin' fast, one afther th' other;
An' two or three times he endeavored to spake,
But the sthrong manly voice used to falther and break;
But at last, by the strength of his high-mountin' pride,
He conquered and masthered his grief's swelling tide,
"An'," says he, "mother, darlin', do n't break your poor
    heart,
For, sooner or later, the dearest must part;
And God knows it's betther than wandering in fear
On the bleak, trackless mountain, among the wild deer,
To lie in the grave, where the head, heart, and breast,
From thought, labor, and sorrow, forever shall rest.
Then, mother, my darlin', do n't cry any more,
Do n't make me seem broken, in this, my last hour,
For I wish, when my head's lyin' undher the raven,
No thrue man can say that I died like a craven!"
Then towards the Judge SHAMUS bent down his head,
An' that minute the solemn death-sentence was said.

The mornin' was bright, an' the mists rose on high,
An' the lark whistled merrily in the clear sky;
But why are the men standin' idle so late?
An' why do the crowds gather fast in the strate?
What come they to talk of? what come they to see?
An' why does the long rope hang from the cross-tree?
O SHAMUS O'BRIEN! pray fervent and fast,
May the saints take your soul, for this day is your last;
Pray fast an' pray sthrong, for the moment is nigh,
When, sthrong, proud, an' great as you are, you must die.

At last they threw open the big prison-gate,
An' out came the sheriffs and sodgers in state,
An' a cart in the middle an' SHAMUS was in it,
Not paler, but prouder than ever, that minute.
An' as soon as the people saw SHAMUS O'BRIEN,

Wid prayin' and blessin', and all the girls cryin',
A wild, wailin' sound kem on by degrees,
Like the sound of the lonesome wind blowin' through
     trees.
On, on to the gallows the sheriffs are gone,
An' the cart an' the sodgers go steadily on;
An' at every side swellin' around of the cart,
A wild, sorrowful sound, that id open your heart.
Now under the gallows the cart takes its stand,
An' the hangman gets up with the rope in his hand;
An' the priest, havin' blest him, goes down on the ground,
An' SHAMUS O'BRIEN throws one last look round.

Then the hangman dhrew near, an' the people grew still,
Young faces turned sickly, and warm hearts turn chill;
An' the rope bein' ready, his neck was made bare,
For the grip iv the life-strangling cord to prepare;
An' the good priest has left him, havin' said his last
     prayer.
But the good priest done more, for his hands he unbound,
An' with one daring spring JIM has leaped on the ground;
Bang! bang! goes the carbines, and clash goes the sabers;
He 's not down! he 's alive still! now stand to him, neigh-
     bors!
Through the smoke and the horses he 's into the crowd,—
By the heavens, he 's free!—than thunder more loud,
By one shout from the people the heavens were shaken—
One shout that the dead of the world might awaken.
The sodgers ran this way, the sheriffs ran that,
An' Father MALONE lost his new Sunday hat;
To-night he 'll be sleepin' in Aherloe Glin,
An' the divil 's in the dice if you catch him ag'in.
Your swords they may glitter, your carbines go bang,
But if you want hangin', it 's yourself you must hang.

Well, a week after this time, without firing a cannon,
A sharp, Yankee schooner sailed out of the Shannon,
And the captain left word he was going to Cork,
But the divil a bit, he was bound for New York.
The very next spring, a bright morning in May,
Just six months after the great hangin' day,
A letter was brought to the town of Kildare,
An' on the outside was written out fair,

"To ould Mistress O'Brien in Ireland or elsewhere."
And the inside began, "My dear, good old mother,
I 'm safe—and I 'm happy—and not wishing to bother
You in the readin' (with the help of the priest),
I send you inclosed in this letter at least
Enough to pay him and fetch you away
To this land of the free and the brave, Amerikay.
Here you 'll be happy and never nade cryin'
So long as you 're mother of Shamus O'Brien.
An' give me love to swate Biddy, and tell her beware
Of that spalpeen who calls himself Lord of Kildare.
An' just tell the Judge, I do n't now care a rap
For him or his wig, or his dirty black cap;
An' as for dragoons, them paid men of slaughter,
Just say that I love them as the divil loves holy water.
An' now, my good mother, one word of advice:
Fill your bag with pittatyes and whisky and rice,
An' when you start from ould Ireland, take passage at Cork
An' come straight over to the town of New York,
An' there ax the mayor the best way to go
To the state of Cincinnati in the town of Ohio;
For 'tis there you will find me without much tryin'
At the Harp and the Eagle kept by Shamus O'Brien."

J. S. Le Fanu.

THE GLOVE AND THE LIONS.

King Francis was a hearty king, and loved a royal sport,
And one day as his lions fought, sat looking on the court;
The nobles filled the benches, with the ladies in their pride,
And 'mongst them sat the Count de Lorge, with one for
 whom he sighed:
And truly 'twas a gallant thing to see that crowning show,
Valor and love, and a king above, and the royal beasts
 below.

Ramped and roared the lions, with horrid laughing jaws;
They bit, they glared, gave blows like beams, a wind
 went with their paws;
With wallowing might and stifled roar they rolled on one
 another,

Till all the pit with sand and mane was in a thunderous
    smother,
The bloody foam above the bars came whisking through
    the air;
Said Francis then, "Faith, gentlemen, we 're better here
    than there!"

De Lorge's love o'erheard the King, a beauteous, lively
    dame,
With smiling lips and sharp bright eyes, which always
    seemed the same;
She thought, "The Count, my lover, is brave as brave
    can be.
He surely would do wondrous things to show his love of
    me;
King, ladies, lovers, all look on; the occasion is divine;
I 'll drop my glove, to prove his love; great glory will be
    mine!"

She dropped her glove to prove his love, then looked on
    him and smiled;
He bowed, and in a moment leaped among the lions wild;
The leap was quick, return was quick, he has regained his
    place,
Then threw the glove,—but not with love,—right in the
    lady's face.
"By Heaven!" said Francis, "rightly done!" and he rose
    from where he sat;
"No love," quoth he, "but vanity, sets love a task like
    that."

Leigh Hunt.

A LEGEND OF BREGENZ.

Girt round with rugged mountains
    The fair Lake Constance lies;
In her blue heart reflected,
    Shine back the starry skies;
And watching each white cloudlet
    Float silently and slow,
You think a piece of heaven
    Lies on our earth below!

Midnight is there: and silence,
  Enthroned in heaven, looks down
Upon her own calm mirror,
  Upon a sleeping town;
For Bregenz, that quaint city
  Upon the Tyrol shore,
Has stood above Lake Constance
  A thousand years and more.

Her battlements and towers
  Upon their rocky steep
Have cast their trembling shadow
  For ages on the deep;
Mountain and lake and valley
  A sacred legend know,
Of how the town was saved one night,
  Three hundred years ago.

Far from her home and kindred
  A Tyrol maid had fled,
To serve in the Swiss valleys,
  And toil for daily bread;
And every year that fleeted
  So silently and fast
Seemed to bear farther from her
  The memory of the past.

She served kind, gentle masters,
  Nor asked for rest or change;
Her friends seemed no more new ones,
  Their speech seemed no more strange;
And when she led her cattle
  To pasture every day,
She ceased to look and wonder
  On which side Bregenz lay.

She spoke no more of Bregenz
  With longing and with tears;
Her Tyrol home seemed faded
  In a deep mist of years.
She heeded not the rumors
  Of Austrian war and strife;
Each day she rose contented,
  To the calm toils of life.

Yet, when her master's children
  Would clustering round her stand,
She sang them the old ballads
  Of her own native land;
And when at morn and evening
  She knelt before God's throne,
The accents of her childhood
  Rose to her lips alone.

And so she dwelt: the valley
  More peaceful, year by year;
When suddenly strange portents
  Of some great deed seemed near.
The golden corn was bending
  Upon its fragile stalk,
While farmers, heedless of their fields,
  Paced up and down in talk.

The men seemed stern and altered,
  With looks cast on the ground;
With anxious faces, one by one,
  The women gathered round;
All talk of flax or spinning,
  Or work, was put away;
The very children seemed afraid
  To go alone to play.

One day, out in the meadow,
  With strangers from the town,
Some secret plan discussing,
  The men walked up and down;
Yet now and then seemed watching
  A strange, uncertain gleam,
That looked like lances 'mid the trees
  That stood below the stream.

At eve they all assembled,
  All care and doubt were fled;
With jovial laugh they feasted,
  The board was nobly spread.
The elder of the village
  Rose up, his glass in hand,
And cried, "We drink the downfall
  Of an accursed land!

"The night is growing darker,—
   Ere one more day is flown,
Bregenz, our foeman's stronghold,
   Bregenz shall be our own!"
The women shrank in terror,
   (Yet pride, too, had her part)
But one poor Tyrol maiden
   Felt death within her heart.

Before her stood fair Bregenz,
   Once more her towers arose;
What were the friends beside her?
   Only her country's foes!
The faces of her kinsfolk,
   The days of childhood flown,
The echoes of her mountains,
   Reclaimed her as their own.

Nothing she heard around her
   (Though shouts rang forth again),
Gone were the green Swiss valleys,
   The pasture and the plain;
Before her eyes one vision,
   And in her heart one cry,
That said, "Go forth, save Bregenz,
   And then, if need be, die!"

With trembling haste and breathless,
   With noiseless step she sped;
Horses and weary cattle
   Were standing in the shed;
She loosed the strong white charger,
   That fed from out her hand;
She mounted, and she turned his head
   Towards her native land.

Out—out into the darkness,—
   Faster, and still more fast;
The smooth grass flies behind her,
   The chestnut wood is past;
She looks up; clouds are heavy:
   Why is her steed so slow?—
Scarcely the wind beside them
   Can pass them as they go.

"Faster!" she cries, "O, faster!"
　　Eleven the church-bells chime;
"O God," she cries, "help Bregenz,
　　And bring me there in time!"
But louder than bells' ringing,
　　Or lowing of the kine,
Grows nearer in the midnight
　　The rushing of the Rhine.

Shall not the roaring waters
　　Their headlong gallop check?
The steed draws back in terror,
　　She leans above his neck
To watch the flowing darkness,—
　　The bank is high and steep,—
One pause—he staggers forward
　　And plunges in the deep.

She strives to pierce the blackness
　　And looser throws the rein;
Her steed must breast the waters
　　That dash above his mane.
How gallantly, how nobly,
　　He struggles through the foam!
And see—in the fair distance
　　Shine out the lights of home!

Up the steep bank he bears her,
　　And now they rush again
Towards the heights of Bregenz,
　　That tower above the plain.
They reach the gate of Bregenz
　　Just as the midnight rings,
And out come serf and soldier,
　　To meet the news she brings.

Bregenz is saved! ere daylight
　　Her battlements are manned;
Defiance greets the army
　　That marches on the land.
And if to deeds heroic
　　Should endless fame be paid,
Bregenz does well to honor
　　The noble Tyrol maid.

Three hundred years are vanished,
   And yet upon the hill
An old stone gateway rises,
   To do her honor still;
And there, when Bregenz women
   Sit spinning in the shade,
They see in quaint old carving
   The Charger and the Maid.

And when, to guard old Bregenz,
   By gateway, street, and tower,
The warder paces all night long,
   And calls each passing hour,
"Nine," "ten," "eleven," he cries aloud,
   And then (O crown of Fame!)
When midnight pauses in the skies,
   He calls the maiden's name!

Adelaide A. Procter.

THE ELF-CHILD AND THE MINISTER.

Hester Prynne went, one day, to the mansion of Governor Bellingham, with a pair of gloves which she had fringed and embroidered to his order. Lifting the iron hammer that hung at the portal, Hester Prynne gave a summons.

"Is the worshipful Governor Bellingham within?"

"Yea, forsooth," replied the bond servant, "but he hath a godly minister or two with him, and likewise a leech. Ye may not see his worship now."

"Nevertheless, I will enter."

Just then adown the vista of the garden avenue, a number of persons were seen approaching towards the house.

Governor Bellingham, in a loose gown and easy cap, walked foremost, and appeared to be showing off his estates, and expatiating on his projected improvements. The venerable pastor, John Wilson, with beard white as the snowdrift, was seen over Governor Bellingham's shoulder. Behind the Governor and Mr. Wilson came two other guests; one the Reverend Arthur Dimmesdale, and in close companionship with him, old Roger Chilling-worth, a person of great skill in physic. The Governor ascended one or two steps, and, throwing open the leaves of the great hall window, found himself close to little Pearl.

"What have we here?" said Governor Bellingham, looking with surprise at the scarlet little figure before him. "I profess I have never seen the like since my days of vanity, in old King James' time, when I was wont to esteem it a high favor to be admitted to a court mask. There used to be a swarm of these small apparitions in holiday time, and we called them children of the Lord of Misrule. But how got such a guest into my hall?"

"Ay, indeed!" cried good old Mr. Wilson. "What little bird of scarlet plumage may this be? Methinks I have seen just such figures when the sun has been shining through a richly painted window, and tracing out the golden and crimson images across the floor. But that was in the old land. Prithee, young one, who art thou, and what has ailed thy mother to bedizen thee in this strange fashion? Art thou a Christian child—ha? Dost know thy catechism? Or art thou one of those naughty elfs or fairies, whom we thought to have left behind us in merry old England?"

"I am mother's child, and my name is Pearl!"

"Pearl?—Ruby, rather!—or Coral—or Red Rose, at the very least, judging from thy hue! But where is this mother of thine? Ah! I see. This is the self-same child of whom we have had speech together; and behold here the unhappy woman, Hester Prynne, her mother!"

"Sayest thou so?" said the Governor. "She comes at a good time; and we will look into this matter forthwith. Hester Prynne, there hath been much question concerning thee, of late. The point hath been weightily discussed whether we, that are of authority and influence, do well discharge our consciences by trusting an immortal soul, such as there is in yonder child, to the guidance of one who hath stumbled and fallen, amid the pitfalls of this world. Speak thou, the child's own mother! Were it not, thinkest thou, for thy little one's temporal and eternal welfare that she be taken out of thy charge, and clad soberly, and disciplined strictly, and instructed in the truths of heaven and earth? What canst thou do for the child in this kind?"

"I can teach my little Pearl what I have learned from this!" answered Hester Prynne, laying her finger on the red token. "This badge hath taught me—it daily teaches me—it is teaching me at this moment—lessons whereof my child may be the wiser and better, albeit they can profit nothing to myself."

"We will judge warily, and look well what we are about to do. Good Master Wilson, I pray you, examine this Pearl—since that is her name—and see whether she hath had such Christian nurture as befits a child of her age."

The old minister seated himself in an armchair, and made an effort to draw Pearl betwixt his knees. But the child, unaccustomed to the touch of any but her mother, escaped through the open window, and stood on the upper step, looking like a wild tropical bird of rich plumage, ready to take flight into the upper air.

"Pearl," said he, with great solemnity, "thou must take heed to instruction, that so, in due season, thou mayest wear in thy bosom the pearl of great price. Canst thou tell me, my child, who made thee?"

Now, Pearl knew well enough who made her. But that perversity which all children have more or less, and of which little Pearl had a tenfold portion, now took thorough possession of her, and closed her lips, or impelled her to speak words amiss. After putting her finger in her mouth, with many ungracious refusals to answer, the child finally announced that she had not been made at all, but had been plucked by her mother off the bush of wild roses that grew by the prison door.

"This is awful!" said the Governor. "Here is a child of three years old, and she cannot tell who made her! Without question she is equally in the dark as to her soul, its present depravity and future destiny! Methinks, gentlemen, we need inquire no further."

Hester caught hold of Pearl and drew her forcibly into her arms, confronting the old Puritan magistrate with almost a fierce expression. Alone in the world, cast off by it, and with this sole treasure to keep her heart alive, she felt that she possessed indefeasible rights against the world, and was ready to defend them to the death.

"God gave me the child!" she cried. "He gave her in requital of all things else which ye had taken from me.

She is my happiness —she is my torture, none the less. Pearl keeps me here in life. Pearl punishes me, too. Ye shall not take her; I will die first.''

"My poor woman," said the old minister, "the child shall be well cared for—far better than thou canst do it."

"God gave her into my keeping," repeated Hester Prynne, raising her voice almost to a shriek. "I will not give her up!" And here by a sudden impulse she turned to the young clergyman. "Speak thou for me! Thou wast my pastor, and hadst charge of my soul, and knowest me better than these men can. I will not lose the child. Speak for me. Thou knowest—for thou hast sympathies which these men lack—thou knowest what is in my heart, and what are a mother's rights, and how much the stronger they are when that mother has but her child and the scarlet letter. Look thou to it. I will not lose the child. Look to it!"

The young minister at once came forward. "There is truth in what she says, truth in what Hester says, and in the feeling which inspires her. God gave her the child, and gave her, too, an instinctive knowledge of its nature and requirements—but seemingly so peculiar—which no other mortal can possess. And, moreover, is there not a quality of awful sacredness in the relation between this mother and this child? This child hath come from the hand of God, to work in many ways upon her heart, who pleads so earnestly and with such bitterness of spirit, the right to keep her. It was meant for a blessing, for the one blessing of her life. It was meant for a retribution, too; a torture to be felt at many an unthought-of moment, a pang, a sting, an ever-recurring agony in the midst of a troubled joy. And may it not be that this boon was meant to keep the mother's soul alive, and to preserve her from blacker depths of sin into which Satan might else have sought to plunge her? Therefore, it is good for this poor, sinful woman that she hath an infant immortality to teach her, by the Creator's sacred pledge, that if she bring the child to heaven, the child also will bring its parent thither. For Hester Prynne's sake, then, and no less for the poor child's sake, let us leave them as Providence has seen fit to place them."

"There is a weighty import in what my young brother hath spoken," added the Reverend Mr. Wilson. "What say you, worshipful Master Bellingham? Hath he not pleaded well for the poor woman?''

"Indeed, hath he,'' answered the magistrate, "and hath adduced such arguments that we will even leave the matter as it now stands. Care must be had, nevertheless, to put the child to due and stated examinations in the catechism, at thy hands or Master Dimmesdale's. Moreover, at the proper season, the tithing-men must take heed that she go both to school and to meeting.''

The affair being so satisfactorily concluded, Hester Prynne, with Pearl, departed from the house. As they descended the steps, the lattice of a chamber window was thrown open, and forth into the sunny day was thrust the face of Mistress Hibbins.

"Hist! hist!'' said she, while her ill-omened physiognomy seemed to cast a shadow. "Wilt thou go with us to-night? There will be a merry company in the forest, and I well-nigh promised the Black Man that comely Hester Prynne should make one.''

"Make my excuse to him, so please you,'' answered Hester, with a triumphant smile. "I must tarry at home and keep watch over my little Pearl. Had they taken her from me, I would willingly have gone with thee into the forest, and signed my name in the Black Man's book too, and that with my own blood.''

"We shall have thee there anon,'' said the witch-lady.
Nathaniel Hawthorne.

AUX ITALIENS.

At Paris it was, at the opera there;
   And she looked like a queen in a book that night,
With the wreath of pearl in her raven hair,
   And the brooch on her breast so bright.

Of all the operas that Verdi wrote,
   The best, to my taste, is the Trovatoré;
And Mario can soothe, with a tenor note,
   The souls in purgatory.

The moon on the tower slept soft as snow;
   And who was not thrilled in the strangest way,
As we heard him sing, while the gas burned low,
   "Non ti scordar di me?"

The emperor there, in his box of state,
   Looked grave; as if he had just then seen
The red flag wave from the city gate,
   Where his eagles in bronze had been.

The empress, too, had a tear in her eye:
   You 'd have said that her fancy had gone back again,
For one moment, under the old blue sky,
   To the old glad life in Spain.

Well! there in our front-row box we sat
   Together, my bride betrothed and I;
My gaze was fixed on my opera hat,
   And hers on the stage hard by.

And both were silent, and both were sad;—
   Like a queen she leaned on her full white arm,
With that regal, indolent air she had;
   So confident of her charm!

I have not a doubt she was thinking then
   Of her former lord, good soul that he was,
Who died the richest and roundest of men,
   The Marquis of Carabas.

I hope that, to get to the kingdom of heaven,
   Through a needle's eye he had not to pass;
I wish him well for the jointure given
   To my lady of Carabas.

Meanwhile, I was thinking of my first love
   As I had not been thinking of aught for years;
Till over my eyes there began to move
   Something that felt like tears.

I thought of the dress that she wore last time,
   When we stood 'neath the cypress-trees together,
In that lost land, in that soft clime,
   In the crimson evening weather;

Of that muslin dress (for the eve was hot);
  And her warm white neck in its golden chain;
And her full soft hair, just tied in a knot,
  And falling loose again;

And the jasmine flower in her fair young breast;
  (O the faint, sweet smell of that jasmine flower!)
And the one bird singing alone to his nest;
  And the one star over the tower.

I thought of our little quarrels and strife,
  And the letter that brought me back my ring;
And it all seemed then, in the waste of life,
  Such a very little thing!

For I thought of her grave below the hill,
  Which the sentinel cypress-tree stands over;
And I thought, "Were she only living still,
  How I could forgive her and love her!"

And I swear, as I thought of her thus in that hour,
  And of how, after all, old things are best,
That I smelt the smell of that jasmine flower
  Which she used to wear in her breast.

It smelt so faint, and it smelt so sweet,
  It made me creep, and it made me cold!
Like the scent that steals from the crumbling sheet
  Where a mummy is half unrolled;

And I turned and looked; she was sitting there,
  In a dim box over the stage; and drest
In that muslin dress, with that full soft hair,
  And that jasmine in her breast!

I was here, and she was there;
  And the glittering horse-shoe curved between:—
From my bride betrothed, with her raven hair
  And her sumptuous scornful mien,

To my early love, with her eyes downcast,
  And over her primrose face the shade,
(In short, from the future back to the past,)
  There was but a step to be made.

To my early love from my future bride
   One moment I looked. Then I stole to the door,
I traversed the passage; and down at her side
   I was sitting, a moment more.

My thinking of her, or the music's strain,
   Or something which never will be exprest,
Had brought her back from the grave again,
   With the jasmine in her breast.

She is not dead, and she is not wed!
   But she loves me now, and she loved me then!
And the very first word that her sweet lips said,
   My heart grew youthful again.

The marchioness there, of Carabas,
   She is wealthy, and young, and handsome still;
And but for her . . . well, we 'll let that pass;
   She may marry whomever she will.

But I will marry my own first love,
   With her primrose face, for old things are best;
And the flower in her bosom, I prize it above
   The brooch in my lady's breast.

The world is filled with folly and sin,
   And love must cling where it can, I say:
For beauty is easy enough to win;
   But one is n't loved every day.

And I think in the lives of most women and men,
   There 's a moment when all would go smooth and even
If only the dead could find out when
   To come back and be forgiven.

But O the smell of that jasmine flower!
   And O that music! and O the way
That voice rang out from the donjon tower,
   Non ti scordar di me,
     Non ti scordar di me!

                 Robert Bulwer Lytton.

COUNT CANDESPINA'S STANDARD.

Scarce were the splintered lances dropped,
   Scarce were the swords drawn out,
Ere recreant Lara, sick with fear,
   Had wheeled his steed about;

His courser reared, and plunged, and neighed,
   Loathing the fight to yield;
But the coward spurred him to the bone,
   And drove him from the field.

Gonzalez in his stirrups rose:
   "Turn, turn, thou traitor knight!
Thou bold tongue in a lady's bower,
   Thou dastard in a fight!"

But vainly valiant Gomez cried
   Across the waning fray:
Pale Lara and his craven band
   To Burgos scoured away.

"Now, by the God above me, sirs,
   Better we all were dead,
Than a single knight among ye all
   Should ride where Lara led!

"Yet ye who fear to follow me,
   As yon traitor, turn and fly;
For I lead ye not to win a field;
   I lead ye forth to die.

"Olea, plant my standard here—
   Here on this little mound;
Here raise the war-cry of thy house,
   Make this our rallying ground.

"Forget not, as thou hop'st for grace,
   The last care I shall have
Will be to hear thy battle-cry,
   And see that standard wave."

Down on the ranks of Aragon
   The bold Gonzalez drove,
And Olea raised his battle-cry,
   And waved the flag above.

Slowly Gonzalez' little band
   Gave ground before the foe;
But not an inch of the field was won
   Without a deadly blow;

And not an inch of the field was won
   That did not draw a tear
From the widowed wives of Aragon,
   That fatal news to hear.

Backward and backward Gomez fought,
   And high o'er the clashing steel,
Plainer and plainer rose the cry,
   "Olea for Castile!"

Backward fought Gomez, step by step,
   Till the cry was close at hand,
Till his dauntless standard shadowed him;
   And there he made his stand.

Mace, sword, and axe rang on his mail,
   Yet he moved not where he stood,
Though each gaping joint of armor ran
   A stream of purple blood.

As, pierced with countless wounds he fell,
   The standard caught his eye,
And he smiled like an infant hushed asleep,
   To hear the battle-cry.

Now, one by one the wearied knights
   Have fallen, or basely flown;
And on the mound where his post was fixed
   Olea stood alone.

"Yield up thy banner, gallant knight!
   Thy lord lies on the plain;
Thy duty has been nobly done;
   I would not see thee slain."

"Spare pity, King of Aragon!
　I would not hear thee lie:
My lord is looking down from heaven
　To see his standard fly."

"Yield, madman, yield! thy horse is down,
　Thou hast nor lance nor shield;
Fly!—I will grant thee time." "This flag
　Can neither fly nor yield!"

They girt the standard round about,
　A wall of flashing steel;
But still they heard the battle-cry,
　"Olea for Castile!"

And there, against all Aragon,
　Full-armed with lance and brand,
Olea fought until the sword
　Snapped in his sturdy hand.

Among the foe with that high scorn
　Which laughs at earthly fears,
He hurled the broken hilt, and drew
　His dagger on the spears.

They hewed the hauberk from his breast,
　The helmet from his head;
They hewed the hands from off his limbs;
　From every vein he bled.

Clasping the standard to his heart,
　He raised one dying peal,
That rang as if a trumpet blew,—
　"Olea for Castile!"

George H. Boker.

HER LETTER.

I 'm sitting alone by the fire,
　Dressed just as I came from the dance,
In a robe even *you* would admire,—
　It cost a cool thousand in France;

I 'm be-diamonded out of all reason,
   My hair is done up in a cue:
In short, sir, "the belle of the season"
   Is wasting an hour on you.

A dozen engagements I 've broken;
   I left in the midst of a set;
Likewise a proposal, half spoken,
   That waits—on the stairs—for me yet.
They say he 'll be rich,—when he grows up,—
   And then he adores me indeed.
And you, sir, are turning your nose up,
   Three thousand miles off, as you read.

"And how do I like my position?"
   "And what do I think of New York?"
"And now, in my higher ambition,
   With whom do I waltz, flirt, or talk?"
"And is n't it nice to have riches,
   And diamonds, and silks, and all that?"
"And are n't it a change to the ditches
   And tunnels of Poverty Flat?"

Well, yes,—if you saw us out driving
   Each day in the park, four-in-hand,—
If you saw poor, dear mamma contriving
   To look supernaturally grand,—
If you saw papa's picture as taken
   By Brady, and tinted at that,—
You 'd never suspect he sold bacon
   And flour at Poverty Flat.

And yet, just this moment, when sitting
   In the glare of the grand chandelier,—
In the bustle and glitter befitting
   The "finest *soirée* of the year,"
In the mists of a *gauze de Chambéry*,
   And the hum of the smallest of talk,—
Somehow, Joe, I thought of the "Ferry,"
   And the dance that we had on "The Fork;"

Of Harrison's barn, with its muster
   Of flags festooned over the wall;
Of the candles that shed their soft luster
   And tallow on head-dress and shawl;

Of the steps that we took to one fiddle;
  Of the dress of my queer *vis-à-vis;*
And how I once went down the middle
  With the man that shot Sandy McGee;

Of the moon that was quietly sleeping
  On the hill, when the time came to go;
Of the few baby peaks that were peeping
  From under their bedclothes of snow;
Of that ride,—that to me was the rarest;
  Of—the something you said at the gate,—
Ah, Joe, then I was n't an heiress
  To "the best-paying lead in the State."

Well, well, it 's all past; yet it 's funny
  To think, as I stood in the glare
Of fashion, and beauty, and money,
  That I should be thinking, right there,
Of some one who breasted highwater,
  And swam the North Fork, and all that,
Just to dance with old Folinsbee's daughter,
  The Lily of Poverty Flat.

But goodness! what nonsense I 'm writing!
  (Mamma says my taste still is low,)
Instead of my triumphs reciting,
  I 'm spooning on Joseph,—heigh-ho!
And I 'm to be "finished" by travel,—
  Whatever 's the meaning of that,—
Oh! why did papa strike pay gravel
  In drifting on Poverty Flat?

Good-night,—here 's the end of my paper;
  Good-night,—if the longitude please,—
For maybe while wasting my taper,
  Your sun 's climbing over the trees.
But know if you have n't got riches,
  And are poor, dearest Joe, and all that,
That my heart 's somewhere there in the ditches,
  And you 've struck it,—on Poverty Flat.

                                        Bret Harte.

THE BUGLE SONG.

The splendor falls on castle walls
    And snowy summits old in story;
The long light shakes across the lakes,
    And the wild cataract leaps in glory.
Blow, bugle, blow, set the wild echoes flying,
Blow, bugle; answer, echoes, dying, dying, dying.

    O hark! O hear! how thin and clear,
        And thinner, clearer, farther going!
    O sweet and far, from cliff and scar,
        The horns of Elfland faintly blowing!
Blow, let us hear the purple glens replying:
Blow, bugle; answer, echoes, dying, dying, dying.

    O love, they die in yon rich sky,
        They faint on hill, or field, or river:
    Our echoes roll from soul to soul,
        And grow forever and forever.
Blow, bugle, blow, set the wild echoes flying,
And answer, echoes, answer, dying, dying, dying.
                    Lord Tennyson.

THE GREEN GNOME.

Ring, sing! ring, sing! pleasant Sabbath bells!
Chime, rhyme! chime, rhyme! through dales and dells!

And I galloped and I galloped on my palfrey white as milk,
My robe was of the sea-green woof, my serk was of the
    silk;
My hair was golden yellow, and it floated to my shoe;
My eyes were like two harebells bathed in little drops of
    dew;
My palfrey, never stopping, made a music sweetly blent
With the leaves of autumn dropping all around me as I
    went;
And I heard the bells, grown fainter, far behind me peal
    and play,
Fainter, fainter, fainter, till they seemed to die away;

And beside a silver runnel, on a little heap of sand,
I saw the green gnome sitting, with his cheek upon his
    hand.
Then he started up to see me, and he ran with cry and
    bound,
And drew me from my palfrey white and set me on the
    ground.
O crimson, crimson were his locks, his face was green to
    see,
But he cried, "O light-haired lassie, you are bound to
    marry me!"
He clasped me round the middle small, he kissed me on
    the cheek,
He kissed me once, he kissed me twice,—I could not stir
    or speak;
He kissed me twice, he kissed me thrice,—but when he
    kissed again,
I called aloud upon the name of Him who died for men.

Sing, sing! ring, ring! pleasant Sabbath bells!
Chime, rhyme! chime, rhyme! through dales and dells!

O faintly, faintly, faintly, calling men and maids to pray,
So faintly, faintly, faintly, rang the bells far away;
And as I named the Blessed Name, as in our need we can,
The ugly green, green gnome became a tall and comely
    man:
His hands were white, his beard was gold, his eyes were
    black as sloes,
His tunic was of scarlet woof, and silken were his hose;
A pensive light from Faëryland still lingered on his cheek,
His voice was like the running brook, when he began to
    speak;
"O, you have cast away the charm my step-dame put on
    me,
Seven years I dwelt in Faëryland, and you have set me
    free.
O, I will mount thy palfrey white, and ride to kirk with
    thee,
And, by those little dewy eyes, we twain will wedded be!"

Back we galloped, never stopping, he before and I behind,
And the autumn leaves were dropping, red and yellow, in
    the wind:

And the sun was shining clearer, and my heart was high
    and proud,
As nearer, nearer, nearer rang the kirk bells sweet and
    loud,
And we saw the kirk before us, as we trotted down the
    fells,
And nearer, clearer, o'er us, rang the welcome of the bells.

Ring, sing! ring, sing! pleasant Sabbath bells!
Chime, rhyme! chime, rhyme! over fields and fells!
                      Robert Buchanan.

ROMOLA AND SAVONAROLA.

By the early morning light, a woman in the dress of a
nun was seen walking along a road which led from Florence. She passed the gate, paused under a cypress-tree,
lifted up the hanging roof of her cowl, and looked before
her. It was Romola hurrying away from the breath of
soft hated lips warm upon her cheek, the breath of an
odious mind stifling her own.

All things conspired to give her the sense of freedom
and solitude; her escape from the accustomed walls and
streets, the widening distance from her husband, the morning stillness, the great dip of ground on the roadside
making a gulf between her and the somber calm of the
mountains. She was alone in the presence of the earth
and sky, with no human presence interposing and making
law for her.

Suddenly a voice close to her said—"You are Romola
de Bardi, the wife of Tito Melema." She knew the voice;
it had vibrated through her more than once before; and
because she knew it, she did not turn round or look up.
She sat shaken by awe, and yet inwardly rebelling against
the awe. It was one of those black-skirted monks who
was daring to speak to her, that was all. And yet she
was shaken, as if that destiny which men thought of as a
sceptered deity had come to her and grasped her with
fingers of flesh.

"What right have you to speak to me, or to hinder
me?"

"The right of a messenger. You have put on a religious garb, and you have no religious purpose. You have sought the garb as a disguise. But you were not suffered to pass me without being discerned. It was declared to me who you were; it is declared to me that you are seeking to escape from the lot God has laid upon you. You wish your true name and your true place in life to be hidden, that you may choose for yourself a new name and a new place, and have no rule but your own will. And I have a command to call you back. My daughter, you must return to your place."

"I will not return. I acknowledge no right of priest or monk to interfere with my actions. You have no power over me."

"But it is not the poor monk who claims to interfere with you; it is the truth that commands you. And you cannot escape it. Either you must obey it, and it will lead you; or you must disobey it, and it will hang on you with the weight of a chain which you will drag forever."

Romola turned with anger in her eyes and faced the speaker, Savonarola. She was nearly as tall as he was, and their faces were almost on a level. At the look on his face, the defiant words fell back without utterance, and she was constrained to plead: "My father, you cannot know the reasons which compel me to go. None can know them but myself. None can judge for me. I have been driven by a great sorrow. I am resolved to go."

"I know enough, my daughter! You are not happy in your married life; you were warned by a message from heaven, delivered in my presence—you were warned before marriage, when you might still have lawfully chosen to be free from the marriage bond. But you chose the bond; and in willfully breaking it, you are breaking a pledge. Of what wrongs will you complain when you yourself are breaking the simplest law that lies at the foundation of the trust which binds man to man—faithfulness to the spoken word? And to break that pledge you fly from Florence; Florence, where there are the only men and women in the world to whom you owe the debt of fellow-citizen. I have a divine warrant to stop you!"

"I was not going away to ease and self-indulgence. I was going away to hardship. I expect no joy; it is gone from my life."

"You are seeking your own will, my daughter. You are seeking some good other than the law you are bound to obey. But how will you find good? It is not a thing of choice; it is a river that flows from the Invisible Throne, and flows in the path of obedience. I say again, man cannot choose his duties. You may choose to forsake your duties, and choose not to have the sorrow they bring. But you will go forth; and what will you find, my daughter? Sorrow without duty—bitter herbs, and no bread with them."

"But if you knew, if you knew what it is to me—how impossible it seemed to me to bear it!"

"My daughter, you carry something within your mantle; draw it forth and look at it."

She drew forth the crucifix. Still pointing toward it, he said:

"There, my daughter, is the image of a supreme offering, made by a supreme love, because the need of man was great. Conform your life to that image. If you forsake your place, who will fill it? Ask your conscience, my daughter. You are a wife. You seek to break ties in self-will and anger, not because the higher life calls upon you to renounce them. The higher life begins for us when we renounce our own will to bow before a Divine Law. If there is wickedness in the streets, your steps should shine with the light of purity; if there is a cry of anguish, you, because you know the meaning of the cry, should be there to still it. My beloved daughter, sorrow has come to teach you a new worship; the sign of it hangs before you."

"My husband—he is not—my love is gone!"

"My daughter, there is the bond of higher love. If the cross comes to you as a wife, you must carry it as a wife. You may say, 'I will forsake my husband,' but you cannot cease to be a wife. Live for Florence—for your own people. Bear the anguish and the smart. The iron is sharp—I know, I know—it rends the tender flesh. The draught is bitterness on the lips. But there is rapture in the cup—there is the vision which makes all life below it lost forever. Come, my daughter, come back to your place!"

"Father, I will be guided. Teach me! I will go back."

Almost unconsciously she sank on her knees. Savona-rola stretched out his hands over her; but feeling would no longer pass through the channel of speech, and he was silent.

George Eliot.

THE FORGING OF THE ANCHOR.

Come, see the Dolphin's anchor forged; 'tis at a white
    heat now:
The billows ceased, the flames decreased; though on the
    forge's brow
The little flames still fitfully play through the sable mound;
And fitfully you still may see the grim smiths ranking
    round,
All clad in leathern panoply, their broad hands only bare;
Some rest upon their sledges here, some work the wind-
    lass there.

The windlass strains the tackle-chains, the black mound
    heaves below,
And red and deep a hundred veins burst out at every
    throe;
It rises, roars, rends all outright,—O Vulcan, what a
    glow!
'Tis blinding white, 'tis blasting bright, the high sun
    shines not so!
The high sun sees not, on the earth, such fiery fearful
    show,—
The roof-ribs swarth, the candent hearth, the ruddy, lurid
    row
Of smiths that stand, an ardent band, like men before the
    foe;
As, quivering through his fleece of flame, the sailing
    monster slow
Sinks on the anvil,—all about the faces fiery grow;
"Hurrah!" they shout, "leap out, leap out:" bang, bang,
    the sledges go;
Hurrah! the jetted lightnings are hissing high and low;
A hailing fount of fire is struck at every squashing blow;
The leathern mail rebounds the hail; the rattling cinders
    strew

The ground around; at every bound the sweltering fountains flow;
And thick and loud the swinking crowd, at every stroke,
pant "Ho!"

Leap out, leap out, my masters; leap out and lay on load!
Let 's forge a goodly anchor, a bower, thick and broad;
For a heart of oak is hanging on every blow, I bode,
And I see the good ship riding, all in a perilous road;
The low reef roaring on her lee, the roll of ocean poured
From stem to stern, sea after sea, the mainmast by the
board,
The bulwarks down, the rudder gone, the boats stove
at the chains;
But courage still, brave mariners, the bower still remains,
And not an inch to flinch he deigns save when ye pitch
sky-high,
Then moves his head, as though he said, "Fear nothing,
—here am I!"
Swing in your strokes in order, let foot and hand keep time,
Your blows make music sweeter far than any steeple's
chime!
But while ye swing your sledges, sing; and let the burden
be,
The Anchor is the Anvil King, and royal craftsmen we;
Strike in, strike in, the sparks begin to dull their rustling
red!
Our hammers ring with sharper din, our work will soon
be sped;
Our anchor soon must change his bed of fiery rich array
For a hammock at the roaring bows, or an oozy couch of
clay;
Our anchor soon must change the lay of merry craftsmen
here,
For the Yeo-heave-o, and the Heave-away, and the sigh-
ing seaman's cheer;
When, weighing slow, at eve they go far, far from love
and home,
And sobbing sweethearts, in a row, wail o'er the ocean foam.

In livid and obdurate gloom, he darkens down at last.
A shapely one he is, and strong as e'er from cat was cast.
A trusted and trustworthy guard, if thou hadst life like me,

What pleasures would thy toils reward beneath the deep
    green sea!
O deep sea-diver, who might then behold such sights as
    thou?
The hoary monsters' palaces! methinks what joy ' twere
    now
To go plump plunging down amid the assembly of the
    whales,
And feel the churned sea round me boil beneath their
    scourging tails!

    ·   ·   ·   ·   ·

                        Samuel Ferguson.

JOCK JOHNSTONE, THE TINKLER.

"O, came ye ower by the Yoke-burn Ford,
    Or down the King's Road of the cleuch? *
Or saw ye a knight and a lady bright,
    Wha ha'e gane the gate they baith shall rue?"

"I saw a knight and a lady bright
    Ride up the cleuch at the break of day,
The knight upon a coal-black steed,
    And the dame on one of a silver-gray.

"And the lady's palfrey flew the first,
    With many a clang of silver bell:
Swift as the raven's morning flight
    The two went scouring ower the fell.

"By this time they are man and wife,
    And standing in St. Mary's fane;
And the lady in the grass-green silk
    A maid you will never see again."

"But I can tell thee, saucy wight,—
    And that the runaway shall prove,—
Revenge to a Douglas is as sweet
    As maiden charms, or maiden's love."

* Dell.

"Since thou say'st that, my Lord Douglas,
    Good faith some clinking there will be;
Beshrew my heart but and my sword,
    If I winna turn and ride with thee!"

They whipped out ower the Shepherd Cleuch,
    And doun the links o' the Corsecleuch Burn;
And aye the Douglas swore by his sword
    To win his love, or ne'er return.

"First fight your rival, Lord Douglas,
    And then brag after, if you may;
For the Earl of Ross is as brave a lord
    As ever gave good weapon sway.

"But I for ae poor siller merk,
    Or thirteen pennies and a bawbee,
Will tak in hand to fight you baith,
    Or beat the winner, whiche'er it be."

The Douglas turned him on his steed,
    And I wat a loud laughter leuch he:
"Of a' the fools I have ever met,
    Man, I ha'e never met ane like thee.

"Art thou akin to lord or knight,
    Or courtly squire or warrior leal?"
"I am a tinkler," quo' the wight,
    "But I like croun-cracking unco weel."

When they came to St. Mary's kirk,
    The chaplain shook for very fear;
And aye he kissed the cross, and said,
    "What deevil has sent that Douglas here!

"He neither values book nor ban,
    But curses all without demur;
And cares nae mair for a holy man
    Than I do for a worthless cur."

"Come here, thou bland and brittle priest,
    And tell to me without delay
Where you have hid the lord of Ross
    And the lady that came at the break of day."

"No knight or lady, good Lord Douglas,
　Have I beheld since break of morn;
And I never saw the lord of Ross
　Since the woful day that I was born."

Lord Douglas turned him round about,
　And looked the Tinkler in the face;
Where he beheld a lurking smile,
　And a deevil of a dour grimace.

"How 's this, how 's this, thou Tinkler loun?
　Hast thou presumed to lie on me?"
"Faith that I have!" the Tinkler said,
　"And a right good turn I have done to thee;

"For the lord of Ross and thy own true love,
　The beauteous Harriet of Thirlestane,
Rade west away, ere the break of day;
　And you 'll never see the dear maid again;

"So I thought it best to bring you here,
　On a wrang scent, of my own accord;
For had you met the Johnstone clan,
　They wad ha'e made mince-meat of a lord."

At this the Douglas was so wroth
　He wist not what to say or do;
But he strak the Tinkler o'er the croun,
　Till the blood came dreeping ower his brow.

"Beshrew my heart," quo' the Tinkler lad,
　"Thou bear'st thee most ungallantlye!
If these are the manners of a lord,
　They are manners that winna gang doun wi' me."

"Hold up thy hand," the Douglas cried,
　"And keep thy distance, Tinkler loun!"
"That will I not," the Tinkler said,
　"Though I and my mare should both go doun!"

"I have armor on," cried the Lord Douglas,
　"Cuirass and helm, as you may see."
"The deil me care!" quo' the Tinkler lad;
　"I shall have a skelp at them and thee."

"You are not horsed," quo' the Lord Douglas,
  "And no remorse this weapon brooks."
"Mine 's a right good yaud," quo' the Tinkler lad,
  "And a great deal better nor she looks.

"So stand to thy weapons, thou haughty lord,
  What I have taken I needs must give;
Thou shalt never strike a tinkler again,
  For the langest day thou hast to live."

Then to it they fell, both sharp and snell,
  Till the fire from both their weapons flew;
But the very first shock that they met with,
  The Douglas his rashness 'gan to rue.

For though he had on a sark of mail,
  And a cuirass on his breast wore he,
With a good steel bonnet on his head,
  Yet the blood ran trickling to his knee.

The Douglas sat upright and firm,
  Aye as together their horses ran;
But the Tinkler laid on like a very deil,—
  Siccan strokes were never laid on by man.

"Hold up thy hand, thou Tinkler loun,"
  Cried the poor priest, with whining din;
"If thou hurt the brave Lord James Douglas,
  A curse be on thee and all thy kin!"

"I care no more for Lord James Douglas
  Than Lord James Douglas cares for me;
But I want to let his proud heart know
  That a tinkler 's a man as well as he."

So they fought on, and they fought on,
  Till good Lord Douglas' breath was gone;
And the Tinkler bore him to the ground,
  With rush, with rattle, and with groan.

"O hon! O hon!" cried the proud Douglas,
  "That I this day should have lived to see!
For sure my honor I have lost,
  And a leader again I can never be!

"But tell me of thy kith and kin,
    And where was bred thy weapon hand?
For thou art the wale of tinkler louns
    That ever was born in fair Scotland."

"My name 's Jock Johnstone," quo' the wight;
    "I winna keep in my name frae thee;
And here, tak thou thy sword again,
    And better friends we two shall be."

But the Douglas swore a solemn oath,
    That was a debt he could never owe;
He would rather die at the back of the dike
    Than owe his sword to a man so low.

"But if thou wilt ride under my banner,
    An' bear my livery and my name,
My right-hand warrior thou shalt be
    And I 'll knight thee on the field of fame."

"Woe worth thy wit, good Lord Douglas,
    To think I 'd change my trade for thine;
Far better and wiser would you be,
    To live a journeyman of mine,

"To mend a kettle or a casque,
    Or clout a goodwife's yettlin' pan,—
Upon my life, good Lord Douglas,
    You 'd make a noble tinkler-man!

"I would give you drammock twice a day,
    And sunkets on a Sunday morn,
And you should be a rare adept
    In steel and copper, brass and horn!

"I 'll fight you every day you rise,
    Till you can act the hero's part;
Therefore, I pray you, think of this,
    And lay it seriously to heart."

The Douglas writhed beneath the lash,
    Answering with an inward curse,—
Like salmon wriggling on a spear,
    That makes his deadly wound the worse.

But up there came two squires renowned;
    In search of Lord Douglas they came;
And when they saw their master down,
    Their spirits mounted in a flame.

And they flew upon the Tinkler wight,
    Like perfect tigers on their prey:
But the Tinkler heaved his trusty sword,
    And made him ready for the fray.

"Come one to one, ye coward knaves,—
    Come hand to hand, and steed to steed;
I would that ye were better men,
    For this is glorious work indeed!"

Before you could have counted twelve,
    The Tinkler's wondrous chivalrye
Had both the squires upon the sward,
    And their horses galloping o'er the lea.

The Tinkler tied them neck and heel,
    And mony a biting jest gave he:
"O fie, for shame!" said the Tinkler lad;
    "Siccan fighters I did never see!"

He slit one of their bridle reins,—
    O, what disgrace the conquered feels!—
And he skelpit the squires with that good tawse,
    Till the blood ran off at baith their heels.

The Douglas he was forced to laugh
    Till down his cheeks the salt tear ran:
"I think the deevil be come here
    In the likeness of a tinkler man!"

Then he has to Lord Douglas gone,
    And he raised him kindly by the hand,
And he set him on his gallant steed,
    And bore him away to Henderland:

"Be not cast down, my Lord Douglas,
    Nor writhe beneath a broken bane;
For the leech's art will mend the part,
    And your honor lost will spring again.

" 'Tis true, Jock Johnstone is my name;
　　I 'm a right good tinkler, as you see;
For I can crack a casque betimes,
　　Or clout one, as my need may be.

"Jock Johnstone is my name, 'tis true,
　　But noble hearts are allied to me;
For I am the lord of Annandale,
　　And a knight and earl as well as thee."

Then Douglas strained the hero's hand,
　　And took from it his sword again:
"Since thou art the lord of Annandale,
　　Thou hast eased my heart of meikle pain.

"I might have known thy noble form
　　In that disguise thou 'rt pleased to wear;
All Scotland knows thy matchless arm,
　　And England by experience dear.

"We have been foes as well as friends,
　　And jealous of each other's sway;
But little can I comprehend
　　Thy motive for these pranks to-day."

"Sooth, my good lord, the truth to tell,
　　'Twas I that stole your love away,
And gave her to the lord of Ross
　　An hour before the break of day;

"For the lord of Ross is my brother,
　　By all the laws of chivalrye;
And I brought with me a thousand men
　　To guard him to my ain countrye.

"But I thought meet to stay behind,
　　And try your lordship to waylay,
Resolved to breed some noble sport,
　　By leading you so far astray.

"Judging it better some lives to spare,—
　　Which fancy takes me now and then,—
And settle our quarrel hand to hand,
　　Than each with our ten thousand men.

"God send you soon, my Lord Douglas,
　　To Border foray sound and haill!
　But never strike a tinkler again,
　　If he be a Johnstone of Annandale."

James Hogg.

THE VOICES AT THE THRONE.

A little child,
A little meek-faced, quiet village child,
Sat singing by her cottage door at eve
A low, sweet Sabbath song.　No human ear
Caught the faint melody,—no human eye
Beheld the upturned aspect, or the smile
That wreathed her innocent lips while they breathed
The oft-repeated burden of the hymn,
"Praise God! Praise God!"

　　　　　　　　　　　　A seraph by the throne
In full glory stood.　With eager hand
He smote the golden harp-string, till a flood
Of harmony on the celestial air
Welled forth, unceasing.　There, with a great voice
He sang the "Holy, holy evermore,
Lord God Almighty!" and the eternal courts
Thrilled with the rapture, and the hierarchies,
Angel, and rapt archangel, throbbed and burned
With vehement adoration.

　　　　　　　　　　　Higher yet
Rose the majestic anthem, without pause,
Higher, with rich magnificence of sound,
To its full strength; and still the infinite heavens
Rang with the "Holy, holy evermore!"
Till, trembling with excessive awe and love,
Each sceptered spirit sank before the throne
With a mute hallelujah.

　　　　　　　　　　But even then,
While the ecstatic song was at its height,
Stole in an alien voice—a voice that seemed
To float, float upward from some world afar—

A meek and childlike voice, faint, but how sweet!
That blended with the spirits' rushing strain,
Even as a fountain's music with the roll
Of the reverberate thunder.

       Loving smiles
Lit up the beauty of each angel's face
At that new utterance, smiles of joy that grew
More joyous yet, as ever and anon
Was heard the simple burden of the hymn,
"Praise God! Praise God!"

       And when the seraph's song
Had reached its close, and o'er the golden lyre
Silence hung brooding,—when the eternal courts
Rang with the echoes of his chant sublime,
Still through the abysmal space that wandering voice
Came floating upward from its world afar,
Still murmured sweet on the celestial air,
"Praise God! Praise God!"

         T. Westwood.

LADY CLARE.

It was the time when lilies blow,
 And clouds are highest up in air,
Lord Ronald brought a lily-white doe
 To give his cousin, Lady Clare.

I trow they did not part in scorn:
 Lovers long-betroth'd were they:
They two will wed the morrow morn;
 God's blessing on the day!

"He does not love me for my birth,
 Nor for my lands so broad and fair;
He loves me for my own true worth,
 And that is well," said Lady Clare.

In there came old Alice the nurse,
 Said, "Who was this that went from thee?"
"It was my cousin," said Lady Clare,
 "To-morrow he weds with me."

"O, God be thank'd!" said Alice the nurse,
  "That all comes round so just and fair;
Lord Ronald is heir of all your lands,
  And you are not the Lady Clare."

"Are ye out of your mind, my nurse, my nurse,"
  Said Lady Clare, "that ye speak so wild?"
"As God 's above," said Alice the nurse,
  "I speak the truth: you are my child.

"The old Earl's daughter died at my breast;
  I speak the truth, as I live by bread!
I buried her like my own sweet child,
  And put my child in her stead."

"Falsely, falsely have ye done,
  O mother," she said, "if this be true;—
To keep the best man under the sun
  So many years from his due."

"Nay, now, my child," said Alice the nurse,
  "But keep the secret for your life,
And all you have will be Lord Ronald's,
  When you are man and wife."

"If I 'm a beggar born," she said,
  "I will speak out, for I dare not lie.
Pull off, pull off the brooch of gold,
  And fling the diamond necklace by."

"Nay, now, my child," said Alice the nurse,
  "But keep the secret all ye can."
She said, "Not so; but I will know
  If there be any faith in man."

"Nay, now, what faith?" said Alice the nurse;
  "The man will cleave unto his right."
"And he shall have it," the lady replied,
  "Though I should die to-night."

"Yet give one kiss to your mother dear!
  Alas, my child, I sinn'd for thee."
"O mother, mother, mother," she said,
  "So strange it seems to me.

"Yet here 's a kiss for my mother dear,
 My mother dear, if this be so,
And lay your hand upon my head,
 And bless me, mother, ere I go."

She clad herself in a russet gown,
 She was no longer Lady Clare:
She went by dale, and she went by down,
 With a single rose in her hair.

The lily-white doe Lord Ronald had brought
 Leapt up from where she lay,
Dropt her head in the maiden's hand,
 And follow'd her all the way.

Down stept Lord Ronald from his tower:
 "O Lady Clare, you shame your worth!
Why come you drest like a village maid,
 That are the flower of the Earth?"

"If I come drest like a village maid,
 I am but as my fortunes are:
I am a beggar born," she said,
 "And not the Lady Clare."

"Play me no tricks," said Lord Ronald,
 "For I am yours in word and in deed;
Play me no tricks," said Lord Ronald,
 "Your riddle is hard to read."

O, and proudly stood she up!
 Her heart within her did not fail:
She look'd into Lord Ronald's eyes,
 And told him all her nurse's tale.

He laugh'd a laugh of merry scorn;
 He turn'd and kiss'd her where she stood:
"If you are not the heiress born,
 And I," said he, "the next in blood,—

"If you are not the heiress born,
 And I," said he, "the lawful heir,
We two will wed to-morrow morn,
 And you shall still be Lady Clare."

Lord Tennyson.

THE ROMANCE OF THE SWAN'S NEST.

Little Ellie sits alone
'Mid the beaches of a meadow
  By a stream-side on the grass;
  And the trees are showering down
Doubles of their leaves in shadow
  On her shining hair and face.

She has thrown her bonnet by,
And her feet she has been dipping
  In the shallow water's flow:
  Now she holds them nakedly
In her hands, all sleek and dripping,
  While she rocketh to and fro.

Little Ellie sits alone,
And the smile she softly uses
  Fills the silence like a speech,
  While she thinks what shall be done,
And the sweetest pleasure chooses
  For her future within reach.

Little Ellie in her smile
Chooses—"I will have a lover,
  Riding on a steed of steeds:
  He shall love me without guile,
And to him I will discover
  The swan's nest among the reeds.

"And the steed shall be red-roan,
And the lover shall be noble,
  With an eye that takes the breath:
  And the lute he plays upon
Shall strike ladies into trouble,
  As his sword strikes men to death.

"And the steed it shall be shod
All in silver, housed in azure,
  And the mane shall swim the wind;
  And the hoofs along the sod
Shall flash onward and keep measure,
  Till the shepherds look behind.

"But my lover will not prize
All the glory that he rides in,
  When he gazes in my face:
  He will say, 'O Love, thine eyes
Build the shrine my soul abides in,
  And I kneel here for thy grace!'

"Then, ay, then he shall kneel low,
With the red-roan steed anear him,
  Which shall seem to understand,
  Till I answer, 'Rise and go!
For the world must love and fear him
  Whom I gift with heart and hand.'

"Then he will arise so pale,
I shall feel my own lips tremble
  With a yes I must not say:
  Nathless maiden-brave, 'Farewell,'
I will utter, and dissemble—
  'Light to-morrow with to-day!'

"Then he 'll ride among the hills
To the wide world past the river,
  There to put away all wrong,
  To make straight distorted wills,
And to empty the broad quiver
  Which the wicked bear along.

"Three times shall a young foot-page
Swim the stream and climb the mountain
  And kneel down beside my feet—
  'Lo, my master sends this gage,
Lady, for thy pity's counting!
  What wilt thou exchange for it?'

"And the first time, I will send
A white rosebud for a guerdon;
  And the second time, a glove;
  But the third time—I may bend
From my pride, and answer—'Pardon,
  If he comes to take my love.'

"Then the young foot-page will run,
Then my lover will ride faster,
  Till he kneeleth at my knee:
  'I am a duke's eldest son,
Thousand serfs do call me master,
  But, O Love, I love but thee!'

"He will kiss me on the mouth
Then, and lead me as a lover
  Through the crowds that praise his deeds:
  And, when soul-tied by one troth,
Unto him I will discover
  That swan's nest among the reeds."

Little Ellie, with her smile
Not yet ended, rose up gayly,
  Tied the bonnet, donn'd the shoe,
  And went homeward, round a mile,
Just to see, as she did daily,
  What more eggs were with the two.

Pushing through the elm-tree copse,
Winding up the stream, light-hearted,
  Where the osier pathway leads,
  Past the boughs she stoops—and stops.
Lo, the wild swan had deserted,
  And a rat had gnaw'd the reeds!

Ellie went home sad and slow.
If she found the lover ever,
  With his red-roan steed of steeds,
  Sooth I know not; but I know
She could never show him,—never,
  That swan's nest among the reeds!

Elizabeth Barrett Browning.

SCENE FROM HENRY THE FOURTH.

Enter King HENRY, NORTHUMBERLAND, WORCESTER, HOTSPUR, *Sir* WALTER BLUNT, *and others.*

King. My blood hath been too cold and temperate,
Unapt to stir at these indignities,
As you have found me; for, accordingly,
You tread upon my patience: but be sure
I will from hénceforth rather be myself,
Mighty and to be fear'd, than my condition.
    Wor. Our House, my sovereign liege, little deserves
The scourge of greatness to be used on it;
And that same greatness too which our own hands
Have holp to make so portly.
    King. Worcester, get thee gone; for I do see
Danger and disobedience in thine eye:
You were about to speak, my Lord Northumberland.
    North.   Yea, my good lord.
Those prisoners in your Highness' name demanded,
Which Harry Percy here at Holmedon took,
Were, as he says, not with such strength denied
As is deliver'd to your Majesty:
Either envy, therefore, or misprision
Is guilty of this fault, and not my son.
    Hot. My liege, I did deny no prisoners.
But, I remember, when the fight was done,
When I was dry with rage and éxtreme toil,
Breathless and faint, leaning upon my sword,
Came there a certain lord, neat, trimly dress'd,
Fresh as a bridegroom; and his chin, new reap'd,
Show'd like a stubble-land at harvest-home:
He was perfumèd like a milliner;
And 'twixt his finger and his thumb he held
A pouncet-box, which ever and anon
He gave his nose, and took 't away again;
And still he smiled and talk'd;
And, as the soldiers bore dead bodies by,
He call'd them untaught knaves, unmannerly,
To bring a slovenly unhandsome corse
Betwixt the wind and his nobility.
With many holiday and lady terms

He question'd me; among the rest, demanded
My prisoners in your Majesty's behalf.
I then, all smarting with my wounds being cold,
Out of my grief and my impatience
To be so pester'd with a popinjay,
Answer'd neglectingly, I know not what,—
He should, or he should not; for 't made me mad
To see him shine so brisk and smell so sweet,
And talk so like a waiting-gentlewoman
Of guns and drums and wounds,—God save the mark!—
And telling me the sovereign'st thing on Earth
Was parmaceti for an inward bruise;
And that it was great pity, so it was,
This villainous salt-petre should be digg'd
Out of the bowels of the harmless earth,
Which many a good tall fellow had destroy'd
So cowardly; and, but for these vile guns,
He would himself have been a soldier.
This bald unjointed chat of his, my lord,
I answer'd indirectly, as I said;
And I beseech you, let not his report
Come current for an accusation
Betwixt my love and your high Majesty.
    Blunt.   The circumstance consider'd, good my lord,
Whatever Harry Percy then had said
To such a person, and in such a place,
At such a time, with all the rest re-told,
May reasonably die, and never rise
To do him wrong, or any way impeach
What then he said, so he unsay it now.
    King.   Why, yet he doth deny his prisoners,
But with proviso and exception,
That we at our own charge shall ransom straight
His brother-in-law, the foolish Mortimer;
Who, on my soul, hath willfully betray'd
The lives of those that he did lead to fight
Against the great magician, damn'd Glendower.
Shall our coffers, then,
Be emptied to redeem a traitor home?
Shall we buy treason? and indent with fears
When they have lost and forfeited themselves?
No, on the barren mountains let him starve;
For I shall never hold that man my friend

Whose tongue shall ask me for one penny cost
To ransom home revolted Mortimer.

Hot. Revolted Mortimer!
He never did fall off, my sovereign liege,
But by the chance of war: to prove that true
Needs no more but one tongue for all those wounds,
Those mouthèd wounds, which valiantly he took,
When on the gentle Severn's sedgy bank,
In single opposition, hand to hand,
He did confound the best part of an hour
In changing hardiment with great Glendower.
Three times they breathed, and three times did they drink,
Upon agreement, of swift Severn's flood;
Who then, affrighted with their bloody looks,
Ran fearfully among the trembling reeds,
And hid his crisp head in the hollow bank
Blood-stainèd with these valiant combatants.
Never did base and rotten policy
Color her working with such deadly wounds;
Nor never could the noble Mortimer
Receive so many, and all willingly:
Then let him not be slander'd with revolt.

King. Thou dost belie him, Percy, thou dost belie him;
He never did encounter with Glendower:
I tell thee,
He durst as well have met the Devil alone
As Owen Glendower for an enemy.
Art not ashamed? But, sirrah, from henceforth
Let me not hear you speak of Mortimer:
Send me your prisoners with the speediest means,
Or you shall hear in such a kind from me
As will displease you.—My Lord Northumberland,
We license your departure with your son.—
Send us your prisoners, or you 'll hear of it.

[*Exeunt King* HENRY, BLUNT, *and train.*

Hot. An if the Devil come and roar for them,
I will not send them: I will after straight,
And tell him so; for I will ease my heart,
Although it be with hazard of my head.

North. What, drunk with choler? stay, and pause awhile:
Here comes your uncle.

Re-enter WORCESTER.

Hot.   Speak of Mortimer!
Zounds, I will speak of him; and let my soul
Want mercy, if I do not join with him:
Yea, on his part I 'll empty all these veins,
And shed my dear blood drop by drop i' the dust,
But I will lift the down-trod Mortimer
As high i' the air as this unthankful King,
As this ingrate and canker'd Bolingbroke.

    Wor.   Who struck this heat up after I was gone?

    Hot.   He will, forsooth, have all my prisoners;
And when I urged the ransom once again
Of my wife's brother, then his cheek look'd pale,
And on my face he turn'd an eye of death,
Trembling even at the name of Mortimer.

    Wor.   Peace, cousin, say no more:
And now I will unclasp a secret book,
And to your quick-conceiving discontent
I 'll read you matter deep and dangerous;
As full of peril and adventurous spirit
As to o'er-walk a current roaring loud
On the unsteadfast footing of a spear.

    Hot.   If we fall in, good night, or sink or swim!
Send danger from the east unto the west,
So honor cross it from the north to south,
And let them grapple. O, the blood more stirs
To rouse a lion than to start a hare!
By Heaven, methinks it were an easy leap,
To pluck bright honor from the pale-faced Moon;
Or dive into the bottom of the deep,   •
Where fathom-line could never touch the ground,
And pluck up drownèd honor by the locks;
But out upon this half-faced fellowship!

    Wor.   Good cousin, give me audience for awhile.

    Hot.   I cry you mercy.

    Wor.   Those same noble Scots
That are your prisoners,—

    Hot.   I 'll keep them all;
By Heaven, he shall not have a Scot of them;
No, if a Scot would save his soul, he shall not:
I 'll keep them, by this hand.

    Wor.   You start away,
And lend no ear unto my purposes.
Those prisoners you shall keep;—

Hot.   Nay, I will; that 's flat.
He said he would not ransom Mortimer;
Forbade my tongue to speak of Mortimer;
But I will find him when he lies asleep,
And in his ear I 'll holla *Mortimer!*
Nay,
I 'll have a starling shall be taught to speak
Nothing but *Mortimer*, and give it him,
To keep his anger still in motion.

William Shakespeare.

BOAT SONG.

FROM "THE LADY OF THE LAKE."

Hail to the Chief who in triumph advances!
  Honor'd and bless'd be the ever-green Pine!
Long may the tree, in his banner that glances,
  Flourish, the shelter and grace of our line!
    Heaven send it happy dew,
    Earth lend it sap anew,
Gayly to bourgeon, and broadly to grow,
    While every Highland glen
    Sends back our shout again,
"Roderigh Vich Alpine dhu, ho! ieroe!"

Ours is no sapling, chance-sown by the fountain,
  Blooming in Beltane, in winter to fade;
When the whirlwind has stripp'd every leaf on the
    mountain,
  The more shall Clan-Alpine exult in her shade.
    Moor'd in the rifted rock,
    Proof to the tempest's shock,
Firmer he roots him the ruder it blow;
    Menteith and Breadalbane, then,
    Echo his praise agen,
"Roderigh Vich Alpine dhu, ho! ieroe!"

Proudly our pibroch has thrill'd in Glen Fruin,
  And Bannochar's groans to our slogan replied;
Glen Luss and Ross-dhu, they are smoking in ruin,
  And the best of Loch-Lomond lie dead on her side.

   Widow and Saxon maid
   Long shall lament our raid,
  Think of Clan-Alpine with fear and with woe;
   Lennox and Leven-glen
   Shake when they hear agen,
"Roderigh Vich Alpine dhu, ho! ieroe!"

 Row, vassals, row, for the pride of the Highlands!
  Stretch to your oars, for the ever-green Pine!
 O that the rosebud that graces yon islands,
  Were wreathed in a garland around him to twine!
   O that some seedling gem,
   Worthy such noble stem,
  Honor'd and bless'd in their shadow might grow!
   Loud should Clan-Alpine then
   Ring from her deepmost glen,
"Roderigh Vich Alpine dhu, ho! ieroe!"
         Sir Walter Scott.

THE TRIAL OF BEN THOMAS.

It was a sultry noon and Jeffersonville was brisk. As Jeffersonville is brisk only during court week, it may be inferred that court was in session.

About the large square building little groups of farmers were gathered. Within were the usual courthouse habitués,—jurors who hope in vain to "get off," and citizens of limited income who yet hope to "get on."

Apparently, there was nothing exciting on hand just then, though a murder trial had been interrupted by a temporary adjournment. But the defendant was a negro, and a murder by a negro was not a novelty. While the court was assembling, the curious might have noted the prisoner's points. His face, if it had any marked characteristic, was noted chiefly for its inexpressive lines, and its appearance was one of supreme indifference. His stout, heavy frame was clad in a common jean suit stained with months of wear, and his kinky hair was sprinkled with gray. He sat quietly, allowing his eyes to roam from face to face as the genial conversation drifted about in the groups around him. He was evidently not impressed by any sense of peril, though, when the court had adjourned, a clear case of murder had been proved against him, and only his statement and the argument remained.

Slowly the court assembled. The prisoner's counsel had introduced no testimony. A man had been stabbed by his client, had fallen dead, his hand clasped over the wound; and a knife had dropped, which the defendant's wife had seized and concealed. This had been proved by the state's witnesses.

The prisoner took the stand to make his statement. He declared emphatically that the deceased, knife in hand, had assaulted him, and that he had killed him in self-defense; that the knife which fell from the relaxing hand was the dead man's. He told the story simply, and as he began it a tall, thick-set gentleman in a gray suit, walking with the aid of a stout stick, entered the room and stood silently at the door. As the prisoner resumed his seat, the newcomer entered within the rail. He shook hands gravely with a number of the older lawyers, and took the hand the court extended to him across the desk. Then he turned, and, to the astonishment of every one, shook hands with the defendant, into whose face a light had suddenly dawned, which resolved itself into a broad, silent grin. This done, the old gentleman seated himself near the defendant's lawyer, and, leaning heavily on his massive cane, listened attentively to the speech.

The speaker was not verbose. He rapidly summed up, and laid the case before the jury in its best light. Really there was not much to be said, and he soon reached his peroration. He pictured the blasted home of the negro; his wife and babe deprived of his labor; and dwelt long on the good name he had always borne. After summing up, he took his hat and books and retired to a secluded part of the room.

The prosecuting attorney arose, and, with a few cold words, swept away the cobwebs of the case. "The man had stabbed another wantonly. If the knife were the property of the deceased, why was it not produced in court? The defendant's wife had picked it up."

He passed the case to the jury, and the judge prepared to deliver his charge, when the old gentleman in gray rose to his feet. "If your Honor please, the prisoner is entitled to the closing, and, in absence of other counsel, I beg you to mark my name for the defendant."

"Mr. Clerk," said the court, "mark General Robert Thomas for the defense." The silence was absolute; something new was coming. Only this old man, gray, grim, and majestically defiant, stood between the negro and the grave.

"The knife that was found by the dead man's side was his own. He had drawn it before he was stabbed. Ben Thomas is a brave man, a strong man; he would not have used a weapon upon him unarmed." As he spoke he drew from his bosom a long, keen knife, and rested its point gently on the table.

"It has been asked, 'Where is the dead man's knife?' Let me give you my theory: When Bill Fowler staggered back under the blow of Ben Thomas, clutching his wound, and the knife fell to the ground, the lightning's flash was not quicker than the change born in a moment in the bosom of that erring woman, the unwitting cause of the tragedy. Up to this time she had been weak and yielding; she had turned aside from the little home to gamble with strange men. In the awful moment of that tragedy, when the dancers stood horrified, this woman became, by an inspiration, a wife again. Deceived herself, she caught up the tell-tale knife, and hurled it into the swamp, destroying evidence of her husband's innocence, when she thought to have destroyed one proof of his guilt. This I say is a theory. You remember her cry was, 'Run!'

"But there is another evidence, gentlemen of the jury. Should I be forced to ask for a new trial, it will be developed that this poor woman, repentant now, thank God, walked, in three days, from the scene of that tragedy to my home, seventy miles, to ask my aid and counsel; that eluding me at Macon, though footsore and weary and crazed with grief, she returned to the swamp, and laboring under an excitement that brought the scene so vividly to her mind that she was enabled to find the knife, did find it, and but that an accident to my vehicle delayed me, it would have been produced here in evidence—"

"May it please your Honor, much as I dislike to interrupt the honorable gentleman, I do not think it is proper to introduce with the argument, evidence that has not been given upon trial."

"If your Honor please, a decision upon such a proposition is not needed. I willingly admit all that is claimed. But, sir, I offer no evidence, not even this knife, with the name of the deceased upon it, though it comes to me direct from the hand of the woman who, it has been proved, snatched from under his hand a weapon when he fell to the ground. I am , but arguing a theory to account for the facts that have been proved. But, gentlemen of the jury, not upon this theory, not upon these facts, do I base the assertion that the deceased had a knife in his hand when he made the assault. I speak from a knowledge of men. Ben Thomas would never have stabbed an unarmed man. Why do I say this? Because I know he is as brave a man as ever faced death; a faithful man; a powerful man, and conscious of his power. Such men do not use weapons upon unarmed assailants. I speak to men who reason. True reasoning with such is as strong as proof. A brave man who is full of strength never draws a weapon to repel a single assailant. The defendant drew when he saw a glittering weapon in the hand of his foe,—not from fear, because he could have fled, but to equalize the combat.

"Why do I say he is brave? Every man on this jury shouldered his musket during the war. Most of you followed the lamented Pickett. Some, perhaps, were at Gettysburg. I was there, too! I, and the only brother God ever gave me! A part of him is there yet—a part of him, but not all; for, praise God, we picked up whatever was left of him and brought it back to Georgia. I well remember that fight. The enemy stood brave and determined, and met our charges with a courage and grit that could not be shaken. Line after line melted away during those days, and at last came Pickett's charge. When that magnificent command went in, a negro man, a captain's body-servant, stood behind it waiting.

"You know the result.

"Out of that vortex of flame and that storm of lead and iron, a handful drifted back. From one to another this man of black skin ran, then returned and followed in the track of the charge. On, on he went, on through the smoke and flame; on up to the flaming cannon themselves. There he bent and lifted a form from the ground. Together they fell and rose, until, meeting them half-way, I took the burden from the hero and myself bore it on in safety. That burden was the senseless form of my brother; gashed, and bleeding, and mangled, but alive, thank God! And the man who bore him out, who came to me with him in his arms, himself shot with the fragments of a shell until his great heart was nearly dropping from his breast—that man, O my friends, sits here under my hand. See if I speak not the truth. Do you see that scar which marks his breast from left to right? That scar was won by a slave in an hour that tried the souls of freemen, and put to its test the best manhood of the South. No man who wins such wounds can thrust a knife into an unarmed assailant. I have come seventy miles in my old age to say it."

It may have been contrary to the evidence, but the jury, without leaving the room, returned a verdict of "Not guilty."

H. S. Edwards.

THE REVOLUTIONARY RISING.

Out of the North the wild news came,
Far flashing on its wings of flame,
Swift as the boreal light which flies
At midnight through the startled skies.
And there was tumult in the air,
  The fife's shrill note, the drum's loud beat,
And through the wide land everywhere
  The answering tread of hurrying feet;
While the first oath of Freedom's gun
Came on the blast from Lexington;
And Concord roused, no longer tame,
Forgot her old baptismal name,
Made bare her patriot arm of power,
And swelled the discord of the hour.

Within its shade of elm and oak
  The church of Berkley Manor stood;
There Sunday found the rural folk,
  And some esteemed of gentle blood.
  In vain their feet with loitering tread
Passed mid the graves where rank is naught;
All could not read the lesson taught
  In that republic of the dead.

How sweet the hour of Sabbath talk,
　The vale with peace and sunshine full,
Where all the happy people walk,
　Decked in their homespun flax and wool;
　Where youth's gay hats with blossoms bloom;
And every maid, with simple art,
Wears on her breast, like her own heart,
　A bud whose depths are all perfume;
While every garment's gentle stir
Is breathing rose and lavender.

The pastor came; his snowy locks
　Hallowed his brow of thought and care;
And calmly, as shepherds lead their flocks,
　He led into the house of prayer,
Then soon he rose; the prayer was strong;
The Psalm was warrior David's song;
The text, a few short words of might—
"*The Lord of Hosts shall arm the right!*"

He spoke of wrongs too long endured,
Of sacred rights to be secured;
Then from his patriot tongue of flame
The startling words for freedom came.
The stirring sentences he spake
Compelled the heart to glow or quake,
And, rising on his theme's broad wing,
　And grasping in his nervous hand
　The imaginary battle-brand,
In face of death he dared to fling
Defiance to a tyrant king.

Even as he spoke, his frame, renewed
In eloquence of attitude,
Rose, as it seemed, a shoulder higher;
Then swept his kindling glance of fire
From startled pew to breathless choir;
When suddenly his mantle wide,
His hands impatient flung aside,
And, lo! he met their wondering eyes
Complete in all a warrior's guise.

A moment there was awful pause—
When Berkley cried, "Cease, traitor, cease!
God's temple is the house of peace!"
    The other shouted, "Nay, not so,
When God is with our righteous cause;
His holiest places then are ours,
His temples are our forts and towers
    That frown upon the tyrant foe;
In this, the dawn of Freedom's day,
There is a time to fight and pray!"

And now before the open door—
    The warrior priest had ordered so—
The enlisting trumpet's sudden roar
Rang through the chapel, o'er and o'er,
    Its long·reverberating blow,
So loud and clear, it seemed the ear
Of dusty death must wake and hear.

And there the startling drum and fife
Fired the living with fiercer life;
While overhead, with wild increase,
Forgetting its ancient toll of peace,
    The great bell swung as ne'er before:
It seemed as it would never cease;
And every word its ardor flung
From off its jubilant iron tongue
    Was "War! War! War!"

"Who dares?"—this was the patriot's cry,
    As striding from the desk he came,—
"Come out with me, in Freedom's name,
For her to live, for her to die?"
A hundred hands flung up reply,
A hundred voices answered, "I!"

                              Thomas Buchanan Read.

WILLIAM TELL AMONG THE MOUNTAINS.

Ye crags and peaks, I'm with you once again!
I hold to you the hands you first beheld,
To show they still are free. Methinks I hear
A spirit in your echoes answer me,
And bid your tenant welcome to his home
Again! O, sacred forms, how proud ye look!
How high you lift your heads into the sky!
How huge you are! how mighty and how free!
Ye are the things that tower, that shine, whose smile
Makes glad, whose frown is terrible, whose forms,
Robed or unrobed, do all the impress wear
Of awe divine. Ye guards of liberty!
I'm with you once again!—I call to you
With all my voice! I hold my hands to you
To show they still are free. I rush to you,
As though I could embrace you!

Scaling yonder peak,
I saw an eagle wheeling, near its brow,
O'er the abyss. His broad, expanded wings
Lay calm and motionless upon the air,
As if he had floated there, without their aid,
By the sole act of his unlorded will,
That buoyed him proudly up! Instinctively
I bent my bow; yet wheeled he, heeding not
The death that threatened him! I could not shoot!
'Twas liberty! I turned my bow aside,
And let him soar away.

Once Switzerland was free! O, with what pride
I used to walk these hills, look up to heaven,
And bless God that it was so! It was free!
From end to end, from cliff to lake, 'twas free!
Free as our torrents are, that leap our rocks,
And plough our valleys without asking leave;
Or as our peaks, that wear their caps of snow
In very presence of the regal sun!
How happy was I in it then! I loved
Its very storms! Ay, often have I sat
In my boat, at night, when down the mountain gorge

The wind came roaring—sat in it, and eyed
The thunder breaking from his cloud, and smiled
To see him shake his lightnings o'er my head,
And think I had no master, save his own!

You know the jutting cliff, round which a track
Up hither winds, whose base is but the brow
To such another one, with scanty room
For two to pass abreast? O'ertaken there
By the mountain-blast, I 've laid me flat along;
And while gust followed gust more furiously,
As if 't would sweep me o'er the horrid brink,
And I have thought of other lands, whose storms
Are summer-flaws to those of mine, and just
Have wished me there,—the thought that mine was free
Has checked that wish; and I have raised my head,
And cried, in thraldom, to that furious wind,
"Blow on!—This is the land of liberty!"

Sheridan Knowles.

THE DYING CHRISTIAN TO HIS SOUL.

Vital spark of heavenly flame,
Quit, oh! quit this mortal frame!
Trembling, hoping, lingering, flying,—
Oh, the pain—the bliss of dying!
Cease, fond nature, cease thy strife,
And let me languish into life!

Hark! they whisper: angels say,
"Sister spirit, come away!"
What is this absorbs me quite,—
Steals my senses, shuts my sight,
Drowns my spirit, draws my breath?—
Tell me, my soul! can this be death?

The world recedes—it disappears;
Heaven opens on my eyes; my ears
    With sounds seraphic ring:
Lend, lend your wings! I mount, I fly!
O Grave! where is thy victory?
    O Death! where is thy sting?

Alexander Pope.

THE ROMANCE OF A ROSE.

It is nearly a hundred years ago
Since the day that the Count De Rochambeau,
Our ally, against the British crown,
Met Washington in Newport town.

'Twas the month of March, and the air was chill;
But bareheaded, over Aquidneck Hill,
Guest and host they took their way,
While on either side, in grand display,

A gallant army, French and fine,
Was ranged three deep in glittering line;
And the French fleet sent a welcome roar
Of a hundred guns from Conanicut shore.

And the bells rang out from every steeple,
And from street to street the Newport people
Followed and shouted with a hearty zest,
De Rochambeau and his honored guest.

And women out of the windows leant,
And out of the windows smiled and sent
Many a coy and admiring glance
To the fine young officers of France.

And the story goes that the belle of the town
Kissed a rose and flung it down
Straight at the foot of De Rochambeau;
And the gallant Frenchman, bending low,

Lifted it up with a Frenchman's grace,
And kissed it back with a smile at the face
Of the daring maiden where she stood,
Blushing out of her silken hood.

At the ball that night, so the story goes,
The Marshal of France wore a faded rose
In his gold-laced coat; but he looked in vain
For the giver's beautiful face again.

Night after night, and day after day,
She was speeding farther and farther away
From the fatal window, the fatal street,
Where her passionate heart had suddenly beat

A throb too much for the cool control
A Puritan teaches to heart and soul;
A throb too much for the wrathful eyes
Of one who watched in dismayed surprise

From the street below; and, taking gauge
Of a woman's heart in a moment's rage,
He swore, this old colonial squire,
That before the daylight should expire

This daughter of his, with her wit and grace,
Her dangerous heart and her beautiful face,
Should be on her way to a safe retreat,
Where no rose of hers could fall at the feet

Of a curséd Frenchman, high or low:
And so, while the Count De Rochambeau,
On his gold-laced coat wore a faded flower,
And awaited the giver, hour by hour,

She was sailing away in the wild March night,
On the little deck of the sloop Delight;
Guarded, even in darkness there,
By the watchful eyes of a jealous care.

Three weeks after, a brig bore down
Into the harbor of Newport town,
Towing a wreck—'twas the sloop Delight!
Off Hampton Rocks, in the very sight

Of the land she sought, she and her crew,
All on board of her, full in view
Of the storm-bound fishermen o'er the bay,
Went to their doom on that April day.

When Rochambeau heard the terrible tale
He muttered a prayer—for a moment grew pale;
Then "Mon Dieu!" he exclaimed; "so my fine
    romance,
From beginning to end, is a rose and a glance."

A rose and a glance, with a kiss thrown in—
That was all; but enough for a promise of sin,
Thought the stern old squire, when he took the gauge
Of a woman's heart in a moment's rage.

So the sad old story comes to a close;
'Tis a century since; but the world still goes
O'er the same base round, still takes the gauge
Of its brightest hearts in a moment's rage.

Nora Perry.

THE REVENGE.

At Flores in the Azores Sir Richard Grenville lay,
And a pinnace, like a flutter'd bird, came flying from
    far away:
"Spanish ships of war at sea! we have sighted fifty-
    three!"
Then sware Lord Thomas Howard: " 'Fore God, I am
    no coward;
But I cannot meet them here, for my ships are out of
    gear,
And the half my men are sick. I must fly, but follow
    quick.
We are six ships of the line; can we fight with fifty-
    three?"

Then spake Sir Richard Grenville: "I know you are no
    coward;
You fly them for a moment to fight with them again.
But I 've ninety men and more that are lying sick ashore.
I should count myself the coward if I left them, my
    Lord Howard,
To these Inquisition dogs and the devildoms of Spain."

So Lord Howard past away with five ships of war that
    day,
Till he melted like a cloud in the silent summer heaven;
But Sir Richard bore in hand all his sick men from the
    land
Very carefully and slow,
Men of Bideford in Devon,

And we laid them on the ballast down below;
For we brought them all aboard,
And they blest him in their pain, that they were not
    left to Spain,
To the thumbscrew and the stake, for the glory of the
    Lord.

He had only a hundred seamen to work the ship and to
    fight,
And he sailed away from Flores till the Spaniard came
    in sight,
With his huge sea-castles heaving upon the weather
    bow.
"Shall we fight, or shall we fly?
Good Sir Richard, tell us now,
For to fight is but to die!
There 'll be little of us left by the time this sun be set."
And Sir Richard said again: "We be all good English
    men.
Let us bang these dogs of Seville, the children of the
    devil,
For I never turn'd my back upon Don or devil yet."

Sir Richard spoke and he laugh'd, and we roar'd a hur-
    rah, and so
The little Revenge ran on sheer into the heart of the
    foe,
With her hundred fighters on deck, and her ninety sick
    below;
For half of their fleet to the right and half to the left
    were seen,
And the little Revenge ran on thro' the long sea-lane
    between.

Thousands of their soldiers look'd down from their
    decks and laugh'd,
Thousands of their seamen made mock at the mad
    little craft
Running on and on, till delay'd
By their mountain-like San Philip that, of fifteen hun-
    dred tons,
And up-shadowing high above us with her yawning
    tiers of guns,
Took the breath from our sails, and we stay'd.

And while now the great San Philip hung above us like
    a cloud
Whence the thunderbolt will fall
Long and loud,
Four galleons drew away
From the Spanish fleet that day,
And two upon the larboard and two upon the starboard
    lay,
And the battle-thunder broke from them all.

But anon the great San Philip, she bethought herself
    and went,
Having that within her womb that had left her ill-con-
    tent;
And the rest they came aboard us, and they fought us
    hand to hand,
For a dozen times they came with their pikes and
    musqueteers,
And a dozen times we shook 'em off as a dog that
    shakes his ears
When he leaps from the water to the land.

And the sun went down, and the stars came out far
    over the summer sea,
But never a moment ceased the fight of the one and
    the fifty-three.
Ship after ship, the whole night long, their high-built
    galleons came,
Ship after ship, the whole night long, with her battle-
    thunder and flame;
Ship after ship, the whole night long, drew back with
    her dead and her shame.
For some were sunk and many were shatter'd, and so
    could fight us no more—
God of battles, was ever a battle like this in the world
    before?

For he said, "Fight on! fight on!"
Tho' his vessel was all but a wreck;
And it chanced that, when half of the short summer
    night was gone,
With a grisly wound to be drest he had left the deck,
But a bullet struck him that was dressing it suddenly
    dead,

And himself he was wounded again in the side and the
head
And he said, "Fight on! fight on!"

And the night went down, and the sun smiled out far
over the summer sea,
And the Spanish fleet with broken sides lay round us all
in a ring;
But they dared not touch us again, for they fear'd that
we still could sting,
So they watch'd what the end would be.
And we had not fought them in vain,
But in perilous plight were we,
Seeing forty of our poor hundred were slain,
And half of the rest of us maim'd for life
In the crash of the cannonades and the desperate strife;
And the sick men down in the hold were most of them
stark and cold,
And the pikes were all broken or bent, and the powder
was all of it spent;
And the masts and the rigging were lying over the side;
But Sir Richard cried in his English pride,
"We have fought such a fight for a day and a night
As may never be fought again!
We have won great glory, my men!
And a day less or more
At sea or ashore,
We die—does it matter when?
Sink me the ship, Master Gunner—sink her, split her
in twain!
Fall into the hands of God, not into the hands of
Spain!"

And the gunner said, "Ay, ay," but the seamen made
reply:
"We have children, we have wives,
And the Lord hath spared our lives.
We will make the Spaniard promise, if we yield, to let
us go;
We shall live to fight again, and to strike another
blow."
And the lion there lay dying, and they yielded to the
foe.

And the stately Spanish men to their flagship bore him
 then,
Where they laid him by the mast, old Sir Richard caught
 at last,
And they praised him to his face with their courtly for-
 eign grace;
But he rose upon their decks, and he cried:
"I have fought for Queen and Faith like a valiant man
 and true;
I have only done my duty as a man is bound to do:
With a joyful spirit I Sir Richard Grenville die!"
And he fell upon their decks, and he died.

And they stared at the dead that had been so valiant
 and true,
And had holden the power and glory of Spain so cheap
That he dared her with one little ship and his English
 few;
Was he devil or man? He was devil for aught they knew,
But they sank his body with honor down into the deep,
And they mann'd the Revenge with a swarthier alien
 crew,
And away she sail'd with her loss and long'd for her
 own;
When a wind from the lands they had ruin'd awoke
 from sleep,
And the water began to heave and the weather to moan,
And or ever that evening ended a great gale blew,
And a wave like the wave that is raised by an earth-
 quake grew,
Till it smote on their hulls and their sails and their
 masts and their flags,
And the whole sea plunged and fell on the shot-shat-
 ter'd navy of Spain,
And the little Revenge herself went down by the island
 crags
To be lost evermore in the main.

         Lord Tennyson.

THE DEATH OF THE OWD SQUIRE.

'Twas a wild, mad kind of night, as black as the bottomless pit,
The wind was howling away, like a Bedlamite in a fit,
Tearing the ash boughs off, and mowing the poplars down,
In the meadows beyond the old flour mill, where you turn off to the town.

And the rain (well, it *did* rain) dashing against the window glass,
And deluging on the roof, as the Devil were come to pass;
The gutters were running in floods outside the stable-door,
And the spouts splashed from the tiles, as they would never give o'er.

Lor' how the winders rattled! you 'd almost ha' thought that thieves
Were wrenching at the shutters; while a ceaseless pelt of leaves
Flew to the doors in gusts; and I could hear the beck
Calling so loud I knew at once it was up to a tall man's neck.

We was huddling in the harness-room, by a little scrap of fire,
And Tom, the coachman, he was there, a practicing for the choir;
But it sounded dismal, anthem did, for Squire was dying fast,
And the doctor said, "Do what he would, Squire's breaking up at last."

The Death watch, sure enough, ticked loud just over th' owd mare's head,
Though he had never once been heard up there since master's boy lay dead;
And the only sound, beside Tom's toon, was the stirring in the stalls,
And the gnawing and the scratching of the rats in the owd walls.

We could n't hear Death's foot pass by, but we knew
that he was near;
And the chill rain, and the wind and cold made us all
shake with fear;
We listened to the clock upstairs, 'twas breathing soft
and low,
For the nurse said, "At the turn of the night the old
Squire's soul would go."

Master had been a wildish man, and led a roughish life;
Did n't he shoot the Bowton squire, who dared write to
his wife?
He beat the Rads at Hindon town, I heard in twenty-
nine,
When every pail in market-place was brimmed with red
port wine.

And as for hunting, bless your soul, why for forty years
or more
He'd kept the Marley hounds, man, as his fayther did
afore;
And now to die, and in his bed—the season just begun—
"It made him fret," the doctor said, "as it might do
any one."

And when the young sharp lawyer came to see him sign
his will,
Squire made me blow my horn outside as we were going
to kill;
And we turned the hounds out in the court—that seemed
to do him good;
For he swore, and sent us off to seek a fox in Thornhill
wood.

But then the fever it rose high, and he would go see the
room
Where mistress died ten years ago when Lammastide
shall come;
I mind the year, because our mare at Salisbury broke
down;
Moreover, the town hall was burnt at Steeple Dinton
town.

It might be two, or half-past two, the wind seemed
    quite asleep;
Tom, he was off, but I awake, sat watch and ward to
    keep;
The moon was up, quite glorious like, the rain no longer
    fell,
When all at once out clashed and clanged the rusty
    turret bell,

That had n't been heard for twenty year, not since the
    Luddite days;
Tom he leaped up, and I leaped up, for all the house
    ablaze
Had sure not scared us half as much, and out we ran
    like mad,
I, Tom, and Joe, the whipper in, and t' little stable lad.

"He 's killed himself," that 's the idea that came into
    my head;
I felt as sure as though I saw Squire Barrowby was
    dead;
When all at once a door flew back, and he met us face
    to face;
His scarlet coat was on his back, and he looked like
    the old race.

The nurse was clinging to his knees, and crying like a
    child;
The maids were sobbing on the stairs, for he looked
    fierce and wild;
"Saddle my Lightning Bess, my men," that 's what he
    said to me:
"The moon is up, we 're sure to find at Stop or Etterly.

"Get out the dogs; I 'm well to-night, and young again
    and sound,
I 'll have a run once more before they put me under-
    ground;
They brought my father home feet first, and it never
    shall be said
That his son Joe, who rode so straight, died quietly in
    his bed.

"Brandy!" he cried; "a tumbler full, you women howl-
    ing there;"
Then clapped the old black velvet cap upon his long
    gray hair,
Thrust on his boots, snatched down his whip, though he
    was old and weak,
There was a devil in his eye, that would not let me
    speak.

We loosed the dogs to humor him, and sounded on the
    horn;
The moon was up above the woods, just east of Hag-
    gard Bourne;
I buckled Lightning's throat-latch fast; the Squire was
    watching me;
He let the stirrups down himself so quick, yet care-
    fully.

Then up he got and spurred the mare, and, ere I well
    could mount,
He drove the yard gate open, man; and called to old
    Dick Blount,
Our huntsman, dead five years ago—for the fever rose
    again,
And was spreading like a flood of flame, fast up into his
    brain.

Then off he flew before the dogs, yelling to call us on,
While we stood there, all pale and dumb, scarce know-
    ing he was gone;
We mounted, and below the hill we saw the fox break
    out
And down the covert ride we heard the old squire's
    parting shout.

And in the moonlit meadow mist we saw him fly the
    rail
Beyond the hurdles by the beck, just half way down
    the vale;
I saw him breast fence after fence—nothing could turn
    him back;
And in the moonlight after him streamed out the brave
    old pack.

'Twas like a dream, Tom cried to me, as we rode free
    and fast,
Hoping to turn him at the brook, that could not well
    be past,
For it was swollen with the rain; but ah, 'twas not to
    be;
Nothing could stop old Lightning Bess but the broad
    breast of the sea.

The hounds swept on, and well in front the mare had
    got her stride;
She broke across the fallow land that runs by the down
    side;
We pulled up on Chalk Linton Hill, and as we stood us
    there,
Two fields beyond we saw the Squire fall stone dead
    from the mare.

Then she swept on, and in full cry, the hounds went
    out of sight;
A cloud came over the broad moon and something
    dimmed our sight,
As Tom and I bore master home, both speaking under
    breath;
And that's the way I saw th' owd Squire ride boldly to
    his death.

Anonymous.

THE DREAM OF EUGENE ARAM.

'Twas in the prime of summer time,
    An evening calm and cool,
And four-and-twenty happy boys
    Came bounding out of school;
There were some that ran, and some that leapt
    Like troutlets in a pool.

Away they sped with gamesome minds
    And souls untouched by sin;
To a level mead they came, and there
    They drave the wickets in;
Pleasantly shone the setting sun
    Over the town of Lynn.

Like sportive deer they coursed about,
    And shouted as they ran,
Turning to mirth all things of earth
    As only boyhood can;
But the usher sat remote from all,
    A melancholy man!

His hat was off, his vest apart,
    To catch heaven's blessed breeze;
For a burning thought was in his brow,
    And his bosom ill at ease;
So he leaned his head on his hands, and read
    The book between his knees.

Leaf after leaf he turned it o'er,
    Nor ever glanced aside, —
For the peace of his soul he read that book
    In the golden eventide;
Much study had made him very lean,
    And pale, and leaden-eyed.

At last he shut the ponderous tome;
    With a fast and fervent grasp
He strained the dusky covers close,
    And fixed the brazen hasp:
"O God! could I so close my mind,
    And clasp it with a clasp!"

Then leaping on his feet upright,
    Some moody turns he took, —
Now up the mead, then down the mead,
    And past a shady nook, —
And, lo! he saw a little boy
    That pored upon a book.

"My gentle lad, what is 't you read, —
    Romance or fairy fable?
Or is it some historic page,
    Of kings and crowns unstable?"
The young boy gave an upward glance, —
    "It is 'The Death of Abel.'"

The usher took six hasty strides,
   As smit with sudden pain,—
Six hasty strides beyond the place,
   Then slowly back again;
And down he sat beside the lad,
   And talked to him of Cain;

And, long since then, of bloody men,
   Whose deeds tradition saves;
Of lonely folk cut off unseen,
   And hid in sudden graves;
Of horrid stabs, in groves forlorn,
   And murders done in caves;

And how the sprites of injured men
   Shriek upward from the sod,—
Ay, how the ghostly hand will point
   To show the burial clod;
And unknown facts of guilty acts
   Are seen in dreams from God!

He told how murderers walked the earth,
   Beneath the curse of Cain,—
With crimson clouds before their eyes,
   And flames about their brain;
For blood has left upon their souls
   Its everlasting stain.

"And well," quoth he, "I know for truth,
   Their pangs must be extreme,—
Woe, woe, unutterable woe,—
   Who spill life's sacred stream!
For why? Methought, last night, I wrought
   A murder, in a dream!

"One that had never done me wrong—
   A feeble man and old;
I led him to a lonely field,—
   The moon shone clear and cold:
Now here, said I, this man shall die,
   And I will have his gold!

"Two sudden blows with a ragged stick,
  And one with a heavy stone,
One hurried gash with a hasty knife,—
  And then the deed was done:
There was nothing lying at my foot
  But lifeless flesh and bone!

"Nothing but lifeless flesh and bone,
  That could not do me ill;
And yet I feared him all the more,
  For lying there so still:
There was a manhood in his look,
  That murder could not kill!

"And, lo! the universal air
  Seemed lit with ghastly flame,—
Ten thousand, thousand dreadful eyes
  Were looking down in blame;
I took the dead man by his hand,
  And called upon his name.

"O God! it made me quake to see
  Such sense within the slain;
But, when I touched the lifeless clay,
  The blood gushed out amain!
For every clot a burning spot
  Was scorching in my brain!

"My head was like an ardent coal,
  My heart as solid ice;
My wretched, wretched soul, I knew,
  Was at the Devil's price.
A dozen times I groaned,—the dead
  Had never groaned but twice.

"And now, from forth the frowning sky,
  From the heaven's topmost height,
I heard a voice,—the awful voice
  Of the blood-avenging sprite:
'Thou guilty man! take up thy dead,
  And hide it from my sight!'

"And I took the dreary body up,
  And cast it in a stream,—
The sluggish water black as ink,
  The depth was so extreme;
My gentle boy, remember, this
  Is nothing but a dream!

"Down went the corse with a hollow plunge,
  And it vanished in the pool;
Anon I cleansed my bloody hands,
  And washed my forehead cool,
And sat among the urchins young,
  That evening, in the school.

"O Heaven! to think of their white souls,
  And mine so black and grim!
I could not share in childish prayer,
  Nor join in evening hymn;
Like a devil of the pit I seemed,
  'Mid holy cherubim!

"And peace went with them, one and all,
  And each calm pillow spread;
But Guilt was my grim Chamberlain
  That lighted me to bed;
And drew my midnight curtains round,
  With fingers bloody red!

"All night I lay in agony,
  In anguish dark and deep;
My fevered eyes I dared not close,
  But stared aghast at Sleep:
For Sin had rendered unto her
  The keys of Hell to keep!

"All night I lay in agony,
  From weary chime to chime,
With one besetting, horrid hint,
  That racked me all the time;
A mighty yearning, like the first
  Fierce impulse unto crime!

"One stern tyrannic thought, that made
  All other thoughts its slave;
Stronger and stronger every pulse
  Did that temptation crave,—
Still urging me to go and see
  The dead man in his grave!

"Heavily I rose up, as soon
  As light was in the sky,
And sought the black, accurséd pool
  With a wild misgiving eye;
And I saw the Dead in the river bed,
  For the faithless stream was dry.

"Merrily rose the lark, and shook
  The dewdrop from its wing;
But I never marked its morning flight,
  I never heard it sing:
For I was stooping once again
  Under the horrid thing.

"With breathless speed, like a soul in chase,
  I took him up and ran;—
There was no time to dig a grave
  Before the day began:
In a lonesome wood, with heaps of leaves,
  I hid the murdered man!

"And all that day I read in school,
  But my thought was other where;
As soon as the midday task was done,
  In secret I was there:
And a mighty wind had swept the leaves,
  And still the corpse was bare!

"Then down I cast me on my face,
  And first began to weep,
For I knew my secret then was one
  That earth refused to keep:
Or land or sea, though he should be
  Ten thousand fathoms deep.

"So wills the fierce avenging Sprite,
   Till blood for blood atones!
Ay, though he 's buried in a cave,
   And trodden down with stones,
And years have rotted off his flesh,—
   The world shall see his bones!

"Oh, God! that horrid, horrid dream
   Besets me now awake!
Again—again, with dizzy brain,
   The human life I take;
And my right red hand grows raging hot,
   Like Cranmer's at the stake.

"And still no peace for the restless clay,
   Will wave or mold allow;
The horrid thing pursues my soul,—
   It stands before me now!"
The fearful boy looked up and saw
   Huge drops upon his brow.

That very night, while gentle sleep
   The urchin eyelids kissed,
Two stern-faced men set out from Lynn,
   Through the cold and heavy mist;
And Eugene Aram walked between,
   With gyves upon his wrist.

Thomas Hood.

JEAN VALJEAN.

Jean Valjean was an escaped convict. In his youth he had stolen a loaf of bread for his sister's starving children, for which crime he had spent nineteen years as a galley slave.

Through the influence of a Bishop, the only man who had ever been kind to him, Jean Valjean had taken a new departure in life. He went to a town where he was not known, worked hard, and soon became a rich man at the head of a great factory. He became so well known and so dearly beloved for his many deeds of kindness that he was unanimously elected Mayor of the city.

He had held this position for about five years, having assumed the name of Monsieur Madeleine, when he learned that in a neighboring town an old man was to be tried for stealing, and that this man was strongly suspected of being the long-lost Jean Valjean, in which case the punishment would be the galleys for life. The real Jean Valjean would have to reach Arras the next day in order to prevent an innocent man from being convicted. He passed the night in awful conflict with himself. . . .

He examined the situation and found it an unheard of one, so unheard of that, in the midst of his reverie, by some strange impulse of almost inexplicable anxiety, he rose from his chair and bolted his door. He feared lest something might yet enter. A moment after he blew out his light. It annoyed him. It seemed to him that somebody could see him. Somebody? Who? Alas! what he wanted to keep out of doors had entered; what he wanted to render blind was looking upon him — his conscience.

"Well, what am I afraid of? Why do I ponder over these things? Have I the right to disarrange what Providence arranges? No, let the matter alone! let us not interfere with God."

But the current of his thoughts had not changed. He still saw his duty, written in luminous letters which flared out before his eyes. "Go! Avow the name! Denounce thyself."

Denounce himself! Great God! Give himself up! He saw with infinite despair all that he must leave, all that he must resume. He must then bid farewell to this existence, so good, so pure, so radiant, to this respect of all, to honor, to liberty! No more would he go out in the fields; never again would he hear the birds singing in the month of May; never more give alms to the little children; no longer would he feel the sweetness of gratitude and love; instead of that, the galley crew, the iron collar, the red blouse, the chain at his foot, fatigue, the dungeon, the plank-bed, all these horrors which he knew so well! At his age, after being what he was! If he were still young! But so old, to be tumbled about by the prison guard, to be struck by the jailer's stick, to endure the curiosity of strangers, who would be told, "This one is the famous Jean Valjean, who was Mayor of M——m!!"

At that moment there was a rap at the door of his room. He shuddered from head to foot.

"Who is there?"

"I, Monsieur Mayor."

He recognized the voice of the old woman, his portress.

"The driver says he has come for Monsieur, the Mayor."

There was a long silence. He examined the flame of the candle with a stupid air, took some of the melted wax from around the wick and rolled it in his fingers. The old woman ventured to speak again.

"Monsieur Mayor, what shall I say?"

"Say that it is right, and that I am coming down."

It was broad day when he arrived at Herdin. He stopped before an inn to let his horse breathe and to give him some oats. The stable-boy stooped down suddenly and examined the left wheel, then asked:

"Have you come far?"

"Five leagues from here."

It is a miracle that you have come five leagues without tumbling you and your horse into some ditch on the way. Look for yourself."

The wheel, in fact, was badly damaged. The wheel-wright came and examined it.

"Can you mend that wheel on the spot? I must leave in an hour at the latest."

"Impossible to-day! There are two spokes and a hub to be repaired. Monsieur cannot start again before to-morrow."

"My business cannot wait until to-morrow. Instead of mending this wheel, cannot it be replaced?"

"It's of no use, Monsieur. I have nothing but cart wheels to sell. We are a small place here."

"But I can surely find in the village a horse to let?"

"It would take a better horse than there is in these parts to reach Arras before to-morrow."

"Is there no livery stable in the village?"

"No!"

He felt an immense joy. It was evident that Providence was in the matter. It was Providence that had broken the wheel of the tilbury, and stopped him on his way. He had not yielded to the first summons; he had made all possible effort to continue his journey; he had faithfully and scrupulously exhausted every means.

"Monsieur," said a woman standing near, "my boy tells me that you are anxious to hire a carriage?" This simple speech, made by a poor woman, made him cold. He thought he saw the hand he was but now freed from reappear in the shadow behind him, all ready to seize him again.

"Yes, good woman, I am looking for a carriage to hire, but there is none in the place."

"Yes, there is." He shuddered. The fatal hand had closed on him again. The poor woman had, in fact, under a shed, a sort of willow cariole. It was a frightful go-cart; it had no springs, but it went upon two wheels, and could go to Arras. He paid what was asked, and resumed the route he had followed since morning. It was nearly eight o'clock in the evening when the cariole drove into the yard of the Hotel de la Poste at Arras. He was not acquainted with the city; the streets were dark, and he went haphazard. A citizen came along with a lantern.

"Monsieur, the courthouse, if you please?"

"If Monsieur wishes to see a trial he is rather late. Ordinarily, the sessions close at six o'clock." However, when they reached the great square, the citizen showed him four long, lighted windows on the front of a vast dark building.

"Faith, Monsieur, you are in time, you are fortunate."

Suddenly, without knowing how, he found himself near the door; he seized the knob convulsively; the door opened; he was in the courtroom.

It was a large hall, dimly lighted, and noisy and silent by turns, where all the machinery of a criminal trial was exhibited with its petty, yet solemn gravity.

No man in this multitude paid any attention to him. All eyes converged on a single point, a wooden bench placed along the wall at the left hand of the judge.

Upon this bench, which was lighted by several candles, was a man between two officers. This was the man. He did not look for him, he saw him. His eyes went towards him naturally, as if they had known in advance where he was.

Judges, clerks, a throng of heads cruelly curious—he had seen all these once before, twenty-seven years ago. He had fallen again upon these fearful things; they were before him; they moved, they had being; it was no longer an effort of his memory, a mirage of his fancy; he saw reappearing and living again around him, with all the frightfulness of reality, the monstrous visions of the past.

All this was yawning before him. Stricken with horror he closed his eyes and exclaimed from the depths of his soul, "Never!"

The judge gave an order, and a moment afterwards a door opened and an officer led in the first witness, the convict Brevet.

"Brevet, look well upon the prisoner, collect your remembrance, and say on your soul and conscience whether you still recognize this man as your former friend in the galleys, Jean Valjean."

"Yes, your honor, I was the first to recognize him, and still do so. This man is Jean Valjean, who came to Toulon in 1796 and left in 1815. I recognize him now positively."

Another witness was brought in, a convict for life, as was shown by his red cloak and green cap.

The judge addressed nearly the same words to him as to Brevet.

"Gad, do I recognize him? We were five years on the same chain."

An officer brought in Cochepaille, another convict for life. His testimony was: "It is Jean Valjean, the same they called Jean the Jack, he was so strong."

A buzz ran through the crowd and almost invaded the jury. It was evident that the man was lost.

"Officers," said the judge, "enforce order; I am about to sum up the case."

At this moment there was a movement near the judge. Monsieur Madeleine, who had been sitting among the privileged spectators behind the court, had risen, pushed open the low door which separated the tribunal from the bar, and was standing in the center of the hall. All eyes were strained towards him as he exclaimed, "Gentlemen of the jury, release the accused. Your honor, order my arrest. He is not the man whom you seek; it is I! I am Jean Valjean!!

Victor Hugo.

THE BOY ORATOR OF ZEPATA CITY.

It seemed a particularly happy and appropriate circumstance that the first business in the new courtroom should be, of itself, of an important and momentous nature, something that dealt not only with the present, but with the past of Zepata.

Abe Barrow had been closely associated with the early history of Zepata; he had killed in his day several of the Zepata citizens, and two visiting brother-desperadoes, and the corner where his gambling-house had stood was still known as Barrow's Corner. Ten years before, the murder of Deputy-Sheriff Welsh had led him to the penitentiary, and a month previous to the opening of the new courthouse he had been freed, and arrested at the prison gate to stand trial for the murder of Hubert Thompson. The fight with Thompson had been a fair fight—as those said who remembered it—and Thompson was a man they could well spare; but the case against Barrow had been prepared during his incarceration by the new and youthful district attorney, "Judge" Henry Harvey, and as it offered a fitting sacrifice for the dedication of the new temple of justice, the people were satisfied and grateful.

Barrow's wife, a thin, yellow-faced woman in a mean-fitting, showy gown, sat at the district attorney's elbow. She was the only woman in the room.

Harry Harvey, "The Boy Orator of Zepata City," as he was called, turned slowly on his heels, and swept the courtroom carelessly with a glance of his clever black eyes. The moment was his. He saw all the men he knew — the men who made his little world — crowding silently forward, forgetful of the heat, of the suffocating crush of those about them, of the wind that rattled the doors in the corridors, and conscious only of him.

"This man," he said, and as he spoke even the wind in the corridors hushed for the moment, "is no part or parcel of Zepata City of to-day. He comes to us a relic of the past, a past that was full of hardships and glorious efforts in the face of daily disappointments, embitterments, and rebuffs. But the part *this* man played in that past, lives only in the rude court-records of that day, in the traditions of the gambling-hell and the saloons, and on the headstones of his victims. Gentlemen, the 'bad man' has become an unknown quantity in Zepata City. It lies with you to see that he remains so. This man, Abe Barrow, has enjoyed a reputation as a 'bad man,' a desperate and brutal ruffian. Free him to-day, and you set a premium on such reputations. Acquit him of this crime, and you encourage others to like evil. Let him go, and he will walk the streets with a swagger, and boast that you were afraid to touch him—*afraid*, gentlemen—and children and women will point after him as the man who has sent nine others into eternity, and who yet walks the street a free man.

"For the last ten years, your honor, this man, Abner Barrow, has been serving a term of imprisonment in the state penitentiary; I ask you to send him back there again for the remainder of his life. Abe Barrow is out of date. He has missed step with the march of progress, and has been out of step for ten years. It cannot be said of us that we have sat idle in the market-place. We have advanced and advanced in the last ten years, until we have reached the very foremost place with civilized people. This Rip Van Winkle of the past returns to find a city where he left a prairie town; a bank where he spun his roulette-wheel; this magnificent courthouse instead of a vigilance committee! He is there, in the prisoner's pen, a convicted murderer and an unconvicted assassin, the last of his race—the bullies and bad men of the border —a thing to be forgotten and put away forever from the sight of men. And I ask you, gentlemen, to put him away where he will not hear the voice of man nor children's laughter, nor see a woman smile; where he will not even see the face of the warden who feeds him, nor sunlight except as it is filtered through the iron bars of a jail. Bury him with the bitter past, with the lawlessness that has gone — that has gone, thank God! — and which must *not* return."

The district attorney sat down suddenly, and was conscious of nothing until the foreman pronounced the prisoner at the bar guilty of murder in the second degree.

Judge Truax leaned across his desk and said, simply, that it lay in his power to sentence the prisoner to not less than two years confinement in the state penitentiary, or for the remainder of his life.

"Before I deliver sentence on you, Abner Barrow," he said, with an old man's kind severity, "is there anything you have to say on your own behalf?"

The district attorney turned his face, as did all the others, but he did not see the prisoner—he still saw himself holding the courtroom with a spell, and heard his own periods ringing against the whitewashed ceiling. The others saw a tall, broad-shouldered man leaning heavily forward over the bar of the prisoner's box. His face was white with the prison tan, markedly so in contrast with those sunburnt by the wind and sun turned towards him, and pinched and hollow-eyed and worn. When he spoke, his voice had the huskiness which comes from non-use, and cracked and broke like a child's.

"I do n't know, Judge, that I have anything to say in my own behalf. I guess what the gentleman said about me is all there is to say. I *am* a back number, I *am* out of date; I *was* a loafer and a blackguard. He told you I had no part or parcel in this city, or in this world; that I belonged to the past; that I ought to be dead. Now that 's not so. I have just one thing that belongs to this city, and to this world—and to me; one thing that I could n't take to jail with me, and that I 'll have to leave behind me when I go back to it. I mean my wife. You, sir, remember her, sir, when I married her twelve years ago. She was Henry Holman's daughter. I took her from the home she had with her father against that gentleman's wishes, sir, to live with me over my dance-hall. You may remember her as she was then. She gave up everything a woman ought to have, to come to me. She thought she was going to be happy with me; that 's why she come, I guess. Maybe she was happy for about two weeks. After that first two weeks her life, sir, was a hell, and I made it a hell. Respectable women would n't speak to her because she was my wife; even them that were friends of hers when she lived on the ranch, would n't speak to her because she was my wife—and she had no children. That was her life. She lived alone over the dance-hall, and sometimes when I was drunk—I beat her.

"At the end of two years I killed Welsh, and they sent me to the penitentiary for ten years, and she was free. She could have gone back to her folks and got a divorce if she 'd wanted to, and never seen me again. It was an escape most women 'd gone down on their knees and thanked their Maker for.

"But what did this woman do—my wife, the woman I misused and beat and dragged down in the mud with me? She was too mighty proud to go back to her people, or to the friends who shook her when she was in trouble; and she sold out the place, and bought a ranch with the money, and worked it by herself, worked it day and night, until in ten years she had made herself an old woman, as you see she is to-day.

"And for what? To get *me* free again; to bring *me* things to eat in jail, and picture papers, and tobacco— when she was living on bacon and potatoes, and drinking alkali water—working to pay for a lawyer to fight for *me* —to pay for the *best* lawyer."

The man stopped suddenly and turned with a puzzled look towards where his wife sat, for she had dropped her head on the table in front of her, and he had heard her sobbing.

"And what I want to ask of you, sir, is to let me have two years out of jail to show her how I feel about it. It 's all I 've thought of when I was in jail, to be able to see her sitting in her own kitchen with her hands folded, and me working and sweating in the fields for her, working till every bone ached, trying to make it up to her.

"And I can't," the man cried, suddenly, losing the control he had forced upon himself, and tossing his hands up above his head, and with his eyes fixed hopelessly on the bowed head before him. "I can't! It 's too late! It 's too late! Do n't send me back for life! Give me a few years to work for her—two years, one year,—to show her what I feel here, what I never felt for her before. Look at her, gentlemen, look how worn she is, and poorly, and look at her hands, and you men must feel how I feel —I do n't ask you for myself. I do n't want to go free on my own account. My God! Judge, do n't bury me alive, as that man asked you to. I only want to live with her. Give me this last chance. Let me prove that what I 'm saying is true."

The man stopped and stood, searching with desperate eagerness from face to face. The gentlemen of the jury sat quite motionless, looking straight ahead. No one moved until there was a sudden stir around the district attorney's table, and the men stepped aside and let the woman pass them and throw herself against the prisoner's box. The prisoner bent his tall, gaunt figure over the rail, and as the woman pressed his one hand against her face, touched her shoulders with the other awkwardly.

"There now, do n't you take on so. Now you know how I feel, it 's all right; do n't take on."

Judge Truax looked at the paper on his desk for some seconds, and raised his head, coughing as he did so. "It lies—" Judge Truax began, and then stopped, and began again in a more certain tone. "It lies at the discretion of this court to sentence the prisoner to a term of imprisonment of two years, or for an indefinite period, or for life. Owing to— On account of certain circumstances which were—have arisen—this sentence is suspended. This court stands adjourned."

As he finished, he sprang out of his chair impulsively, and placed his hand upon the district attorney's shoulder.

"Harry! Harry, my boy, could you go to Austin and repeat the speech that man has just made to the governor?"

The boy orator laughed, and took one of the older man's hands in both of his, and pressed it quickly. "I 'd like mighty well to try," he said.

Richard Harding Davis.

YE MARINERS OF ENGLAND.

Ye mariners of England,
    That guard our native seas;
Whose flag has braved, a thousand years,
    The battle and the breeze!
Your glorious standard launch again
    To match another foe!
And sweep through the deep,
    While the stormy winds do blow;
While the battle rages loud and long,
    And the stormy winds do blow.

The spirit of your fathers
   Shall start from every wave;
For the deck it was their field of fame,
   And Ocean was their grave.
Where Blake and mighty Nelson fell,
   Your manly hearts shall glow,
As ye sweep through the deep,
   While the stormy winds do blow;
While the battle rages loud and long,
   And the stormy winds do blow.

Britannia needs no bulwarks,
   No towers along the steep;
Her march is o'er the mountain waves,
   Her home is on the deep.
With thunders from her native oak,
   She quells the floods below,—
As they roar on the shore,
   When the stormy winds do blow;
When the battle rages loud and long,
   And the stormy winds do blow.

The meteor flag of England
   Shall yet terrific burn;
Till danger's troubled night depart,
   And the star of peace return.
Then, then, ye ocean warriors!
   Our song and feast shall flow
To the fame of your name,
   When the storm has ceased to blow;
When the fiery fight is heard no more
   And the storm has ceased to blow.
               Thomas Campbell.

BATTLE HYMN OF THE REPUBLIC.

Mine eyes have seen the glory of the coming of the
      Lord;
He is trampling out the vintage where the grapes of
      wrath are stored;
He hath loosed the fateful lightning of His terrible
      swift sword,
          His truth is marching on.

I have seen Him in the watch-fires of a hundred circling
      camps;
They have builded Him an altar in the evening dews and
      damps;
I can read His righteous sentence by the dim and flaring
      lamps,
          His days are marching on.

I have read a fiery gospel, writ in burnished rows of
      steel;
"As ye deal with My contemners, so with you My grace
      shall deal;
Let the Hero born of woman, crush the serpent with
      His heel,
          Since God is marching on."

He has sounded forth the trumpet that shall never call
      retreat;
He is sifting out the hearts of men before His judgment
      seat;
O, be swift, my soul, to answer Him! be jubilant my
      feet!
          Our God is marching on.

In the beauty of the lilies Christ was born across the sea,
With a glory in His bosom that transfigures you and
      me;
As He died to make men holy, let us die to make men
      free,
          While God is marching on.
                Julia Ward Howe.

HIGH-TIDE ON THE COAST OF LINCOLNSHIRE.

The old mayor climbed the belfry tower,
 The ringers run by two, by three;
"Pull! if ye never pulled before;
 Good ringers, pull your best," quoth hee.
"Play uppe, play uppe, O Boston bells!
Ply all your changes, all your swells!
  Play uppe *The Brides of Enderby!*"

Men say it was a "stolen tyde,"—
 The Lord that sent it, He knows all,
But in myne ears doth still abide
 The message that the bells let fall;
And there was naught of strange, beside
The flights of mews and peewits pied,
 By millions crouched on the old sea-wall.

I sat and spun within the doore;
 My thread brake off, I raised myne eyes:
The level sun, like ruddy ore,
 Lay sinking in the barren skies;
And dark against day's golden death
She moved where Lindis wandereth!—
My sonne's faire wife, Elizabeth.

"Cusha! Cusha! Cusha!" calling
 Ere the early dews were falling,
 Farre away I heard her song.
"Cusha! Cusha!" all along
Where the reedy Lindis floweth
  Floweth, floweth,
From the meads where melick groweth
Faintly came her milking-song.

"Cusha! Cusha! Cusha!" calling
"For the dews will soone be falling;
Leave your meadow grasses mellow,
  Mellow, mellow,
Quit your cowslips, cowslips yellow!
Come uppe, Whitefoot! come uppe, Lightfoot!
Quit the stalks of parsley hollow,
  Hollow, hollow!

Come uppe, Jetty! rise and follow;
From the clovers lift your head!
Come uppe, Whitefoot! come uppe, Lightfoot!
Come uppe, Jetty! rise and follow,
Jetty, to the milking-shed.''

If it be long—ay, long ago—
    When I beginne to think howe long,
Againe I hear the Lindis flow,
    Swift as an arrowe, sharpe and strong;
And all the aire, it seemeth mee,
Bin full of floating bells (sayth shee),
That ring the tune of *Enderby*.

Alle fresh the level pasture lay,
    And not a shadowe mote be seene,
Save where, full fyve good miles away,
    The steeple towered from out the greene.
And lo! the great belle farre and wide
Was heard in all the country side
That Saturday at eventide.

The swannerds, where their sedges are,
    Moved on in sunset's golden breath;
The shepherde lads I heard afarre,
    And my sonne's wife, Elizabeth;
Till, floating o'er the grassy sea,
Came downe that kyndly message free,
The Brides of Mavis Enderby.

Then some looked uppe into the sky,
    And all along where Lindis flows
To where the goodly vessels lie,
    And where the lordly steeple shows.
They sayde, ''And why should this thing be,
What danger lowers by land or sea?
They ring the tune of *Enderby*.

''For evil news from Mablethorpe,
    Of pyrate galleys, warping down,—
For shippes ashore beyond the scorpe,
    They have not spared to wake the towne;

But while the west bin red to see,
And storms be none, and pyrates flee,
Why ring *The Brides of Enderby?*"

I looked without, and lo! my sonne
    Came riding downe with might and main;
He raised a shout as he drew on,
    Till all the welkin rang again:
"Elizabeth! Elizabeth!"
(A sweeter woman ne'er drew breath
Than my sonne's wife, Elizabeth.)

"The old sea-wall" (he cried) "is downe!
    The rising tide comes on apace;
And boats adrift in yonder towne
    Go sailing uppe the market-place!"
He shook as one that looks on death:
"God save you, mother!" straight he sayth;
"Where is my wife, Elizabeth?"

"Good sonne, where Lindis winds away
    With her two bairns I marked her long;
And ere yon bells beganne to play,
    Afar I heard her milking-song."
He looked across the grassy sea,
To right, to left, *Ho, Enderby!*
They rang *The Brides of Enderby.*

With that he cried and beat his breast;
    For lo! along the river's bed
A mighty eygre reared his crest,
    And uppe the Lindis raging sped.
It swept with thunderous noises loud,—
Shaped like a curling snow-white cloud,
Or like a demon in a shroud.

And rearing Lindis, backward pressed,
    Shook all her trembling bankes amaine;
Then madly at the eygre's breast
    Flung uppe her weltering walls again.
Then bankes came downe with ruin and rout,
Then beaten foam flew round about,—
Then all the mighty floods were out.

So tarre, so fast, the eygre drave,
    The heart had hardly time to beat
Before a shallow seething wave
    Sobbed in the grasses at oure feet:
The feet had hardly time to flee
Before it brake against the knee,—
And all the world was in the sea.

Upon the roofe we sate that night;
    The noise of bells went sweeping by;
I marked the lofty beacon light
    Stream from the church tower, red and high,—
A lurid mark, and dread to see;
And awsome bells they were to mee,
That in the dark rang *Enderby.*

They rang the sailor lads to guide,
    From roofe to roofe who fearless rowed;
And I,—my sonne was at my side,
    And yet the ruddy beacon glowed;
And yet he moaned beneath his breath,
"O, come in life, or come in death!
O lost! my love, Elizabeth!"

And didst thou visit him no more?
    Thou didst, thou didst, my daughter deare,
The waters laid thee at his doore
    Ere yet the early dawn was clear!
Thy pretty bairns in fast embrace,
The lifted sun shone on thy face,
Downe drifted to thy dwelling-place.

That *flow* strewed wrecks about the grass,
    That *ebbe* swept out the flocks to sea,—
A fatal *ebbe* and *flow*, alas!
    To manye more than myne and mee;
But each will mourne his own (she sayth),
And sweeter woman ne'er 'drew breath
Than my sonne's wife, Elizabeth.

I shall never hear her more
By the reedy Lindis shore,
"Cusha! Cusha! Cusha!" calling,
    Ere the early dews be falling;

I shall never hear her song,
"Cusha! Cusha!" all along,
  Where the sunny Lindis floweth,
      Goeth, floweth,
  From the meads where melick groweth,
  Where the water winding down,
  Onward floweth to the town.
  I shall never see her more,
  Where the reeds and rushes quiver,
      Shiver, quiver,
  Stand beside the sobbing river,—
  Sobbing, throbbing, in its falling
  To the sandy lonesome shore.

Jean Ingelow.

HER FIRST APPEARANCE.

It was the first night of "The Sultana," and every member of the Lester Comic Opera Company, from Lester himself down to the wardrobe woman's son, who would have had to work if his mother lost her place, was sick with anxiety.

As Van Bibber passed the stage door, Lester came off the stage and beckoned to him violently. "Come here," he said, "you ought to see this; the children are doing their turn. You want to hear them. They 're great!"

There were over a dozen children before the footlights, with the prima donna in the center. They seemed entirely too much at home and too self-conscious to please Van Bibber, but there was one exception. The one exception was the smallest of them, a very, very little girl, with long auburn hair and black eyes; such a very little girl that every one in the house looked at her first, and then looked at no one else. She had big gentle eyes and two wonderful dimples, and in the excitement of the dancing and the singing, her eyes laughed and flashed, and the dimples deepened and disappeared and reappeared again. She was as happy and innocent looking as though it were nine in the morning and she were playing school at some kindergarten. From all over the house the women were murmuring their delight, and the men were laughing and pulling their mustaches, and nudging each other to "look at the littlest one."

There was a roar from the house that went to Lester's head like wine. There were four encores, and then the children came off jubilant and happy, with the littlest girl's arms full of flowers.

Van Bibber hunted up the wardrobe woman, and told her he wanted to meet the littlest girl.

"This is the little girl, sir. Her name is Madeline. Speak to the gentleman, Madeline; he wants to tell you what a great big hit youse made."

The little girl was seated on one of the cushions of a double throne, so high from the ground that the young woman who was pulling off the child's silk stockings and putting woolen ones on in their place did so without stooping.

Van Bibber took the littlest girl's small hand in his and shook it solemnly and said, "I am very glad to know you. Can I sit up here beside you, or do you rule alone?"

"Yes, ma'am—yes, sir."

He did not know exactly what to say next, and yet he wanted to talk to the child very much. There was a doll lying on the top of a chest near them, and he picked this up and surveyed it critically. "Is this your doll?"

"No, it's 'at 'ittle durl's; my doll he's dead."

"Dear me!" said Van Bibber, "that's very sad. But dead dolls do come to life again."

But Madeline yawned a very polite and sleepy yawn, closed her eyes, and let her curly head fall on his elbow and rest there.

Van Bibber was looking a long way ahead at what the future was to bring to the confiding little being at his side, and of the evil knowledge and temptations that would mar the beauty of her quaintly sweet face, and its strange mark of gentleness and refinement.

"Does she come of professional people?" Van Bibber asked of the wardrobe woman.

"Yes."

"Are—are you her mother?"

"No."

"Who is her mother?"

The woman looked at the sleeping child and then up at him, almost defiantly. "Ida Clare was her mother."

Van Bibber's protecting hand left the child as suddenly as though something had burned it, and he drew back so quickly that her head slipped from his arm, and she awoke and raised her eyes and looked up at him question- ingly. He looked back at her with a glance of the strang- est concern and of the deepest pity. Then he stooped and drew her towards him very tenderly, put her head back in the corner of his arm, and watched her in silence while she smiled drowsily and went to sleep again.

"And who takes care of her now?" he asked.

"I do," she said. "After the divorce Ida came to me; I used to be in her company when she was doing 'Alad- din,' and then when I left the stage and started to keep an actors' boarding-house, she came to me. She lived on with us a year, until she died, and she made me the guardian of the child. I train children for the stage, you know, me and my sister, Ada Dyer. You 've heard of her, I guess. I 'm expecting to get what I spent on her from what she makes on the stage. She 's great, she is; she 'll be just as good as her mother was."

Van Bibber winced visibly, but turned it off into a cough. "And her father,—does he—"

"Her father," said the woman, tossing back her head, "he looks after himself, he does. We do n't ask no favors of *him*. She 'll get along without him or his folks, thank you. Call him a gentleman? Nice gentleman he is! But perhaps he 's a friend of yourn?"

"I just know him."

Van Bibber sat for several minutes thinking, and then looked up quickly, dropped his eyes again as quickly, and said, with an effort to speak quietly and unconcernedly: "If the little girl is not on in this act, would you mind if I took her home? I have a cab at the stage door, and she 's so sleepy it seems a pity to keep her up. The sister you spoke of or some one could put her to bed."

"Yes," the woman said doubtfully, "Ada 's home. Yes, you can take her around, if you want to."

He stepped into the cab at the stage entrance, and after looking about to see that no one was near enough to hear him, said to the driver: "To the Berkeley Flats, on Fifth avenue." The hall-boy at the Berkeley said, Yes, Mr. Caruthers was in, and the young English servant who opened the hall door to Mr. Caruthers's apartment watched Van Bibber with alarm as he laid the child on the divan in the hall, and pulled a covert coat from the rack to throw over her.

Mr. Caruthers was standing by the mantel over the empty fireplace, wrapped in a long, loose dressing-gown, which he was tying around him as Van Bibber entered.

"Excuse my costume, will you?" he said. "I turned in rather early to-night, it was so hot."

"Yes, it is hot. I was at the first night of 'The Sultana' this evening."

"Oh, yes, Lester's new piece. Was it any good?"

"I do n't know—yes, I think it was. I did n't see it from the front. There were a lot of children in it—little ones; they danced and sang, and made a great hit. One of them had never been on the stage before. It was her first appearance.

"It seems to me that it is a great pity—I say, it seems a pity that a child like that should be allowed to go on in that business. A grown woman can go into it with her eyes open, or a girl who has had decent training can, too. But it 's different with a child. She has no choice in the matter; they do n't ask her permission, and she is n't old enough to know what it means; and she gets used to it and fond of it before she grows to know what the danger is. And then it 's too late. It seemed to me that if there was any one who had the right to stop it, it would be a very good thing to let that person know about her—about this child, I mean; the one who made the hit—before it was too late. It seems to me a responsibility I would n't care to take myself. I would n't care to think that I had the chance to stop it, and had let the chance go by. You know what the life is and what the temptations a woman —I mean we all know—every man knows."

Mr. Caruthers was looking at him with his lips pressed closely together, and his eyebrows drawn into the shape of the letter V. He leaned forward and looked at Van Bibber intently.

"What is all this about? Did you come here, Mr. Van Bibber, simply to tell me this? Why did you come?"

"Because of your child."

Young Van Bibber was quite prepared for an outbreak of some sort, and mentally braced himself to receive it. In consequence he was quite unprepared for what followed. For Mr. Caruthers raised his face without a trace of feeling in it. When he spoke, it was in a tone of quiet politeness.

"Mr. Van Bibber, you are a very brave young man. You have dared to say to me what those who are my best friends—what even my own family would not care to say. They are afraid it might hurt me, I suppose. They have some absurd regard for my feelings; they hesitate to touch upon a subject which in no way concerns them, and which they know must be very painful to me. But you come here, unasked and uninvited, to let me know what you think of my conduct; to let me understand that it does not agree with your own ideas of what I ought to do, and to tell me how I, who am old enough to be your father, should behave. You have rushed in where angels fear to tread. I suppose I ought to thank you for it; but I have always said that it is not the wicked people who are to be feared in this world, or who do the most harm. It is the well-meaning fool who makes all the trouble. I think, if you will allow me to say so, that you have demonstrated my theory pretty thoroughly, and have done about as much needless harm for one evening as you can possibly wish. And so, if you will excuse me, I will ask to say good-night, and will request of you that you grow older and wiser and much more considerate before you come to see me again."

"It is very easy to call a man a fool, but it is much harder to be called a fool, and not to throw the other man out of the window. But that, you see, would not do any good, and I have something to say to you first. I am quite well aware that I did an unconventional thing in coming here—a bold thing or a foolish thing, as you choose—but the situation is pretty bad, and I did as I would have wished to be done by if I had had a child going to the devil and did n't know it. I should have been glad to learn of it even from a stranger. However, there are other kindly disposed people in the world besides fathers. There is an aunt perhaps, or an uncle or two; and sometimes, even to-day, there is the chance Samaritan —Good-night."

"Wait just one minute, please, Mr. Van Bibber. Before you go, I want to say—I want you to understand my position."

"Oh, that's all right."

"No, it is not all right. Since you have done me the honor to make my affairs your business, I would prefer that you should understand them fully. I do not care to have you discuss my conduct at clubs and afternoon teas with young women until you—"

"Oh, I would n't say that if I were you."

"I beg your pardon. That was a mistake. I was wrong. I beg your pardon. But you have tried me very sorely. You have intruded upon a private trouble that you ought to know must be very painful to me. But I believe you meant well. I know you to be a gentleman, and I am willing to think you acted on impulse, and that you will see to-morrow what a mistake you have made. It is not a thing I talk about; I do not speak of it to my friends, and they are far too considerate to speak of it to me. But you have put me on the defensive; you have made me out more or less of a brute, and I do n't intend to be so far misunderstood. There are two sides to every story, and there is something to be said about this, even for me. When I married, I did so against the wishes of my people and the advice of all my friends. You know all about that. God help us! who does n't? It was very rich, rare reading for you, and for every one else who saw the daily papers, and we gave them all they wanted of it. I took her out of that life and married her because I believed she was as good a woman as any of those who had never had to work for their living, and I was bound that my friends and your friends should recognize her and respect her as my wife had a right to be respected; and I took her abroad that I might give all you sensitive, fine people a chance to get used to the idea of being polite to a woman who had once been a burlesque actress. It began over there in Paris. She had every chance when she married me that a woman ever had—all that a man's whole thought and love and money could bring to her. And you know what she did. And after the divorce—and she was free to go where she pleased, and to live as she pleased, and with whom she pleased,—I swore to my God that I would never see her nor her child again. I loved the mother, and she deceived me and disgraced me and broke my heart, and I only wish she had killed me. Was I to love and worship and care for this child, and have

her grow up with all her mother's vanity and animal nature, and have her turn on me some day and show me
that what is bred in the bone must tell, and that I was a
fool again—a pitiful fond fool? I could not trust her; I
can never trust any woman or child again, and least of
all that woman's child. She is as dead to me as though
she were buried with her mother, and it is nothing to me
what she is or what her life is. I know in time what it
will be. She has begun earlier than I had supposed, that
is all; but she is nothing to me. Oh, I care too much.
I cannot let her mean anything to me; when I do care, it
means so much more to me than to other men. They
may pretend to laugh and to forget and to outgrow it,
but it is not so with me. It means too much. Why,
man, I loved that child's mother to the day of her death.
I loved that woman then, and, God help me! I love that
woman still.''

He covered his face with his hands, and sat leaning
forward and breathing heavily as he rocked himself to
and fro. Van Bibber still stood looking gravely out at
the lights that picketed the black surface of the city. He
was, to all appearances, as unmoved by the outburst of
feeling into which the older man had been surprised, as
though it had been something in a play. There was an
unbroken silence for a moment, and then it was Van
Bibber who was the first to speak.

"I came here as you say, on impulse; but I am glad I
came, for I have your decisive answer now about the child.
I have been thinking, since you have been speaking, and
before, when I saw her dancing in front of the footlights,
when I did not know who she was, that I could give up a
horse or two, if necessary, and support this child instead.
Children are worth more than horses. As you say, it's
a good deal of an experiment, but I think I'll run the
risk.''

He walked quickly to the door and disappeared in the
hall, and then came back, kicking the door open as he
returned, and holding the child in his arms.

"This is she; this is your child. She will need to be
fed a bit; they did not treat her very well, I fancy. She
is thin and peaked and tired looking.'' He drew up the
loose sleeve of her jacket, and showed the bare forearm to
the light. "It is very thin, and under her eyes you can

see how deep the lines are. This red spot on her cheek is where the chorus girls kissed her, but they will never kiss her again. She is going to grow up a sweet, fine, beautiful woman—are you not? She does not look like her mother; she has her father's auburn hair and straight nose and finer-cut lips and chin. She looks very much like her father. It seems a pity—she will grow up without knowing him, or who he is—or was, if he should die. She will never speak with him, or see him, or take his hand. She may pass him some day on the street and she will not know him, and he will not know her—''

The child in his arms stirred, shivered slightly, and awoke. The two men watched her breathlessly, with silent intentness. She raised her head and stared around the unfamiliar room doubtfully, then turned to where her father stood, looking at him a moment, and passed him by; and then looking up into Van Bibber's face, recognized him, and gave a gentle, sleepy smile, and with a sigh of content and confidence, drew her arm up closer around his neck, and let her head fall back upon his breast.

The father sprang to his feet with a quick, jealous gasp of pain. "Give her to me! She is mine; give her to me!"

Van Bibber closed the door gently behind him, and went jumping down the winding stairs of the Berkeley, three steps at a time.

And an hour later, when the English servant came to his master's door, he found him still awake and sitting in the dark by the open window, holding something in his arms and looking out over the sleeping city. "James, you can make up a place for me here on the lounge. Miss Caruthers, my daughter, will sleep in my room to-night."

Richard Harding Davis.

AN ENCOUNTER WITH AN INTERVIEWER.

The nervous, dapper, "peart" young man took the chair I offered him, and said he was connected with the *Daily Thunderstorm*, and added:

"Hoping it 's no harm, I 've come to interview you."

"Come to what?"

"*Interview* you."

"Ah! I see. Yes—yes. Um! Yes—yes."

I was not feeling bright that morning. Indeed, my powers seemed a bit under a cloud. However, I went to the bookcase, and when I had been looking six or seven minutes, I found I was obliged to refer to the young man. I said:

"How do you spell it?"

"Spell what?"

"Interview."

"O my goodness! what do you want to spell it for?"

"I do n't want to spell it; I want to see what it means."

"Well, this is astonishing, I must say. *I* can tell you what it means, if you—if you——"

"O, all right! That will answer, and much obliged to you, too."

"I n, *in*, t e r, *ter*, *in*ter——"

"Then you spell it with an *I*?"

"Why, certainly!"

"O, that is what took me so long."

"Why, my *dear* sir, what did *you* propose to spell it with?"

"Well, I—I—hardly know. I had the Unabridged, and I was ciphering around in the back end, hoping I might tree her among the pictures. But it 's a very old edition."

"Why, my friend, they would n't have a *picture* of it in even the latest e—— My dear sir, I beg your pardon, I mean no harm in the world, but you do not look as—as—intelligent as I had expected you would. No harm—I mean no harm at all."

"O, do n't mention it! It has often been said, and by people who would not flatter and who could have no inducement to flatter, that I am quite remarkable in that way. Yes—yes; they always speak of it with rapture."

"I can easily imagine it. But about this interview. You know it is the custom, now, to interview any man who has become notorious."

"Indeed, I had not heard of it before. It must be very interesting. What do you do it with?"

"Ah, well—well—well—this is disheartening. It *ought* to be done with a club in some cases; but customarily it consists in the interviewer asking questions, and the interviewed answering them. It is all the rage now. Will you let me ask you certain questions calculated to bring out the salient points of your public and private history?"

"O, with pleasure—with pleasure. I have a very bad memory, but I hope you will not mind that. That is to say, it is an irregular memory—singularly irregular. Sometimes it goes in a gallop, and then again it will be as much as a fortnight passing a given point. This is a great grief to me."

"O, it is no matter, so you will try to do the best you can."

"I will. I will put my whole mind on it."

"Thanks. Are you ready to begin?"

"Ready."

Q. How old are you?

A. Nineteen, in June.

Q. Indeed! I would have taken you to be thirty-five or six. Where were you born?

A. In Missouri.

Q. When did you begin to write?

A. In 1836.

Q. Why, how could that be, if you are only nineteen now?

A. I do n't know. It does seem curious, somehow.

Q. It does, indeed. Whom do you consider the most remarkable man you ever met?

A. Aaron Burr.

Q. But you never could have met Aaron Burr, if you are only nineteen years——

A. Now, if you know more about me than I do, what do you ask me for?

Q. Well, it was only a suggestion; nothing more. How did you happen to meet Burr?

A. Well, I happened to be at his funeral one day, and he asked me to make less noise, and——

Q. But, good heavens! if you were at his funeral, he must have been dead; and if he was dead, how could he care whether you made a noise or not?

A. I do n't know. He was always a particular kind of a man that way.

Q. Still, I do n't understand it at all. You say he spoke to you and that he was dead.

A. I did n't say he was dead.

Q. But was n't he dead?

A. Well, some said he was, some said he was n't.

Q. What did you think?

A. Oh, it was none of my business! It was n't any of my funeral.

Q. Did you— However, we can never get this matter straight. Let me ask you something else. What was the date of your birth?

A. Monday, October 31, 1693.

Q. What! Impossible! That would make you a hundred and ninety years old. How do you account for that?

A. I do n't account for it at all.

Q. But you said at first you were only nineteen, and now you make yourself out to be one hundred and ninety. It is an awful discrepancy.

A. Why, have you noticed that? (Shaking hands.) Many a time it has seemed to me like a discrepancy, but somehow I could n't make up my mind. How quick you notice a thing!

Q. Thank you for the compliment, as far as it goes. Had you, or have you, any brothers or sisters?

A. Eh! I—I—I think so—yes—but I do n't remember.

Q. Well, that is the most extraordinary statement I ever heard.

A. Why, what makes you think that?

Q. How could I think otherwise? Why, look here! Who is this a picture of on the wall? Is n't that a brother of yours?

A. Oh, yes, yes, yes! Now you remind me of it; that *was* a brother of mine. That 's William—*Bill* we called him. Poor old Bill!

Q. Why? Is he dead then?

A. Ah! well, I suppose so. We never could tell. There was a great mystery about it.

Q. That is sad, very sad. He disappeared, then?

A. Well, yes, in a sort of general way. We buried him.

Q. *Buried* him! *Buried* him, without knowing whether he was dead or not?

A. Oh, no! Not that. He was dead enough.

Q. Well, I confess that I can't understand this. If you buried him, and you knew he was dead—

A. No! no! We only thought he was.

Q. Oh, I see. He came to life again?

A. I bet he did n't.

Q. Well, I never heard anything like this. *Somebody* was dead. *Somebody* was buried. Now, where was the mystery?

A. Ah! that 's just it! That 's it exactly. You see, we were twins—defunct and I—and we got mixed in the bathtub when we were only two weeks old, and one of us was drowned. But we did n't know which. Some think it was Bill. Some think it was me.

Q. Well, that *is* remarkable. What do *you* think?

A. Goodness knows! I would give whole worlds to know. This solemn, this awful mystery has cast a gloom over my whole life. But I will tell you a secret now, which I never have revealed to any creature before. One of us had a peculiar mark—a large mole on the back of his left hand—that was *me*. *That child was the one that was drowned!*

Q. Very well, then, I do n't see that there is any mystery about it, after all.

A. You do n't? Well, *I* do. Anyway, I do n't see how they could ever have been such a blundering lot as to go and bury the wrong child. But, 'sh!—do n't mention it where the family can hear of it. Heaven knows they have heart-breaking troubles enough without adding this.

Q. Well, I believe I have got material enough for the present, and I am very much obliged to you for the pains you have taken. But I was a good deal interested in that account of Aaron Burr's funeral. Would you mind telling me what particular circumstance it was that made you think Burr was such a remarkable man?

A. Oh! it was a mere trifle! Not one man in fifty would have noticed it at all. When the sermon was over, and the procession all ready to start for the cemetery, and the body all arranged nice in the hearse, he said he wanted to take a last look at the scenery, and so he *got up and rode with the driver.*

Then the young man reverently withdrew. He was very pleasant company, and I was sorry to see him go. I need not say that I have never been troubled with interviewers since.

Samuel L. Clemens.

VIRGINIA.

Ye good men of the Commons, with loving hearts and true,
Who stand by the bold Tribunes that still have stood
    by you,
Come, make a circle round me, and mark my tale with
    care,
A tale of what Rome once hath borne, of what Rome
    yet may bear.
This is no Grecian fable, of fountains running wine,
Of maids with snaky tresses, or sailors turned to swine;
Here, in this very Forum, under the noonday sun,
In sight of all the people, the bloody deed was done.
Old men still creep among us who saw that fearful day,
Just seventy years and seven ago, when the wicked Ten
    bare sway.

Of all the wicked Ten still the names are held accursed,
And of all the wicked Ten, Appius Claudius was the worst.
He stalked along the Forum like King Tarquin in his
    pride:
Twelve axes waited on him, six marching on a side;
The townsmen shrank to right and left, and eyed askance
    with fear
His lowering brow, his curling mouth, which always
    seemed to sneer.

Nor lacks he fit attendance; for close behind his heels,
With outstretched chin and crouching pace, the client
    Marcus steals.
Where'er ye shed the honey, the buzzing flies will crowd;
Where'er ye fling the carrion, the raven's croak is loud;

Where'er down Tiber garbage floats, the greedy pike you
    see;
And wheresoe'er such lord is found, such client still will be.

Just then, as through one cloudless chink in a black
    stormy sky
Shines out the dewy morning star, a fair young girl
    came by,
With her small tablets in her hand, and her satchel on her
    arm
Home she went bounding from the school, nor dreamed
    of shame or harm;
And past those dreaded axes she innocently ran,
With bright, frank brow that had not learned to blush at
    gaze of man;
And up the Sacred Street she turned, and, as she danced
    along,
She warbled gaily to herself lines of the good old song.
And Appius heard her sweet young voice, and saw her
    sweet young face,
And loved her with the accurséd love of his accurséd race,
And all along the Forum, and up the Sacred Street,
His vulture eye pursued the trip of those small glancing
    feet.

She crossed the Forum, shining with stalls in alleys gay,
And just had reached the very spot whereon I stand this
    day,
When up the varlet Marcus came; not such as when,
    erewhile,
He crouched behind his patron's heels, with the true client
    smile;
He came with lowering forehead, swollen features, and
    clenched fist,
And strode across Virginia's path, and caught her by the
    wrist.
Hard strove the frightened maiden, and screamed with
    look aghast;
And at her scream, from right and left, the folks came
    running fast;
The money-changer Crispus, with his thin silver hairs,
And Hanno from the stately booth glittering with Punic
    wares,

And the strong smith Muræna, grasping a half-forged
    brand,
And Volero, the flesher, his cleaver in his hand.
All came in wrath and wonder; for all knew that fair child;
And, as she passed them twice a day, all kissed their
    hands and smiled;
And the strong smith Muræna gave Marcus such a blow,
The caitiff reeled three paces back, and let the maiden go.
Yet glared he fiercely round him, and growled in harsh,
    fell tone,
"She's mine, and I will have her. I seek but for my own:
She is my slave, born in my house, and stolen away and
    sold,
The year of the sore sickness, ere she was twelve hours
    old.
I wait on Appius Claudius; I waited on his sire:
Let him who works the client wrong, beware the patron's
    ire!"

So spake the varlet Marcus; and dread and silence came
On all the people at the sound of the great Claudian name.
Straightway Virginius led his child a little space aside,
To where the reeking shambles stood, piled up with horn
    and hide.
Hard by, a flesher on a block had laid his whittle down:
Virginius caught the whittle up, and hid it in his gown.
And then his eyes grew very dim, and his throat began
    to swell,
And in a hoarse, changed voice he spake, "Farewell,
    sweet child! Farewell!
The house that was the happiest within the Roman walls,
The house that envied not the wealth of Capua's marble
    halls,
Now, for the brightness of thy smile, must have eternal
    gloom,
And for the music of thy voice, the silence of the tomb.

"The time is come. See how he points his eager hand this
    way!
See how his eyes gloat on thy grief, like a kite's upon the
    prey!
With all his wit, he little deems, that, spurned, betrayed,
    bereft,

Thy father hath in his despair one fearful refuge left.
He little deems that in this hand I clutch what still can
    save
Thy gentle youth from taunts and blows, the portion of
    the slave;
Then clasp me round the neck once more, and give me
    one more kiss;
And now, mine own dear little girl, there is no way but
    this.''

With that he lifted high the steel, and smote her in the
    side,
And in her blood she sank to earth, and with one sob she
    died.
Then for a little moment all people held their breath;
And through the crowded Forum was stillness as of death;
And in another moment brake forth from one and all
A cry as if the Volscians were coming o'er the wall.
Some with averted faces shrieking fled home amain;
Some ran to call a leech, and some ran to lift the slain;
Some felt her lips and little wrist, if life might there be
    found;
And some tore up their garments fast, and strove to
    stanch the wound.
In vain they ran, and felt, and stanched; for never truer
    blow
That good right arm had dealt in fight against a Volscian
    foe.

When Appius Claudius saw that deed he shuddered and
    sank down,
And hid his face some little space with the corner of his
    gown,
Till, with white lips and bloodshot eyes, Virginius tottered
    nigh,
And stood before the judgment-seat, and held the knife
    on high.
"Oh, dwellers in the nether gloom, avengers of the slain,
By this dear blood I cry to you, do right between us twain;
And even as Appius Claudius hath dealt by me and mine,
Deal you by Appius Claudius and all the Claudian line!''
So spake the slayer of his child, and turned, and went his
    way;

But first he cast one haggard glance to where the body
    lay,
And writhed and groaned a fearful groan; and then with
    steadfast feet,
Strode right across the market-place unto the Sacred
    Street.
Then up sprang Appius Claudius: "Stop him; alive or
    dead!
Ten thousand pounds of copper to the man who brings
    his head!"
He looked upon his clients, but none would work his will.
He looked upon his lictors, but they trembled and stood
    still.
And as Virginius through the press his way in silence
    cleft,
Ever the mighty multitude fell back to right and left,
And he hath passed in safety into his woeful home,
And there ta'en horse to tell the camp what deeds are
    done in Rome.

                       Lord Macaulay.

CUDDLE DOON.

    The bairnies cuddle doon at nicht
        Wi' muckle fash an' din.
"Oh, try and sleep, ye waukrife rogues;
        Your father's comin' in."
    They never heed a word I speak.
        I try to gie a froon;
    But aye I hap them up, an' cry,
    "Oh, bairnies, cuddle doon!"

    Wee Jamie, wi' the curly heid—
        He aye sleeps next the wa'—
    Bangs up an' cries, "I want a piece"—
        The rascal starts them a'.
    I rin an' fetch them pieces, drinks—
        They stop awee the soun'—
    Then draw the blankets up, an' cry,
    "Noo, weanies, cuddle doon!"

But ere five minutes gang, wee Rab
  Cries oot, frae 'neath the claes,
"Mither, mak' Tam gie ower at ance:
  He's kittlin' wi' his taes."
The mischief's in that Tam for tricks;
  He'd bother half the toon.
But aye I hap them up, an' cry,
  "Oh, bairnies, cuddle doon!"

At length they hear their father's fit;
  An', as he steeks the door,
They turn their faces to the wa',
  While Tam pretends to snore.
"Hae a' the weans been gude?" he asks,
  As he pits aff his shoon.
"The bairnies, John, are in their beds,
  An' lang since cuddled doon."

An' just afore we bed oorsels,
  We look at oor wee lambs.
Tam has his airm roun' wee Rab's neck,
  An' Rab his airm roun' Tam's.
I lift wee Jamie up the bed,
  An' as I straik each croon,
I whisper, till my heart fills up,
  "Oh, bairnies, cuddle doon!"

The bairnies cuddle doon at nicht
  Wi' mirth that's dear to me;
But soon the big warl's cark an' care
  Will quaten doon their glee.
Yet, come what will to ilka ane,
  May He who sits aboon
Aye whisper, though their pows be bauld,
  "Oh, bairnies, cuddle doon!"

               Alexander Anderson.

FITZ-JAMES AND RODERICK DHU.

At length they came where, stern and steep,
The hill sinks down upon the deep.
Here Vennachar in silver flows,
There, ridge on ridge, Benledi rose;
Ever the hollow path twined on
Beneath steep bank and threatening stone;
An hundred men might hold the post
With hardihood against an host.

So toilsome was the road to trace,
The guide, abating of his pace,
Led slowly through the pass's jaws,
And asked Fitz-James, by what strange cause
He sought these wilds? traversed by few,
Without a pass from Roderick Dhu.

"A warrior thou, and ask me why!
Moves our free course by such fixed cause,
As gives the poor mechanic laws?
Enough, I am by promise tied
To match me with this man of pride:
Twice have I sought Clan-Alpine's glen
In peace; but when I come again,
I come with banner, brand, and bow,
As leader seeks his mortal foe.
For love-lorn swain, in lady's bower,
Ne'er panted for the appointed hour,
As I, until before me stand
This rebel Chieftain and his band."

"Have, then, thy wish!" He whistled shrill,
And he was answered from the hill;
Wild as the scream of the curlieu,
From crag to crag the signal flew.
Instant, through copse and heath, arose
Bonnets and spears and bended bows;
On right, on left, above, below,
Sprung up at once the lurking foe;
From shingles gray their lances start,
The bracken-bush sends forth the dart,
The rushes and the willow-wand

Are bristling into ax and brand,
And every tuft of broom gives life
To plaided warrior armed for strife.
That whistle garrisoned the glen
At once with full five hundred men,
As if the yawning hill to heaven
A subterranean host had given.
Watching their leader's beck and will,
All silent there they stood, and still.
Like the loose crags whose threatening mass
Lay tottering o'er the hollow pass,
As if an infant's touch could urge
Their headlong passage down the verge,
With step and weapon forward flung,
Upon the mountain-side they hung.
The mountaineer cast glance of pride
Along Benledi's living side,
Then fixed his eye and sable brow
Full on Fitz-James: ''How say'st thou now?
These are Clan-Alpine's warriors true;
And, Saxon,—I am Roderick Dhu!''

Fitz-James was brave:—though to his heart
The life-blood thrilled with sudden start,
He manned himself with dauntless air,
Returned the Chief his haughty stare,
His back against a rock he bore,
And firmly placed his foot before:
''Come one, come all! this rock shall fly
From its firm base as soon as I.''
Sir Roderick marked—and in his eyes
Respect was mingled with surprise,
And the stern joy which warriors feel
In foemen worthy of their steel.
Short space he stood—then waved his hand:
Down sunk the disappearing band;
Each warrior vanished where he stood,
In broom or bracken, heath or wood;
Sunk brand and spear and bended bow,
In osiers pale and copses low;
It seemed as if their mother Earth
Had swallowed up her warlike birth.

Fitz-James looked round—yet scarce believed
The witness that his sight received;

Such apparition well might seem
Delusion of a dreadful dream.
Sir Roderick in suspense he eyed,
And to his look the Chief replied,
'Fear nought—nay, that I need not say—
But—doubt not aught from mine array.
Thou art my guest; I pledged my word
As far as Coilantogle ford:
Nor would I call a clansman's brand
For aid against one valiant hand,
Though on our strife lay every vale
Rent by the Saxon from the Gael.
So move we on; I only meant
To show the reed on which you leant,
Deeming this path you might pursue
Without a pass from Roderick Dhu.''

The Chief in silence strode before,
And reached the torrent's sounding shore,
And here his course the Chieftain staid,
Threw down his target and his plaid,
And to the Lowland warrior said:—
''Bold Saxon! to his promise just,
Vich-Alpine has discharged his trust.
This murderous Chief, this ruthless man,
This head of a rebellious clan,
Hath led thee safe through watch and ward,
Far past Clan-Alpine's outmost guard.
Now, man to man, and steel to steel,
A Chieftain's vengeance thou shalt feel.
See, here all vantageless I stand,
Armed, like thyself, with single brand;
For this is Coilantogle ford,
And thou must keep thee with thy sword.''

The Saxon paused: ''I ne'er delayed,
When foeman bade me draw my blade;
Nay, more, brave Chief, I vowed thy death;
Yet sure thy fair and generous faith,
And my deep debt for life preserved,
A better meed have well deserved:
Can naught but blood our feud atone?
Are there no means?'' ''No. Stranger, none!
And here—to fire thy flagging zeal—

The Saxon cause rests on thy steel;
For thus spoke Fate by prophet bred
Between the living and the dead;
'Who spills the foremost foeman's life,
His party conquers in the strife.'"

"Then, by my word," the Saxon said,
"The riddle is already read:
Seek yonder brake beneath the cliff,—
There lies Red Murdock, stark and stiff.
Thus Fate hath solved her prophecy;
Then yield to Fate, and not to me."

Dark lightning flashed from Roderick's eye—
"Soars thy presumption then so high,
Because a wretched kern ye slew,
Homage to name to Roderick Dhu?
He yields not, he, to man nor Fate!
Thou add'st but fuel to my hate:
My clansman's blood demands revenge,—
Not yet prepared?　By heaven, I change
My thought, and hold thy valor light
As that of some vain carpet-knight,
Who ill deserved my courteous care,
And whose best boast is but to wear
A braid of his fair lady's hair."
"I thank thee, Roderick, for the word!
It nerves my heart, it steels my sword;
For I have sworn this braid to stain
In the best blood that warms thy vein.
Now, truce, farewell! and, ruth, begone!"

Then each at once his falchion drew,
Each on the ground his scabbard threw,
Each looked to sun, and stream, and plain,
As what they ne'er might see again:
Then foot, and point, and eye opposed,
In dubious strife they darkly closed.
Ill fared it then with Roderick Dhu,
That on the field his targe he threw,
Whose brazen studs and tough bull hide
Had death so often dashed aside;
For trained abroad his arms to wield,
Fitz-James's blade was sword and shield.

He practiced every pass and ward,
To thrust, to strike, to feint, to guard;
While less expert, though stronger far,
The Gael maintained unequal war.
Three times in closing strife they stood,
And thrice the Saxon blade drank blood;
No stinted draught, no scanty tide,
The gushing flood the tartans dyed.
Fierce Roderick felt the fatal drain,
And showered his blows like wintry rain;
And as firm rock, or castle roof,
Against the winter shower is proof,
The foe, invulnerable still,
Foiled his wild rage by steady skill,
Till at advantage ta'en, his brand
Forced Roderick's weapon from his hand;
And backward borne upon the lea,
Brought the proud Chieftain to his knee.
"Now, yield thee, or, by Him who made
The world, thy heart's blood dyes my blade!"

"Thy threats, thy mercy, I defy!
Let recreant yield, who fears to die."—
Like adder darting from his coil,
Like wolf that dashes through the toil,
Like mountain-cat who guards her young,
Full at Fitz-James's throat he sprung;
Received, but recked not of a wound,
And locked his arms his foeman round.
They tug, they strain!—down, down they go,
The Gael above, Fitz-James below.
The Chieftain's gripe his throat compressed,
His knee was planted in his breast;
His clotted locks he backward threw,
Across his brow his hand he drew,
From blood and mist to clear his sight,
Then gleamed aloft his dagger bright!
But, while the dagger gleamed on high,
Reeled soul and sense, reeled brain and eye.
Down came the blow! but in the heath
The erring blade found bloodless sheath.
Unwounded from the dreadful close,
But breathless all, Fitz-James arose.
Sir Walter Scott

PARADISE AND THE PERI.

One morn a Peri at the gate
Of Eden stood, disconsolate;
And as she listened to the Springs
  Of Life within, like music flowing,
And caught the light upon her wings
  Through the half-open portal glowing,
She wept to think her recreant race
Should e'er have lost that glorious place!

The glorious Angel, who was keeping
The Gates of Light, beheld her weeping;
"Nymph of a fair but erring line!"
Gently he said, "One hope is thine.
'Tis written in the Book of Fate,
  The Peri yet may be forgiven
Who brings to this Eternal gate
  The Gift that is most dear to Heaven!
Go seek it, and redeem thy sin—
'Tis sweet to let the Pardoned in."

Rapidly as comets run
To th' embraces of the Sun,
Down the blue vault the Peri flies,
And through the war-field's bloody haze
Beholds a youthful warrior stand,
  Alone beside his native river,
The red blade broken in his hand,
  And the last arrow in his quiver.
"Live ," said the Conqueror, "live to share
The trophies and the crowns I bear!"
Silent that youthful warrior stood,
Silent he pointed to the flood
All crimson with his country's blood,
Then sent his last remaining dart,
For answer, to th' Invader's heart.

False flew the shaft, though pointed well·
The Tyrant lived, the Hero fell!—
Yet marked the Peri where he lay,
  And when the rush of war was past,

Swiftly descending on a ray
   Of morning light, she caught the last—
Last glorious drop his heart had shed,
Before its free-born spirit fled!

"Be this," she cried, as she winged her flight,
"My welcome gift at the Gates of Light.
   Though foul are the drops that oft distil
      On the field of warfare, blood like this,
      For liberty shed, so holy is,
   It would not stain the purest rill,
      That sparkles among the Bowers of Bliss!
Oh, if there be, on this earthly sphere,
A boon, an offering Heaven holds dear,
'Tis the last libation Liberty draws
From the heart that bleeds and breaks in her cause!"

"Sweet," said the Angel, as she gave
   The gift into his radiant hand,—
"Sweet is our welcome of the Brave
   Who die thus for their native Land.—
   But see—alas!—the crystal bar
   Of Eden moves not; holier far
   Than even this drop the boon must be,
   That opes the Gates of Heaven for thee!"

Her first fond hope of Eden blighted,
   Now among Afric's lunar mountains,
Far to the South, the Peri lighted;
   Close by a Lake, she heard the moan
Of one who, at this silent hour,
   Had thither stolen to die alone.
One who, in life, where'er he moved,
   Drew after him the hearts of many;
Yet now, as though he ne'er were loved,
   Dies here unseen, unwept by any!
Deserted youth! one thought alone
   Shed joy around his soul in death—
That she, whom he for years had known,
And loved, and might have called his own,
   Was safe from this foul midnight's breath.

"Sleep," said the Peri, as softly she stole
   The farewell sigh of that vanishing soul;

Again the Peri soars above,
Bearing to Heaven that precious sigh
  Of pure, self-sacrificing love.
High throbbed her heart, with hope elate,
  Th' Elysian palm she soon shall win,
For the bright Spirit at the gate
  Smiled as she gave that offering in.

But, ah! even Peris' hopes are vain—
Again the Fates forbade, again
Th' immortal barrier closed: "Not yet,"
The Angel said, as, with regret,
He shut from her that glimpse of glory;
"Peri, see—the crystal bar
  Of Eden moves not; holier far
Than even this sigh the boon must be
That opes the Gates of Heaven for thee."

Now naught can charm the luckless Peri;
Her soul is sad, her wings are weary,
When, o'er the vale of Balbec winging
  Slowly, she sees a child at play,
Among the rosy wild flowers singing,
  As rosy and as wild as they.
And near the boy, who tired with play
Now nestling 'mid the roses lay,
She saw a wearied man dismount
  From his hot steed, and on the brink
Of a small imaret's rustic fount
  Impatient fling him down to drink.
Then swift his haggard brow he turned,
In which the Peri's eye could read
Dark tales of many a ruthless deed;
The ruined maid, the shrine profaned,
Oaths broken, and the threshold stained
With blood of guests! *there* written all,
Black as the damning drops that fall
From the denouncing Angel's pen,
Ere Mercy weeps them out again.
But hark! the vesper call to prayer!
The boy has started from the bed
Of flowers, where he had laid his head,
  And down upon the fragrant sod
Kneels, with his forehead to the south,
  Lisping th' eternal name of God.

And how felt *he*, the wretched Man
Reclining there—while memory ran
O'er many a year of guilt and strife,
Flew o'er the dark flood of his life,
Nor found one sunny resting-place,
Nor brought him back one branch of grace.
"There *was* a time," he said, in mild
Heart-humbled tones,—"thou blessèd child!
When, young and haply pure as thou,
I looked and prayed like thee; but now——"
He hung his head; each nobler aim,
  And hope, and feeling, which had slept
From boyhood's hour, that instant came
  Fresh o'er him, and he wept—he wept!
Blest tears of soul-felt penitence!
  In whose benign, redeeming flow
Is felt the first, the only sense
  Of guiltless joy that guilt can know.

And now, behold him kneeling there
By the child's side, in humble prayer,
While the same sunbeam shines upon
The guilty and the guiltless one;
And hymns of joy proclaim through Heaven
The triumph of a Soul Forgiven!
'Twas when the golden orb had set,
While on their knees they lingered yet,
There fell a light more lovely far
Than ever came from sun or star,
Upon the tear that, warm and meek,
Dewed that repentant sinner's cheek.

But well th' enraptured Peri knew
'Twas a bright smile the Angel threw
From Heaven's gate, to hail that tear
Her harbinger of glory near!
"Joy, joy forever! My task is done—
The Gates are passed, and Heaven is won!"
                              Thomas Moore.

THE BOWER SCENE FROM "BECKET."

CHARACTERS:

ROSAMUND DE CLIFFORD, the real love of Henry II., of England.

GEOFFREY, son of Rosamund and Henry.

ELEANOR, Queen of England.

THOMAS BECKET, Chancellor of England.

SIR REGINALD FITZURSE, suitor for the hand of Rosamund, and enemy to Becket.

Scene: ROSAMUND's bower. This place was built by Henry in a garden called "Labyrinthus," so that no one might approach ROSAMUND. ELEANOR, however, induces GEOFFREY to pilot her to the hiding-place, and comes to wreak vengeance on ROSAMUND.

ROSAMUND. The boy is so late; pray God, he be not
    lost.
        [*Enter* GEOFFREY *and* ELEANOR.]
Geoffrey, the pain thou has put me to!
        [*Seeing* ELEANOR.] Ha, you!
How came you hither?

ELEANOR. Your own child brought me hither!

ROS. How dared you? Know you not this bower is
    secret,
Of and belonging to the King of England,
More sacred than his forests for the chase?
Nay, nay, Heaven help you! Get you hence in haste
Lest worse befall you.

EL. Child, I am mine own self
Of and belonging to the King. The King
Hath divers ofs and ons, ofs and belongings,
Whom it pleases him
To call his wives; but so it chances, child,
That I am his sultana.
Do you believe that you are married to him?

ROS. I *should* believe it.

EL. You must not believe it,
Because I have a wholesome medicine here
Puts that belief asleep. Your answer, beauty!
Do you believe that you are married to him?

ROS. Geoffrey, my boy, I saw the ball you lost in the
fork of the great willow over the brook. Go. See that
you do not fall in. Go. [*Exit* GEOFFREY.]

EL. He is easily found again. *Do* you believe it?

I pray you, then, to take my sleeping-draught;
But if you should not care to take it—see! [*Draws a
        dagger.*]
What! have I scared the red rose from your face
Into your heart?   But this will find it there,
And dig it from the root forever.

   Ros. I do beseech you—my child is so young,
So backward, too; I cannot leave him yet.
I am not so happy I could not die myself,
But the child is so young.   You have children—his;
And mine is the King's child; so, if you love him—
Nay, if you love him, there is great wrong done
Somehow; but if you do not—there are those
Who say you do not love him—let me go
With my young boy, and I will hide my face,
Blacken and gipsyfy it; none shall know me;
The King shall never hear of me again,
But I will beg my bread along the world
With my young boy, and God will be our guide.
I never meant you harm in any way.
See, I can say no more.

   El. Will you not say you are not married to him?
   Ros. Ay, madam, I can *say* it, if you will.
   El. Then art thou a proven wanton?
   Ros.   No,
I am none such.   I never loved but one.
I have heard of such that range from love to love,
Like the wild beast—if you can call it love.
I have heard of such—yea, even among those
Who sit on thrones—I never saw any such,
Never knew any such, and howsoever
You do misname me, match'd with any such,
I am snow to mud.

   El.   The more the pity then
That thy true home—the heavens—cry out for thee
Who art too pure for earth.

             [*Enter* Fitzurse.]

   Fitzurse. Give her to me.

   El. The Judas-lover of our passion-play
Hath track'd us hither.

   Fitz. Well, why not?   I follow'd
You and the child; he babbled all the way.
Give her to me to make my honeymoon.

Come with me, love,
And I will love thee.   Madame, let her live
I have a far-off burrow where the King
Would miss her and forever.

  EL. How sayst thou, sweetheart?
Wilt thou go with him?   He will marry thee.

  ROS. Give me the poison; set me free of him!
   [ELEANOR *offers the vial.*]
No, no!   I will not have it.

  EL.   Then this other,
The wiser choice, because my sleeping-draught
May bloat thy beauty out of shape, and make
Thy body loathsome even to thy child;
While this but leaves thee with a broken heart,
A doll-face blanch'd and bloodless, over which,
If pretty Geoffrey do not break his own,
It must be broken for him.

  ROS.   O I see now
Your purpose is to fright me—a troubadour,
You play with words.   You had never used so many,
Not if you meant it, I am sure.   The child—
No—mercy!   No!

  EL. Play!   That bosom never
Heaved under the King's hand with such true passion
As at this loveless knife that stirs the riot,
Which it will quench in blood!   Slave, if he love thee
Thy life is worth the wrestle for it.   Arise,
And dash thyself against me that I may slay thee!
The worm!   shall I let her go?   But ha! what's here?
By very God, the cross I gave the King!
His village darling in some sly caress
Has wheedled it off the King's neck to her own.
By thy leave, beauty.   Ay, the same!   I warrant
Thou hast sworn on this, my cross, a hundred times
Never to leave him—and that merits death,
False oath on holy cross—for thou must leave him
To-day, but not quite yet.   My good Fitzurse,
The running down the chase is kindlier sport
Ev'n than the death.   Who knows but that thy lover
May plead so pitifully, that I may spare thee?
Come hither, man; stand there.   [*To* ROSAMUND.]   Take
  thy one chance;
Catch at the last straw.   Kneel to thy lord Fitzurse;

Crouch even because thou hatest him; fawn upon him
For thy life and thy son's.

Ros. [*rising*].　　　　　I am a Clifford,
My son a Clifford and Plantagenet.
I am to die, then, tho' there stand beside thee
One who might grapple with thy dagger, if he
Had aught of man, or thou of woman; or I
Would bow to such a baseness as would make me
Most worthy of it; both of us will die,
And I will fly with my sweet boy to heaven,
And shriek to all the saints among the stars:
"Eleanor of Aquitaine, Eleanor of England!
Murdered by that adulteress, Eleanor,
Whose doings are a horror to the east,
A hissing in the west!"　Strike!
I challenge thee to meet me before God.
Answer me there.

El. [*raising the dagger.*]　This in thy bosom, fool!
[*Enter* BECKET *from behind.　Catches hold of her arm.*]

Becket.　Murderess!
[*The dagger falls; they stare at one another.　After a pause:*]

El.　My lord, we know you proud of your fine hand,
But having now admired it long enough,
We find that it is mightier than it seems—
At least mine own is frailer—you are laming it.

Becket.　And lamed and maim'd to dislocation, better
Than raised to take a life which Henry bade me
Guard from the stroke that dooms thee after death
To wail in deathless flame.　[*To* ROSAMUND.]
Daughter, the world hath trick'd thee.

　　　　　　　　Leave it, daughter,
Come thou with me to Godstow nunnery,
And live what may be left thee of a life
Saved as by miracle alone with Him
Who gave it.

Lord Tennyson.

COLUMBUS.

Behind him lay the gray Azores,
   Behind the Gates of Hercules;
Before him not the ghost of shores,
   Before him only shoreless seas.
The good mate said: "Now must we pray,
   For lo! the very stars are gone.
Speak, Admiral, what shall I say?"
   "Why say, 'Sail on! sail on! and on!' "

"My men grow mutinous day by day;
   My men grow ghastly wan and weak."
The stout mate thought of home; a spray
   Of salt wave washed his swarthy cheek.
"What shall I say, brave Admiral, say,
   If we sight naught but seas at dawn?"
"Why, you shall say at break of day,
   'Sail on! sail on! sail on! and on!' "

They sailed and sailed, as winds might blow
   Until at last the blanched mate said:
"Why, now not even God would know
   Should I and all my men fall dead.
These very winds forget their way,
   For God from these dread seas is gone.
Now speak, brave Admiral, speak and say—"
   He said: "Sail on! sail on! and on!"

They sailed. They sailed. Then spoke the mate:
   "This mad sea shows its teeth to-night.
He curls his lip, he lies in wait,
   With lifted teeth, as if to bite!
Brave Admiral, say but one good word:
   What shall we do when hope is gone?"
The words leapt as a leaping sword:
   "Sail on! sail on! sail on! and on!"

Then, pale and worn, he kept his deck,
   And peered through darkness. Ah, that night
Of all dark nights! And then a speck—
   A light! A light! A light! A light!

It grew, a starlit flag unfurled!
　It grew to be Time's burst of dawn.
He gained a world; he gave that world
　Its grandest lesson: "On and on!"

Joaquin Miller.

LORRAINE.

"Are you ready for your steeplechase, Lorraine, Lorraine,
　　Lorree?
　You 're booked to ride your capping race to-day at
　　Coulterlee,
　You 're booked to ride Vindictive, for all the world to
　　see,
　To keep him straight, and keep him first, and win the
　　run for me.

She clasped her new-born baby, poor Lorraine, Lor-
　　raine, Lorree.
"I cannot ride Vindictive, as any man might see,
　And I will not ride Vindictive, with this baby on my
　　knee;
　He 's killed a boy, he 's killed a man, and why must he
　　kill me?"

"Unless you ride Vindictive, Lorraine, Lorraine, Lorree,
　Unless you ride Vindictive to-day at Coulterlee,
　And land him safe across the brook, and win the blank
　　for me,
　It 's you may keep your baby, for you 'll get no keep
　　from me."

"That husbands could be cruel," said Lorraine, Lor-
　　raine, Lorree,
"That husbands could be cruel, I have known for seasons
　　three;
　But oh! to ride Vindictive while a baby cries for me,
　And be killed across a fence at last, for all the world
　　to see?"

She mastered young Vindictive—oh! the gallant lass
    was she!—
And she kept him straight, and won the race, as near
    as near could be:
But he killed her at the brook against a pollard willow
    tree,
Oh! he killed her at the brook—the brute!—for all the
    world to see,
And no one but the baby cried for poor Lorraine,
    Lorree.

Charles Kingsley.

LADY CLARA VERE DE VERE.

Lady Clara Vere de Vere,
  Of me you shall not win renown:
You thought to break a country heart
  For pastime, ere you went to town.
At me you smiled, but unbeguiled
  I saw the snare, and I retired:
The daughter of a hundred earls,
  You are not one to be desired.

Lady Clara Vere de Vere,
  I know you proud to bear your name,
Your pride is yet no mate for mine,
  Too proud to care from whence I came.
Nor would I break for your sweet sake
  A heart that dotes on truer charms.
A simple maiden in her flower
  Is worth a hundred coats-of-arms.

Lady Clara Vere de Vere,
  Some meeker pupil you must find,
For were you queen of all that is,
  I could not stoop to such a mind.
You sought to prove how I could love,
  And my disdain is my reply.
The lion on your old stone gates
  Is not more cold to you than I.

Lady Clara Vere de Vere,
  You put strange memories in my head.
Not thrice your branching limes have blown
  Since I beheld young Laurence dead.
Oh! your sweet eyes, your low replies;
  A great enchantress you may be;
But there was that across his throat
  Which you had hardly cared to see.

Lady Clara Vere de Vere,
  When thus he met his mother's view,
She had the passions of her kind,
  She spake some certain truths of you.
Indeed, I heard one bitter word
  That scarce is fit for you to hear;
Her manners had not that repose
  Which stamps the caste of Vere de Vere.

Lady Clara Vere de Vere,
  There stands a specter in your hall:
The guilt of blood is at your door:
  You changed a wholesome heart to gall.
You held your course without remorse,
  To make him trust his modest worth,
And, last, you fixed a vacant stare,
  And slew him with your noble birth.

Trust me, Clara Vere de Vere,
  From yon blue heavens above us bent
The grand old gardener and his wife
  Smile at the claims of long descent.
Howe'er it be, it seems to me,
  'Tis only noble to be good.
Kind hearts are more than coronets,
  And simple faith than Norman blood.

I know you, Clara Vere de Vere:
  You pine among your halls and towers:
The languid light of your proud eyes
  Is wearied of the rolling hours.
In glowing health, with boundless wealth,
  But sickening of a vague disease,
You know so ill to deal with time,
  You needs must play such pranks as these.

Clara, Clara Vere de Vere,
If time be heavy on your hands,
Are there no beggars at your gate,
Nor any poor about your lands?
Oh! teach the orphan boy to read,
Or teach the orphan girl to sew,
Pray Heaven for a human heart,
And let the foolish yeoman go.

Lord Tennyson.

THE RAVEN.

Once upon a midnight dreary, while I pondered, weak
and weary,
Over many a quaint and curious volume of forgotten
lore,—
While I nodded, nearly napping, suddenly there came
a tapping,
As of some one gently rapping, rapping at my chamber-
door.
" 'Tis some visitor," I muttered, "tapping at my chamber-door—
Only this, and nothing more."

Ah, distinctly I remember, it was in the bleak Decem-
ber,
And each separate dying ember wrought its ghost upon
the floor.
Eagerly I wished the morrow: vainly I had sought to
borrow
From my books surcease of sorrow—sorrow for the lost
Lenore—
For the rare and radiant maiden whom the angels name
Lenore—
Nameless here forevermore.

And the silken, sad, uncertain rustling of each purple
curtain
Thrilled me—filled me with fantastic terrors never felt
before;

So that now, to still the beating of my heart, I stood
    repeating,
" 'Tis some visitor entreating entrance at my chamber
    door,—
Some late visitor entreating entrance at my chamber
    door;
        That it is, and nothing more."

Presently my soul grew stronger; hesitating then no
    longer,
"Sir," said I, "or Madam, truly your forgiveness I im-
    plore;
But the fact is, I was napping, and so gently you came
    rapping,
And so faintly you came tapping, tapping at my cham-
    ber door,
That I scarce was sure I heard you"—here I opened
    wide the door:
        Darkness there, and nothing more.

Deep into that darkness' peering, long I stood there,
    wondering, fearing,
Doubting, dreaming dreams no mortal ever dared to
    dream before;
But the silence was unbroken, and the stillness gave no
    token,
And the only word there spoken was the whispered word,
    "Lenore!"
This I whispered, and an echo murmured back the word,
    "LENORE!"
        Merely this, and nothing more.

Back into the chamber turning, all my soul within me
    burning,
Soon again I heard a tapping, something louder than
    before.
"Surely," said I, "surely that is something at my win-
    dow-lattice,
Let me see then what thereat is, and this mystery ex-
    plore,—
Let my heart be still a moment, and this mystery ex-
    plore;—
        'Tis the wind, and nothing more."

Open here I flung the shutter, when, with many a flirt
and flutter,
In there stepped a stately raven of the saintly days of
yore.
Not the least obeisance made he; not a minute stopped
or stayed he;
But, with mien of lord or lady, perched above my
chamber door,—
Perched upon a bust of Pallas, just above my chamber
door—
Perched and sat and nothing more.

Then this ebony bird beguiling my sad fancy into smiling,
By the grave and stern decorum of the countenance it
wore,
"Though thy crest be shorn and shaven, thou," I said,
"art sure no craven;
Ghastly, grim, and ancient raven, wandering from the
nightly shore,
Tell me what thy lordly name is on the Night's Pluto-
nian shore."
Quoth the raven, "Nevermore!"

Much I marveled this ungainly fowl to hear discourse so
plainly,
Though its answer little meaning—little relevancy bore;
For we cannot help agreeing that no living human being
Ever yet was blessed with seeing bird above his cham-
ber door—
Bird or beast upon the sculptured bust above his cham-
ber door,
With such name as "Nevermore!"

But the raven sitting lonely on the placid bust, spoke only
That one word, as if his soul in that one word he did
outpour.
Nothing further then he uttered—not a feather then he
fluttered—
Till I scarcely more than muttered, "Other friends have
flown before—
On the morrow he will leave me, as my hopes have
flown before."
Then the bird said, "Nevermore!"

Startled at the stillness, broken by reply so aptly spoken,
"Doubtless," said I, "what it utters is its only stock
and store,
Caught from some unhappy master, whom unmerciful
disaster
Followed fast and followed faster, till his songs one bur-
den bore,—
Till the dirges of his hope that melancholy burden bore,
Of—Never—nevermore!"

But the raven still beguiling all my sad soul into smiling,
Straight I wheeled a cushioned seat in front of bird, and
bust, and door.
Then, upon the velvet sinking, I betook myself to link-
ing
Fancy unto fancy, thinking what this ominous bird of
yore—
What this grim, ungainly, ghastly, gaunt, and ominous
bird of yore
Meant in croaking "Nevermore!"

This I sat engaged in guessing, but no syllable expressing
To the fowl, whose fiery eyes now burned into my
bosom's core,
This and more I sat divining, with my head at ease
reclining
On the cushion's velvet lining that the lamplight
gloated o'er,
But whose velvet violet lining, with the lamplight
gloating o'er,
She shall press—ah! nevermore!

Then methought the air grew denser, perfumed from an
unseen censer
Swung by seraphim, whose footfalls tinkled on the
tufted floor.
"Wretch," I cried, "thy God hath lent thee—by these
angels he hath sent thee
Respite—respite and nepenthe from thy memories of
Lenore!
Quaff, oh, quaff this kind nepenthe, and forget this lost
Lenore!"
Quoth the raven, "Nevermore!"

"Prophet!" said I, "thing of evil!—prophet still, if bird
    or devil!
  Whether tempter sent, or whether tempest tossed thee
    here ashore,
  Desolate, yet all undaunted, on this desert land en-
    chanted—
  On this home by Horror haunted—tell me truly, I im-
    plore—
  Is there—is there balm in Gilead?—tell me—tell me, I
    implore!"
        Quoth the raven, "Nevermore!"

"Prophet!" said I, "thing of evil!—prophet still, if bird
    or devil!
  By that heaven that bends above us—by that God we
    both adore,
  Tell this soul, with sorrow laden, if, within the distant
    Aidenn,
  It shall clasp a sainted maiden, whom the angels name
    Lenore;
  Clasp a rare and radiant maiden, whom the angels name
    Lenore!"
        Quoth the raven, "Nevermore!"

"Be that word our sign of parting, bird cr fiend!" I
    shrieked, upstarting—
"Get thee back into the tempest and the Night's Pluto-
    nian shore!
  Leave no black plume as a token of that lie thy soul
    hath spoken!
  Leave my loneliness unbroken!—quit the bust above my
    door!
  Take thy beak from out my heart, and take thy form
    from off my door!"
        Quoth the raven, "Nevermore!"

  And the raven, never flitting, still is sitting, still is sit-
    ting
  On the pallid bust of Pallas, just above my chamber
    door;
  And his eyes have all the seeming of a demon's that is
    dreaming,

And the lamplight o'er him streaming throws his
    shadow on the floor;
And my soul from out that shadow that lies floating on
    the floor
        Shall be lifted—NEVERMORE!
            Edgar Allan Poe.

KNEE-DEEP IN JUNE.

I

Tell you what I like the best—
'Long about knee-deep in June,
'Bout the time strawberries melts
On the vine,—some afternoon
Like to jes' git out and rest,
And not work at nothin' else!

II

Orchard 's where I'd ruther be—
Need n't fence it in fer me!—
Jes' the whole sky overhead,
And the whole airth underneath—
Sort o' so 's a man kin breathe
Like he ort, and kind o' has
Elbow-room to keerlessly
Sprawl out len'thways on the grass,
Where the shadders thick and soft
As the kivvers on the bed
Mother fixes in the loft
Allus, when they's company!

III

Jes' a sort o' lazin' there—
S'lazy 'at you peek and peer
Through the wavin' leaves above
Like a feller 'at's in love,
And do n't know it, ner do n't keer!
Ever'thing you hear and see
Got some sort o' interest—
Maybe find a bluebird's nest

Tucked up there conveenently
Fer the boys 'at's apt to be
Up some other apple-tree!
Watch the swallers skootin' past—
'Bout as peert as you could ast;
'Er the Bobwhite raise and whiz
Where some other's whistle is.

IV

Ketch a shadder down below,
And look up to find the crow;
Er a hawk away up there,
'Pearantly froze in the air!—
Hear the old hen squawk and squat,
Over every chick she 's got,
Suddent-like!—And she knows where
That air hawk is, well as you!
You jes' bet your life she do!—
Eyes a-glitterin' like glass,
Waitin' till he makes a pass!

V

Pee-wees' singin', to express
My opinion's second class;
Yit you 'll hear 'em more er less;
Sapsucks gittin' down to biz,
Weedin' out the lonesomeness;
Mr. Bluejay, full o' sass,
In them baseball clothes o' his,
Sportin' round the orchard jes'
Like he owned the premises!
Sun out there in the fields kin sizz,
But flat on yer back, I guess,
In the shade 's where glory is!
That 's jes' what I 'd like to do
Stiddy fer a year er two!

VI

Plague if they ain't sompin' in
Work 'at kind o' goes agin
My convictions!—'long about
Here in June especially!—
Under some old apple-tree,

Jes' a-restin' through and through,
I could git along without
Nothin' else at all to do,
Only jes' a-wishin' you
Was a-gittin' there like me,
And June was eternity!

VII

Lay out there and try to see
Jes' how lazy you kin be!
Tumble round and souse yer head
In the clover-bloom, er pull
Yer straw hat acrost yer eyes,
And peak through it at the skies,
Thinkin' of old chums 'at's dead,
Maybe, smilin' back at you
In betwixt the beautiful
Clouds o' gold and white and blue!—
Month a man kin railly love—
June, you know, I'm talkin' of!

VIII

March ain't never nothin' new!—
Aprile's altogether too
Brash fer me! and May—I jes'
'Bominate its promises,—
Little hints o' sunshine and
Green around the timber-land—
A few blossoms, and a few
Chip-birds, and a sprout or two—
Drap asleep, and it turns in
'Fore daylight and snows agin!—
But when June comes—Clear my throat
With wild honey! Rench my hair
In the dew! and hold my coat!
Whoop out loud! and throw my hat!—
June wants me, and I'm to spare!
Spread them shadders anywhere,
I 'll git down and waller there,
And obleeged to you at that!

James Whitcomb Riley.

RING OUT, WILD BELLS!

Ring out, wild bells, to the wild sky,
The flying cloud, the frosty light;
The year is dying in the night;
Ring out, wild bells, and let him die.

Ring out the old, ring in the new,—
Ring, happy bells, across the snow;
The year is going, let him go;
Ring out the false, ring in the true.

Ring out the grief that saps the mind,
For those that here we see no more;
Ring out the feud of rich and poor,
Ring in redress to all mankind.

Ring out a slowly dying cause,
And ancient forms of paltry strife;
Ring in the nobler modes of life,
With sweeter manners, purer laws.

Ring out the want, the care, the sin,
The faithless coldness of the times;
Ring out, ring out my mournful rhymes,
But ring the fuller minstrel in.

Ring out false pride in place and blood,
The civic slander and the spite;
Ring in the love of truth and right,
Ring in the common love of good.

Ring out old shapes of foul disease,
Ring out the narrowing lust of gold,
Ring out the thousand wars of old;
Ring in the thousand years of peace.

Ring in the valiant man, and free,
The larger heart, the kindlier hand;
Ring out the darkness of the land;
Ring in the Christ that is to be.

Lord Tennyson.

HOW GOOD ARE THE POOR!

'Tis night; within the close-shut cabin door
    The room is wrapped in shade, save where there fall
Some twilight rays that creep along the floor,
    And show the fisher's nets upon the wall.

In the dim corner, from the oaken chest,
    A few white dishes glimmer; in the shade
Stands a tall bed with dusky curtains dressed,
    And a rough mattress at its side is laid.

Five children on the long, low mattress lie—
    A nest of little souls, it heaves with dreams:
In the high chimney the last embers die,
    And redden the dark room with crimson gleams.

The mother kneels and thinks, and, pale with fear,
    She prays alone, hearing the billows shout;
While to wild winds, to rocks, to midnight drear,
    The ominous old ocean sobs without.

Poor wives of fishers! Ah! 'tis sad to say
    "Our sons, our husbands, all that we love best,
Our hearts, our souls, are on those waves away,
    Those ravening wolves that know not ruth, nor rest.

"Terrible fear! we seek the pebbly shore,
    Cry to the rising billows, 'Bring them home!'
Alas! what answer gives their troubled roar
    To the dark thoughts that haunt us as we roam?"

The dawn was whitening over the sea's verge
    As she sat pensive, touching broken chords
Of half-remorseful thought, while the hoarse surge
    Howled a sad concert to her broken words.

"Ah! my poor husband! We had five before.
    Already so much care, so much to find,
For he must work for all. I give him more.
    What was that noise? His step? Ah, no! the wind!

"That I should be afraid of him I love!
   I have done ill.   If he should beat me now
I would not blame him.   Does not the door move?
   Not yet, poor man!"   She sits, with careful brow,
Wrapped in her inward grief; nor hears the roar
   Of wind and waves that dash against his prow,
Or the black cormorant shrieking on the shore.

Sudden the door flies open wide, and lets
   Noisily in the dawn-light scarcely clear,
And the good fisher, dragging his damp nets,
   Stands on the threshold, with a joyful cheer.

" 'Tis thou!" she cries, and, eager as a lover,
   Leaps up and holds her husband to her breast;
Her greeting kisses all his vesture cover;
   " 'Tis I, good wife!" and his broad face expressed

How gay his heart that Janet's love made light.
   "What weather was it?" "Hard." "Your fishing?"
      "Bad.
The sea was like a nest of thieves to-night,
   But I embrace thee, and my heart is light.

"There was a devil in the wind that blew;
   I tore my net, caught nothing, broke my line.
And once I thought the bark was broken, too;
   What did you all the night long, Janet mine?"

She, trembling in the darkness, answered, "I!
   Oh, naught—I sewed, I watched, I was afraid.
The waves were loud as thunder from the sky,
   But it is over." Shyly then she said:

"Our neighbor died last night; it must have been
   When you were gone. She left two little ones,
So small, so frail—William and Madeleine;
   The one just lisps, the other scarcely runs."

The man looked grave, and in the corner cast
   His old fur bonnet, wet with rain and sea,
Muttered awhile and scratched his head—at last:
   "We have five children, this makes seven," said he.

"Already in bad weather we must sleep
   Sometimes without our supper. Now! Ah, well—
'Tis not my fault. These accidents are deep;
   It was the good God's will. I cannot tell.

"Why did He take the mother from those scraps
   No bigger than my fist? 'Tis hard to read.
A learned man might understand, perhaps—
   So little, they can neither work nor need.

"Go fetch them, wife; they will be frightened sore,
   If with the dead alone they waken thus.
That was the mother knocking at our door,
   And we must take the children home to us.

"Brother and sister shall they be to ours,
   And they will learn to climb my knee at even.
When He shall see these strangers in our bowers,
   More fish, more food will give the God of Heaven.

"I will work harder; I will drink no wine—
   Go fetch them. Wherefore dost thou linger, dear?
Not thus are wont to move those feet of thine."
   She drew the curtain, saying, "*They are here!*"
      Victor Hugo—Translation of H. W. Alexander.

THE RESURRECTION.

It was our Sabbath eve. By set of sun
Arimathean Joseph craved, and gained
The grace to lay Him in His sepulcher.
Then, while the first day of the week was dark,
Alone I wended to His sepulcher,
Bearing fair water, and the frankincense,
And linen, that my Lord's sweet body sleep
Well in the rock. And, while my woeful feet
Passed through the gate, and up the paved ascent
Along the Second Wall, over the Hill,
Into that Garden, hard by Golgotha,
The morning brightened over Moab's peaks.

Touched the great Temple's dome with crimson fires,
Lit Ophel and Moriah rosy-red,
Made Olivet all gold, and, in the pools
In Hinnom, laid a sudden lance of flame;
And from the thorn-trees, brake the waking songs
Of little birds; and every palm-tree's top
Was full of doves that cooed, as knowing not
How Love was dead, and Life's dear glory gone,
And the World's hope lay in the tomb with Him;
Which now I spied—that hollow in the rock
Under the camphire leaves. Yet, no guards there
To help me roll the stone! Nay, and no stone!
It lay apart, leaving the door a-gape,
And through the door, as I might dimly see,
The scattered wrappings of the burial night,
Pale gleams amidst the gloom. Not waiting, then,
Deeming our treasure taken wickedly—
I sped; and came to Peter, and to John,
And cried: "Our Lord is stolen from His grave,
And none to tell where He is borne away!"
Thereat, they ran together, came, and saw;
And entered in; and found the linen cloths
Scattered; the rock-bed empty; and, amazed,
Back to their house they went. But I drew nigh
A second time, alone; heart-broken now,
The bright day seeming blackest night to me,
The small birds mockers, and the City's noise—
Waking within the walls—hateful and vain.
Why should Earth wake, the Son of Man asleep?
Or that great guilty City rise and live,
With this dear Lord, dead, in her stony skirts?
Fled, too, my last fond hope, to lay Him fair,
And kiss His wounded feet, and wash the blood
From the pierced palms, and comb His tangled hair
To comeliness, and leave Him—like a King— •
To His forgetful Angels. Weeping hard
With these thoughts, like to snake-fangs, stinging me,
My left hand on the stone I laid, and shut
The eager sunshine off with my right hand,
Kneeling, and looking in the sepulcher.
It was not dark within! I deemed at first
A lamp burned there, such radiance mild I saw
Lighting the hewn walls, and the linen bands;

And, in one corner, folded by itself,
The face-cloth. Coming closer, I espied
Two men who sate there—very watchfully—
One at the head, the other at the foot
Of that stone table where my Lord had lain.
Oh! I say "men"—I should have known no men
Had eyes like theirs, shapes so majestical,
Tongues tuned to such a music as the tone
Wherewith they questioned me: "Why weepest thou?"
'Ah, Sirs!" I said, "my Lord is ta'en away,
Nor wot we whither!" and thereat my tears
Blotted all seeing. So, I turned to wipe
The hot drops off; and, look! Another one
Standing behind me, and my foolish eyes
Hard gazing on Him, and not knowing Him!
Indeed, I deemed this was the Gardener
Keeping the trees and tomb, so was He flesh;
So living, natural, and made like man,
Albeit, if I had marked—if any ray
Of watchful hope had helped me—such a look,
Such Presence, beautiful and pure; such light
Of loveliest compassion in His face,
Had told my beating heart and blinded eyes
WHO this must be. But I—my brow i' the dust—
Heard Him say softly: "Wherefore weepest thou?
Whom seekest thou?" A little marveled I—
Still at His feet, too sorrowful to rise,—
He should ask this,—the void grave gaping near,
And He its watchman; yet His accents glad.
"Sir," said I, "if 'tis thou hast borne Him hence,
Tell me where thou hast laid Him.   Then will I
Bear Him away!"

Ah, friend, such answer came, that my sadness turned
Gladness, as suddenly as gray is gold
When the sun springs in glory! such a word
As made my mourning laugh itself to naught,
Like a cloud melting to the blue! Such word
As, with more music than Earth ever heard,
Set my swift-dancing veins full well aware
Why so the Day dawned, and the City stirred,
And the vast idle world went busy on,
And the birds caroled, and, in palm-tree tops,

The wise doves cooed of love!   Oh, a dear word
Spoke first to me, and, after me, to all,
That all may always know He is the Lord,
And Death is dead, and new times come for men;
And Heaven's ways justified, and Christ alive,
Whom we saw die, nailed on the cruel Cross!
For, while I lay there, sobbing at His feet,
The word He spake—My Lord! my King, my Christ!
Was my name:
"MARY!"

No language had I then,
No language have I now! only I turned
My quick glance upward; saw Him; knew Him! sprang,
Crying: "Rabboni!   Lord! my Lord! dear Lord!"
Edwin Arnold.

RICHELIEU.

In this scene, four characters are introduced: Richelieu, the Minister of France and Cardinal of the church of Rome; Louis, the king; Baradas, the chief conspirator; Julie, Richelieu's ward.

The king and Baradas have planned the assassination of Richelieu. The king has also designed to marry Julie; but in order to prevent this, Richelieu has given her in marriage to Adrien de Mauprat, whom Baradas has induced to become the tool in the assassination of Richelieu.

As De Mauprat enters Richelieu's room to commit the murder, Richelieu, having anticipated him, thwarts him in his purpose, and then explains to him the treachery of Baradas; whereupon De Mauprat becomes concerned for Richelieu's safety, and meeting the conspirators after leaving the house, announces to them that Richelieu is dead.

On the following day, the conspirators, together with De Mauprat, convene at the king's palace. While here, Baradas, who has already imprisoned Huguet, a spy, conspires against De Mauprat, and finally, by gaining the consent of the king, succeeds in having him also imprisoned in the Bastile.

And now as the king and the conspirators are rejoicing over the supposed death of Richelieu, and are discussing plans as to the best disposition of public offices, Richelieu enters and says:

RICH. [*fiercely.*]   Room, my lords, room.
The minister of France can need no intercession with the
 King.

LOUIS.   What means this false report of death, Lord
 Cardinal?

Rich. Are you, then, angered, Sire, that I live still?

Louis. No; but such artifice——

Rich. Not mine; look elsewhere, Louis!
My castle swarmed with the assassins.

Bar. [*advancing.*] We have punished them already. Huguet now
In the Bastile. Oh! my lord, we were prompt
To avenge you—we were.

Rich. We? Ha, ha! you hear
My liege! What page, man, in the last court grammar,
Made you a plural? Count, you have seized the *hireling;*
Sire, shall I name the master?

Louis. Tush, my lord,
The old contrivance; ever does your wit
Invent assassins, that ambition may
Slay rivals——

Rich. Rivals, Sire, in what?
Service to France? I have none. Lives the man
Whom Europe deems rival to
    Armand Richelieu?

Louis. What, so haughty!
Remember, he who made, can unmake.

Rich. Never!
Never! Your anger can recall your trust,
Annul my office, spoil me of my lands,
Rifle my coffers—but my name, my deeds
Are loyal in a land beyond your scepter.
Pass sentence on me, if you will; from Kings
Lo! I appeal to time!

Louis [*motions to Baradas and turns haughtily to the Cardinal*]. Enough!
Your Eminence must excuse a longer audience.
To your own palace: for our conference, this
Nor place, nor season.

Rich. Good, my liege, for Justice
All place a temple, and all season summer!
Do you deny me justice? Saints of heaven!
He turns from me! Do you deny me justice?
For fifteen years, while in these hands dwelt Empire,
The humblest craftsman, the obscurest vassal,
The very leper shrinking from the sun,
Though loathed by Charity, might ask for justice!
Not with the fawning tone and crawling mien

Of some I see around you—Counts and Princes
Kneeling for favors; but erect and loud,
As men who ask man's rights!—My liege, my Louis,
Do you refuse me justice—audience even—
In the pale presence of the baffled Murder?

LOUIS.   Lord Cardinal, one by one you have severed
        from me
The bonds of human love; all near and dear
Marked out for vengeance—exile or the scaffold.
You find me now amidst my trustiest friends,
My closest kindred.   You would tear them from me;
They murder you, forsooth, since me they lôve.
Enough of plots and treasons for one reign.
Home! home! and sleep away these phantoms.

RICH.   Sire!
I—patience, Heaven! Sweet Heaven! Sire, from the foot
Of that Great Throne, these hands have raised aloft
On an Olympus, looking down on mortals
And worshiped by their awe—before the foot
Of that high throne, spurn you the gray-haired man
Who gave you empire—and now sues for safety?

LOUIS.   No; when we see your Eminence in truth
At the foot of the throne, we 'll listen to you.

[*Exit King and train.*]

RICH.   Goddess of bright dreams,
My country—shalt thou lose me now, when most
Thou need'st thy worshiper?   My native land!
Let me but ward this dagger from thy heart,
And die—but on thy bosom.

[*Enter* JULIE.]

JULIE.   Heaven!   I thank thee!
It cannot be, or this all-powerful man
Would not stand idly thus.

RICH.   Julie de Mauprat, what dost thou here?
Home!

JULIE.   Home!—is Adrien there?   You 're dumb, yet
        strive
For words; I see them trembling on your lips,
But choked by pity.   It was truth—all truth!
Seized —the Bastile—and in your presence, too!
Cardinal, where is Adrien?   Think! he saved
Your life; your name is infamy, if wrong
Should come to his!

RICH.   Be soothed, child.

JULIE.   Child no more!
I love, and I am woman!   Hope and suffer:
Love, suffering, hope—what else doth make the strength
And majesty of woman?
I ask thee for my home, my fate, my all!
Where is my husband?

RICH.   You are Richelieu's ward,
A soldier's bride; they who insist on truth
Must out-face fear: you ask me for your husband?
There, where the clouds of heaven look darkest o'er
The domes of the Bastile!

JULIE.   O, mercy, mercy!
Save him, restore him, father!   Art thou not
The Cardinal King? the lord of life and death,
Art thou not Richelieu?

RICH.   Yesterday I was;
To-day a very weak old man; to-morrow,
I know not what.

[*Enter* CLERMONT.]

CLER.   Madame de Mauprat!—
Pardon, your Eminence; even now I seek
This lady's home—commanded by the King
To pray her presence.

RICH.   To those who sent you!
And say you found the virtue they would slay
Here, couched upon this heart, as at an altar,
And sheltered by the wings of sacred Rome!
Be gone!

[*Enter* BARADAS.]

BAR.   My lord, the King cannot believe your Eminence
So far forgets your duty, and his greatness,
As to resist his mandate.—Pray you, madame,
Obey the King; no cause for fear.

JULIE.   My father!

RICH.   She shall not stir!

BAR.   You are not of her kindred;
An orphan——

RICH.   And her country is her mother.

BAR.   The country is the King.

RICH.   Ay, is it so?
Then wakes the power which in the age of iron
Bursts forth to curb the great, and raise the low.

Mark, where she stands: around her form I draw
The awful circle of our solemn Church!
Set but a foot within that holy ground,
And on thy head—yea, though it wore a crown—
I launch the curse of Rome!

BAR.   I dare not brave you;
I do but speak the orders of my King:
The Church, your rank, power, very word, my lord,
Suffice you for resistance; blame yourself,
If it should cost your power.

RICH.   That's *my* stake.   Ah!
Dark gamester! *what is thine?*   Look to it well—
Lose not a trick.   By this same hour to-morrow
Thou shalt have France, or I thy head!

BAR.   In sooth, my lord,
You do need rest; the burdens of the state
O'ertask your health.   [*Aside.*]   His mind
And life are breaking fast.

RICH. [*overhearing him.*]   Irreverent ribald!
If so, beware the falling ruins!   Hark!
I tell thee, scorner of these whitening hairs,
When this snow melteth there shall come a flood!
Avaunt! my name is Richelieu—I defy thee!

                                Edward Bulwer-Lytton.

HOW THE GOSPEL CAME TO JIM OAKS.

One Christmas Eve a strange tragedy was enacted in the far Northwest. Away up in Montana a mining camp was established in days when women were as scarce in that country as they were in the early days of the settlement of California; there was, in fact, but one woman in the camp. She was young, of fine appearance, great physical strength and endurance, and indomitable nerve. Two years before, she had left an unhappy home in Wisconsin to become the wife of a reckless dare-devil named Jim Oaks, with whom she had shared the vicissitudes of a long, slow journey across the intervening plains. This man just missed being a ruffian through his wife's influence.

She loved him with a noble devotion, and, although he was incapable of a like attachment, he loved her, too, after a fashion of his own.

The day before Christmas dawned loweringly. Toward the middle of the afternoon, huge, lumbering clouds began to loom in the Northwest. All signs portended one of those fierce, cold storms that occasionally descend upon the border, arresting torrents in chains of ice, and freezing even the shaggy-coated buffaloes.

At nightfall the wind, changing to the northeast, grew stronger and brought snow. As the cold increased, the snow was condensed into fine particles that bit like needles into the cheeks of belated miners struggling toward their cabins. The gusts were so violent that it was impossible to see even a lighted window at a few yards' distance.

It was considerably past Jim Oaks' supper-time. But as Oaks was the only man in the camp who did n't have to cook his own meals, he had lapsed into a habit of coming in late for supper, for which fault his wife, who was not of a complaining disposition, never reproached him.

It was seven o'clock. Mrs. Oaks fed the fire, then stepped to the pane of glass which formed the only window in the diggings, and essayed to look out into the night. The glass was caked inside with frost and covered on the outside by a snowdrift. Sighing, the young wife returned to her seat by the fire, and then, putting her hand into the bosom of her dress, she drew out—what?

A well-worn copy of the New Testament.

There was something covert in the manner in which she brought this volume into the light, and, thinking she heard a noise at the door, she thrust it back again. Jim Oaks had somehow and somewhere acquired so rank a detestation of the Holy Scriptures that he could not bear to hear them quoted from or even mentioned.

Finding that the noise was nothing but the crunch of a settling drift, she opened the little book and began to read.

The passages on which Minerva Oaks was accustomed to dwell were all marked and underscored with a pencil. High-spirited and able to handle a rifle or a revolver on occasion, she was also a sincere Christian, and quiet in her ways.

She sat, with the Testament spread open on her lap, and the Christmas Eve supper growing browner in front of the fire, until nearly eight o'clock. Then, as a mighty throe of the storm threatened to wrench the cabin from its foundations, she started up with a cry:

"Jim! why, Jim was to be off at Wild Swan Gulch this afternoon. He was going to get us some feathers for Christmas. Ah, me! it is eight o'clock. And the storm! How ever can he find his way home?"

Springing to the door, she lifted the hickory latch and drew it toward her. The mass of snow which had been piled against it fell in and streamed across the floor, and the blast, driving in more snow, extinguished the candle.

"Hah!"

In a few moments she had managed to sweep away a part of the drift and close the door. Then she re-lit the candle. Going to an old horsehide-covered trunk in a corner, she pulled out of it her husband's spare suit, dressed herself in it, and put on the long rubber boots Jim wore when he worked in the sluices; then his old cap, tied close to her head with a comforter; then her own thick shawl and mittens. Lighting her lantern and taking a shovel, she opened the door again and attacked the drift until it yielded far enough to let her latch the door behind her.

The night was awful. She could see nothing through the skurry. She hardly dared to turn her face to the yelling blast. She thought of asking some one to accompany her, but the camp lay some distance out of her line. Moreover, she knew the country in every direction. She could feel her way anywhere if necessary; besides, she had her lantern—that would enable her to distinguish objects within a small circle. Turning resolutely in the direction of Wild Swan Gulch, she set out to find her husband and guide him home.

As she emerged from the canyon and gained the level of the surrounding broken plain, a strange pause came. It seemed as though the winds had suddenly forsaken the neighborhood and gone reeling away into the mountains. She took advantage of this sinister calm to hurry onward at a run. Out of breath at last, she stumbled and fell.

The lantern went out.

She had no matches!

Staggering to her feet, she heard the moan of the returning storm. She shouted:

"Jim!"

Again, with all the might of her voice, she lifted the plainsman's call:

"Yip, yip, yip; ya-hoo! Jim!"

No answer.

Then the tempest rushed round her in a baffling, ferocious whirl of sound and wind and snow.

In the meantime, Jim Oaks had been at one of his old diversions. Having returned from Wild Swan Gulch with a splendid trophy in the shape of a black-billed swan drake, he was lounging toward home when the storm came on, and stopped in at the last saloon, as usual, to get a drink. It was always warm and cozy in that liquor-mill, and on Christmas Eve the place was peculiarly inviting. The boys were assembling for a night at poker, and Jim sat down and took a hand.

"It 's kind o' rough on Minerv," he thought once, about midnight, "leavin' her alone up thar such a night as this. Never mind; she 'll worry it through, I reckon."

But when the man entered his cabin next morning and started toward the bed with a peace-offering extended in his hand, he was completely stunned by what he saw. The untouched bed, the fireless hearth, the cold, untasted supper, his wife's clothes strewn on the floor, the open trunk, the absent cap and lantern—these flashed the truth into his brain.

"She 's gone to hunt for me! She 's been gone a long while—all night, p'rhaps—in the storm. O Minerv!"

Out he sprang through the doorway. The storm was over. The air was clear, still, and bitterly cold. The sun was rising. He cast one strenuous look around the narrow horizon, then plunged through the drifts toward the camp.

"Minerv!" he shouted. "Have any of you seen Minerv?"

Immediately the camp roused itself from its slumbers. When it was found that Mrs. Oaks was missing, the miners volunteered as one man to go to her rescue. It was hard work floundering across the gullies and washouts, which were packed to the edge with snow. Often the men shuddered to think of what might be hidden under those heavy white masses.

The first "sign" was discovered by Jim Oaks' partner, one "Spick" Jones, who kept to the left and signaled from a clump of timber. The bark was partially torn off about four feet from the ground, on the side of the tree, not by the teeth or claws of a wild beast, but, as was plainly to be seen, by the hands of a human creature. Almost every miner was familiar with the trick. It was a trick to keep from freezing at the sacrifice of nails and finger-tips.

Jim Oaks set his teeth hard when he saw the frozen blood-spots on the tree.

"Stay with me, boys," he said, hoarsely, "and help me find my wife."

The men struggled on.

Some two hours later a figure on a distant bluff was seen waving a hat. All sought the place, where the wind had blown so fiercely during the preceding night that it had prevented the snow from lodging on the windward ridges. Mrs. Oaks lay on her back there, half covered with snow, frozen to sleep. Her left hand was thrust inside the vest she wore; her right was extended above her head and covered with blood from her poor, torn fingers.

Everybody made way for Jim.

He came up and knelt down reverently beside her, and kissed her rigid lips.

"Minerv," he said, gently. He reached, trying to feel her heart.

"Minerv!"

He looked around on the faces of his fellow-miners with such an expression on his drawn and haggard visage that they turned away.

He touched the cold hand in her bosom. It covered something which she had clutched for when she fell. He drew it forth; it was her Testament. Opening it mechanically at the fly-leaf, he saw the words, written, perhaps, long before:

"This book has been my comfort.

"Read it, Jim."

And below:

"I am the resurrection and the life. He that believeth

in me, though he were dead, yet shall he live; and he that liveth and believeth in me shall never die."

"Boys," said Jim, half rising to his feet, and holding out the open book with both his trembling hands, "she's left me—her Testament. See!"

Anonymous.

THE UTILITY OF BOOING.

This selection is taken from an old English play, "The Man of the World." It was written to satirize a mean old Scotchman who amassed a large fortune by questionable means, and was elevated to the Peerage under the title of the Earl of Eldon. The Earl, who is represented in the play as Sir Pertinax MacSycophant, is giving his son Egerton an account of his successful business ventures.

Sir Pertinax MacSycophant and Egerton.

Sir P. Zounds! sir, I will not hear a word aboot it; I insist upon it you are wrong; you should have paid your court till my lord, and not have scrupled swallowing a bumper or twa, or twenty, till oblige him.

Eger. Sir, I did drink his toast in a bumper.

Sir P. Yes, you did; but how, how?—just as a bairn takes physic—with aversions and wry faces, which my lord observed; then, to mend the matter, the moment that he and the Colonel got intill a drunken dispute aboot religion, you slily slunged away.

Eger. I thought, sir, it was time to go when my lord insisted upon half-pint bumpers.

Sir P. Sir, that was not leveled at you, but at the Colonel, in order to try his bottom; but they aw agreed that you and I should drink out of sma' glasses.

Eger. But, sir, I beg pardon; I did not choose to drink any more.

Sir P. But, zoons! sir, I tell you there was a necessity for your drinking mair.

Eger. A necessity! in what respect, pray, sir?

Sir P. Why, sir, I have a certain point to carry, independent of the lawyers, with my lord, in this agreement of your marriage—aboot which I am afraid we shall have a warm squabble—and therefore I wanted your assistance in it.

Eger. But how, sir, could my drinking contribute to assist you in your squabble?

Sir P. Yes, sir, it would have contributed, and greatly have contributed, to assist me.

Eger. How so, sir?

Sir P. Nay, sir, it might have prevented the squabble entirely; for as my lord is proud of you for a son-in-law, and is fond of your little French songs, your stories, and your bonmots, when you are in the humor; and guin you had but stayed, and been a little jolly, and drunk half a score bumpers with him, till he had got a little tipsy, I am sure, when we had him in that mood, we might have settled the point as I could wish it, among ourselves, before the lawyers came; but now, sir, I do not ken what will be the consequence.

Eger. But when a man is intoxicated, would that have been a seasonable time to settle business, sir?

Sir P. The most seasonable, sir; for, sir, when my lord is in his cups, his suspicion is asleep, and his heart is aw jollity, fun, and guid fellowship; and, sir, can there be a happier moment than that for a bargain, or to settle a dispute with a friend? What is it you shrug up your shoulders at, sir?

Eger. At my own ignorance, sir; for I understand neither the philosophy nor the morality of your doctrine.

Sir P. I know you do not, sir; and, what is worse, you never will understand it, as you proceed—in one word, Charles, I have often told you, and now again I tell you, once for aw, that the manœuvres of pliability are as necessary to rise in the world, as wrangling and logical subtlety are to rise at the bar; why, you see, sir, I have acquired a noble fortune, a princely fortune—and how do you think I raised it?

Eger. Doubtless, sir, by your abilities.

Sir P. Doubtless, sir, you are a blockhead; nae, sir, I 'll tell you how I raised it—sir, I raised it—by booing— [*Bows very low*]—by booing; sir, I never could stand straight in the presence of a great mon, but always booed, and booed, and booed—as it were-by instinct.

Eger. How do you mean by instinct, sir?

Sir P. How do I mean by instinct!—Why, sir, I mean by—by—by the instinct of interest, sir, which is the universal instinct of mankind. Sir, it is wonderful to think what a cordial, what an amicable—nay, what an infallible influence booing has upon the pride and vanity of human nature. Charles, answer me sincerely, have you a mind to be convinced of the force of my doctrine by example and demonstration?

EGER. Certainly, sir.

SIR P. Then, sir, as the greatest favor I can confer upon you, I 'll give you a short sketch of the stages of my booing, as an excitement, and a landmark to boo by, and as an infallible nostrum for a man of the world to rise in the world.

EGER. Sir, I shall be proud to profit by your experience.

SIR P. Vary weel, sir; sit ye down then, sit you down here.—[*They sit.*]—And now, sir, you must recall to your thoughts that your grandfather was a man whose penurious income of captain's half-pay was the sum total of his fortune; and, sir, aw my provision fra him was a modicum of Latin, an expertness in arithmetic, and a short system of worldly counsel; the principal ingredients of which were a persevering industry, a rigid economy, a smooth tongue, a pliability of temper, and a constant attention to make every mon well pleased with himself.

EGER. Very prudent advice, sir.

SIR P. Therefore, sir, I lay it before you. Now, sir, with these materials I set out, a raw-boned stripling, fra the North to try my fortune with them here, in the Sooth; and my first step into the world was a beggarly clerkship in Sawney Gordon's counting-house, here, in the city of London, which you 'll say afforded but a barren sort of a prospect.

EGER. It was not a very fertile one, indeed, sir.

SIR P. The reverse, the reverse. Weel, sir, seeing myself in this unprofitable situation, I reflected deeply; I cast about my thoughts morning, noon, and night, and marked every man and every mode of prosperity; at last I concluded that a matrimonial adventure, prudently conducted, would be the readiest gait I could gang for the bettering of my condition, and accordingly I set aboot it. Now, sir, in this pursuit, beauty!—ah! beauty often struck my een, and played about my heart; and fluttered, and beat, and knocked, and knocked, but the devil an entrance I ever let it get; for I observed, sir, that beauty is, generally, a—proud, vain, saucy, expensive, impertinent sort of a commodity.

EGER. Very justly observed.

SIR P. And therefore, sir, I left it for prodigals and coxcombs, that could afford to pay for it; and, in its stead, sir, mark! I looked out for an ancient, weel-jointured, superannuated dowager; a consumptive, toothless, phthisicky, wealthy widow, or a shriveled, cadaverous piece of deformity, in the shape of an izzard, or an appersi-and—or, in short, ainy thing, ainy thing that had the siller—the siller—for that, sir, was the north-star of my affections. Do you take me, sir? was nae that right?

EGER. O doubtless, doubtless, sir.

SIR P. Now, sir, where do you think I ganged to look for this woman with the siller?—nae till court, nae till playhouses or assemblies—nae, sir, I ganged till the kirk, till the Anabaptist, Independent, Bradlonian, and Muggletonian meetings; till the morning and evening service of churches and chapels-of-ease, and till the midnight, melting, conciliating love-feasts of the Dissenters; and there, sir, at last I fell upon an old, slighted, antiquated, musty maiden, that looked—ha, ha, ha! she looked just like a skeleton in a surgeon's glass case. Now, sir, this miserable object was religiously angry with herself and all the world; had nae comfort but in metaphysical visions and supernatural deliriums—ha, ha, ha! Sir, she was as mad—as mad as a Bedlamite.

EGER. Not improbable, sir; there are numbers of poor creatures in the same condition.

SIR P. Oh, numbers, numbers. Now, sir, this cracked creature used to pray and sing, and sigh and groan, and weep and wail, and gnash her teeth constantly, morning and evening, at the Tabernacle at Moorfields; and as soon as I found she had the siller, aha! guid traith, I plumped me down upon my knees, close by her—cheek by jowl—and prayed, and sighed, and sung, and groaned, and gnashed my teeth as vehemently as she could do for the life of her; ay, and turned up the whites of mine een, till the strings awmost cracked again. I watched her motions, handed her till her chair, waited on her home, got most religiously intimate with her in a week — married her in a fortnight, buried her in a month—

touched the siller, and with a deep suit of mourning, a melancholy port, a sorrowful visage, and a joyful heart, I began the world again; and this, sir, was the first boo—that is, the first effectual boo—I ever made 'till the vanity of human nature.—[*Rises.*]—Now, sir, do you understand this doctrine?

EGER. Perfectly well, sir.

SIR P. Ay, but was it not right? was it not ingenious, and weel hit off?

EGER. Certainly, sir; extremely well.

SIR P. My next boo, sir, was till your ain mother, whom I ran away with fra the boarding-school; by the interest of whose family I got a guid smart place in the Treasury; and, sir, my very next step was intill Parliament; the which I entered with as ardent and determined an ambition as ever agitated the heart of Cæsar himself. Sir, I booed, and watched, and hearkened, and ran aboot, backwards and forwards, and attended and dangled upon the then great mon, till I got intill the vary bowels of his confidence, and then, sir, I wriggled and wrought, and wriggled, till I wriggled myself among the vary thick of them; ha! I got my snack of the clothing, the foraging, the contracts, the lottery tickets, and aw the political bonuses; till at length, sir, I became a much wealthier mon than one-half of the golden calves I had been so long a-booing to; and was nae that booing to some purpose?

EGER. It was, indeed, sir.

SIR P. But are you convinced of the guid effects and the utility of booing?

EGER. Thoroughly.

SIR P. Sir, it is infallible.

Charles Macklin.

RHYME OF THE DUCHESS MAY.

'Twas a Duke's fair orphan girl, and her uncle's ward,
    the Earl,
Who betrothed her, twelve years old, for the sake of
    dowry gold,
        To his son, Lord Leigh, the churl.

But what time she had made good all her years of womanhood,
Unto both those lords of Leigh spake she out right
sovranly,
      "My will runneth as my blood,

"And while this same blood makes red this same right
hand's veins," she said,
" 'Tis my will as lady free, not to wed a Lord of Leigh,
      But Sir Guy of Linteged."

The old Earl he smiled smooth, then he sighed for willful
youth—
"Good my niece, that hand withal looketh somewhat soft
and small
      For so large a will in sooth."

She, too, smiled by that same sign, but her smile was
cold and fine;
"Little hand clasps muckle gold, or it were not worth
the hold
      Of thy son, good uncle mine!"

Then the young lord jerked his breath, and sware
thickly in his teeth,
"He would wed his own betrothed, an she loved him
an she loathed,
      Let the life come or the death."

Up she rose with scornful eyes, as her father's child
might rise,
"Thy hound's blood, my lord of Leigh, stains thy
knightly heel," quoth she,
      "And he moans not where he lies.

"But a woman's will dies hard, in the hall or on the sward!
By that grave, my lords, which made me orphaned girl
and dowered lady,
      I deny you wife and ward."

Unto each she bowed her head, and swept past with
lofty tread.
Ere the midnight bell had ceased, in the chapel had the
priest
      Blessed her, bride of Linteged.

Fast and fain the bridal train along the night-storm
    rode amain;
Hard the steeds of lord and serf struck their hoofs out
    on the turf,
        In the pauses of the rain.

Fast and fain the kinsman's train along the storm pur-
    sued amain—
Steed on steed-track, dashing off, thickening, doubling,
    hoof on hoof,
        In the pauses of the rain.

And the bridegroom led the flight on his red-roan steed
    of might,
And the bride lay on his arm, still, as if she feared no harm,
        Smiling out into the night.

"Dost thou fear?" he said at last. "Nay," she an-
    swered him in haste;
"Not such death as we could find, only life with one be-
    hind—
        Ride on fast as fear—ride fast!"

Up the mountain wheeled the steed—girth to ground,
    and fetlocks spread—
Headlong bounds, and rocking flanks—down he stag-
    gered, down the banks,
        To the towers of Linteged.

High and low the serfs looked out, red the flambeaus
    tossed about;
In the courtyard rose the cry, "Live the Duchess and
    Sir Guy!"
        But she never heard them shout.

On the steed she dropt her cheek, kissed his mane and
    kissed his neck—
"I had happier died by thee, than lived on a Lady Leigh,"
        Were the first words she did speak.

But a three months' joyance lay 'twixt that moment
    and to-day,
When five hundred archers tall stand beside the castle
    wall,
        To recapture Duchess May.

And the castle standeth black, with the red sun at its
   back;
And a fortnight's siege is done, and, except the Duchess,
   none
      Can misdoubt the coming wrack.

* * *

"One last boon, young Ralph and Clare! faithful hearts
   to do and dare!
Bring that steed up from his stall, which she kissed before you all,
      Guide him up the turret stair.

"Ye shall harness him aright, and lead upward to this
   height!
Once in love and twice in war hath he borne me strong
   and far,
      He shall bear me far to-night."

* * *

They have fetched the steed with care, in the harness
   he did wear,
Past the court and through the doors, across the rushes
   of the floors;
      But they goad him up the stair.

Then from out her bower-chambère did the Duchess
   May repair.
"Tell me, now, what is your need," said the lady, "of
   this steed,
      That ye goad him up the stair?"

Calm she stood! unbodkined through, fell her dark hair
   to her shoe,
And the smile upon her face, ere she left the tiring-
   glass,
      Had not time enough to go.

"Get thee back, sweet Duchess May! hope is gone like
   yesterday—
One-half hour completes the breach, and thy lord grows
   wild of speech;
      Get thee in, sweet lady, and pray!"

"In the east tower, high'st of all, loud he cries for steed
    from stall.
"He would ride as far," quoth he, "as for love and vic-
    tory,
        Though he ride the castle wall."

"And we fetch the steed from stall, up where never a hoof
    did fall.
  Wifely prayer meets deathly need! may the sweet
  heavens hear thee plead,
        If he rides the castle wall."

  Low she dropt her head, and lower, till her hair coiled on
    the floor,
  And tear after tear you heard fall distinct as any word
        Which you might be listening for.

"Get thee in, thou soft ladie! here is never a place for thee!
  Braid thy hair and clasp thy gown, that thy beauty in
  its moan
        May find grace with Leigh of Leigh."

  She stood up in bitter case, with a pale yet steady face,
  Like a statue thunderstruck, which, though quivering,
    seems to look
        Right against the thunder-place.

  And her foot trod in, with pride, her own tears i' the
    stone beside—
"Go to, faithful friends, go to! Judge no more what
  ladies do,
        No, nor how their lords may ride!"

  Then the good steed's rein she took, and his neck did
    kiss and stroke;
  Soft he neighed to answer her, and then followed up the
  stair,
        For the love of her sweet look.

  Oh, and steeply, steeply wound up the narrow stair
    around—
  Oh, and closely, closely speeding, step by step beside
  her treading,
        Did he follow, meek as hound.

On the east tower, high'st of all, there, where never a
    hoof did fall—
Out they swept, a vision steady—noble steed and lovely
    lady,
        Calm as if in bower or stall!

Down she knelt at her lord's knee, and she looked up
    silently;
And he kissed her twice and thrice, for that look within
    her eyes
        Which he could not bear to see.

Quoth he, ''Get thee from this strife—and the sweet
    saints bless thy life!
In this hour I stand in need of my noble red-roan
    steed—
        But no more of my noble wife.''

Quoth she, ''Meekly have I done all thy bidding under
    sun;
But by all my womanhood, which is proved so true and
    good,
        I will never do this one.

''Now, by womanhood's degree and by wifehood's verity,
In this hour if thou hast need of thy noble red-roan
    steed,
        Thou hast also need of me.

''By this golden ring ye see on this lifted hand pardiè,
If this hour on castle wall can be room for steed from
    stall,
        Shall be also room for me.

''So the sweet saints with me be'' (did she utter
    solemnly),
''If a man this eventide, on this castle wall will ride,
        He shall ride the same with me.''

  Oh, he sprang up in the selle, and he laughed out bitter-
    well,
''Wouldst thou ride among the leaves, as we used on other
    eves,
        To hear chime a vesper bell?''

She clang closer to his knee. "Ay, beneath the cypress
    tree!
Mock me not, for otherwhere than along the green-
    wood fair
        Have I ridden fast with thee!

"Fast I rode with new-made vows, from my angry kins-
    man's house!
What! and would you men should reck that I dared
    more for love's sake
        As a bride than as a spouse?

"What, and would you it should fall, as a proverb before all,
    That a bride may keep your side while through castle-
    gate you ride,
        Yet eschew the castle-wall?"

Ho! the breach yawns into ruin, and roars up against
    her suing—
With the inarticulate din, and the dreadful falling in—
        Shrieks of doing and undoing!

Twice he wrung her hands in twain, but the small hands
    closed again.
Back he reined the steed—back, back! but she trailed
    along his track
        With a frantic clasp and strain!

Evermore the foemen pour through the crash of win-
    dow and door;
And the shouts of Leigh and Leigh, and the shrieks of
    "Kill!" and "Flee!"
        Strike up clear amid the roar.

Thrice he wrung her hands in twain, but they closed
    and clung again;
Wild she clung, as one, withstood, clasps a Christ upon
    the rood,
        In a spasm of deathly pain.

She clung wild and she clung mute, with her shuddering
    lips half-shut,
Her head fallen as half in swound, hair and knee swept
    on the ground,
        She clung wild to stirrup and foot.

Back he reined his steed back-thrown on the slippery
   coping-stone,
Back the iron hoofs did grind on the battlement behind,
      Whence a hundred feet went down.

And his heel did press and goad on the quivering flank
   bestrode,
"Friends and brothers, save my wife! Pardon, sweet, in
   change for life,—
      But I ride alone to God."

Straight, as if the holy name had upbreathed her like a
   flame,
She upsprang, she rose upright, in his selle she sate in
   sight;
      By her love she overcame.

And her head was on his breast, where she smiled as
   one at rest,—
"Ring," she cried, "O vesper bell, in the beechwood's
   old chapelle!
      But the passing bell rings best."

They have caught out at the rein, which Sir Guy threw
   loose, in vain,—
For the horse in stark despair, with his front hoofs
   poised in air,
      On the last verge rears amain.

Now he hangs, he rocks between, and his nostrils cur-
   dle in,—
And he shivers head and hoof, and the flakes of foam
   fall off;
      And his face grows fierce and thin!

And a look of human woe from his staring eyes did go,
And a sharp cry uttered he, in a foretold agony
      Of the headlong death below.

And "Ring, ring! thou passing bell!" still she cried,
   "i' the old chapelle!"
Then back-toppling, crashing back—a dead weight
   flung out to wrack,
      Horse and riders overfell!
                              Elizabeth Barrett Browning.

INDEX OF AUTHORS.